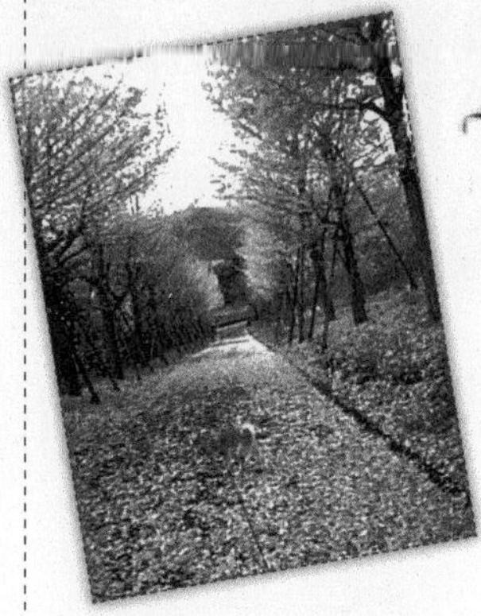

They're different from this pooch above, but the two dogs that were printed on the New Year's card from Mr. Yoshida were just so darn adorable.

—Tsugumi Ohba

The art of drawing manga evolves every day. Muto Ashirogi is always evolving too.

—Takeshi Obata

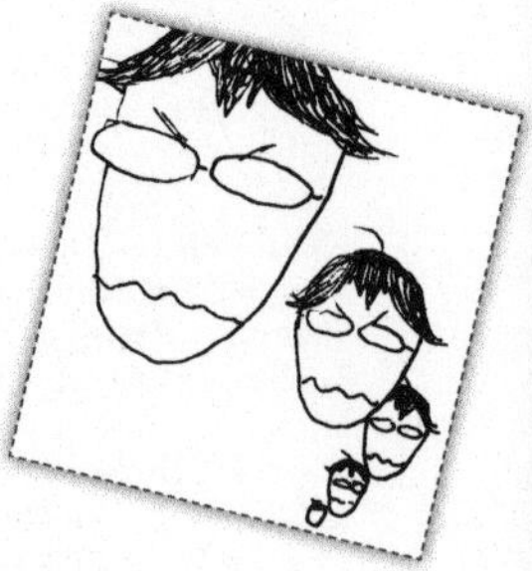

Tsugumi Ohba

Born in Tokyo, Tsugumi Ohba is the author of the hit series *Death Note*. His current series *Bakuman。* is serialized in *Weekly Shonen Jump*.

Takeshi Obata

Takeshi Obata was born in 1969 in Niigata, Japan, and is the artist of the wildly popular SHONEN JUMP title *Hikaru no Go*, which won the 2003 Tezuka Osamu Cultural Prize: Shinsei "New Hope" award and the 2000 Shogakukan Manga award. Obata is also the artist of *Arabian Majin Bokentan Lamp Lamp*, *Ayatsuri Sakon*, *Cyborg Jichan G.*, and the smash hit manga *Death Note*. His current series *Bakuman。* is serialized in *Weekly Shonen Jump*.

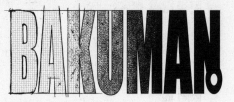

Volume 14

SHONEN JUMP Manga Edition

Story by **TSUGUMI OHBA**
Art by **TAKESHI OBATA**

Translation | **Tetsuichiro Miyaki**
English Adaptation | **Julie Lutz**
Touch-up Art & Lettering | **Elena Diaz**
Design | **Fawn Lau**
Editor | **Alexis Kirsch**

BAKUMAN₀ © 2008 by Tsugumi Ohba, Takeshi Obata
All rights reserved.
First published in Japan in 2008 by SHUEISHA Inc., Tokyo.
English translation rights arranged by SHUEISHA Inc.

Printed in the U.S.A.

Published by VIZ Media, LLC
P.O. Box 77010
San Francisco, CA 94107

10 9 8 7 6 5 4 3 2 1
First printing, September 2012

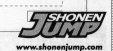

BAKUMAN。

14

MIND GAMES and CATCH-PHRASES

STORY BY
TSUGUMI OHBA

ART BY
TAKESHI OBATA

SHONENJUMP MANGA

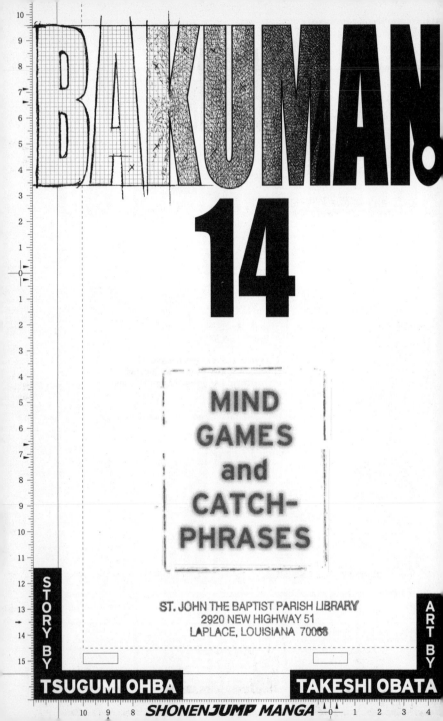

UMAN. バクマン。 vol. 14

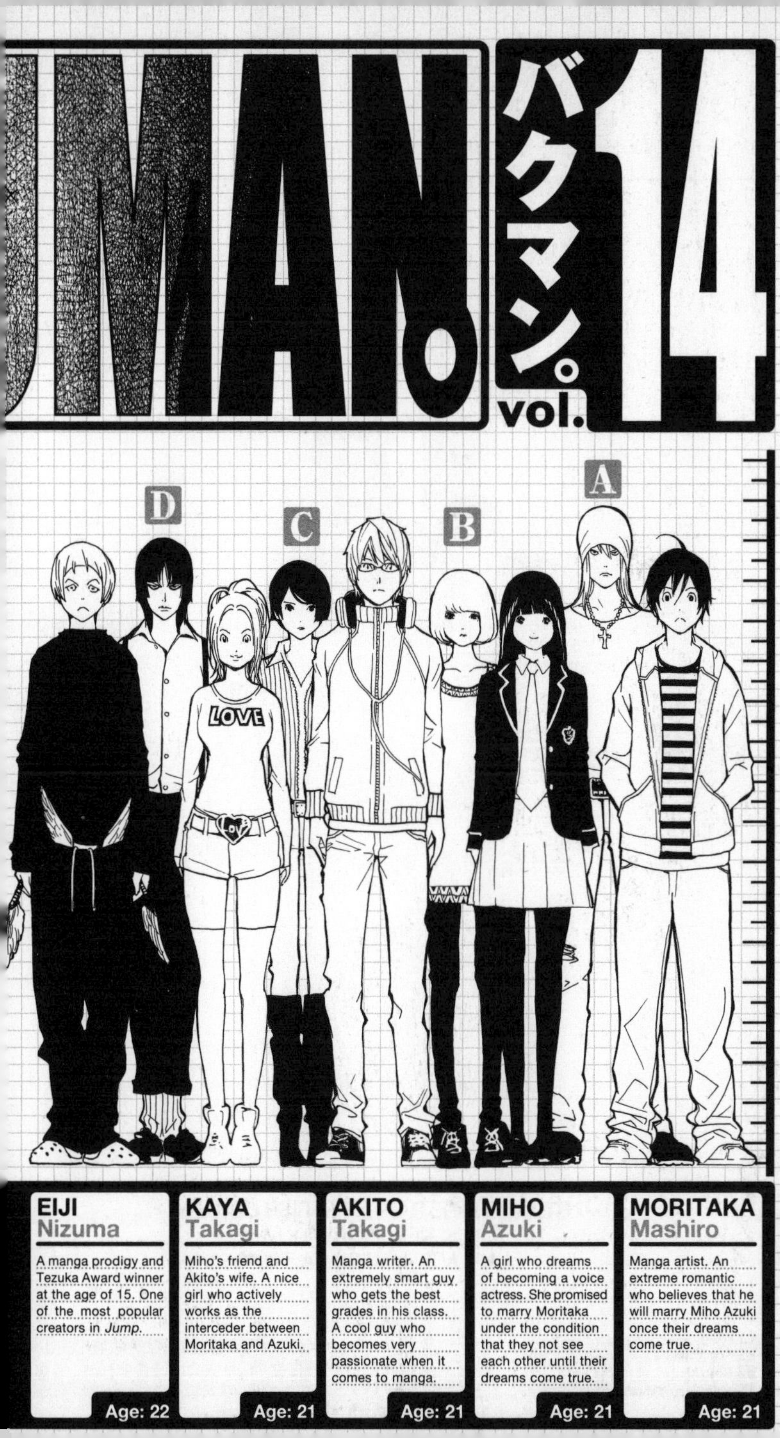
D
C
B
A

EIJI
Nizuma

A manga prodigy and Tezuka Award winner at the age of 15. One of the most popular creators in *Jump*.

Age: 22

KAYA
Takagi

Miho's friend and Akito's wife. A nice girl who actively works as the interceder between Moritaka and Azuki.

Age: 21

AKITO
Takagi

Manga writer. An extremely smart guy who gets the best grades in his class. A cool guy who becomes very passionate when it comes to manga.

Age: 21

MIHO
Azuki

A girl who dreams of becoming a voice actress. She promised to marry Moritaka under the condition that they not see each other until their dreams come true.

Age: 21

MORITAKA
Mashiro

Manga artist. An extreme romantic who believes that he will marry Miho Azuki once their dreams come true.

Age: 21

*These ages are from June 2015.

STORY In order to attain the glory that only a handful of people can, two young men decide to walk the rough "path of manga" and become professional manga creators. This is the story of a great artist, Moritaka Mashiro, a talented writer, Akito Takagi, and their quest to become manga legends!

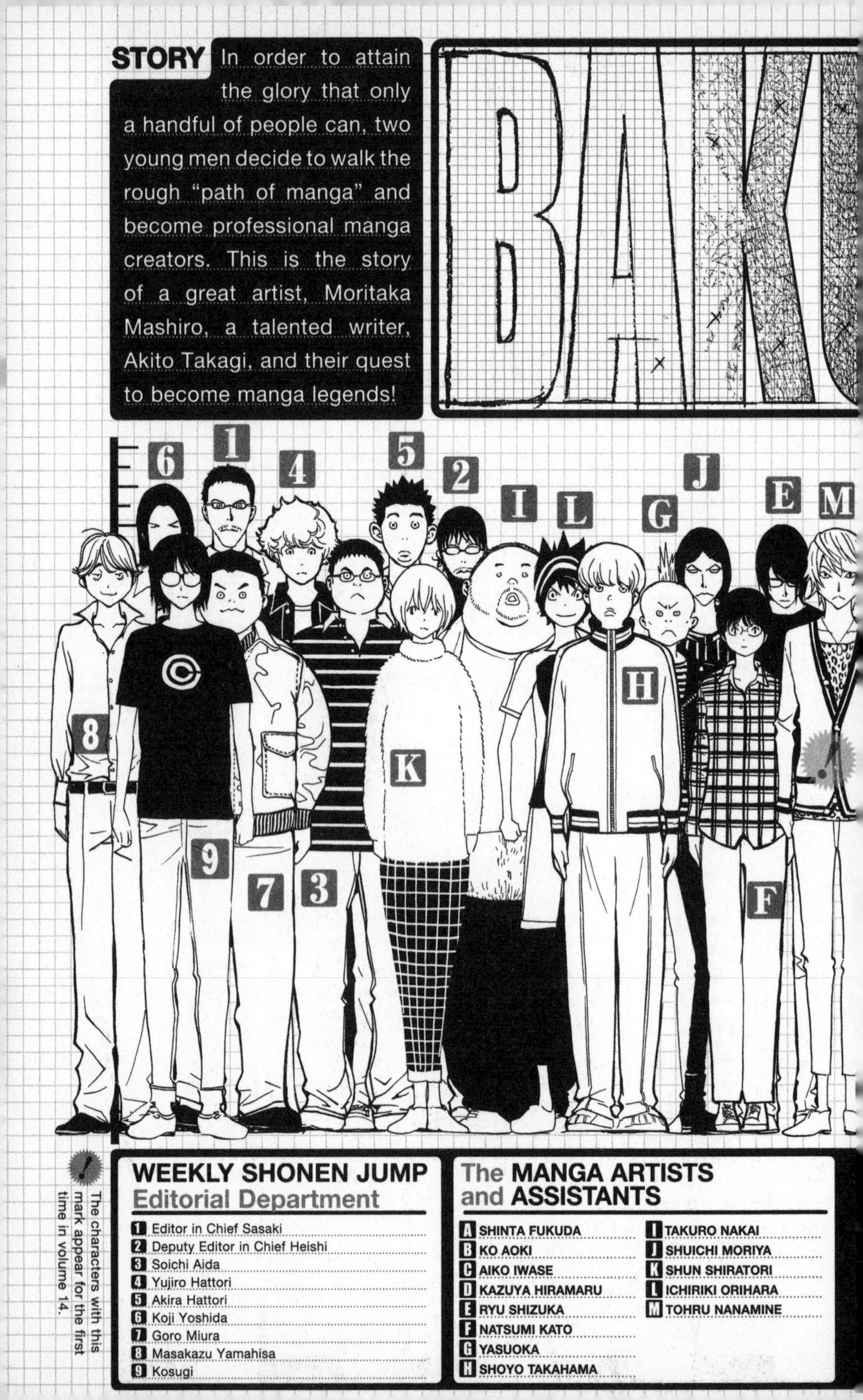
6 1 4 5 2 I L G J E M
8 K H
9 7 3 F

The characters with this mark appear for the first time in volume 14.

WEEKLY SHONEN JUMP Editorial Department

1. Editor in Chief Sasaki
2. Deputy Editor in Chief Heishi
3. Soichi Aida
4. Yujiro Hattori
5. Akira Hattori
6. Koji Yoshida
7. Goro Miura
8. Masakazu Yamahisa
9. Kosugi

The MANGA ARTISTS and ASSISTANTS

- A SHINTA FUKUDA
- B KO AOKI
- C AIKO IWASE
- D KAZUYA HIRAMARU
- E RYU SHIZUKA
- F NATSUMI KATO
- G YASUOKA
- H SHOYO TAKAHAMA
- I TAKURO NAKAI
- J SHUICHI MORIYA
- K SHUN SHIRATORI
- L ICHIRIKI ORIHARA
- M TOHRU NANAMINE

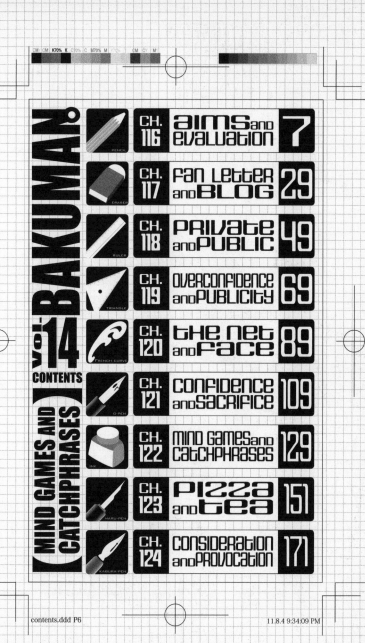

vol. 14 BAKUMAN。

CONTENTS

(MIND GAMES AND CATCHPHRASES)

CH. 116: AIMS AND EVALUATION

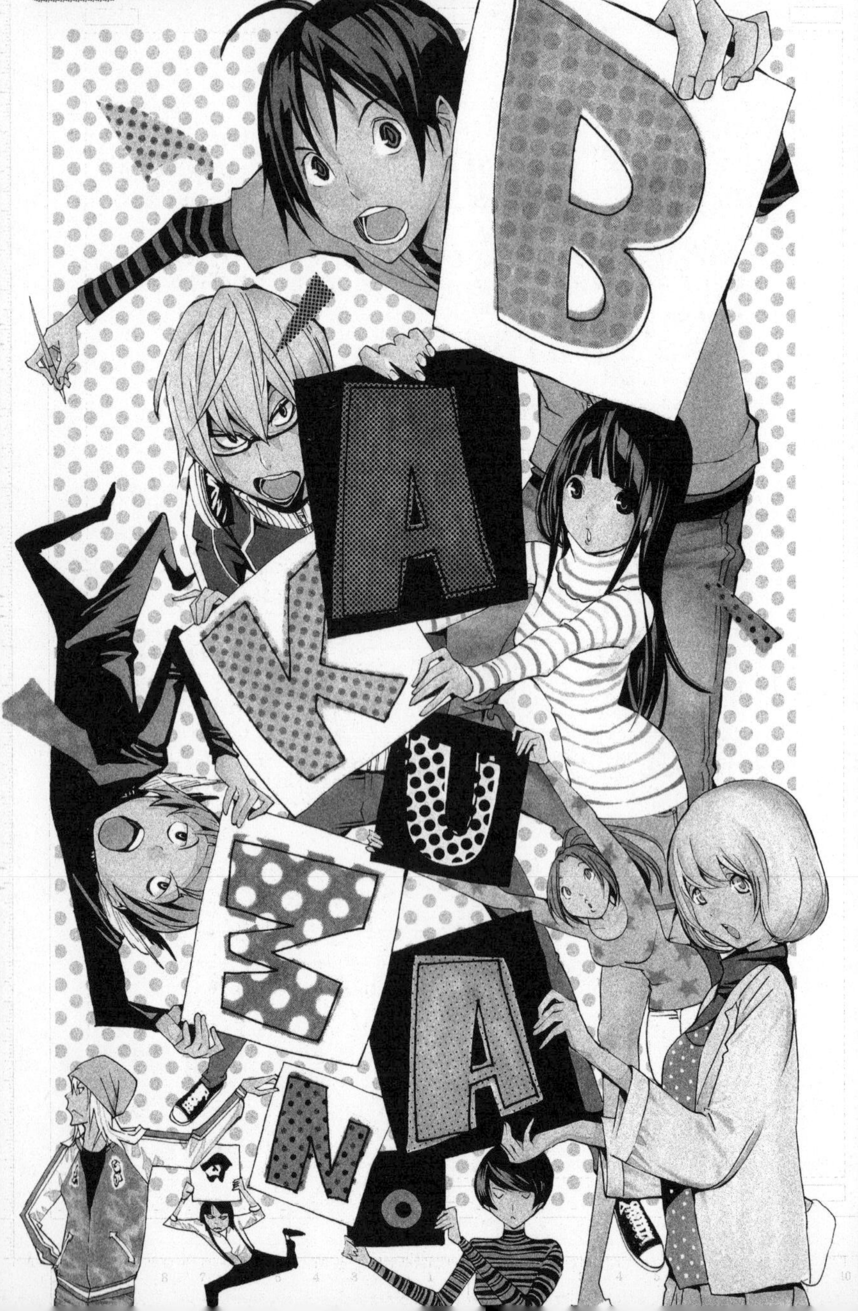
BAKUMAN

BAKUMAN。

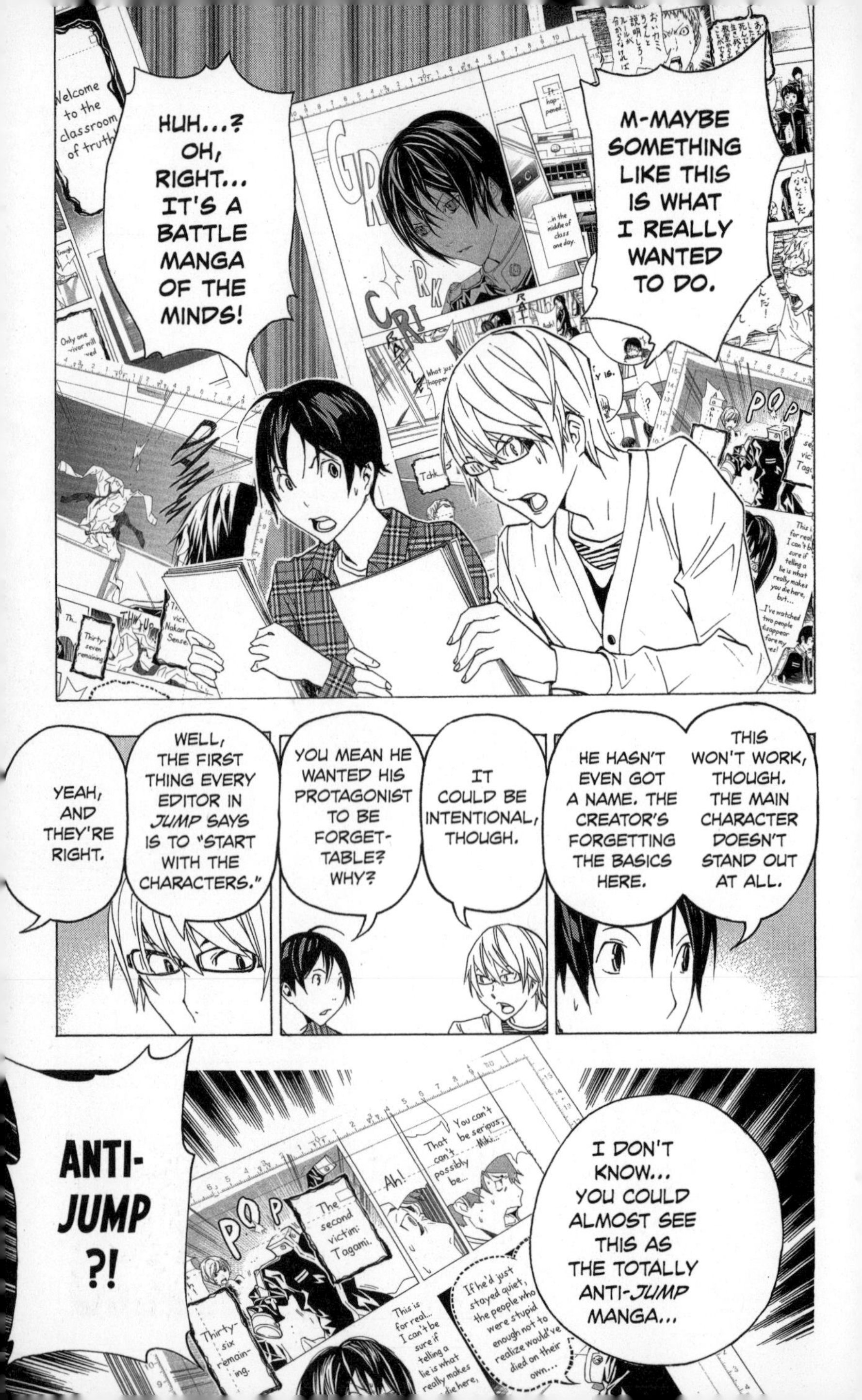
M-MAYBE SOMETHING LIKE THIS IS WHAT I REALLY WANTED TO DO.
HUH...? OH, RIGHT... IT'S A BATTLE MANGA OF THE MINDS!
It happened...
...in the middle of class one day.
Welcome to the classroom of truth
THIS WON'T WORK, THOUGH. THE MAIN CHARACTER DOESN'T STAND OUT AT ALL.
HE HASN'T EVEN GOT A NAME. THE CREATOR'S FORGETTING THE BASICS HERE.
IT COULD BE INTENTIONAL, THOUGH.
YOU MEAN HE WANTED HIS PROTAGONIST TO BE FORGET-TABLE? WHY?
WELL, THE FIRST THING EVERY EDITOR IN *JUMP* SAYS IS TO "START WITH THE CHARACTERS."
YEAH, AND THEY'RE RIGHT.
I DON'T KNOW... YOU COULD ALMOST SEE THIS AS THE TOTALLY ANTI-*JUMP* MANGA...
You can't be serious, Miki...
That can't possibly be...
Ah!
The second victim: Tagami.
POP
If he'd just stayed quiet, the people who were stupid enough not to realize would've died on their own...
This is for real... I can't be sure if telling a lie is what really makes
Thirty-six remaining.
ANTI-*JUMP*?!

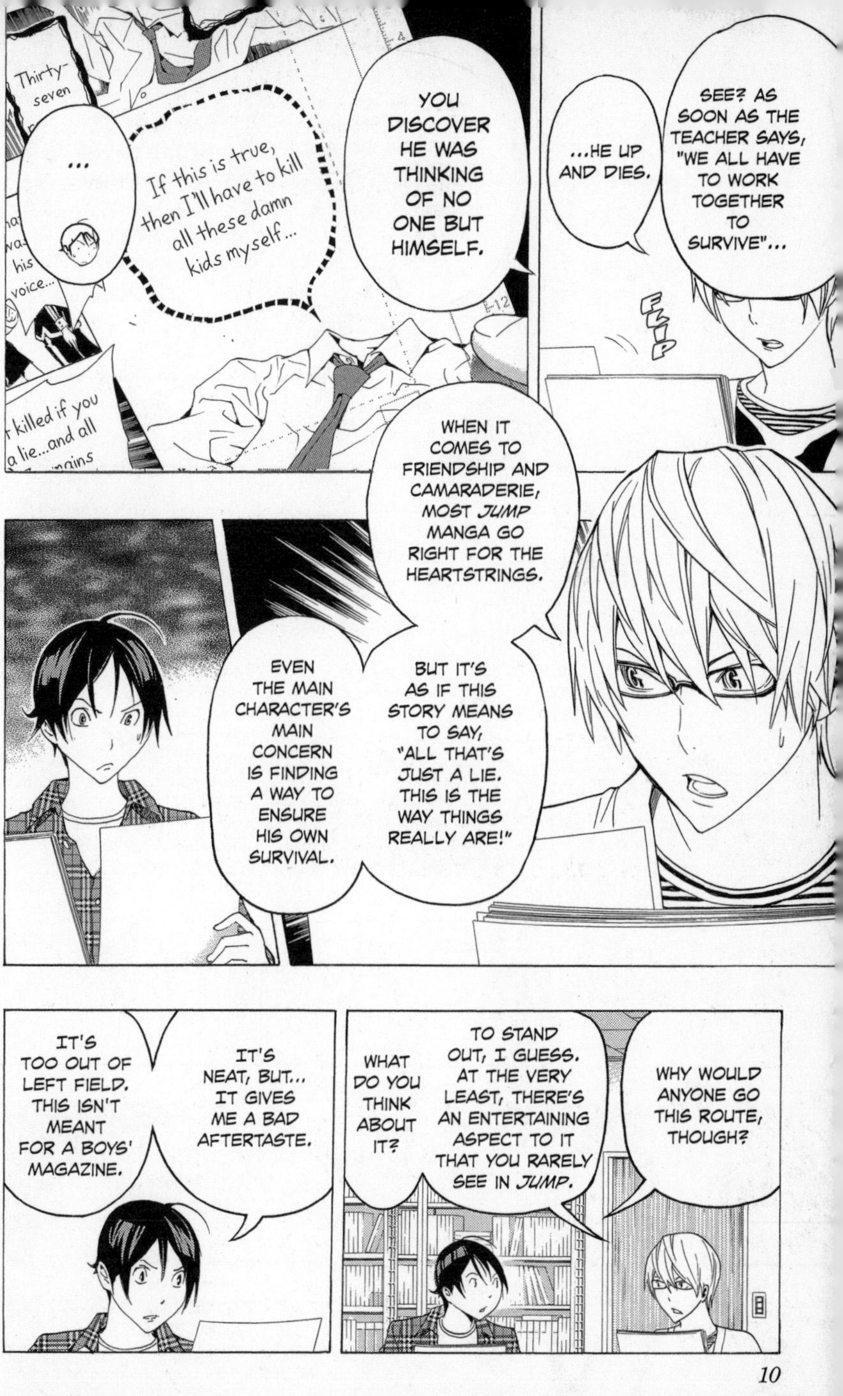
SEE? AS SOON AS THE TEACHER SAYS, "WE ALL HAVE TO WORK TOGETHER TO SURVIVE"...
...HE UP AND DIES.
FLIP
YOU DISCOVER HE WAS THINKING OF NO ONE BUT HIMSELF.
If this is true, then I'll have to kill all these damn kids myself...
...
Thirty-seven
his voice...
killed if you a lie...and all
WHEN IT COMES TO FRIENDSHIP AND CAMARADERIE, MOST JUMP MANGA GO RIGHT FOR THE HEARTSTRINGS.
BUT IT'S AS IF THIS STORY MEANS TO SAY, "ALL THAT'S JUST A LIE. THIS IS THE WAY THINGS REALLY ARE!"
EVEN THE MAIN CHARACTER'S MAIN CONCERN IS FINDING A WAY TO ENSURE HIS OWN SURVIVAL.
WHY WOULD ANYONE GO THIS ROUTE, THOUGH?
TO STAND OUT, I GUESS. AT THE VERY LEAST, THERE'S AN ENTERTAINING ASPECT TO IT THAT YOU RARELY SEE IN JUMP.
WHAT DO YOU THINK ABOUT IT?
IT'S NEAT, BUT... IT GIVES ME A BAD AFTERTASTE.
IT'S TOO OUT OF LEFT FIELD. THIS ISN'T MEANT FOR A BOYS' MAGAZINE.

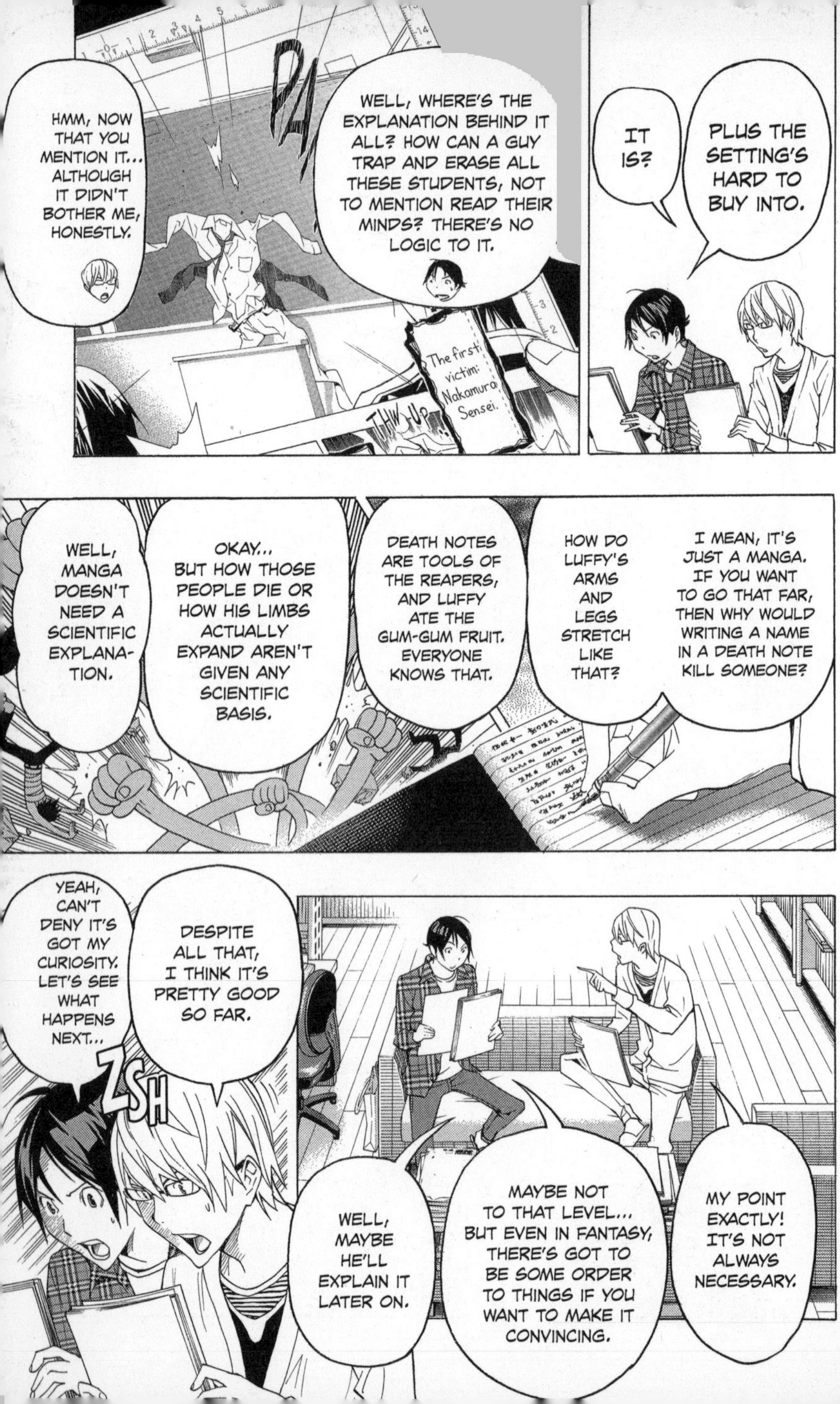
PLUS THE SETTING'S HARD TO BUY INTO.
IT IS?
WELL, WHERE'S THE EXPLANATION BEHIND IT ALL? HOW CAN A GUY TRAP AND ERASE ALL THESE STUDENTS, NOT TO MENTION READ THEIR MINDS? THERE'S NO LOGIC TO IT.
HMM, NOW THAT YOU MENTION IT... ALTHOUGH IT DIDN'T BOTHER ME, HONESTLY.
The first victim: Nakamura Sensei.
THW-UP
I MEAN, IT'S JUST A MANGA. IF YOU WANT TO GO THAT FAR, THEN WHY WOULD WRITING A NAME IN A DEATH NOTE KILL SOMEONE?
HOW DO LUFFY'S ARMS AND LEGS STRETCH LIKE THAT?
DEATH NOTES ARE TOOLS OF THE REAPERS, AND LUFFY ATE THE GUM-GUM FRUIT. EVERYONE KNOWS THAT.
OKAY... BUT HOW THOSE PEOPLE DIE OR HOW HIS LIMBS ACTUALLY EXPAND AREN'T GIVEN ANY SCIENTIFIC BASIS.
WELL, MANGA DOESN'T NEED A SCIENTIFIC EXPLANA-TION.
MY POINT EXACTLY! IT'S NOT ALWAYS NECESSARY.
MAYBE NOT TO THAT LEVEL... BUT EVEN IN FANTASY, THERE'S GOT TO BE SOME ORDER TO THINGS IF YOU WANT TO MAKE IT CONVINCING.
WELL, MAYBE HE'LL EXPLAIN IT LATER ON.
DESPITE ALL THAT, I THINK IT'S PRETTY GOOD SO FAR.
YEAH, CAN'T DENY IT'S GOT MY CURIOSITY. LET'S SEE WHAT HAPPENS NEXT...
ZSH

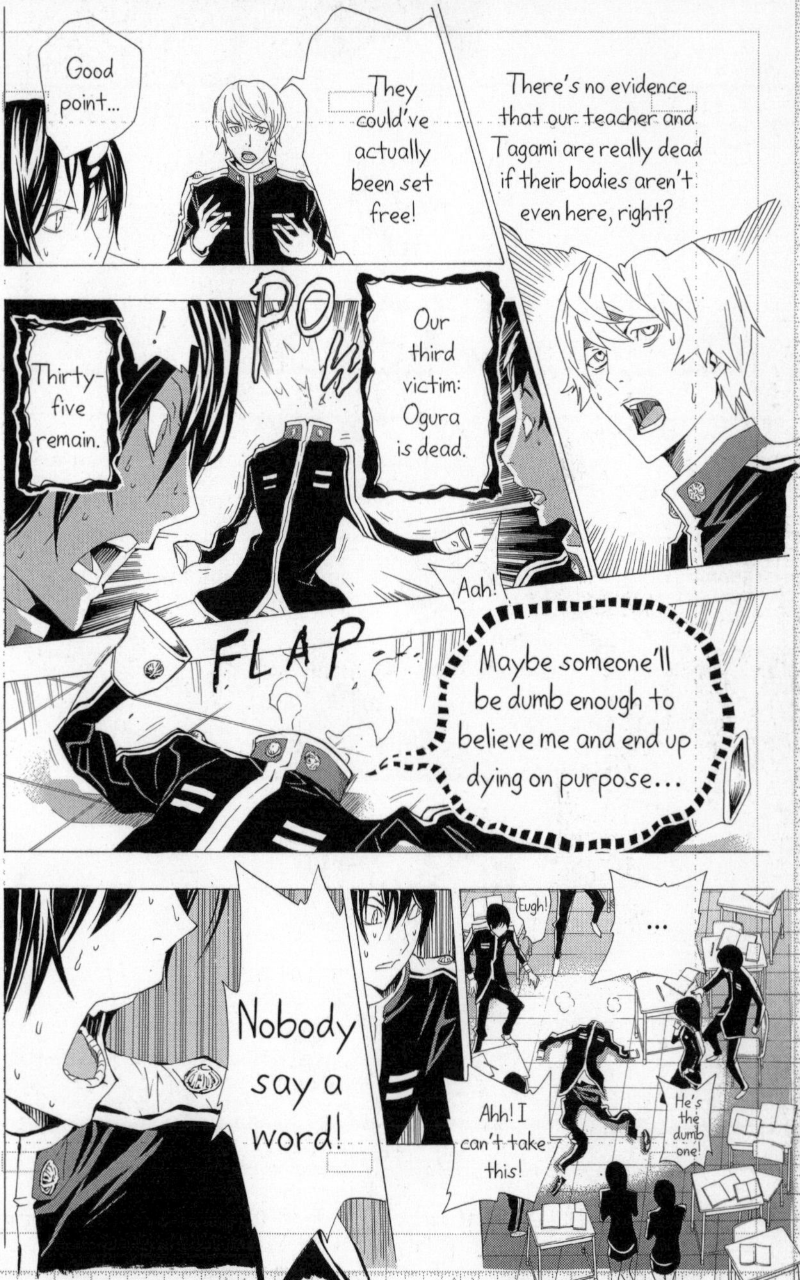
There's no evidence that our teacher and Tagami are really dead if their bodies aren't even here, right?
They could've actually been set free!
Good point...
Our third victim: Ogura is dead.
POW
!
Thirty-five remain.
Aah!
FLAP
Maybe someone'll be dumb enough to believe me and end up dying on purpose...
Eugh!
...
He's the dumb one!
Ahh! I can't take this!
Nobody say a word!

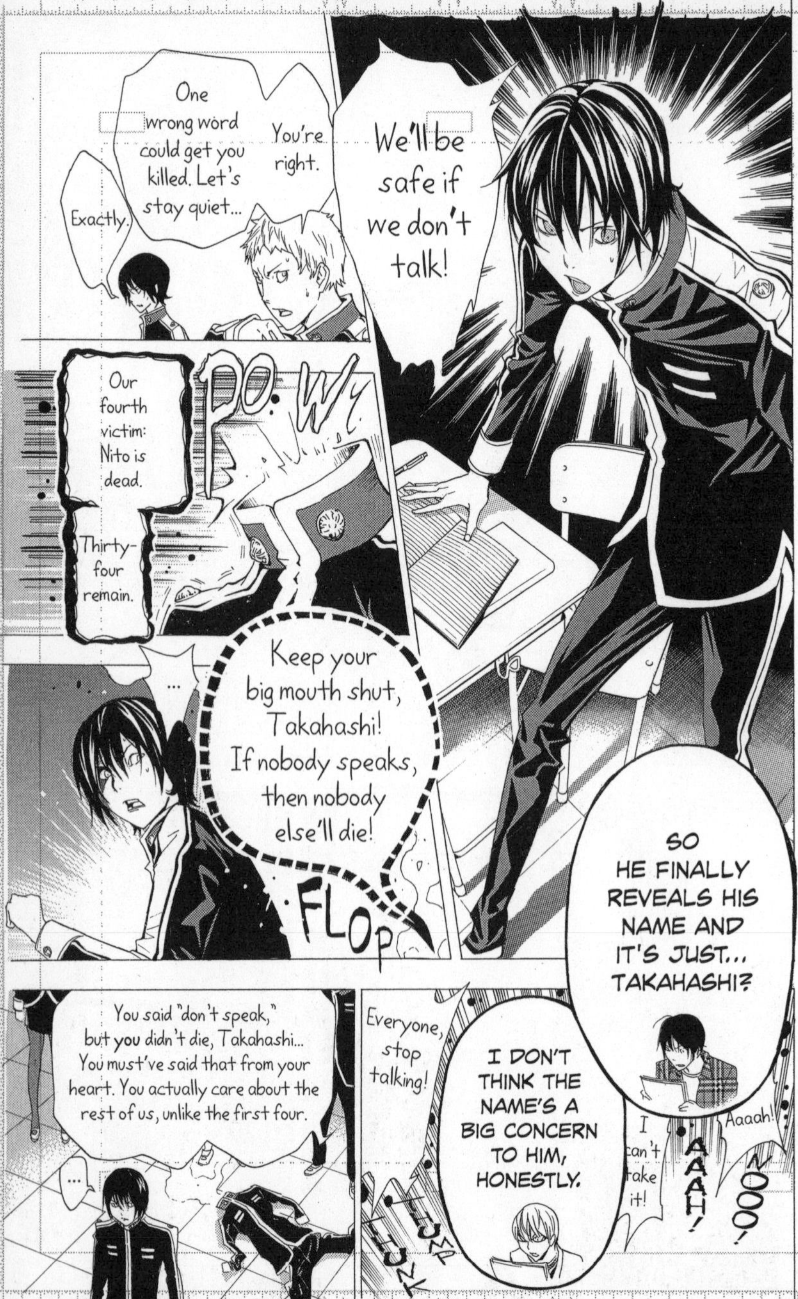
We'll be safe if we don't talk!
One wrong word could get you killed. Let's stay quiet...
You're right.
Exactly.
POW
Our fourth victim: Nito is dead.
Thirty-four remain.
Keep your big mouth shut, Takahashi! If nobody speaks, then nobody else'll die!
...
FLOP
SO HE FINALLY REVEALS HIS NAME AND IT'S JUST... TAKAHASHI?
Aaaah!
NOOO!
AAAH!
I can't take it!
I DON'T THINK THE NAME'S A BIG CONCERN TO HIM, HONESTLY.
Everyone, stop talking!
THUMP
THUNK
You said "don't speak," but **you** didn't die, Takahashi... You must've said that from your heart. You actually care about the rest of us, unlike the first four.
...

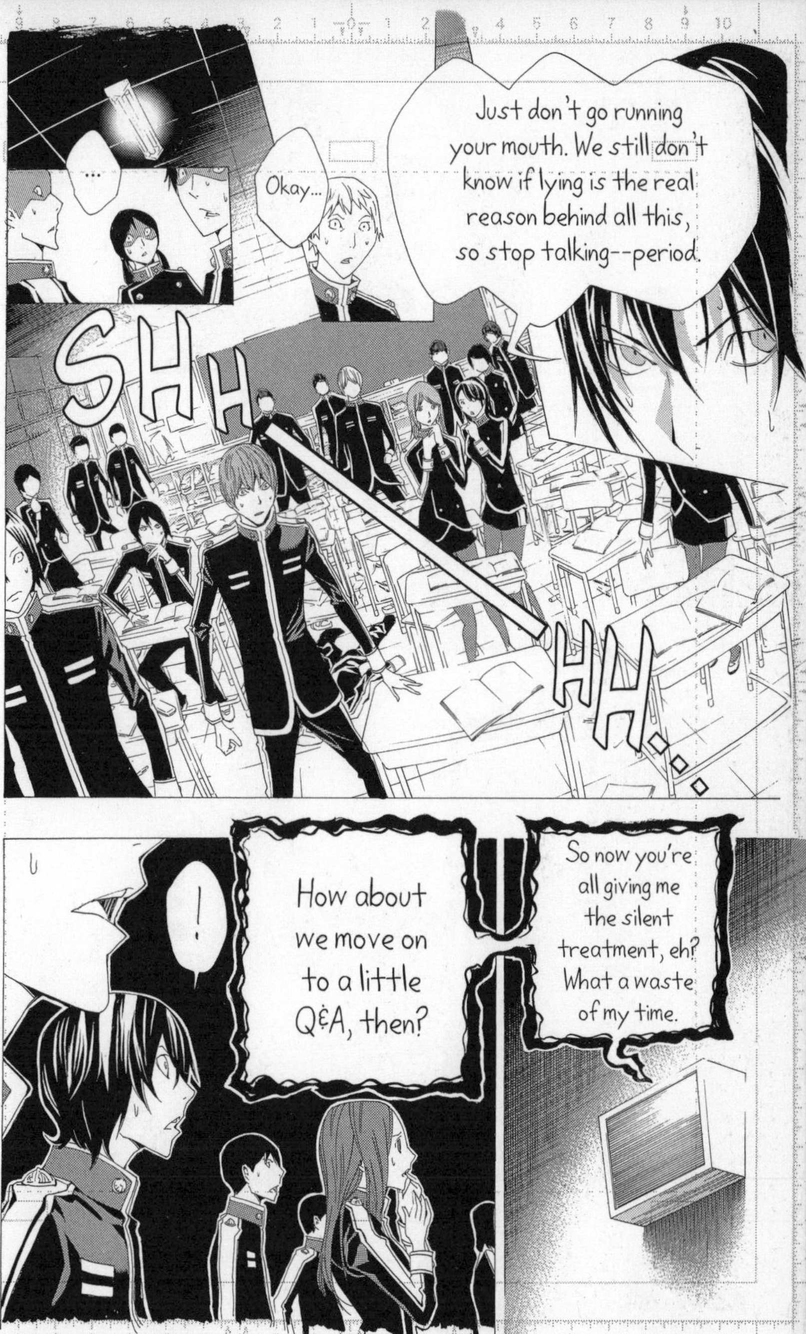
Just don't go running your mouth. We still don't know if lying is the real reason behind all this, so stop talking--period.
Okay...
...
SHHHH...
So now you're all giving me the silent treatment, eh? What a waste of my time.
How about we move on to a little Q&A, then?
!

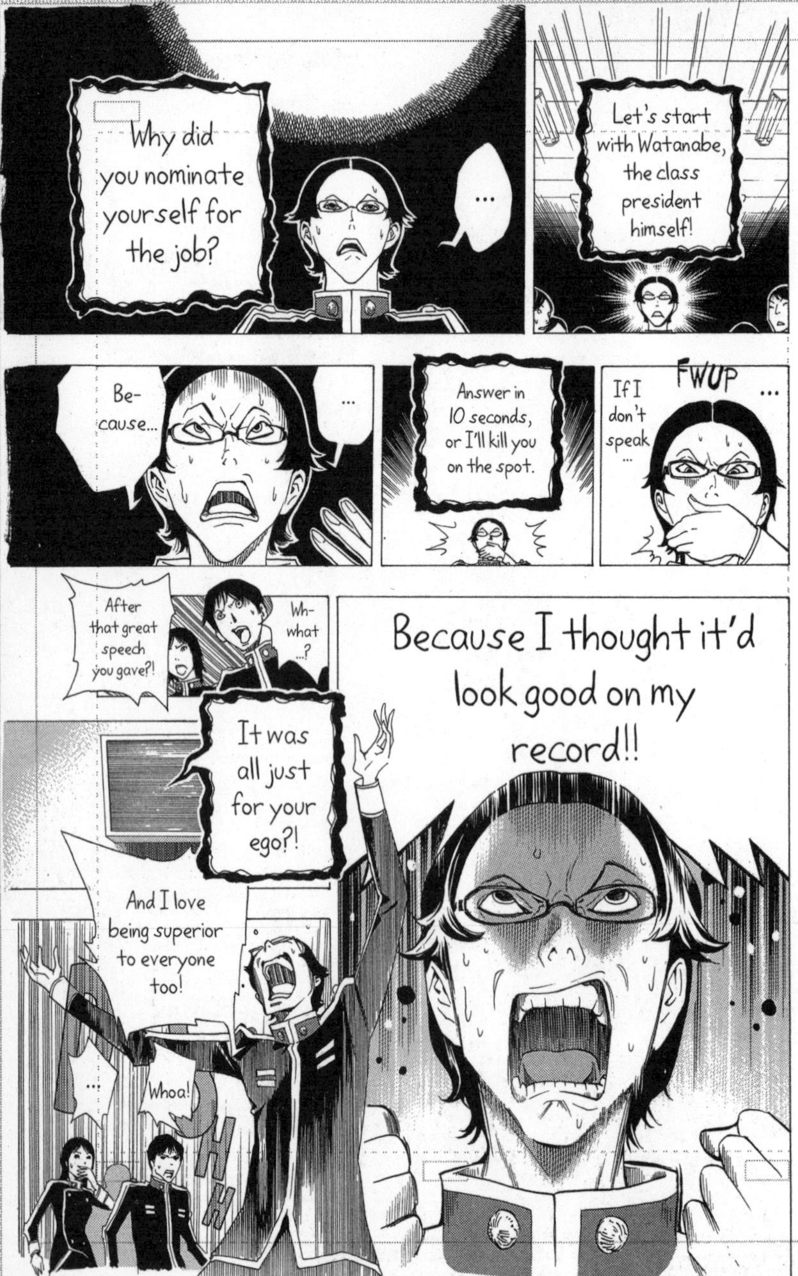
Let's start with Watanabe, the class president himself!
Why did you nominate yourself for the job?
...
...
FWUP
If I don't speak ...
Answer in 10 seconds, or I'll kill you on the spot.
...
Be- cause...
Because I thought it'd look good on my record!!
Wh- what ...?
After that great speech you gave?!
It was all just for your ego?!
And I love being superior to everyone too!
Whoa!
...

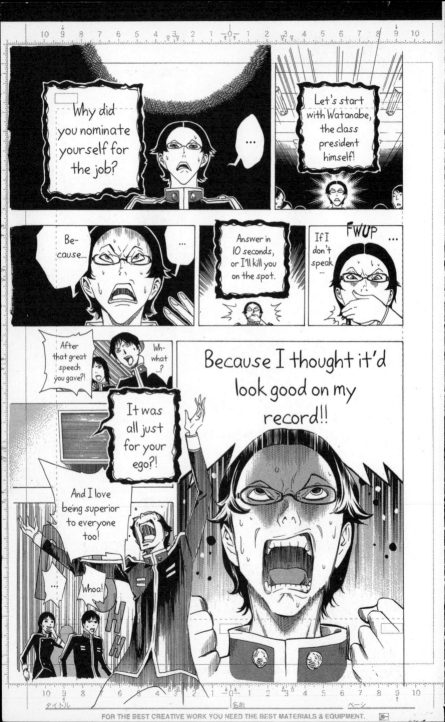

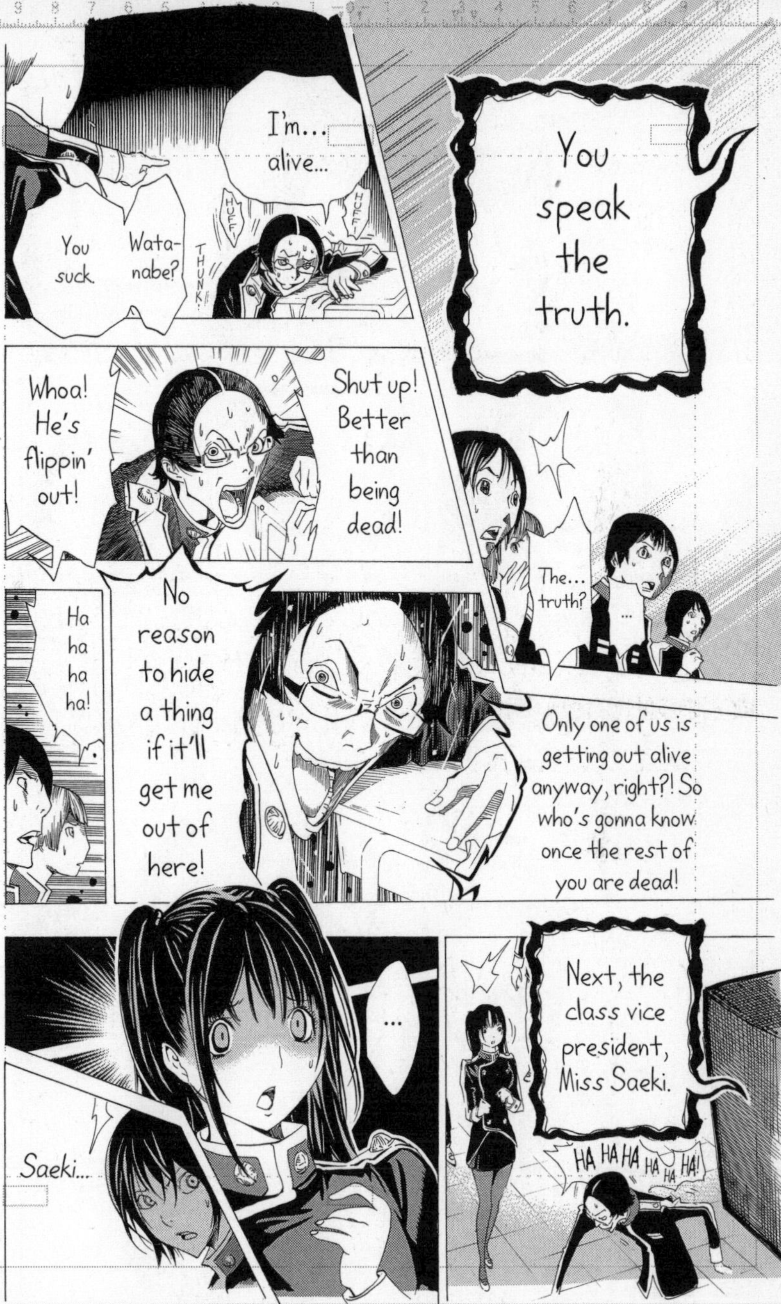

You speak the truth.
I'm... alive...
HUFF! HUFF!
THUNK
Wata-nabe?
You suck.
Shut up! Better than being dead!
Whoa! He's flippin' out!
The... truth?
...
No reason to hide a thing if it'll get me out of here!
Only one of us is getting out alive anyway, right?! So who's gonna know once the rest of you are dead!
Ha ha ha ha!
Next, the class vice president, Miss Saeki.
HA HA HA HA HA HA!
...
Saeki...

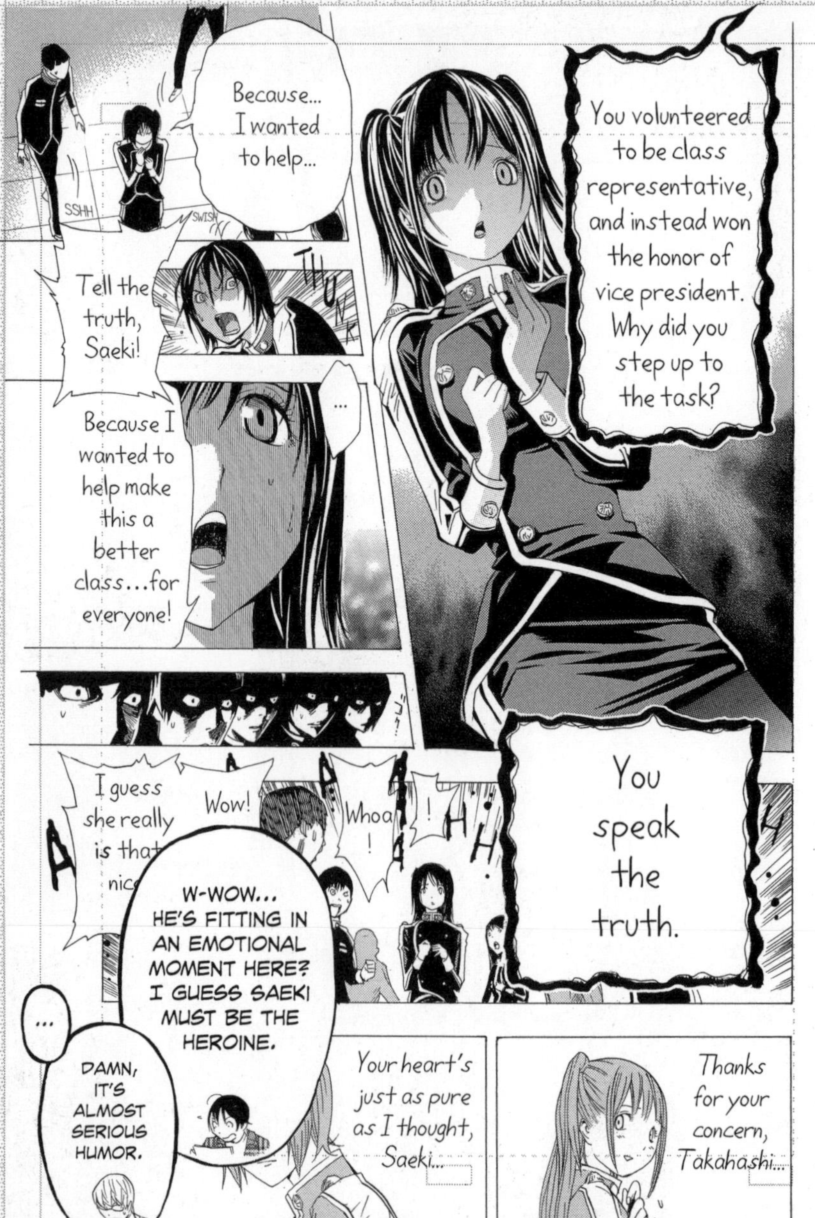
You volunteered to be class representative, and instead won the honor of vice president. Why did you step up to the task?
You speak the truth.
Because... I wanted to help...
SSHH
SWISH
THUNK
Tell the truth, Saeki!
...
Because I wanted to help make this a better class...for everyone!
!
Whoa!
Wow!
I guess she really is that nic
W-WOW... HE'S FITTING IN AN EMOTIONAL MOMENT HERE? I GUESS SAEKI MUST BE THE HEROINE.
DAMN, IT'S ALMOST SERIOUS HUMOR.
...
Thanks for your concern, Takahashi...
Your heart's just as pure as I thought, Saeki...

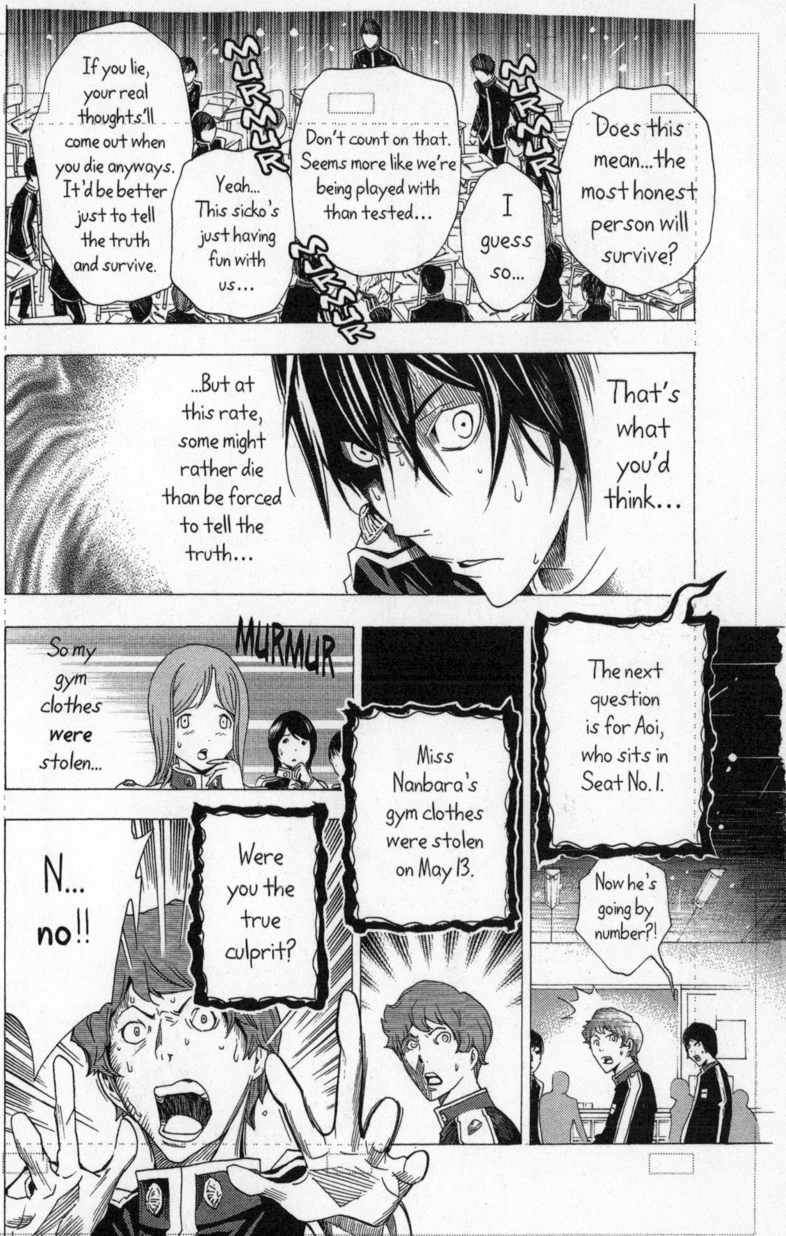
MURMUR
Does this mean...the most honest person will survive?
I guess so...
MURMUR
Don't count on that. Seems more like we're being played with than tested...
Yeah... This sicko's just having fun with us...
MURMUR
If you lie, your real thoughts'll come out when you die anyways. It'd be better just to tell the truth and survive.
That's what you'd think...
...But at this rate, some might rather die than be forced to tell the truth...
The next question is for Aoi, who sits in Seat No. 1.
Now he's going by number?!
Miss Nanbara's gym clothes were stolen on May 13.
MURMUR
So my gym clothes **were** stolen...
Were you the true culprit?
N... **no**!!

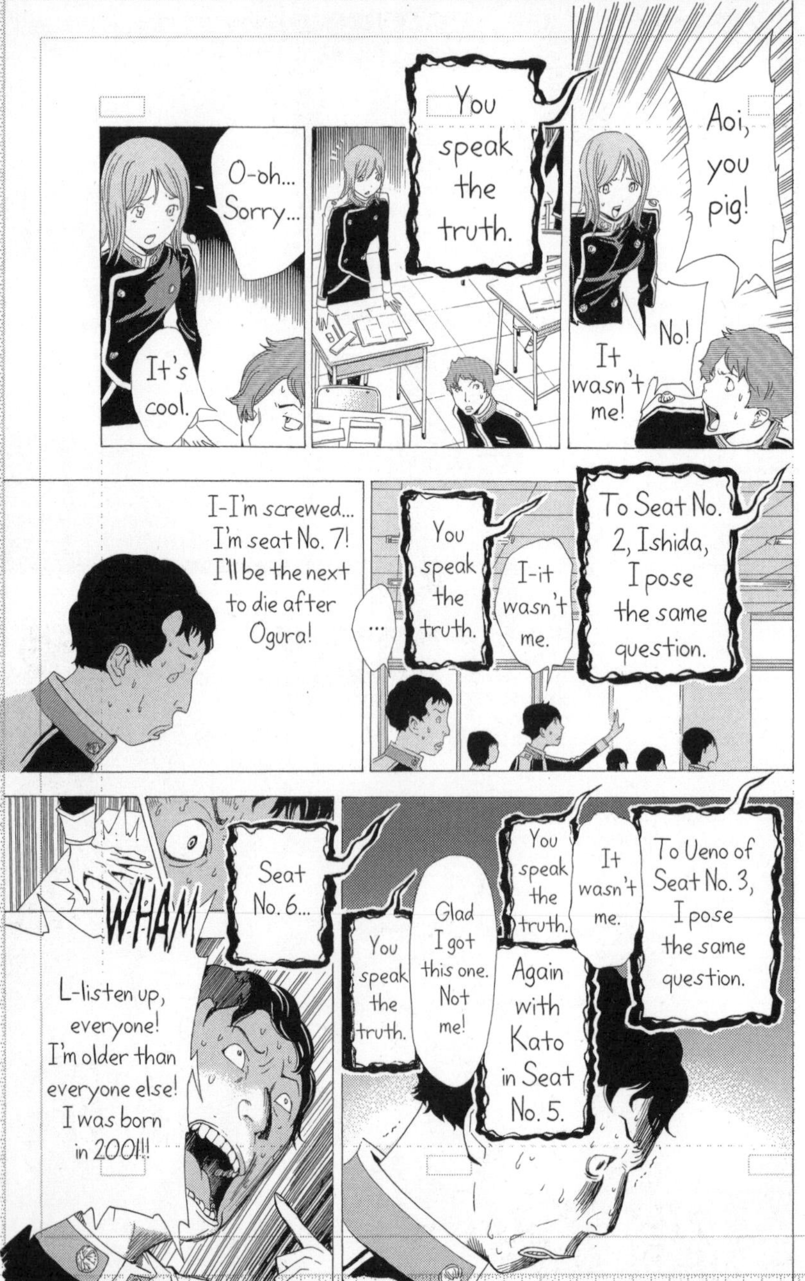
Aoi, you pig!
No!
It wasn't me!
You speak the truth.
O-oh... Sorry...
It's cool.
To Seat No. 2, Ishida, I pose the same question.
I-it wasn't me.
You speak the truth.
...
I-I'm screwed... I'm seat No. 7! I'll be the next to die after Ogura!
To Ueno of Seat No. 3, I pose the same question.
It wasn't me.
You speak the truth.
Again with Kato in Seat No. 5.
Glad I got this one. Not me!
You speak the truth.
Seat No. 6...
WHAM
L-listen up, everyone! I'm older than everyone else! I was born in 2001!!

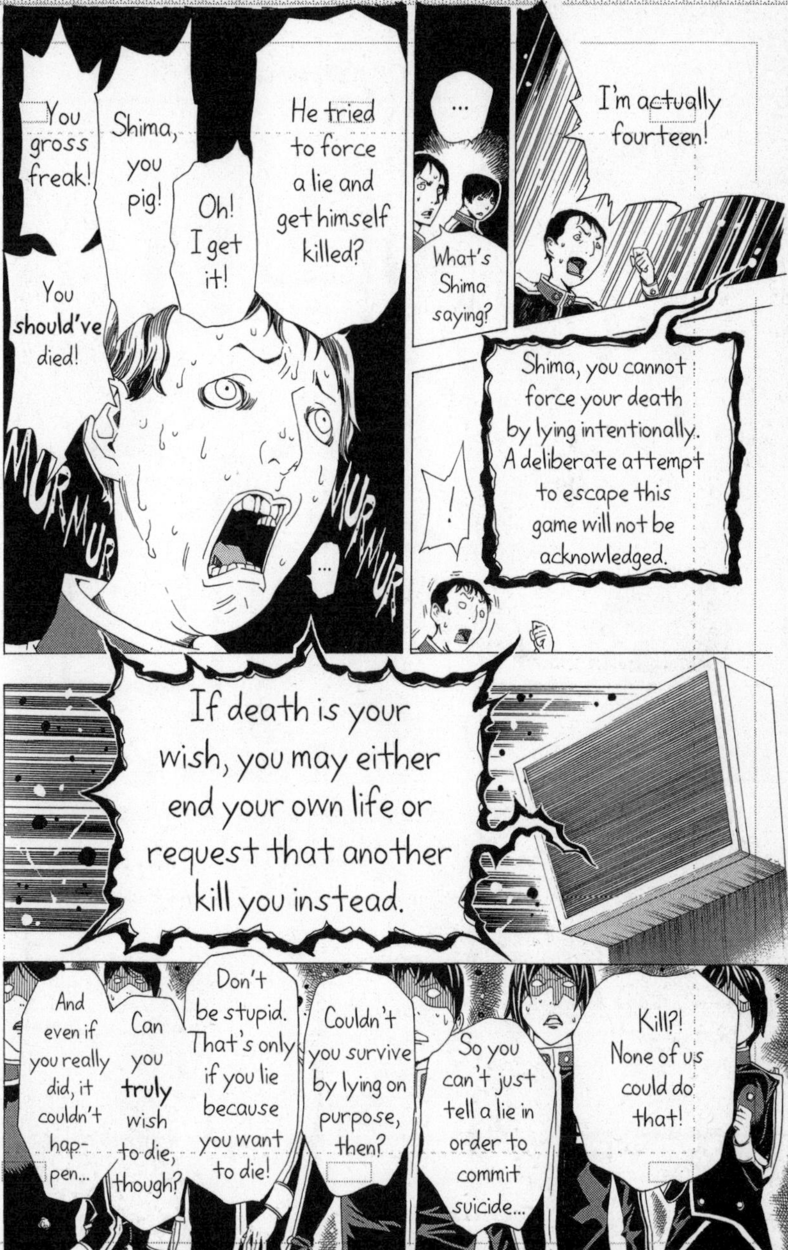

I'm actually fourteen!
...
What's Shima saying?
Shima, you cannot force your death by lying intentionally. A deliberate attempt to escape this game will not be acknowledged.
!
He tried to force a lie and get himself killed?
Oh! I get it!
Shima, you pig!
You gross freak!
You **should've** died!
MURMUR
...
MURMUR
If death is your wish, you may either end your own life or request that another kill you instead.
Kill?! None of us could do that!
So you can't just tell a lie in order to commit suicide...
Couldn't you survive by lying on purpose, then?
Don't be stupid. That's only if you lie because you want to die!
Can you **truly** wish to die, though?
And even if you really did, it couldn't hap-pen...

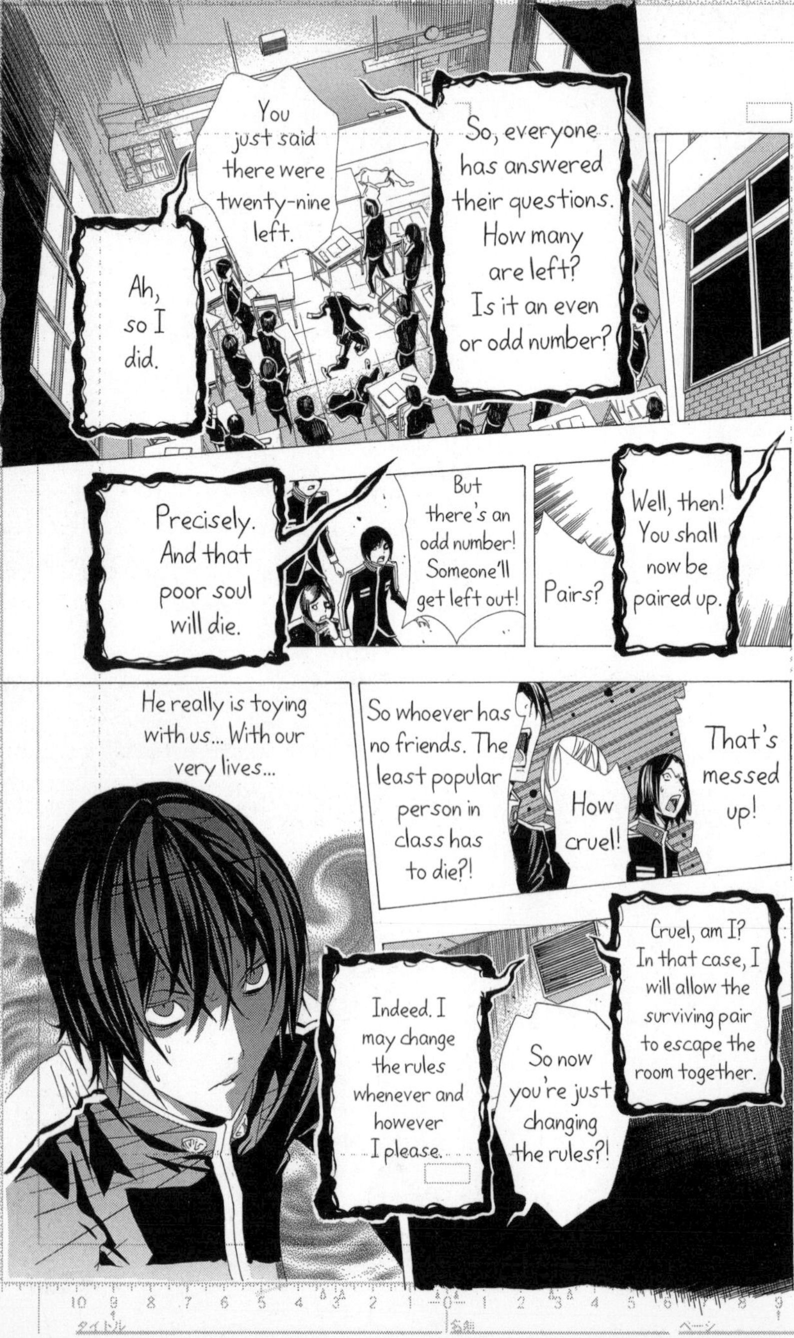
So, everyone has answered their questions. How many are left? Is it an even or odd number?
You just said there were twenty-nine left.
Ah, so I did.
Well, then! You shall now be paired up.
Pairs?
But there's an odd number! Someone'll get left out!
Precisely. And that poor soul will die.
That's messed up!
How cruel!
So whoever has no friends. The least popular person in class has to die?!
Cruel, am I? In that case, I will allow the surviving pair to escape the room together.
So now you're just changing the rules?!
Indeed. I may change the rules whenever and however I please.
He really is toying with us... With our very lives...

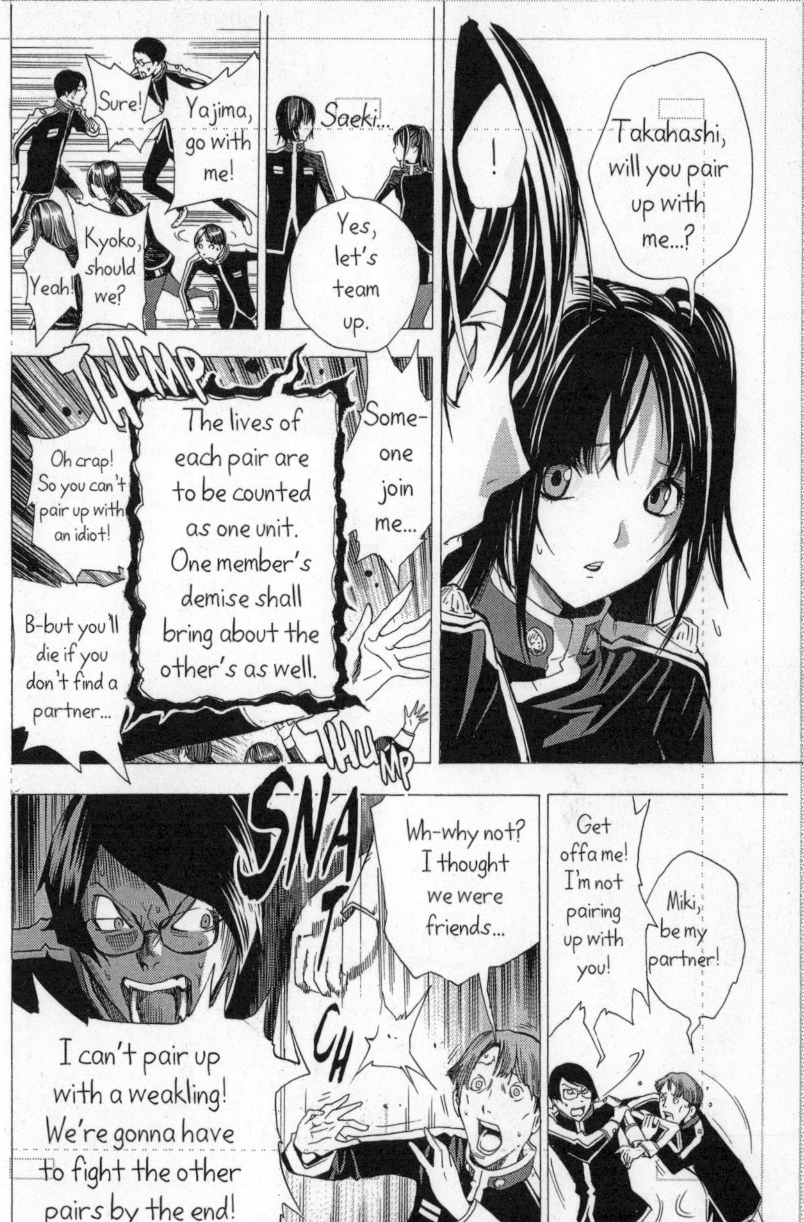
Takahashi, will you pair up with me...?
!
Saeki...
Yes, let's team up.
Yajima, go with me!
Sure!
Kyoko, should we?
Yeah!
THUMP
Some-one join me...
The lives of each pair are to be counted as one unit. One member's demise shall bring about the other's as well.
Oh crap! So you can't pair up with an idiot!
B-but you'll die if you don't find a partner...
THUMP
Miki, be my partner!
Get offa me! I'm not pairing up with you!
Wh-why not? I thought we were friends...
SNATCH
I can't pair up with a weakling! We're gonna have to fight the other pairs by the end!

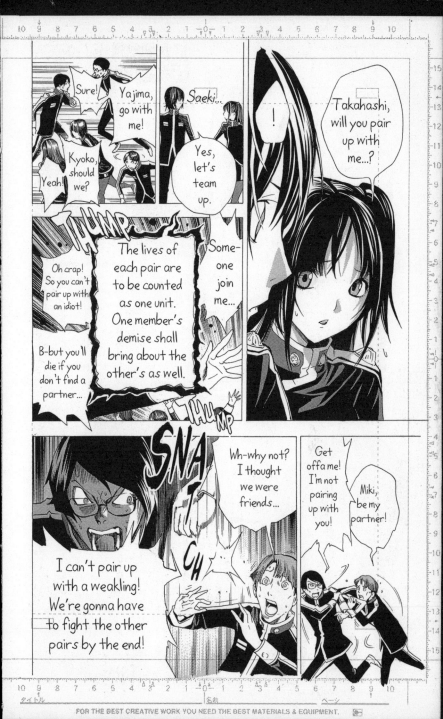

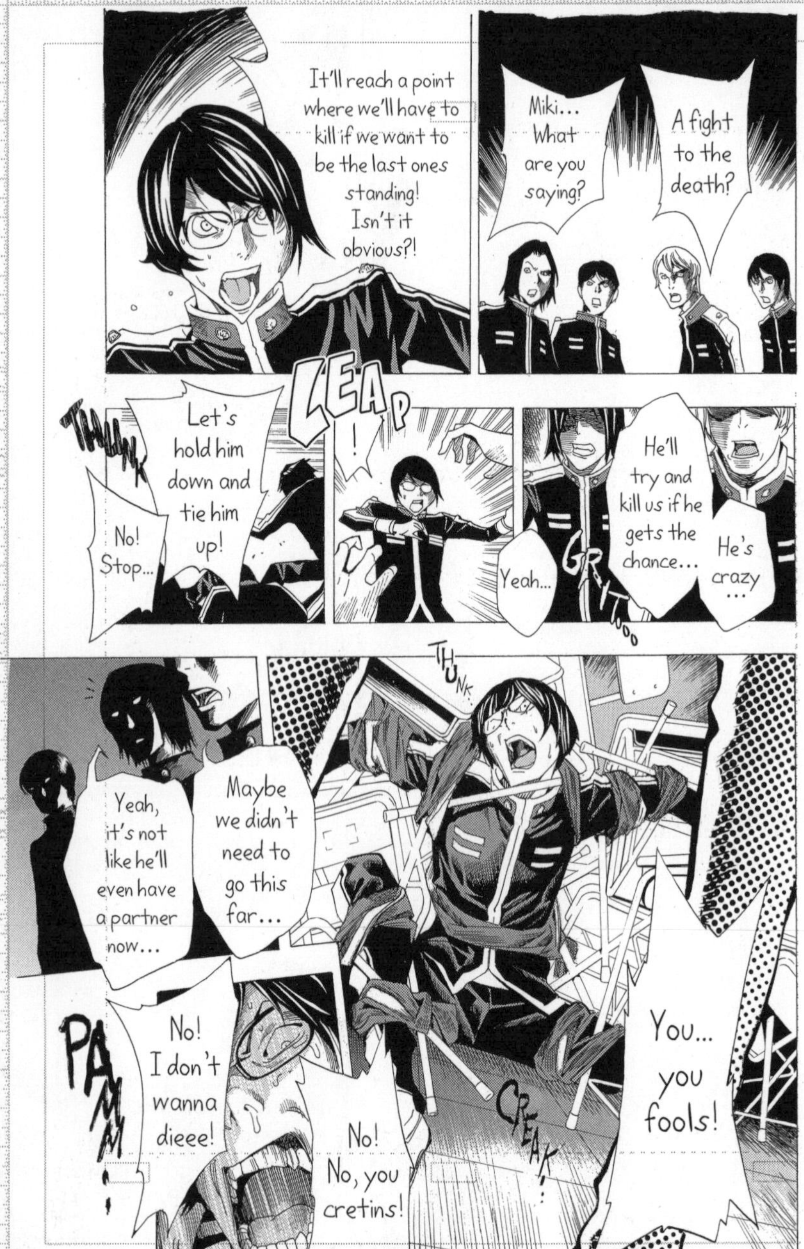

It'll reach a point where we'll have to kill if we want to be the last ones standing! Isn't it obvious?!
Miki... What are you saying?
A fight to the death?
THUNK
No! Stop...
Let's hold him down and tie him up!
LEAP
!
Yeah...
GRIT
He'll try and kill us if he gets the chance...
He's crazy...
THUNK
Maybe we didn't need to go this far...
Yeah, it's not like he'll even have a partner now...
PAM
No! I don't wanna dieee!
No! No, you cretins!
CREAK
You... you fools!

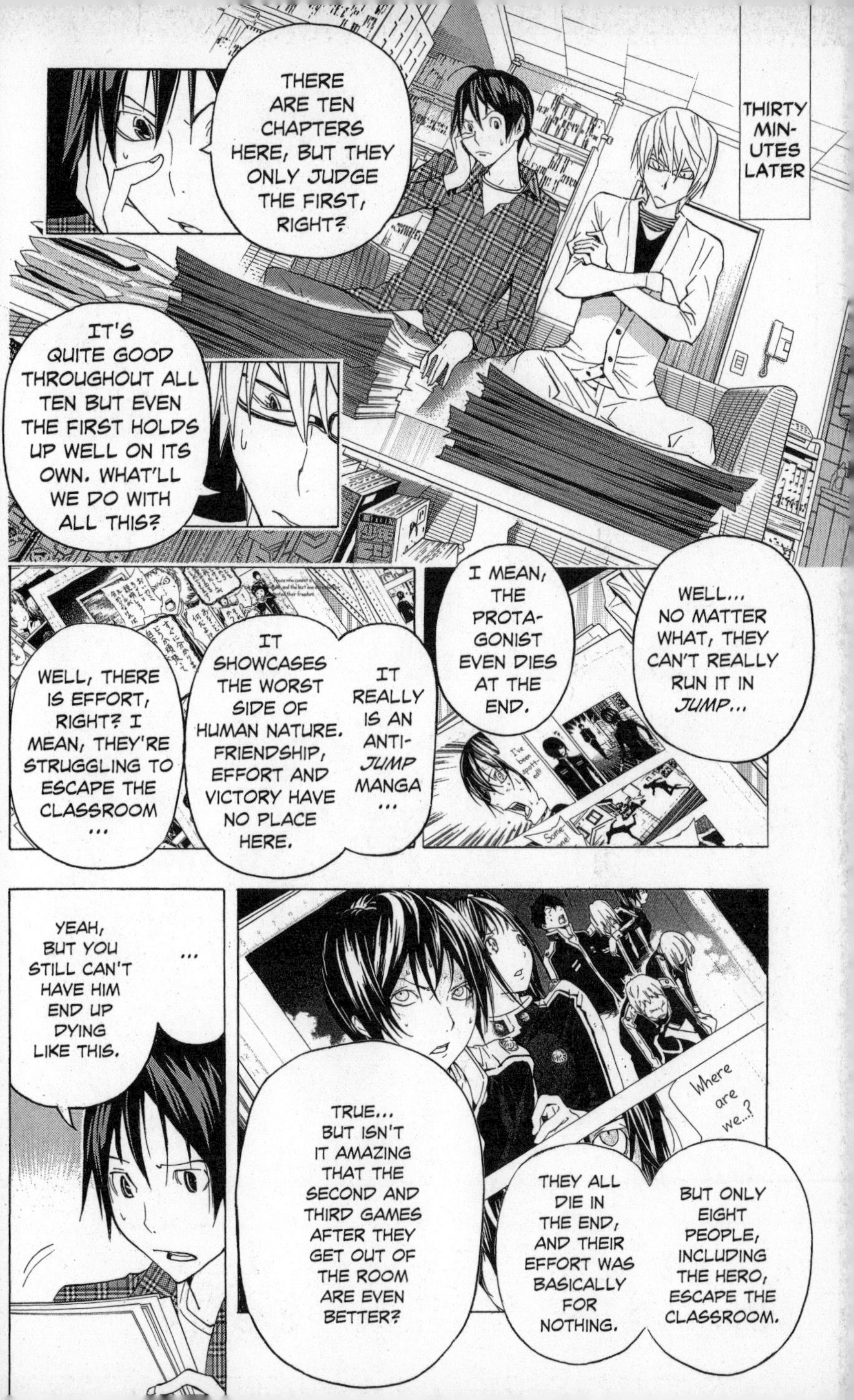
THIRTY MIN-UTES LATER
THERE ARE TEN CHAPTERS HERE, BUT THEY ONLY JUDGE THE FIRST, RIGHT?
IT'S QUITE GOOD THROUGHOUT ALL TEN BUT EVEN THE FIRST HOLDS UP WELL ON ITS OWN. WHAT'LL WE DO WITH ALL THIS?
WELL... NO MATTER WHAT, THEY CAN'T REALLY RUN IT IN *JUMP*...
I MEAN, THE PROTA-GONIST EVEN DIES AT THE END.
I've been spott-ed!
Some-one!
IT REALLY IS AN ANTI-*JUMP* MANGA...
IT SHOWCASES THE WORST SIDE OF HUMAN NATURE. FRIENDSHIP, EFFORT AND VICTORY HAVE NO PLACE HERE.
WELL, THERE IS EFFORT, RIGHT? I MEAN, THEY'RE STRUGGLING TO ESCAPE THE CLASSROOM...
Where are we...?
BUT ONLY EIGHT PEOPLE, INCLUDING THE HERO, ESCAPE THE CLASSROOM.
THEY ALL DIE IN THE END, AND THEIR EFFORT WAS BASICALLY FOR NOTHING.
TRUE... BUT ISN'T IT AMAZING THAT THE SECOND AND THIRD GAMES AFTER THEY GET OUT OF THE ROOM ARE EVEN BETTER?
...
YEAH, BUT YOU STILL CAN'T HAVE HIM END UP DYING LIKE THIS.

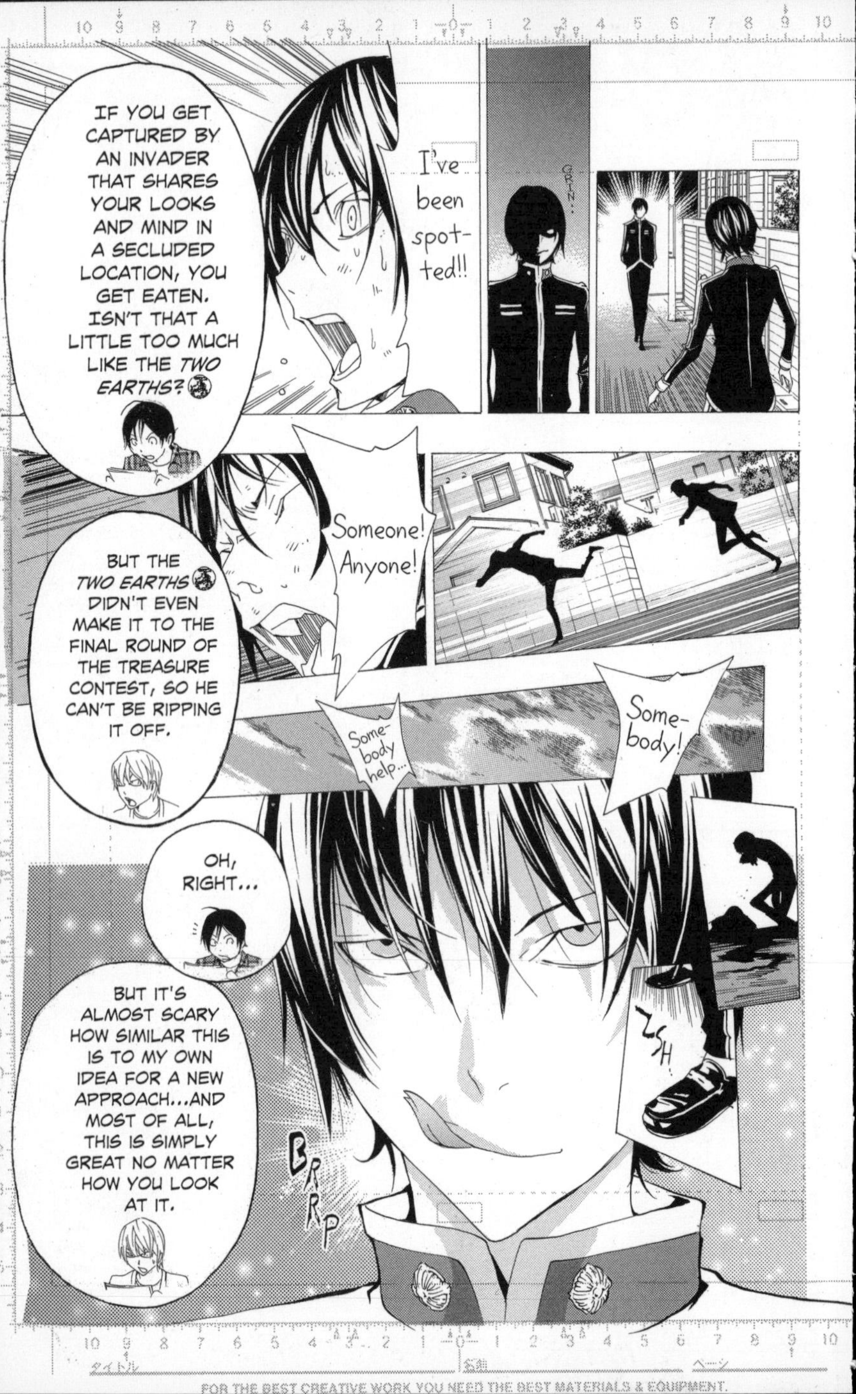
GRIN...
I've been spot-ted!!
IF YOU GET CAPTURED BY AN INVADER THAT SHARES YOUR LOOKS AND MIND IN A SECLUDED LOCATION, YOU GET EATEN. ISN'T THAT A LITTLE TOO MUCH LIKE THE *TWO EARTHS*?
Someone! Anyone!
BUT THE *TWO EARTHS* DIDN'T EVEN MAKE IT TO THE FINAL ROUND OF THE TREASURE CONTEST, SO HE CAN'T BE RIPPING IT OFF.
Some-body!
Some-body help...
ZSH
OH, RIGHT...
BRRP
BUT IT'S ALMOST SCARY HOW SIMILAR THIS IS TO MY OWN IDEA FOR A NEW APPROACH...AND MOST OF ALL, THIS IS SIMPLY GREAT NO MATTER HOW YOU LOOK AT IT.
FOR THE BEST CREATIVE WORK YOU NEED THE BEST MATERIALS & EQUIPMENT

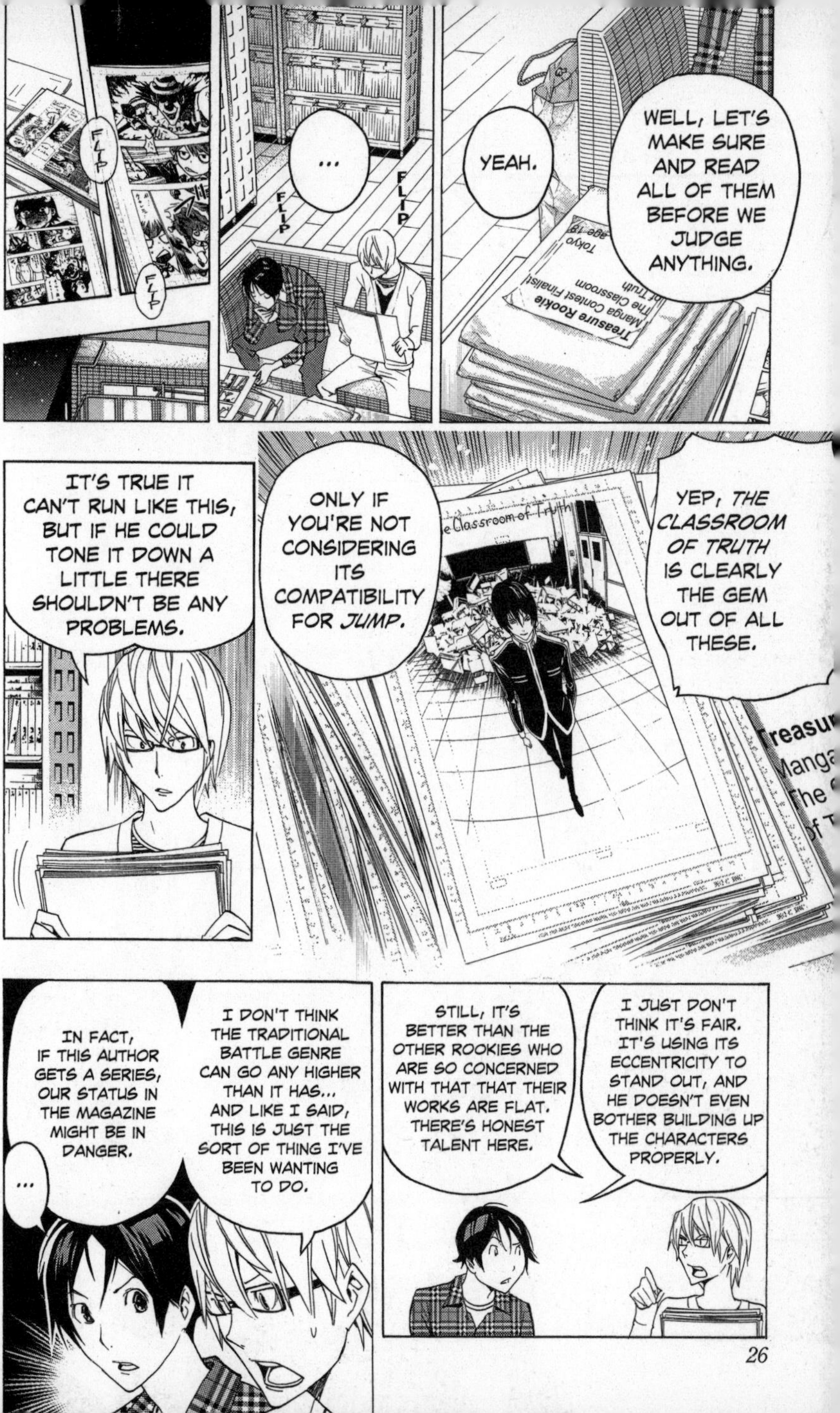
WELL, LET'S MAKE SURE AND READ ALL OF THEM BEFORE WE JUDGE ANYTHING.
YEAH.
Treasure Rookie
Manga Contest Finalist
The Classroom
of Truth
Tokyo
age 18
...
FLIP
FLIP
FLIP
FLIP
YEP, *THE CLASSROOM OF TRUTH* IS CLEARLY THE GEM OUT OF ALL THESE.
ONLY IF YOU'RE NOT CONSIDERING ITS COMPATIBILITY FOR *JUMP*.
IT'S TRUE IT CAN'T RUN LIKE THIS, BUT IF HE COULD TONE IT DOWN A LITTLE THERE SHOULDN'T BE ANY PROBLEMS.
I JUST DON'T THINK IT'S FAIR. IT'S USING ITS ECCENTRICITY TO STAND OUT, AND HE DOESN'T EVEN BOTHER BUILDING UP THE CHARACTERS PROPERLY.
STILL, IT'S BETTER THAN THE OTHER ROOKIES WHO ARE SO CONCERNED WITH THAT THAT THEIR WORKS ARE FLAT. THERE'S HONEST TALENT HERE.
I DON'T THINK THE TRADITIONAL BATTLE GENRE CAN GO ANY HIGHER THAN IT HAS... AND LIKE I SAID, THIS IS JUST THE SORT OF THING I'VE BEEN WANTING TO DO.
IN FACT, IF THIS AUTHOR GETS A SERIES, OUR STATUS IN THE MAGAZINE MIGHT BE IN DANGER.
...

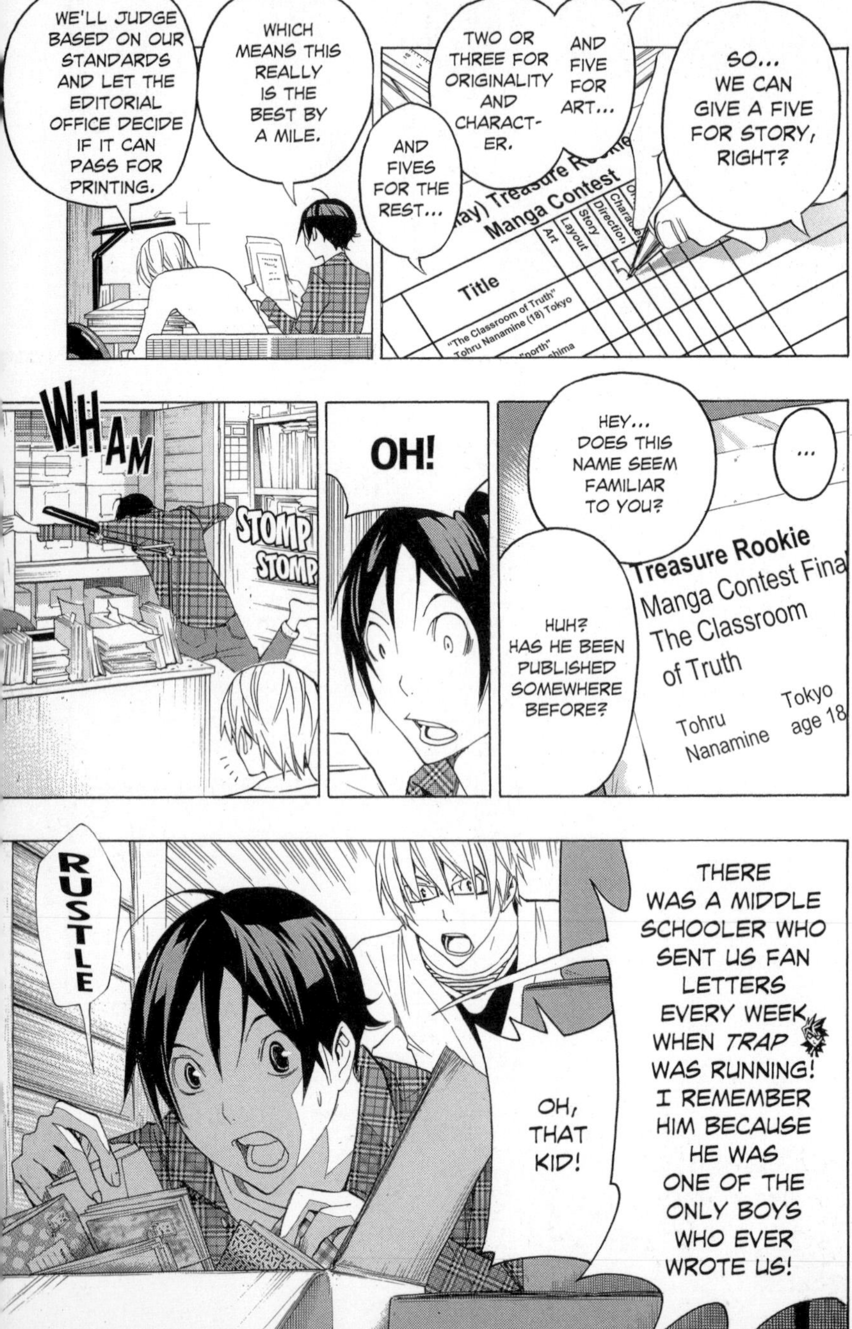
SO... WE CAN GIVE A FIVE FOR STORY, RIGHT?
AND FIVE FOR ART...
TWO OR THREE FOR ORIGINALITY AND CHARACTER.
AND FIVES FOR THE REST...
Treasure Rookie Manga Contest
Art
Layout
Story
Direction
Character
Title
"The Classroom of Truth" Tohru Nanamine (18) Tokyo
WHICH MEANS THIS REALLY IS THE BEST BY A MILE.
WE'LL JUDGE BASED ON OUR STANDARDS AND LET THE EDITORIAL OFFICE DECIDE IF IT CAN PASS FOR PRINTING.
...
HEY... DOES THIS NAME SEEM FAMILIAR TO YOU?
HUH? HAS HE BEEN PUBLISHED SOMEWHERE BEFORE?
Treasure Rookie Manga Contest Fina
The Classroom of Truth
Tohru Nanamine Tokyo age 18
OH!
WHAM
STOMP STOMP
THERE WAS A MIDDLE SCHOOLER WHO SENT US FAN LETTERS EVERY WEEK WHEN *TRAP* WAS RUNNING! I REMEMBER HIM BECAUSE HE WAS ONE OF THE ONLY BOYS WHO EVER WROTE US!
OH, THAT KID!
RUSTLE

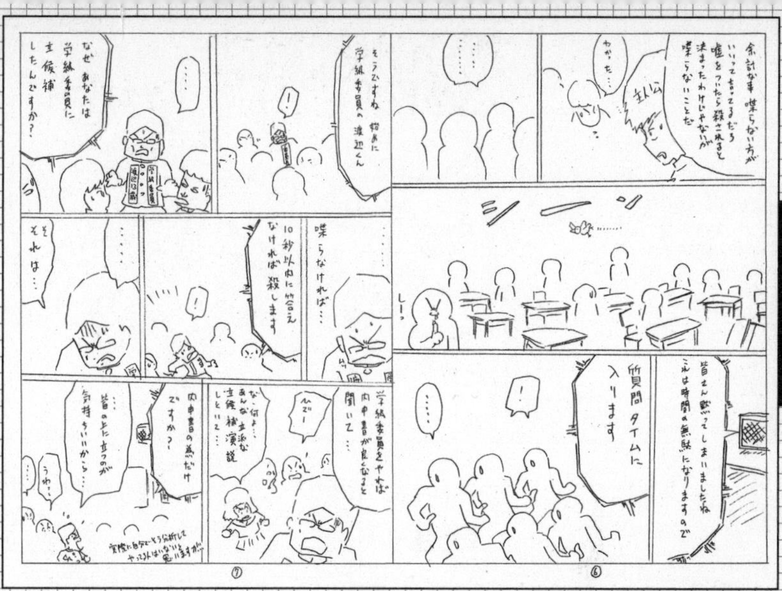
余計な事 喋らない方が
いいって言ってるだろ
嘘をついたら殺されると
決まったわけじゃないが
喋らないことだ
わかった…
……
シーーン
皆さん黙ってしまいましたね
これは時間の無駄になりますので
質問タイムに
入ります
!
……
そうですね 始めに
学級委員の 渡辺くん
!
……
なぜ あなたは
学級委員に
立候補
したんですか？
喋らなければ…
10秒以内に答え
なければ
殺します
!
……
それは…
学級委員をやれば
内申書が良くなると
聞いて…
んでー
な、何よ…
あんな立派な
立候補演説
しといて…
内申書の為だけ
ですか？
皆の上に立つのが
気持ちいいから…
うわ…
……
⑦
⑥

OHBA'S STORYBOARD

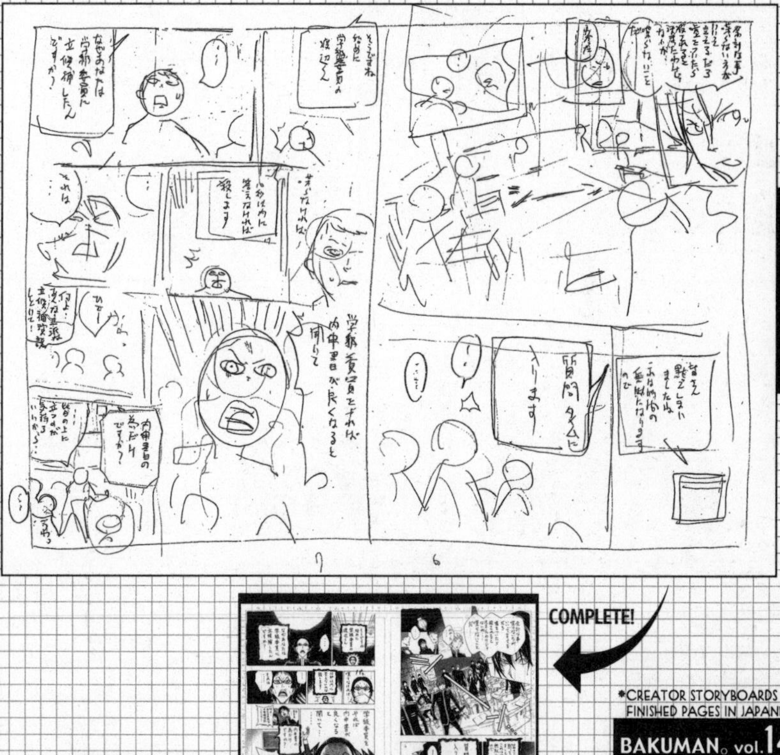

OBATA'S STORYBOARD

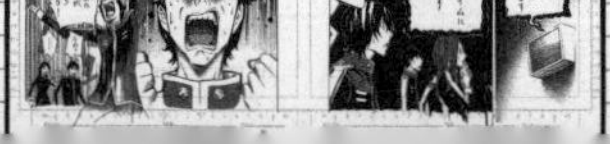

COMPLETE!

*CREATOR STORYBOARDS AND FINISHED PAGES IN JAPANESE

BAKUMAN。 vol.14

"Until the Final Draft Is Complete"

Chapter 116, pp. 14-15

CHAPTER 117 FAN LETTER AND BLOG

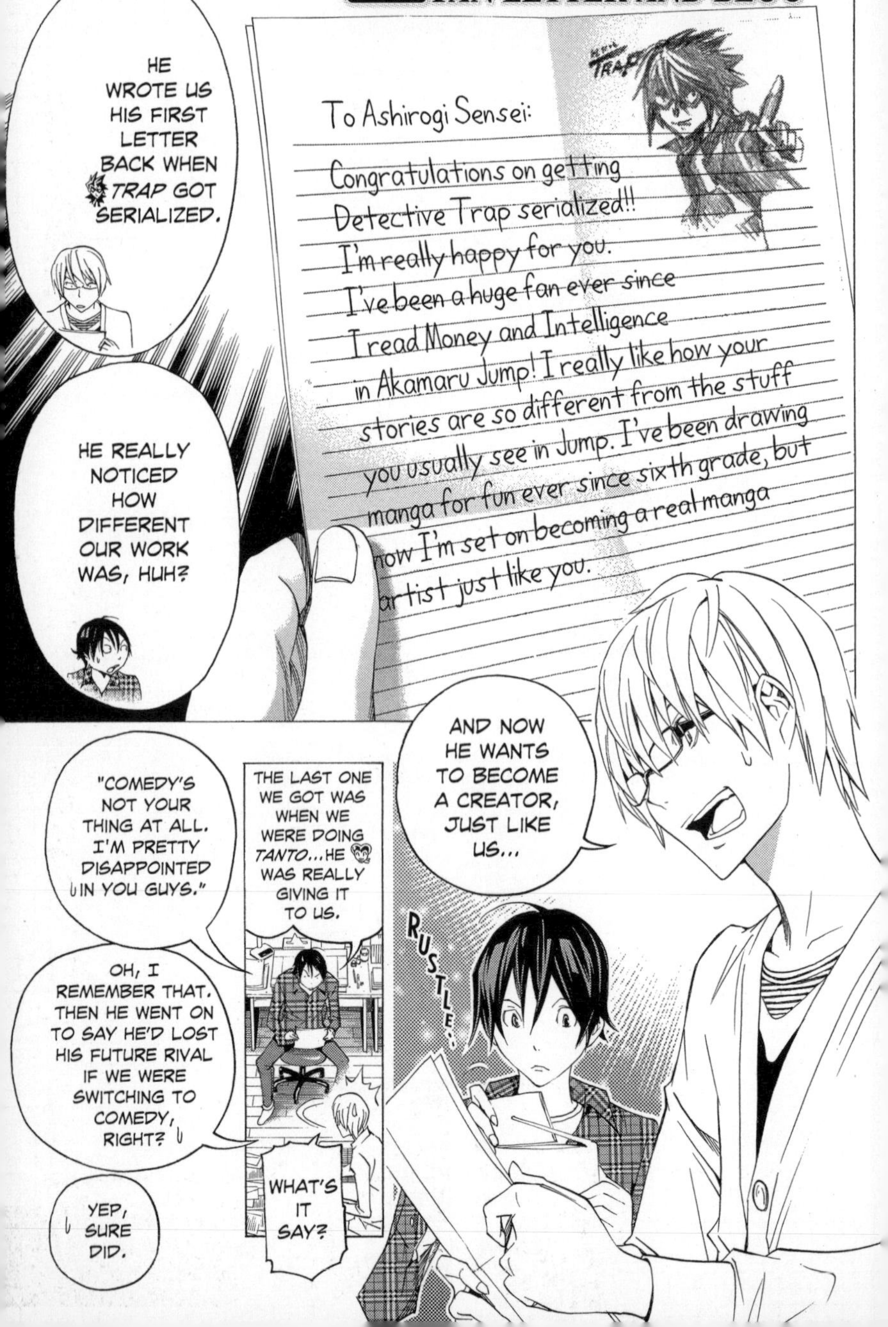
TRAP
To Ashirogi Sensei:
Congratulations on getting Detective Trap serialized!! I'm really happy for you. I've been a huge fan ever since I read Money and Intelligence in Akamaru Jump! I really like how your stories are so different from the stuff you usually see in Jump. I've been drawing manga for fun ever since sixth grade, but now I'm set on becoming a real manga artist just like you.
HE WROTE US HIS FIRST LETTER BACK WHEN TRAP GOT SERIALIZED.
HE REALLY NOTICED HOW DIFFERENT OUR WORK WAS, HUH?
AND NOW HE WANTS TO BECOME A CREATOR, JUST LIKE US...
RUSTLE
THE LAST ONE WE GOT WAS WHEN WE WERE DOING TANTO...HE WAS REALLY GIVING IT TO US.
WHAT'S IT SAY?
"COMEDY'S NOT YOUR THING AT ALL. I'M PRETTY DISAPPOINTED IN YOU GUYS."
OH, I REMEMBER THAT. THEN HE WENT ON TO SAY HE'D LOST HIS FUTURE RIVAL IF WE WERE SWITCHING TO COMEDY, RIGHT?
YEP, SURE DID.

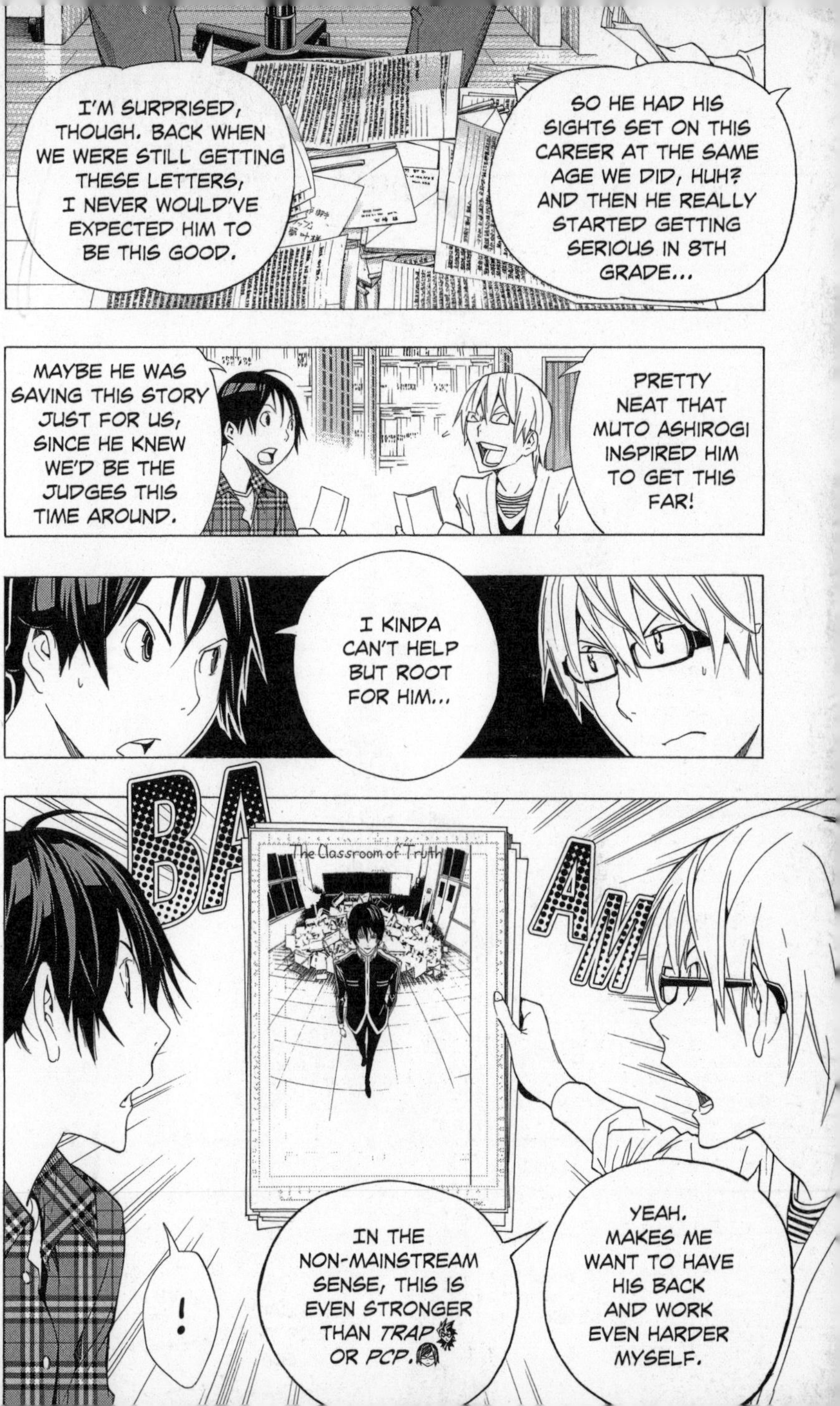
SO HE HAD HIS SIGHTS SET ON THIS CAREER AT THE SAME AGE WE DID, HUH? AND THEN HE REALLY STARTED GETTING SERIOUS IN 8TH GRADE...
I'M SURPRISED, THOUGH. BACK WHEN WE WERE STILL GETTING THESE LETTERS, I NEVER WOULD'VE EXPECTED HIM TO BE THIS GOOD.
PRETTY NEAT THAT MUTO ASHIROGI INSPIRED HIM TO GET THIS FAR!
MAYBE HE WAS SAVING THIS STORY JUST FOR US, SINCE HE KNEW WE'D BE THE JUDGES THIS TIME AROUND.
I KINDA CAN'T HELP BUT ROOT FOR HIM...
BAAM
The Classroom of Truth
YEAH. MAKES ME WANT TO HAVE HIS BACK AND WORK EVEN HARDER MYSELF.
IN THE NON-MAINSTREAM SENSE, THIS IS EVEN STRONGER THAN *TRAP* OR *PCP*.
!

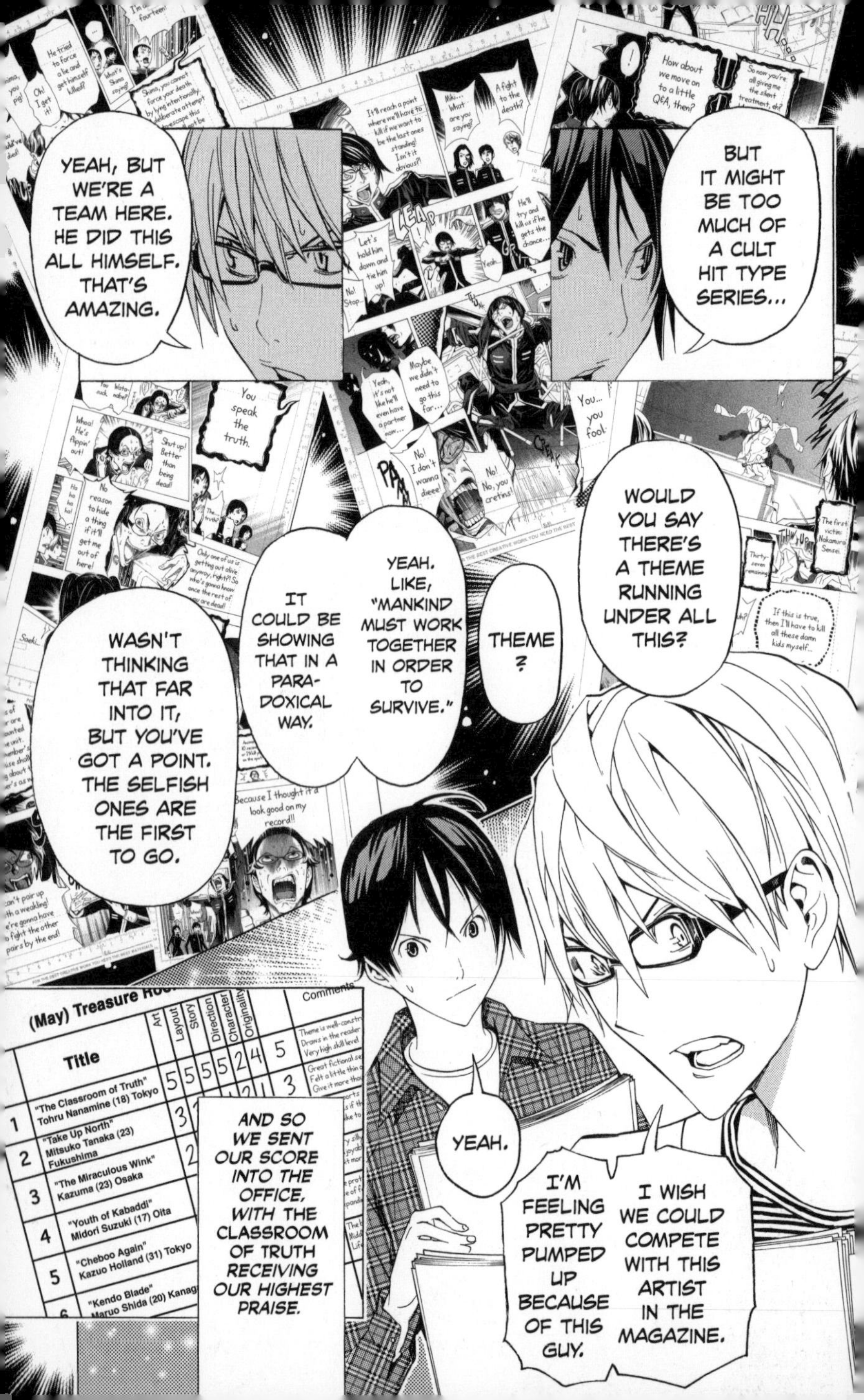
BUT IT MIGHT BE TOO MUCH OF A CULT HIT TYPE SERIES...
YEAH, BUT WE'RE A TEAM HERE. HE DID THIS ALL HIMSELF. THAT'S AMAZING.
WOULD YOU SAY THERE'S A THEME RUNNING UNDER ALL THIS?
THEME?
YEAH. LIKE, "MANKIND MUST WORK TOGETHER IN ORDER TO SURVIVE."
IT COULD BE SHOWING THAT IN A PARA-DOXICAL WAY.
WASN'T THINKING THAT FAR INTO IT, BUT YOU'VE GOT A POINT. THE SELFISH ONES ARE THE FIRST TO GO.
I WISH WE COULD COMPETE WITH THIS ARTIST IN THE MAGAZINE.
I'M FEELING PRETTY PUMPED UP BECAUSE OF THIS GUY.
YEAH.
AND SO WE SENT OUR SCORE INTO THE OFFICE, WITH THE CLASSROOM OF TRUTH RECEIVING OUR HIGHEST PRAISE.
(May) Treasure
Title
Art Layout Story Direction Character Originality
Comments
1 "The Classroom of Truth" Tohru Nanamine (18) Tokyo 5 5 5 5 2 4 5
2 "Take Up North" Mitsuko Tanaka (23) Fukushima
3 "The Miraculous Wink" Kazuma (23) Osaka
4 "Youth of Kabaddi" Midori Suzuki (17) Oita
5 "Cheboo Again" Kazuo Holland (31) Tokyo
"Kendo Blade" Maruo Shida (20)

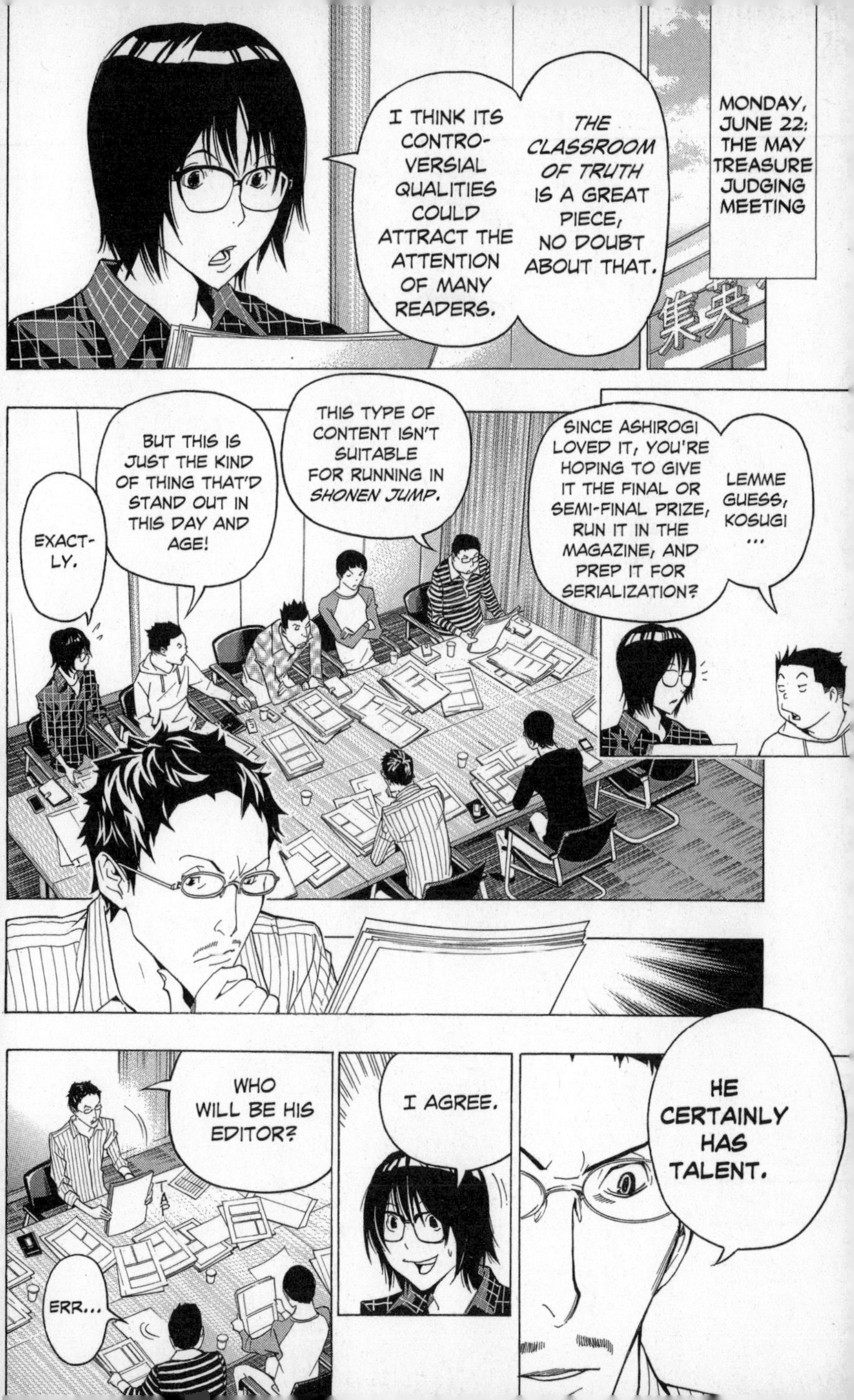
MONDAY, JUNE 22: THE MAY TREASURE JUDGING MEETING
THE CLASSROOM OF TRUTH IS A GREAT PIECE, NO DOUBT ABOUT THAT.
I THINK ITS CONTROVERSIAL QUALITIES COULD ATTRACT THE ATTENTION OF MANY READERS.
LEMME GUESS, KOSUGI...
SINCE ASHIROGI LOVED IT, YOU'RE HOPING TO GIVE IT THE FINAL OR SEMI-FINAL PRIZE, RUN IT IN THE MAGAZINE, AND PREP IT FOR SERIALIZATION?
THIS TYPE OF CONTENT ISN'T SUITABLE FOR RUNNING IN *SHONEN JUMP.*
BUT THIS IS JUST THE KIND OF THING THAT'D STAND OUT IN THIS DAY AND AGE!
EXACTLY.
HE CERTAINLY HAS TALENT.
I AGREE.
WHO WILL BE HIS EDITOR?
TAP
ERR...

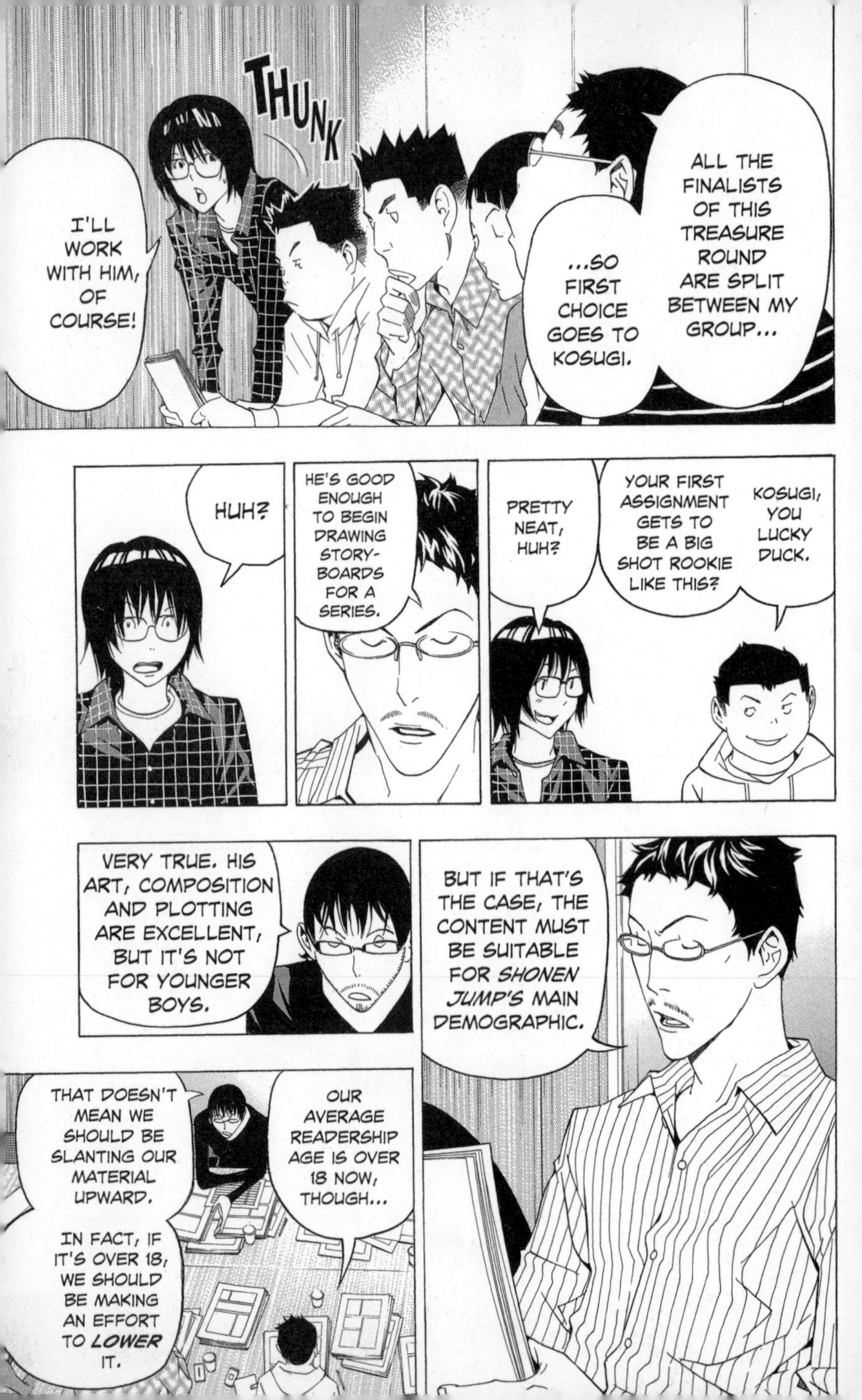
ALL THE FINALISTS OF THIS TREASURE ROUND ARE SPLIT BETWEEN MY GROUP...
...SO FIRST CHOICE GOES TO KOSUGI.
THUNK
I'LL WORK WITH HIM, OF COURSE!
KOSUGI, YOU LUCKY DUCK.
YOUR FIRST ASSIGNMENT GETS TO BE A BIG SHOT ROOKIE LIKE THIS?
PRETTY NEAT, HUH?
HE'S GOOD ENOUGH TO BEGIN DRAWING STORY-BOARDS FOR A SERIES.
HUH?
BUT IF THAT'S THE CASE, THE CONTENT MUST BE SUITABLE FOR *SHONEN JUMP'S* MAIN DEMOGRAPHIC.
VERY TRUE. HIS ART, COMPOSITION AND PLOTTING ARE EXCELLENT, BUT IT'S NOT FOR YOUNGER BOYS.
OUR AVERAGE READERSHIP AGE IS OVER 18 NOW, THOUGH...
THAT DOESN'T MEAN WE SHOULD BE SLANTING OUR MATERIAL UPWARD.
IN FACT, IF IT'S OVER 18, WE SHOULD BE MAKING AN EFFORT TO ***LOWER*** IT.

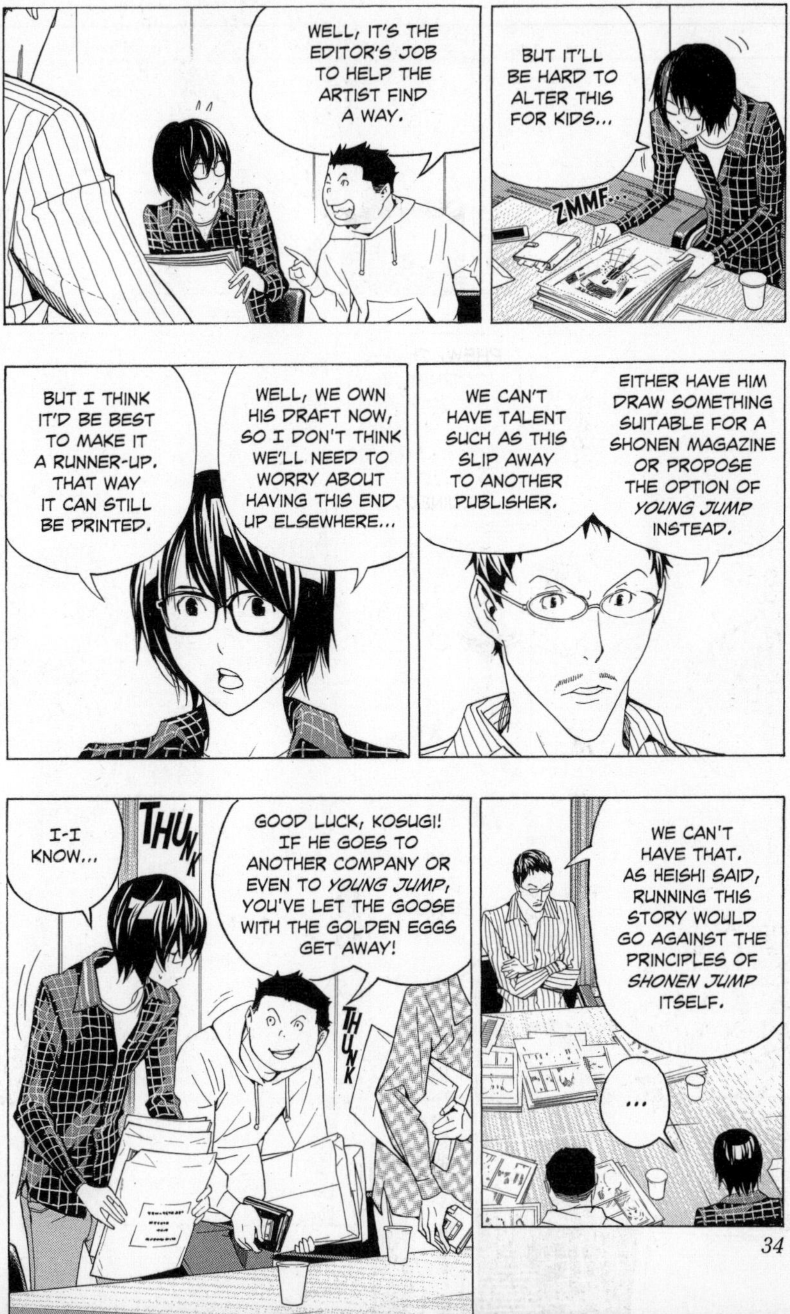
BUT IT'LL BE HARD TO ALTER THIS FOR KIDS...
ZMMF...
WELL, IT'S THE EDITOR'S JOB TO HELP THE ARTIST FIND A WAY.
EITHER HAVE HIM DRAW SOMETHING SUITABLE FOR A SHONEN MAGAZINE OR PROPOSE THE OPTION OF *YOUNG JUMP* INSTEAD.
WE CAN'T HAVE TALENT SUCH AS THIS SLIP AWAY TO ANOTHER PUBLISHER.
WELL, WE OWN HIS DRAFT NOW, SO I DON'T THINK WE'LL NEED TO WORRY ABOUT HAVING THIS END UP ELSEWHERE...
BUT I THINK IT'D BE BEST TO MAKE IT A RUNNER-UP. THAT WAY IT CAN STILL BE PRINTED.
WE CAN'T HAVE THAT. AS HEISHI SAID, RUNNING THIS STORY WOULD GO AGAINST THE PRINCIPLES OF *SHONEN JUMP* ITSELF.
...
THUNK
GOOD LUCK, KOSUGI! IF HE GOES TO ANOTHER COMPANY OR EVEN TO *YOUNG JUMP*, YOU'VE LET THE GOOSE WITH THE GOLDEN EGGS GET AWAY!
THUNK
I-I KNOW...

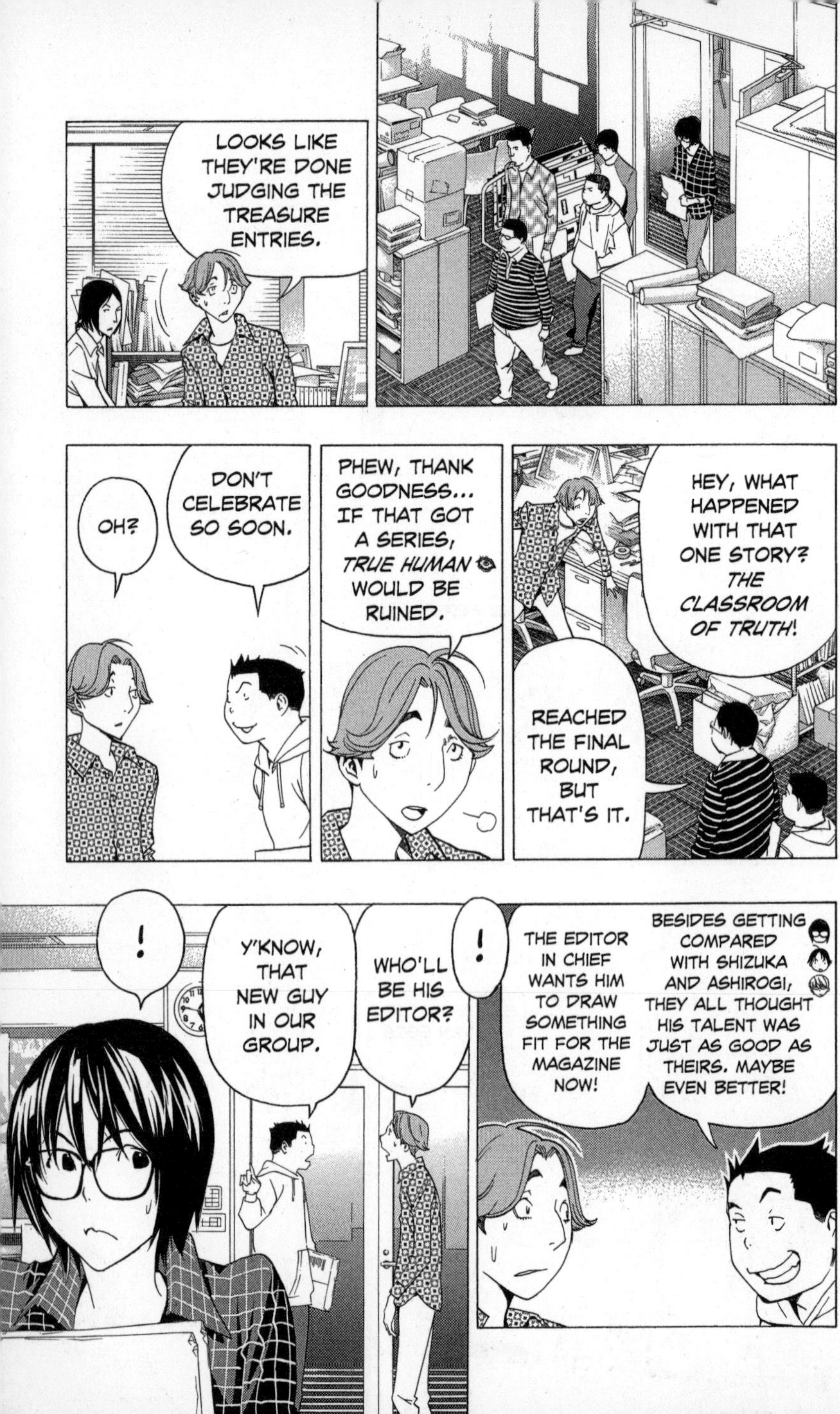
LOOKS LIKE THEY'RE DONE JUDGING THE TREASURE ENTRIES.
HEY, WHAT HAPPENED WITH THAT ONE STORY? *THE CLASSROOM OF TRUTH*!
REACHED THE FINAL ROUND, BUT THAT'S IT.
PHEW, THANK GOODNESS... IF THAT GOT A SERIES, *TRUE HUMAN* WOULD BE RUINED.
DON'T CELEBRATE SO SOON.
OH?
BESIDES GETTING COMPARED WITH SHIZUKA AND ASHIROGI, THEY ALL THOUGHT HIS TALENT WAS JUST AS GOOD AS THEIRS. MAYBE EVEN BETTER!
THE EDITOR IN CHIEF WANTS HIM TO DRAW SOMETHING FIT FOR THE MAGAZINE NOW!
!
WHO'LL BE HIS EDITOR?
Y'KNOW, THAT NEW GUY IN OUR GROUP.
!

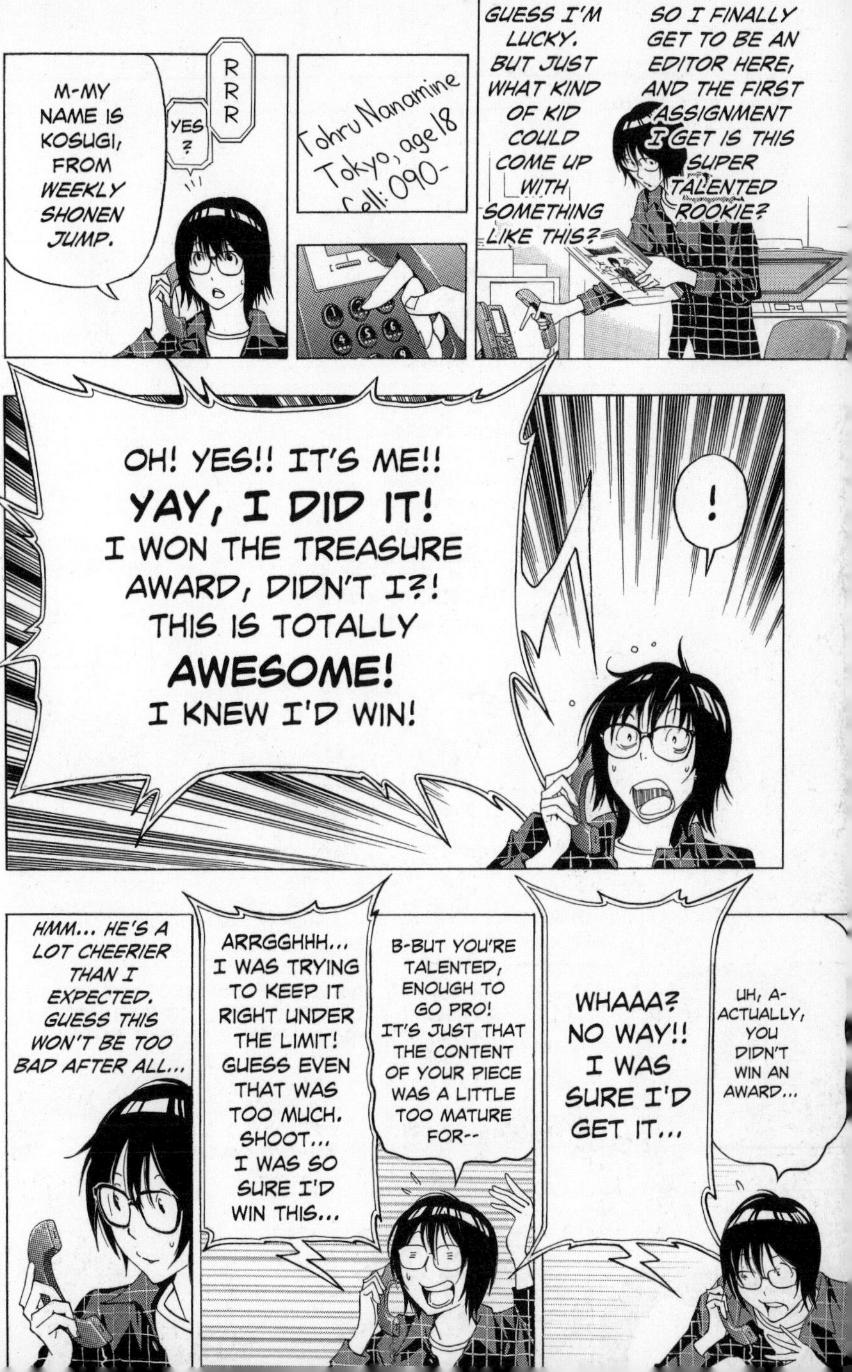
SO I FINALLY GET TO BE AN EDITOR HERE, AND THE FIRST ASSIGNMENT I GET IS THIS SUPER TALENTED ROOKIE?
GUESS I'M LUCKY. BUT JUST WHAT KIND OF KID COULD COME UP WITH SOMETHING LIKE THIS?
Tohru Nanamine Tokyo, age 18 Cell: 090-
RRR
YES?
M-MY NAME IS KOSUGI, FROM WEEKLY SHONEN JUMP.
!
OH! YES!! IT'S ME!! YAY, I DID IT! I WON THE TREASURE AWARD, DIDN'T I?! THIS IS TOTALLY AWESOME! I KNEW I'D WIN!
UH, A-ACTUALLY, YOU DIDN'T WIN AN AWARD...
WHAAA? NO WAY!! I WAS SURE I'D GET IT...
B-BUT YOU'RE TALENTED, ENOUGH TO GO PRO! IT'S JUST THAT THE CONTENT OF YOUR PIECE WAS A LITTLE TOO MATURE FOR--
ARRGGHHH... I WAS TRYING TO KEEP IT RIGHT UNDER THE LIMIT! GUESS EVEN THAT WAS TOO MUCH. SHOOT... I WAS SO SURE I'D WIN THIS...
HMM... HE'S A LOT CHEERIER THAN I EXPECTED. GUESS THIS WON'T BE TOO BAD AFTER ALL...

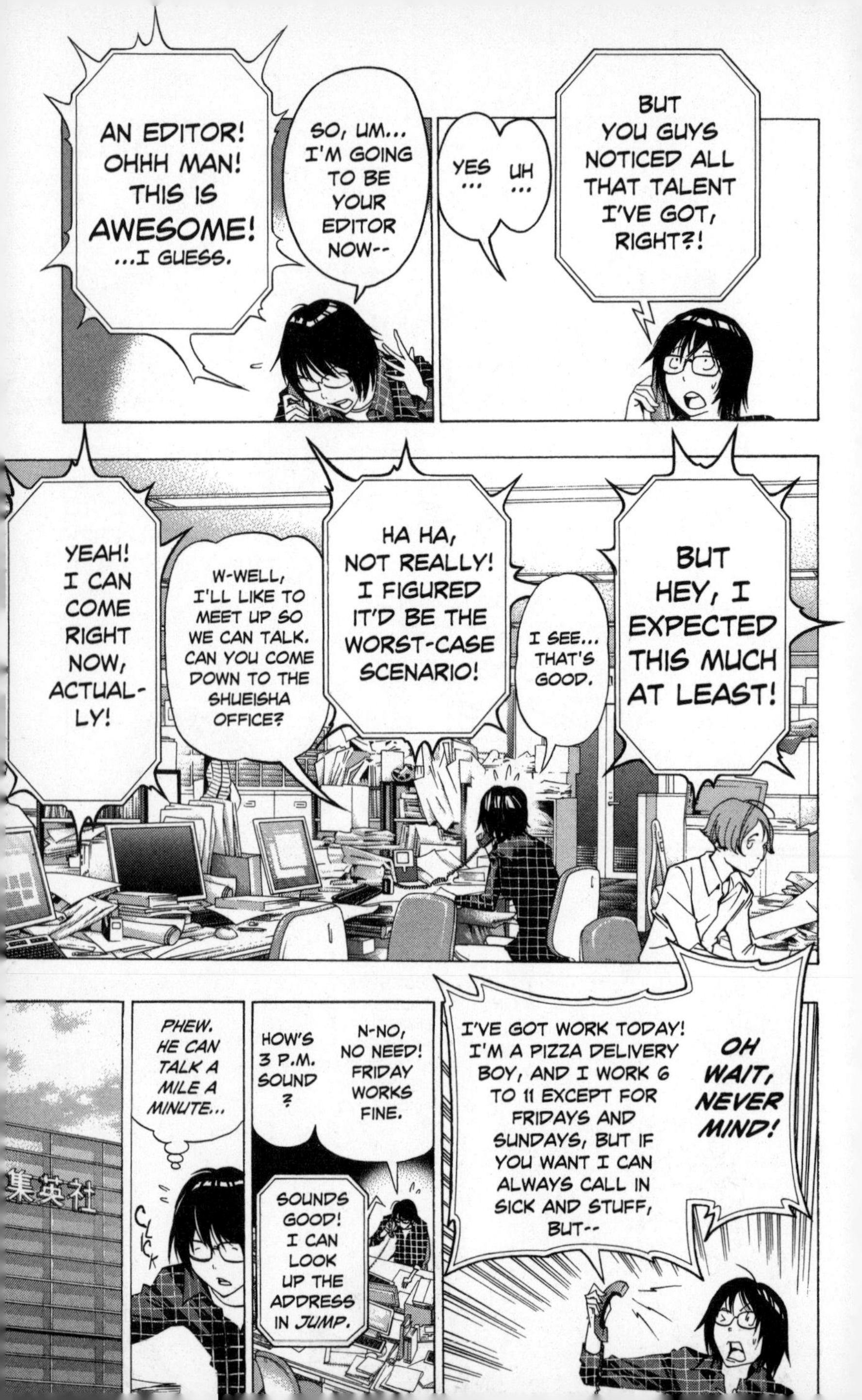
BUT YOU GUYS NOTICED ALL THAT TALENT I'VE GOT, RIGHT?!
UH ...
YES ...
SO, UM... I'M GOING TO BE YOUR EDITOR NOW--
AN EDITOR! OHHH MAN! THIS IS AWESOME! ...I GUESS.
BUT HEY, I EXPECTED THIS MUCH AT LEAST!
I SEE... THAT'S GOOD.
HA HA, NOT REALLY! I FIGURED IT'D BE THE WORST-CASE SCENARIO!
W-WELL, I'LL LIKE TO MEET UP SO WE CAN TALK. CAN YOU COME DOWN TO THE SHUEISHA OFFICE?
YEAH! I CAN COME RIGHT NOW, ACTUAL-LY!
OH WAIT, NEVER MIND!
I'VE GOT WORK TODAY! I'M A PIZZA DELIVERY BOY, AND I WORK 6 TO 11 EXCEPT FOR FRIDAYS AND SUNDAYS, BUT IF YOU WANT I CAN ALWAYS CALL IN SICK AND STUFF, BUT--
N-NO, NO NEED! FRIDAY WORKS FINE.
HOW'S 3 P.M. SOUND?
SOUNDS GOOD! I CAN LOOK UP THE ADDRESS IN *JUMP*.
PHEW. HE CAN TALK A MILE A MINUTE...
CLICK
集英社

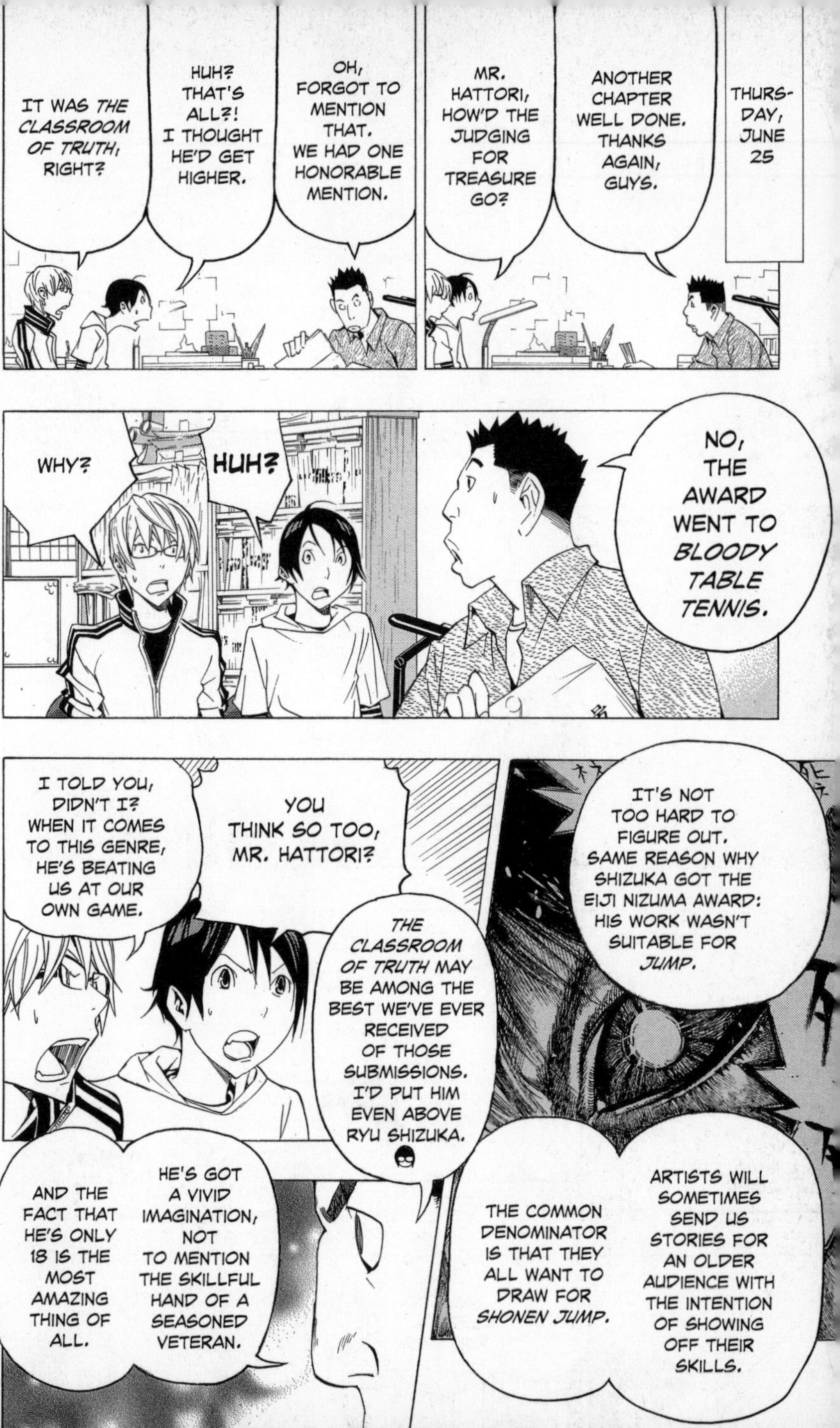
THURSDAY, JUNE 25
ANOTHER CHAPTER WELL DONE. THANKS AGAIN, GUYS.
MR. HATTORI, HOW'D THE JUDGING FOR TREASURE GO?
OH, FORGOT TO MENTION THAT. WE HAD ONE HONORABLE MENTION.
HUH? THAT'S ALL?! I THOUGHT HE'D GET HIGHER.
IT WAS *THE CLASSROOM OF TRUTH*, RIGHT?
NO, THE AWARD WENT TO *BLOODY TABLE TENNIS*.
HUH?
WHY?
IT'S NOT TOO HARD TO FIGURE OUT. SAME REASON WHY SHIZUKA GOT THE EIJI NIZUMA AWARD: HIS WORK WASN'T SUITABLE FOR *JUMP*.
ARTISTS WILL SOMETIMES SEND US STORIES FOR AN OLDER AUDIENCE WITH THE INTENTION OF SHOWING OFF THEIR SKILLS.
THE COMMON DENOMINATOR IS THAT THEY ALL WANT TO DRAW FOR *SHONEN JUMP*.
YOU THINK SO TOO, MR. HATTORI?
I TOLD YOU, DIDN'T I? WHEN IT COMES TO THIS GENRE, HE'S BEATING US AT OUR OWN GAME.
THE CLASSROOM OF TRUTH MAY BE AMONG THE BEST WE'VE EVER RECEIVED OF THOSE SUBMISSIONS. I'D PUT HIM EVEN ABOVE RYU SHIZUKA.
HE'S GOT A VIVID IMAGINATION, NOT TO MENTION THE SKILLFUL HAND OF A SEASONED VETERAN.
AND THE FACT THAT HE'S ONLY 18 IS THE MOST AMAZING THING OF ALL.

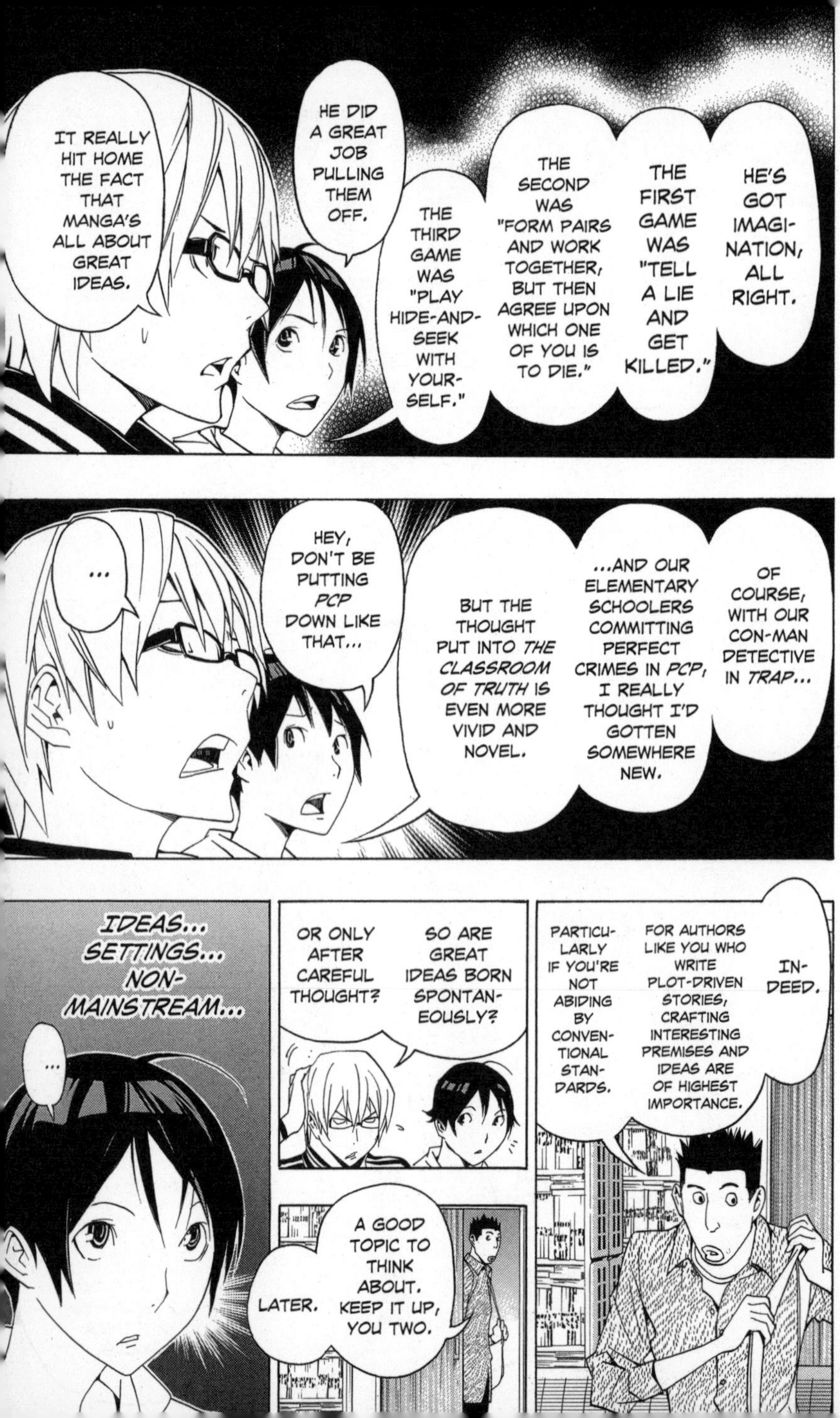
HE'S GOT IMAGINATION, ALL RIGHT.
THE FIRST GAME WAS "TELL A LIE AND GET KILLED."
THE SECOND WAS "FORM PAIRS AND WORK TOGETHER, BUT THEN AGREE UPON WHICH ONE OF YOU IS TO DIE."
THE THIRD GAME WAS "PLAY HIDE-AND-SEEK WITH YOURSELF."
HE DID A GREAT JOB PULLING THEM OFF.
IT REALLY HIT HOME THE FACT THAT MANGA'S ALL ABOUT GREAT IDEAS.
OF COURSE, WITH OUR CON-MAN DETECTIVE IN *TRAP*...
...AND OUR ELEMENTARY SCHOOLERS COMMITTING PERFECT CRIMES IN *PCP*, I REALLY THOUGHT I'D GOTTEN SOMEWHERE NEW.
BUT THE THOUGHT PUT INTO *THE CLASSROOM OF TRUTH* IS EVEN MORE VIVID AND NOVEL.
HEY, DON'T BE PUTTING *PCP* DOWN LIKE THAT...
...
IN-DEED.
FOR AUTHORS LIKE YOU WHO WRITE PLOT-DRIVEN STORIES, CRAFTING INTERESTING PREMISES AND IDEAS ARE OF HIGHEST IMPORTANCE.
PARTICULARLY IF YOU'RE NOT ABIDING BY CONVENTIONAL STANDARDS.
SO ARE GREAT IDEAS BORN SPONTANEOUSLY?
OR ONLY AFTER CAREFUL THOUGHT?
A GOOD TOPIC TO THINK ABOUT. KEEP IT UP, YOU TWO.
LATER.
IDEAS... SETTINGS... NON-MAINSTREAM...
...

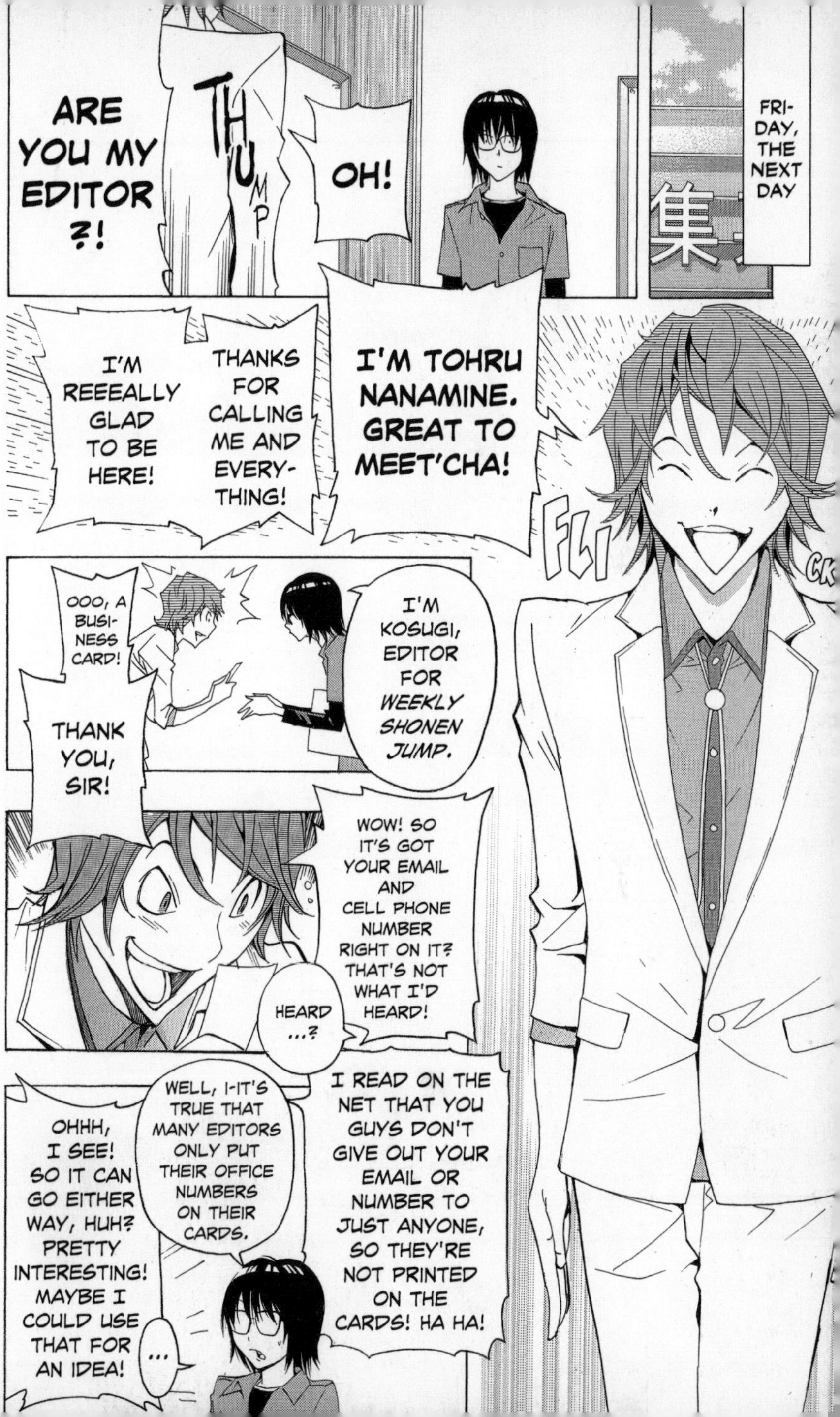
FRI-DAY, THE NEXT DAY
集
OH!
THUMP
ARE YOU MY EDITOR?!
I'M TOHRU NANAMINE. GREAT TO MEET'CHA!
THANKS FOR CALLING ME AND EVERY-THING!
I'M REEEALLY GLAD TO BE HERE!
FLICK
I'M KOSUGI, EDITOR FOR *WEEKLY SHONEN JUMP.*
OOO, A BUSI-NESS CARD!
THANK YOU, SIR!
WOW! SO IT'S GOT YOUR EMAIL AND CELL PHONE NUMBER RIGHT ON IT? THAT'S NOT WHAT I'D HEARD!
HEARD ...?
I READ ON THE NET THAT YOU GUYS DON'T GIVE OUT YOUR EMAIL OR NUMBER TO JUST ANYONE, SO THEY'RE NOT PRINTED ON THE CARDS! HA HA!
WELL, I-IT'S TRUE THAT MANY EDITORS ONLY PUT THEIR OFFICE NUMBERS ON THEIR CARDS.
OHHH, I SEE! SO IT CAN GO EITHER WAY, HUH? PRETTY INTERESTING! MAYBE I COULD USE THAT FOR AN IDEA!
...

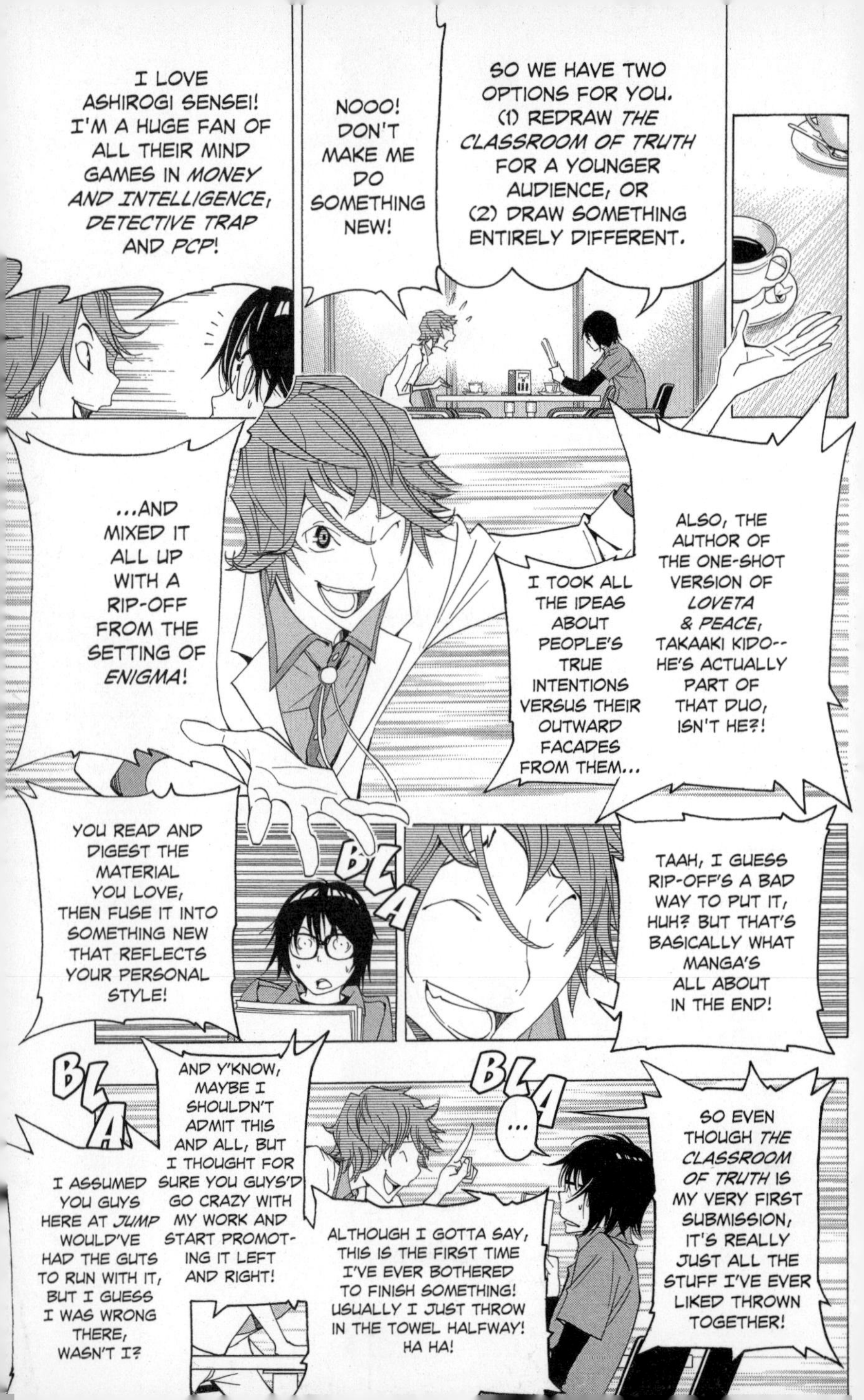
SO WE HAVE TWO OPTIONS FOR YOU. (1) REDRAW *THE CLASSROOM OF TRUTH* FOR A YOUNGER AUDIENCE, OR (2) DRAW SOMETHING ENTIRELY DIFFERENT.
NOOO! DON'T MAKE ME DO SOMETHING NEW!
I LOVE ASHIROGI SENSEI! I'M A HUGE FAN OF ALL THEIR MIND GAMES IN *MONEY AND INTELLIGENCE*, *DETECTIVE TRAP* AND *PCP*!
ALSO, THE AUTHOR OF THE ONE-SHOT VERSION OF *LOVETA & PEACE*, TAKAAKI KIDO-- HE'S ACTUALLY PART OF THAT DUO, ISN'T HE?!
I TOOK ALL THE IDEAS ABOUT PEOPLE'S TRUE INTENTIONS VERSUS THEIR OUTWARD FACADES FROM THEM...
...AND MIXED IT ALL UP WITH A RIP-OFF FROM THE SETTING OF *ENIGMA*!
TAAH, I GUESS RIP-OFF'S A BAD WAY TO PUT IT, HUH? BUT THAT'S BASICALLY WHAT MANGA'S ALL ABOUT IN THE END!
BLA
YOU READ AND DIGEST THE MATERIAL YOU LOVE, THEN FUSE IT INTO SOMETHING NEW THAT REFLECTS YOUR PERSONAL STYLE!
SO EVEN THOUGH *THE CLASSROOM OF TRUTH* IS MY VERY FIRST SUBMISSION, IT'S REALLY JUST ALL THE STUFF I'VE EVER LIKED THROWN TOGETHER!
...
BLA
ALTHOUGH I GOTTA SAY, THIS IS THE FIRST TIME I'VE EVER BOTHERED TO FINISH SOMETHING! USUALLY I JUST THROW IN THE TOWEL HALFWAY! HA HA!
AND Y'KNOW, MAYBE I SHOULDN'T ADMIT THIS AND ALL, BUT I THOUGHT FOR SURE YOU GUYS'D GO CRAZY WITH MY WORK AND START PROMOTING IT LEFT AND RIGHT!
I ASSUMED YOU GUYS HERE AT *JUMP* WOULD'VE HAD THE GUTS TO RUN WITH IT, BUT I GUESS I WAS WRONG THERE, WASN'T I?
BLA

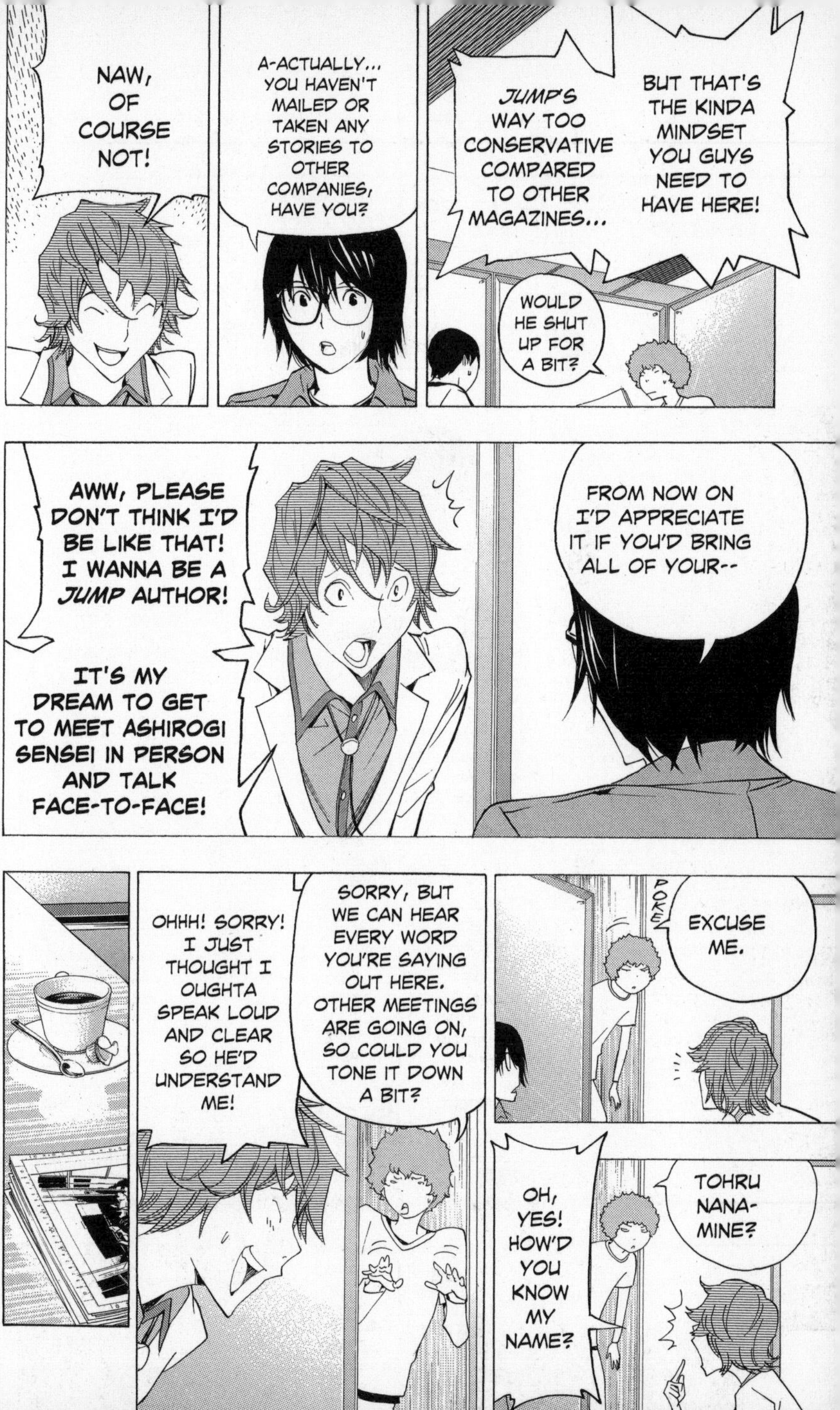
BUT THAT'S THE KINDA MINDSET YOU GUYS NEED TO HAVE HERE!
JUMP'S WAY TOO CONSERVATIVE COMPARED TO OTHER MAGAZINES...
WOULD HE SHUT UP FOR A BIT?
A-ACTUALLY... YOU HAVEN'T MAILED OR TAKEN ANY STORIES TO OTHER COMPANIES, HAVE YOU?
NAW, OF COURSE NOT!
FROM NOW ON I'D APPRECIATE IT IF YOU'D BRING ALL OF YOUR--
AWW, PLEASE DON'T THINK I'D BE LIKE THAT! I WANNA BE A JUMP AUTHOR!
IT'S MY DREAM TO GET TO MEET ASHIROGI SENSEI IN PERSON AND TALK FACE-TO-FACE!
POKE
EXCUSE ME.
TOHRU NANAMINE?
OH, YES! HOW'D YOU KNOW MY NAME?
SORRY, BUT WE CAN HEAR EVERY WORD YOU'RE SAYING OUT HERE. OTHER MEETINGS ARE GOING ON, SO COULD YOU TONE IT DOWN A BIT?
OHHH! SORRY! I JUST THOUGHT I OUGHTA SPEAK LOUD AND CLEAR SO HE'D UNDERSTAND ME!

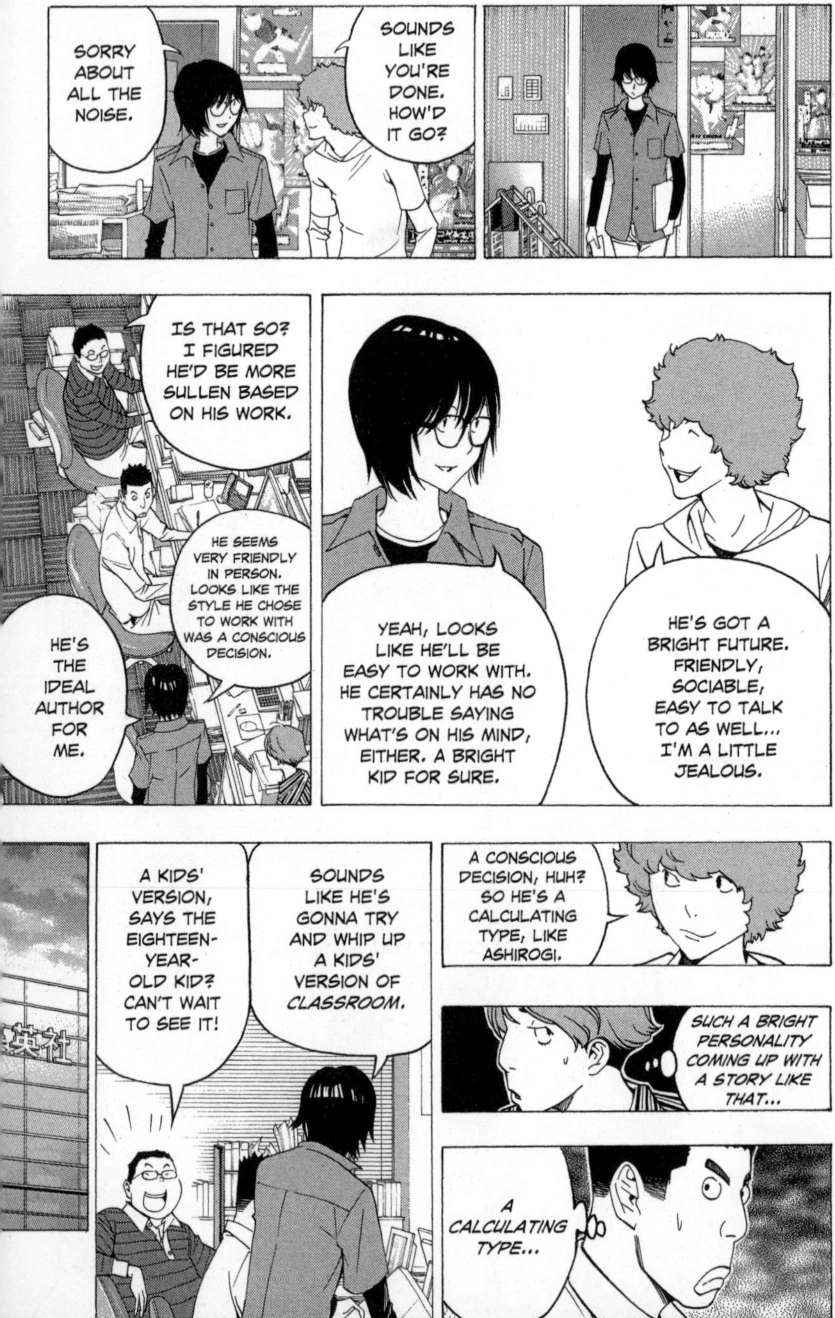

SOUNDS LIKE YOU'RE DONE. HOW'D IT GO?
SORRY ABOUT ALL THE NOISE.
HE'S GOT A BRIGHT FUTURE. FRIENDLY, SOCIABLE, EASY TO TALK TO AS WELL... I'M A LITTLE JEALOUS.
YEAH, LOOKS LIKE HE'LL BE EASY TO WORK WITH. HE CERTAINLY HAS NO TROUBLE SAYING WHAT'S ON HIS MIND, EITHER. A BRIGHT KID FOR SURE.
IS THAT SO? I FIGURED HE'D BE MORE SULLEN BASED ON HIS WORK.
HE SEEMS VERY FRIENDLY IN PERSON. LOOKS LIKE THE STYLE HE CHOSE TO WORK WITH WAS A CONSCIOUS DECISION.
HE'S THE IDEAL AUTHOR FOR ME.
A CONSCIOUS DECISION, HUH? SO HE'S A CALCULATING TYPE, LIKE ASHIROGI.
SUCH A BRIGHT PERSONALITY COMING UP WITH A STORY LIKE THAT...
A CALCULATING TYPE...
SOUNDS LIKE HE'S GONNA TRY AND WHIP UP A KIDS' VERSION OF *CLASSROOM*.
A KIDS' VERSION, SAYS THE EIGHTEEN-YEAR-OLD KID? CAN'T WAIT TO SEE IT!

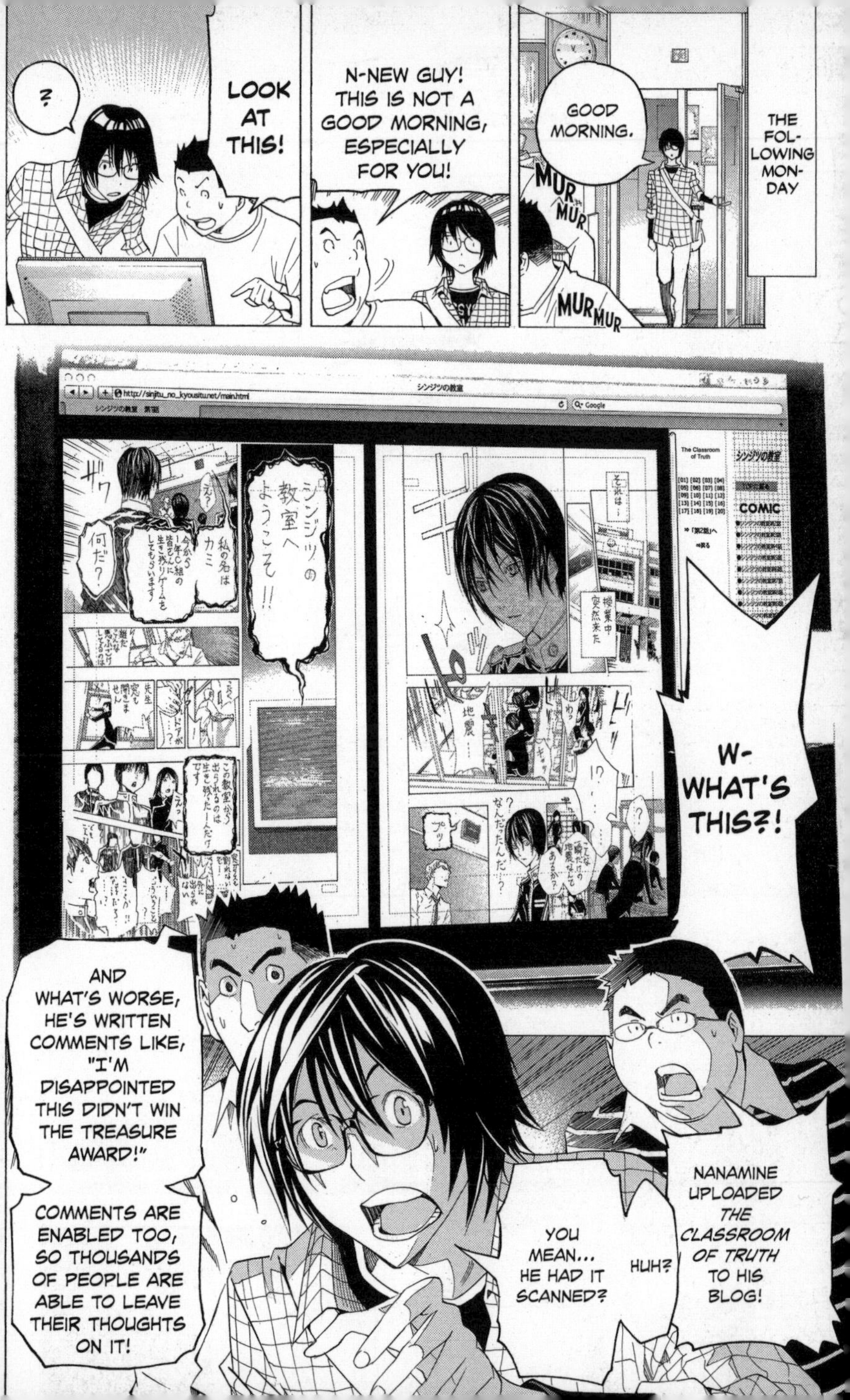

THE FOL-LOWING MON-DAY
GOOD MORNING.
MUR MUR
MUR MUR
N-NEW GUY! THIS IS NOT A GOOD MORNING, ESPECIALLY FOR YOU!
LOOK AT THIS!
?
W-WHAT'S THIS?!
シンジツの教室
http://sinjitu_no_kyousitu.net/main.html
シンジツの教室へようこそ!!
The Classroom of Truth
COMIC
NANAMINE UPLOADED THE CLASSROOM OF TRUTH TO HIS BLOG!
HUH?
YOU MEAN... HE HAD IT SCANNED?
AND WHAT'S WORSE, HE'S WRITTEN COMMENTS LIKE, "I'M DISAPPOINTED THIS DIDN'T WIN THE TREASURE AWARD!"
COMMENTS ARE ENABLED TOO, SO THOUSANDS OF PEOPLE ARE ABLE TO LEAVE THEIR THOUGHTS ON IT!

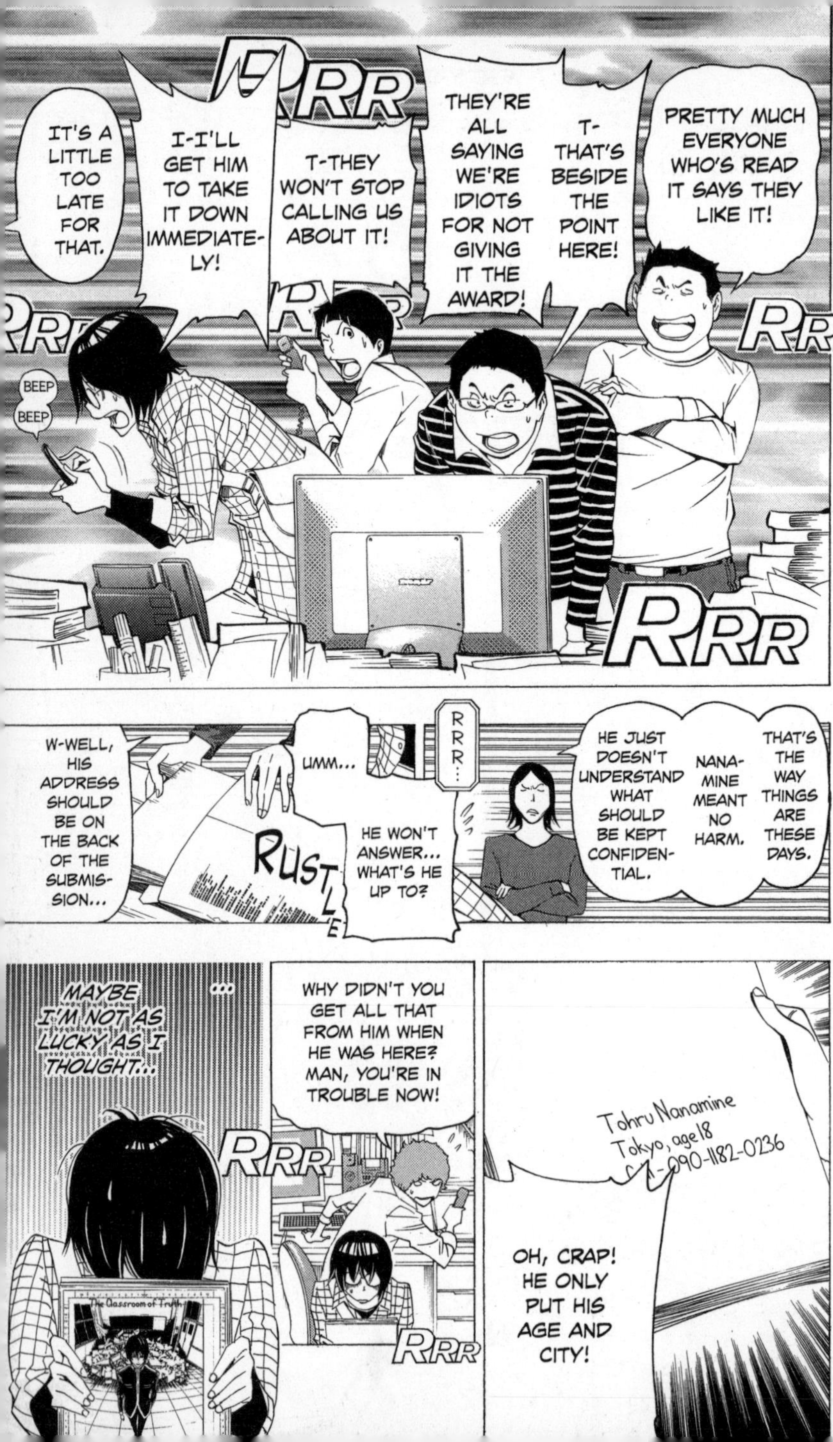
RRR
PRETTY MUCH EVERYONE WHO'S READ IT SAYS THEY LIKE IT!
T-THAT'S BESIDE THE POINT HERE!
THEY'RE ALL SAYING WE'RE IDIOTS FOR NOT GIVING IT THE AWARD!
RRR
T-THEY WON'T STOP CALLING US ABOUT IT!
I-I'LL GET HIM TO TAKE IT DOWN IMMEDIATE-LY!
IT'S A LITTLE TOO LATE FOR THAT.
BEEP
BEEP
RRR
RRR
THAT'S THE WAY THINGS ARE THESE DAYS.
NANAMINE MEANT NO HARM.
HE JUST DOESN'T UNDERSTAND WHAT SHOULD BE KEPT CONFIDEN-TIAL.
RRR...
UMM...
HE WON'T ANSWER... WHAT'S HE UP TO?
RUSTLE
W-WELL, HIS ADDRESS SHOULD BE ON THE BACK OF THE SUBMIS-SION...
Tohru Nanamine
Tokyo, age 18
090-1182-0236
OH, CRAP! HE ONLY PUT HIS AGE AND CITY!
WHY DIDN'T YOU GET ALL THAT FROM HIM WHEN HE WAS HERE? MAN, YOU'RE IN TROUBLE NOW!
RRR
RRR
...
MAYBE I'M NOT AS LUCKY AS I THOUGHT...
The Classroom of Truth

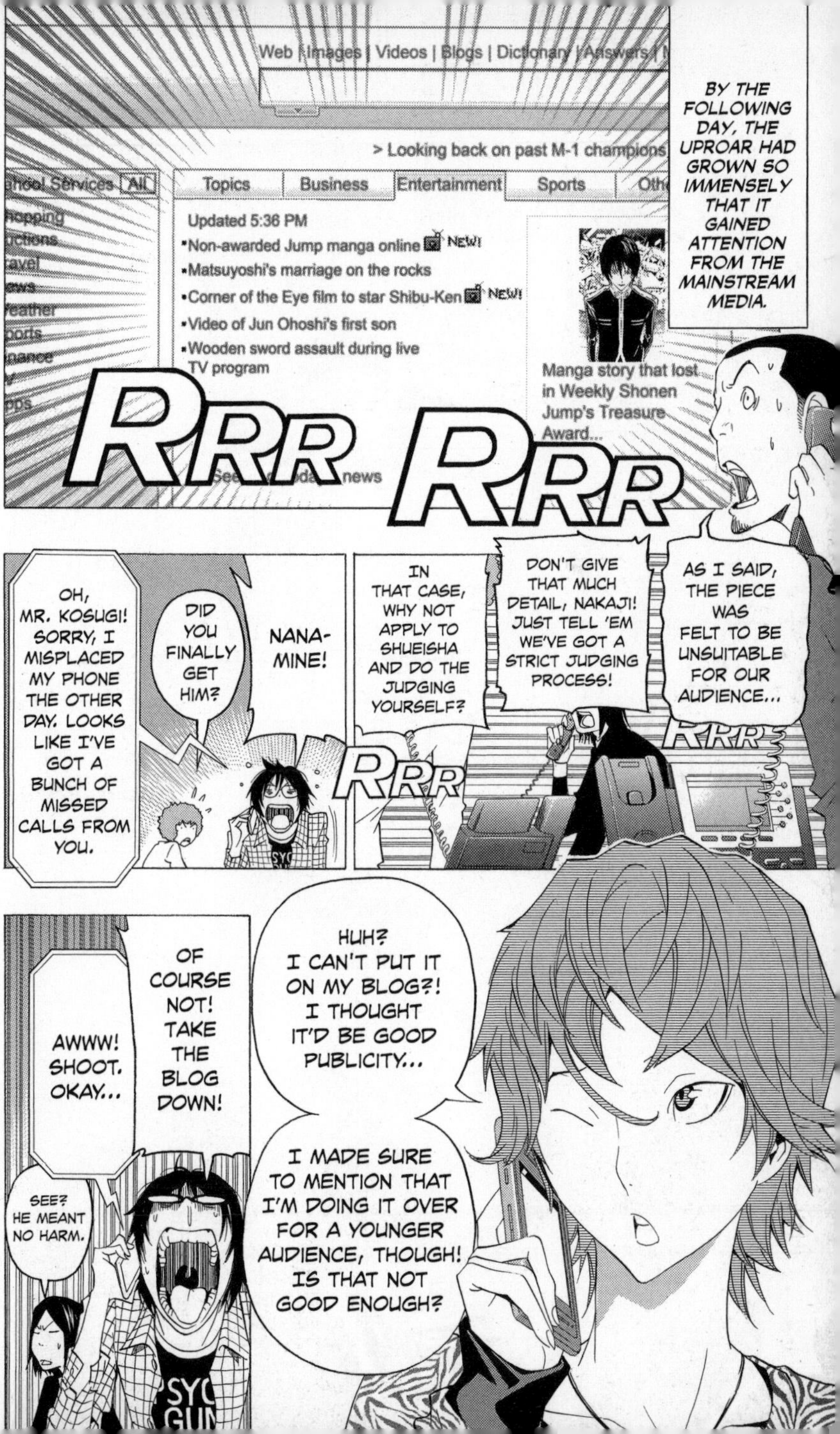
BY THE FOLLOWING DAY, THE UPROAR HAD GROWN SO IMMENSELY THAT IT GAINED ATTENTION FROM THE MAINSTREAM MEDIA.
Web | Images | Videos | Blogs | Dictionary | Answers |
> Looking back on past M-1 champions
Topics | Business | Entertainment | Sports
Updated 5:36 PM
•Non-awarded Jump manga online NEW!
•Matsuyoshi's marriage on the rocks
•Corner of the Eye film to star Shibu-Ken NEW!
•Video of Jun Ohoshi's first son
•Wooden sword assault during live TV program
Manga story that lost in Weekly Shonen Jump's Treasure Award...
RRR RRR
AS I SAID, THE PIECE WAS FELT TO BE UNSUITABLE FOR OUR AUDIENCE...
RRR
DON'T GIVE THAT MUCH DETAIL, NAKAJI! JUST TELL 'EM WE'VE GOT A STRICT JUDGING PROCESS!
IN THAT CASE, WHY NOT APPLY TO SHUEISHA AND DO THE JUDGING YOURSELF?
RRR
NANA-MINE!
DID YOU FINALLY GET HIM?
OH, MR. KOSUGI! SORRY, I MISPLACED MY PHONE THE OTHER DAY. LOOKS LIKE I'VE GOT A BUNCH OF MISSED CALLS FROM YOU.
HUH? I CAN'T PUT IT ON MY BLOG?! I THOUGHT IT'D BE GOOD PUBLICITY...
I MADE SURE TO MENTION THAT I'M DOING IT OVER FOR A YOUNGER AUDIENCE, THOUGH! IS THAT NOT GOOD ENOUGH?
OF COURSE NOT! TAKE THE BLOG DOWN!
AWWW! SHOOT. OKAY...
SEE? HE MEANT NO HARM.

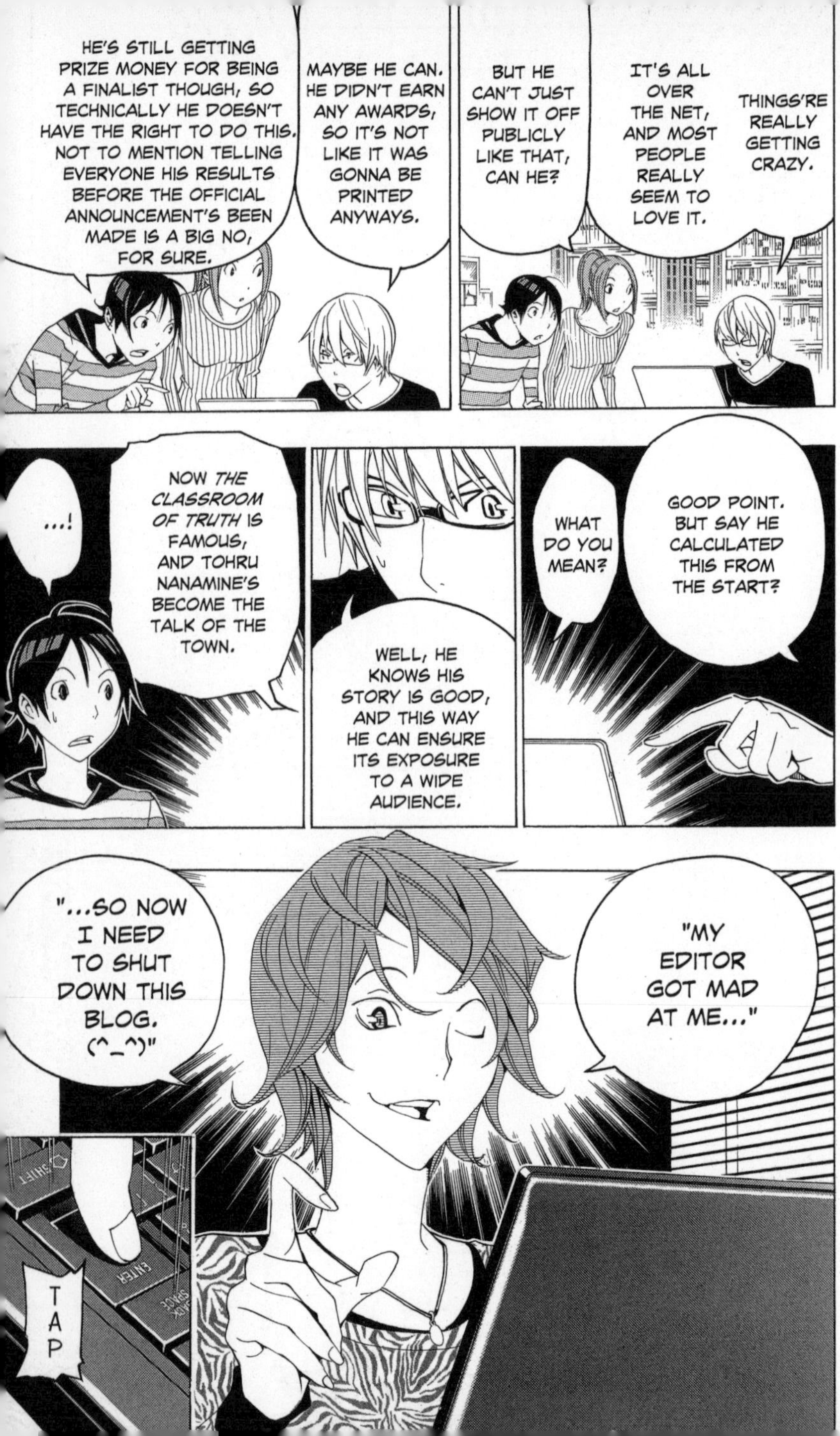
THINGS'RE REALLY GETTING CRAZY.
IT'S ALL OVER THE NET, AND MOST PEOPLE REALLY SEEM TO LOVE IT.
BUT HE CAN'T JUST SHOW IT OFF PUBLICLY LIKE THAT, CAN HE?
MAYBE HE CAN. HE DIDN'T EARN ANY AWARDS, SO IT'S NOT LIKE IT WAS GONNA BE PRINTED ANYWAYS.
HE'S STILL GETTING PRIZE MONEY FOR BEING A FINALIST THOUGH, SO TECHNICALLY HE DOESN'T HAVE THE RIGHT TO DO THIS. NOT TO MENTION TELLING EVERYONE HIS RESULTS BEFORE THE OFFICIAL ANNOUNCEMENT'S BEEN MADE IS A BIG NO, FOR SURE.
GOOD POINT. BUT SAY HE CALCULATED THIS FROM THE START?
WHAT DO YOU MEAN?
WELL, HE KNOWS HIS STORY IS GOOD, AND THIS WAY HE CAN ENSURE ITS EXPOSURE TO A WIDE AUDIENCE.
NOW *THE CLASSROOM OF TRUTH* IS FAMOUS, AND TOHRU NANAMINE'S BECOME THE TALK OF THE TOWN.
...!
"MY EDITOR GOT MAD AT ME..."
"...SO NOW I NEED TO SHUT DOWN THIS BLOG. (^_^)"
TAP

OHBA'S STORYBOARD

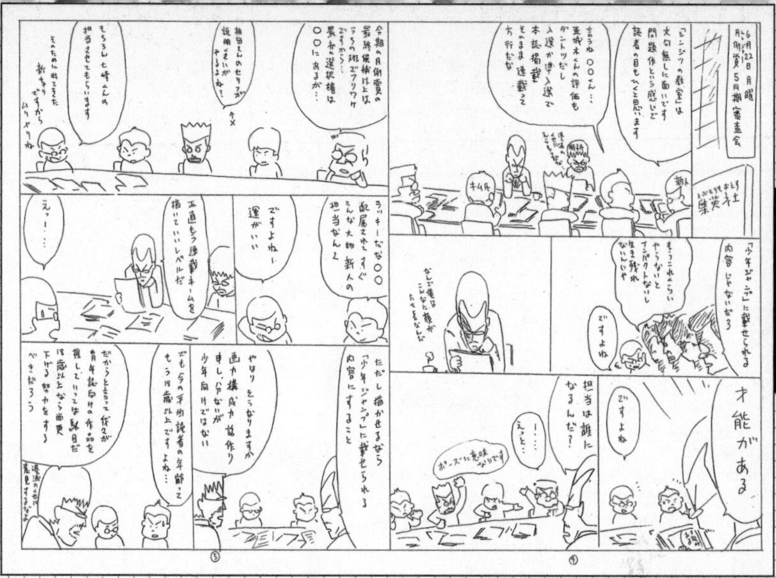
6月22日 月曜 月例賞5月期審査会
集英社
「ジンジツの教室」は文句無しに面白いです 問題作という感じで読者の目もひくと思います
言うね○○くん… 亜城木くんの評価もダントツだし入選か準入選で本誌掲載そのまま連載って方行だな
「少年ジャンプ」に載せられる内容じゃないだろ
もうこれくらいやらないとインパクトないし生き残れないんじゃ
ですよね
なんで俺はこんなに顔がたて長なんだ
才能がある
ですよね
担当は誰になるんだ？
…えっと…
ポーズに意味ないです
今期の月例賞の最終候補以上はうちの班でフリワケですから… 最初の選択権は○○にあるが…
相田さんのセリフが説明くさいがやるよね？
もちろん七峰くんの担当させてもらいます
そのために出てきた新キャラですからムリヤリね
ラッキーだな○○ 配属されてすぐこんな大物新人の担当なんて
ですよねー 運がいい
正直もう連載ネームを描いていいレベルだ
えっー…
ただし描かせるなら「少年ジャンプ」に載せられる内容にすること
やはりそうなりますか 画力構成力話作り申し分ないが少年向けではない
でも今の平均読者の年齢ってもう18歳以上ですよね…
だからといって我々が青年誌向けの作品を推してっては駄目だ 18歳以上なら尚更下げる努力をするべきだろう
⑤
④

OBATA'S STORYBOARD

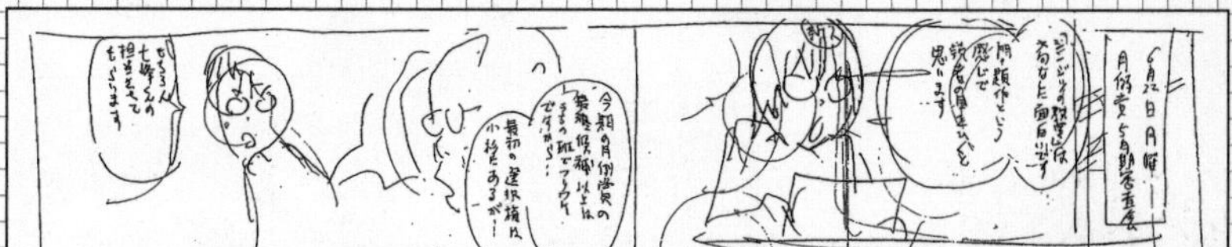

COMPLETE!

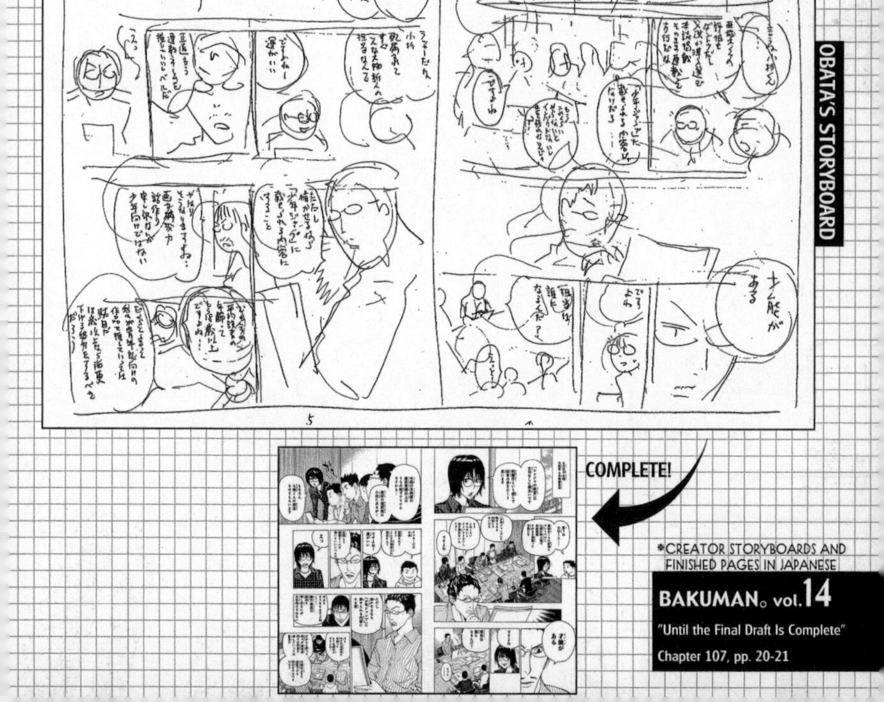

*CREATOR STORYBOARDS AND FINISHED PAGES IN JAPANESE

BAKUMAN。 vol.14

"Until the Final Draft Is Complete"

Chapter 107, pp. 20-21

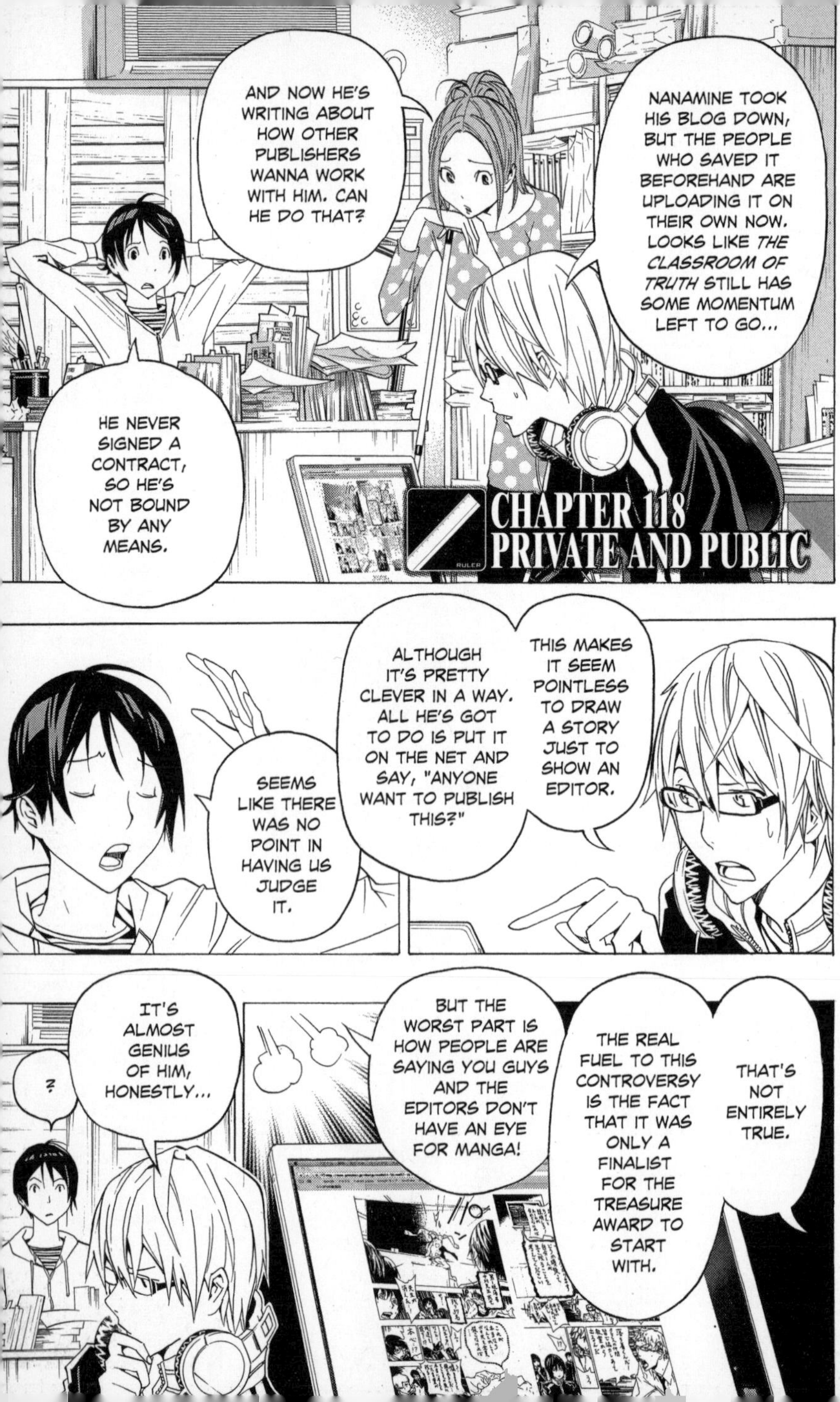
NANAMINE TOOK HIS BLOG DOWN, BUT THE PEOPLE WHO SAVED IT BEFOREHAND ARE UPLOADING IT ON THEIR OWN NOW. LOOKS LIKE *THE CLASSROOM OF TRUTH* STILL HAS SOME MOMENTUM LEFT TO GO...
AND NOW HE'S WRITING ABOUT HOW OTHER PUBLISHERS WANNA WORK WITH HIM. CAN HE DO THAT?
HE NEVER SIGNED A CONTRACT, SO HE'S NOT BOUND BY ANY MEANS.
CHAPTER 118
PRIVATE AND PUBLIC
RULER
THIS MAKES IT SEEM POINTLESS TO DRAW A STORY JUST TO SHOW AN EDITOR.
ALTHOUGH IT'S PRETTY CLEVER IN A WAY. ALL HE'S GOT TO DO IS PUT IT ON THE NET AND SAY, "ANYONE WANT TO PUBLISH THIS?"
SEEMS LIKE THERE WAS NO POINT IN HAVING US JUDGE IT.
THAT'S NOT ENTIRELY TRUE.
THE REAL FUEL TO THIS CONTROVERSY IS THE FACT THAT IT WAS ONLY A FINALIST FOR THE TREASURE AWARD TO START WITH.
BUT THE WORST PART IS HOW PEOPLE ARE SAYING YOU GUYS AND THE EDITORS DON'T HAVE AN EYE FOR MANGA!
IT'S ALMOST GENIUS OF HIM, HONESTLY...
?

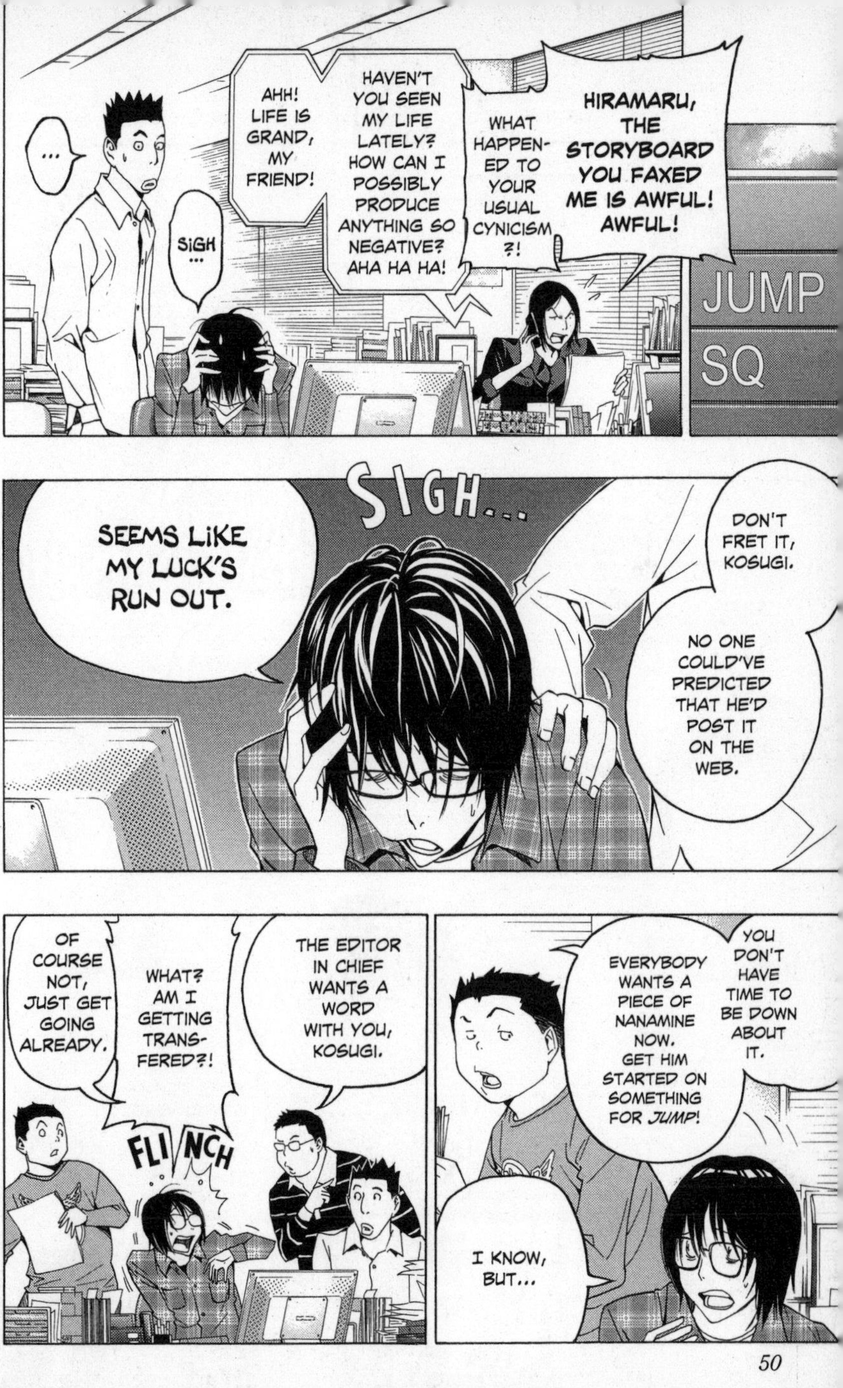
HIRAMARU, THE STORYBOARD YOU FAXED ME IS AWFUL! AWFUL!
WHAT HAPPENED TO YOUR USUAL CYNICISM?!
HAVEN'T YOU SEEN MY LIFE LATELY? HOW CAN I POSSIBLY PRODUCE ANYTHING SO NEGATIVE? AHA HA HA!
AHH! LIFE IS GRAND, MY FRIEND!
SIGH...
...
JUMP SQ
SIGH...
SEEMS LIKE MY LUCK'S RUN OUT.
DON'T FRET IT, KOSUGI.
NO ONE COULD'VE PREDICTED THAT HE'D POST IT ON THE WEB.
YOU DON'T HAVE TIME TO BE DOWN ABOUT IT.
EVERYBODY WANTS A PIECE OF NANAMINE NOW. GET HIM STARTED ON SOMETHING FOR *JUMP*!
I KNOW, BUT...
THE EDITOR IN CHIEF WANTS A WORD WITH YOU, KOSUGI.
WHAT? AM I GETTING TRANS-FERED?!
FLINCH
OF COURSE NOT, JUST GET GOING ALREADY.

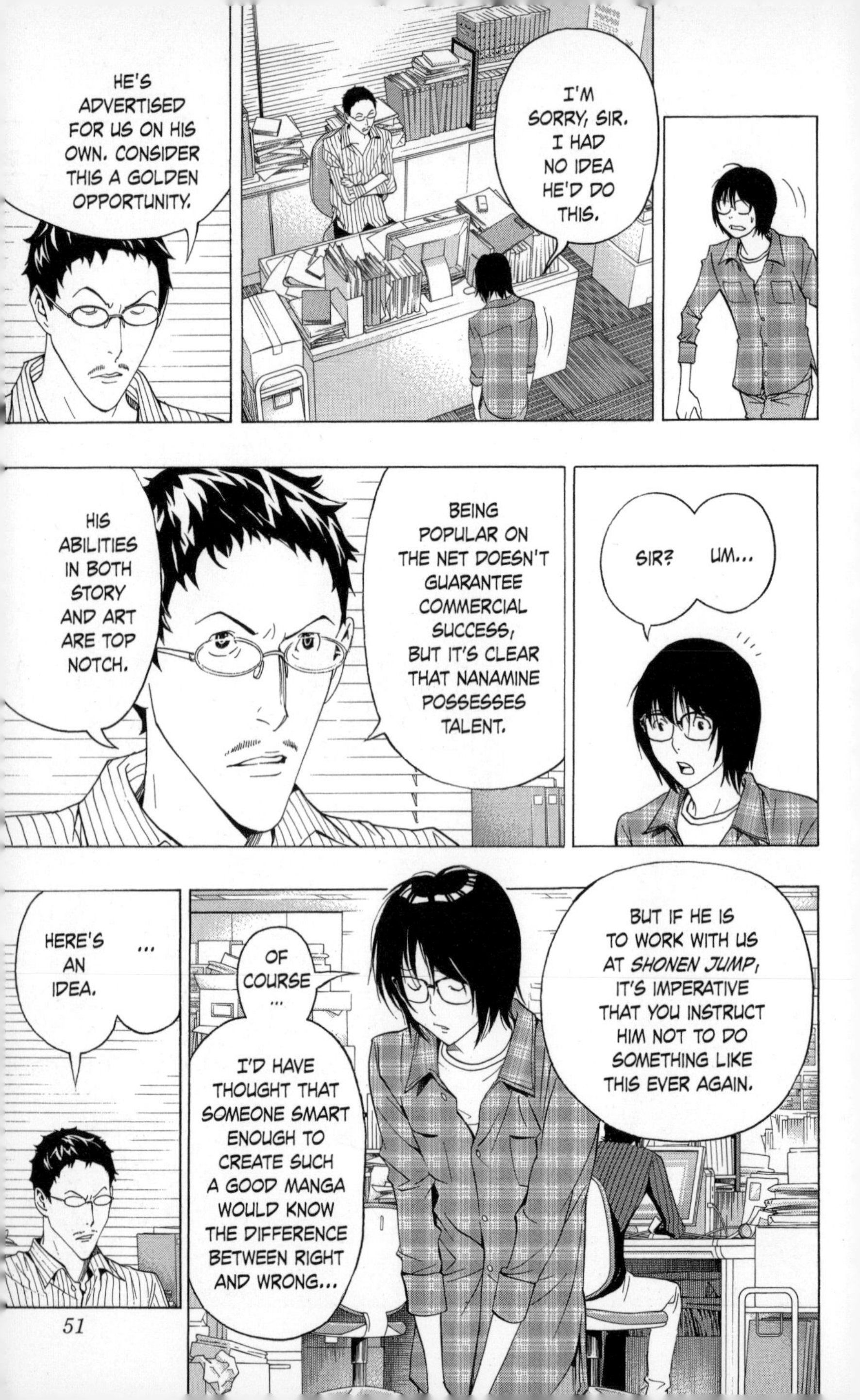
I'M SORRY, SIR. I HAD NO IDEA HE'D DO THIS.
HE'S ADVERTISED FOR US ON HIS OWN. CONSIDER THIS A GOLDEN OPPORTUNITY.
SIR? UM...
BEING POPULAR ON THE NET DOESN'T GUARANTEE COMMERCIAL SUCCESS, BUT IT'S CLEAR THAT NANAMINE POSSESSES TALENT.
HIS ABILITIES IN BOTH STORY AND ART ARE TOP NOTCH.
BUT IF HE IS TO WORK WITH US AT *SHONEN JUMP*, IT'S IMPERATIVE THAT YOU INSTRUCT HIM NOT TO DO SOMETHING LIKE THIS EVER AGAIN.
OF COURSE...
I'D HAVE THOUGHT THAT SOMEONE SMART ENOUGH TO CREATE SUCH A GOOD MANGA WOULD KNOW THE DIFFERENCE BETWEEN RIGHT AND WRONG...
...
HERE'S AN IDEA.

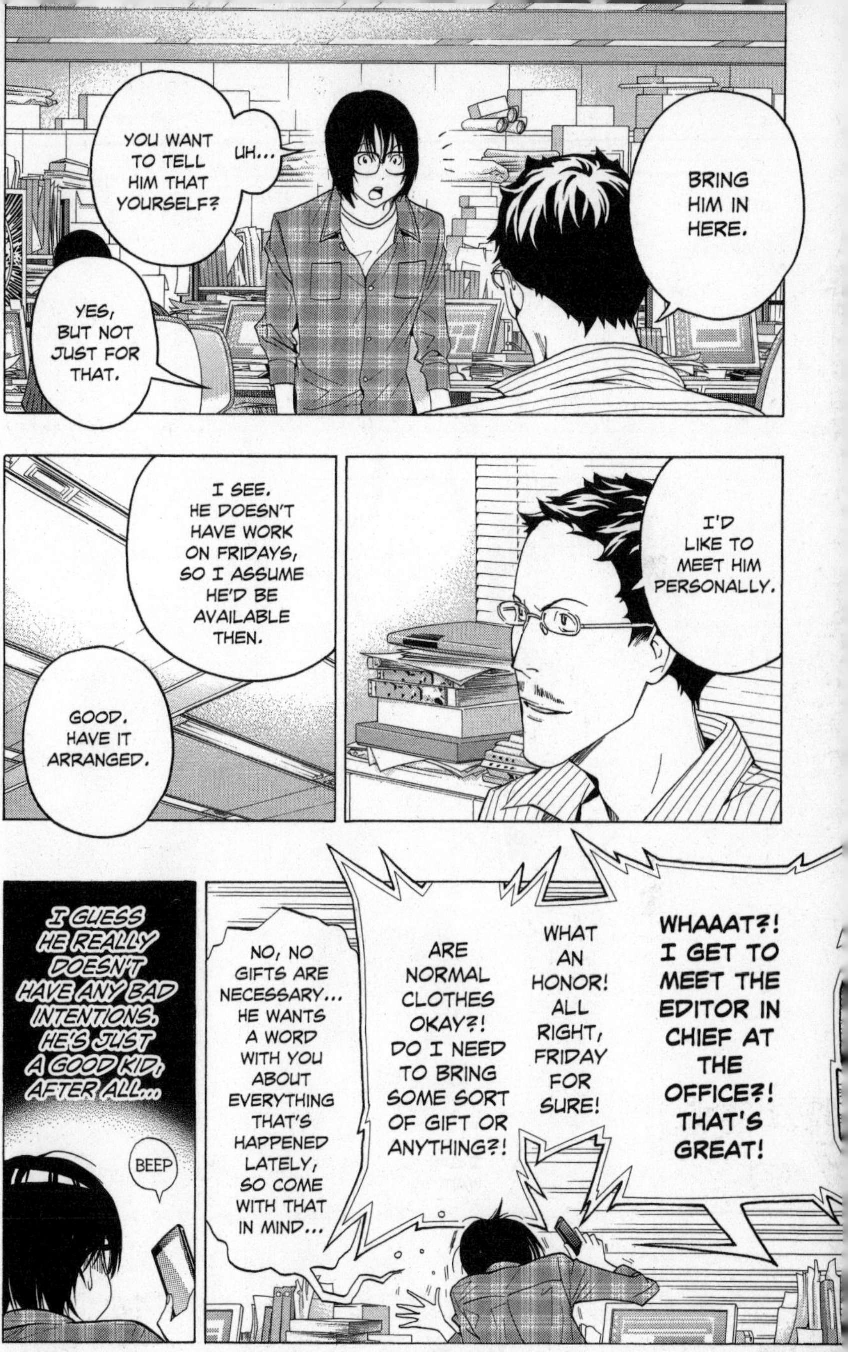
BRING HIM IN HERE.
UH...
YOU WANT TO TELL HIM THAT YOURSELF?
YES, BUT NOT JUST FOR THAT.
I'D LIKE TO MEET HIM PERSONALLY.
I SEE. HE DOESN'T HAVE WORK ON FRIDAYS, SO I ASSUME HE'D BE AVAILABLE THEN.
GOOD. HAVE IT ARRANGED.
WHAAAT?! I GET TO MEET THE EDITOR IN CHIEF AT THE OFFICE?! THAT'S GREAT!
WHAT AN HONOR! ALL RIGHT, FRIDAY FOR SURE!
ARE NORMAL CLOTHES OKAY?! DO I NEED TO BRING SOME SORT OF GIFT OR ANYTHING?!
NO, NO GIFTS ARE NECESSARY... HE WANTS A WORD WITH YOU ABOUT EVERYTHING THAT'S HAPPENED LATELY, SO COME WITH THAT IN MIND...
I GUESS HE REALLY DOESN'T HAVE ANY BAD INTENTIONS. HE'S JUST A GOOD KID, AFTER ALL...
BEEP

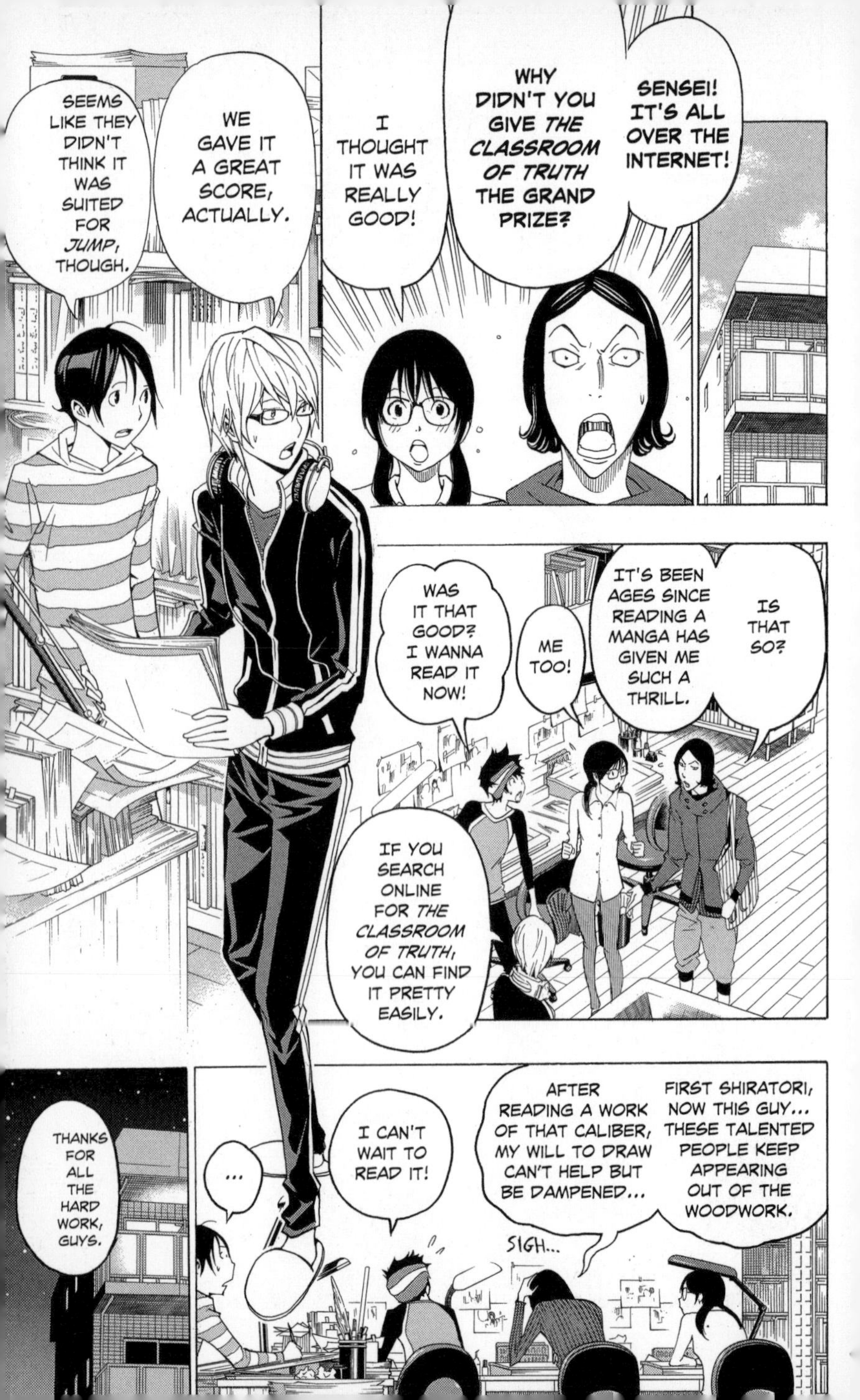
SENSEI! IT'S ALL OVER THE INTERNET!
WHY DIDN'T YOU GIVE *THE CLASSROOM OF TRUTH* THE GRAND PRIZE?
I THOUGHT IT WAS REALLY GOOD!
IS THAT SO?
IT'S BEEN AGES SINCE READING A MANGA HAS GIVEN ME SUCH A THRILL.
ME TOO!
WAS IT THAT GOOD? I WANNA READ IT NOW!
IF YOU SEARCH ONLINE FOR *THE CLASSROOM OF TRUTH*, YOU CAN FIND IT PRETTY EASILY.
WE GAVE IT A GREAT SCORE, ACTUALLY.
SEEMS LIKE THEY DIDN'T THINK IT WAS SUITED FOR *JUMP*, THOUGH.
FIRST SHIRATORI, NOW THIS GUY... THESE TALENTED PEOPLE KEEP APPEARING OUT OF THE WOODWORK.
AFTER READING A WORK OF THAT CALIBER, MY WILL TO DRAW CAN'T HELP BUT BE DAMPENED...
SIGH...
I CAN'T WAIT TO READ IT!
...
THANKS FOR ALL THE HARD WORK, GUYS.

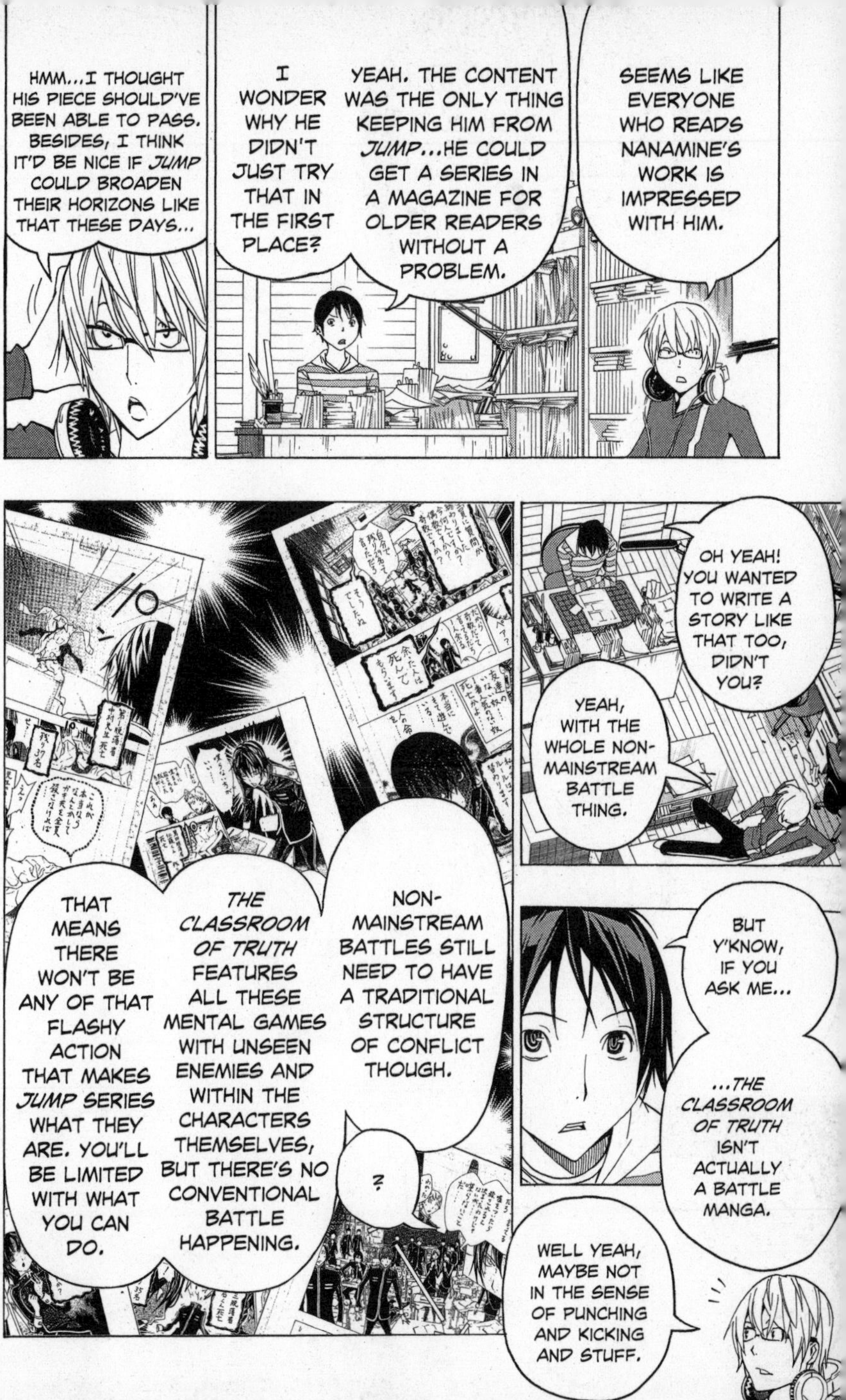
SEEMS LIKE EVERYONE WHO READS NANAMINE'S WORK IS IMPRESSED WITH HIM.
YEAH. THE CONTENT WAS THE ONLY THING KEEPING HIM FROM *JUMP*...HE COULD GET A SERIES IN A MAGAZINE FOR OLDER READERS WITHOUT A PROBLEM.
I WONDER WHY HE DIDN'T JUST TRY THAT IN THE FIRST PLACE?
HMM...I THOUGHT HIS PIECE SHOULD'VE BEEN ABLE TO PASS. BESIDES, I THINK IT'D BE NICE IF *JUMP* COULD BROADEN THEIR HORIZONS LIKE THAT THESE DAYS...
OH YEAH! YOU WANTED TO WRITE A STORY LIKE THAT TOO, DIDN'T YOU?
YEAH, WITH THE WHOLE NON-MAINSTREAM BATTLE THING.
NON-MAINSTREAM BATTLES STILL NEED TO HAVE A TRADITIONAL STRUCTURE OF CONFLICT THOUGH.
THE CLASSROOM OF TRUTH FEATURES ALL THESE MENTAL GAMES WITH UNSEEN ENEMIES AND WITHIN THE CHARACTERS THEMSELVES, BUT THERE'S NO CONVENTIONAL BATTLE HAPPENING.
THAT MEANS THERE WON'T BE ANY OF THAT FLASHY ACTION THAT MAKES *JUMP* SERIES WHAT THEY ARE. YOU'LL BE LIMITED WITH WHAT YOU CAN DO.
?
BUT Y'KNOW, IF YOU ASK ME...
...*THE CLASSROOM OF TRUTH* ISN'T ACTUALLY A BATTLE MANGA.
WELL YEAH, MAYBE NOT IN THE SENSE OF PUNCHING AND KICKING AND STUFF.

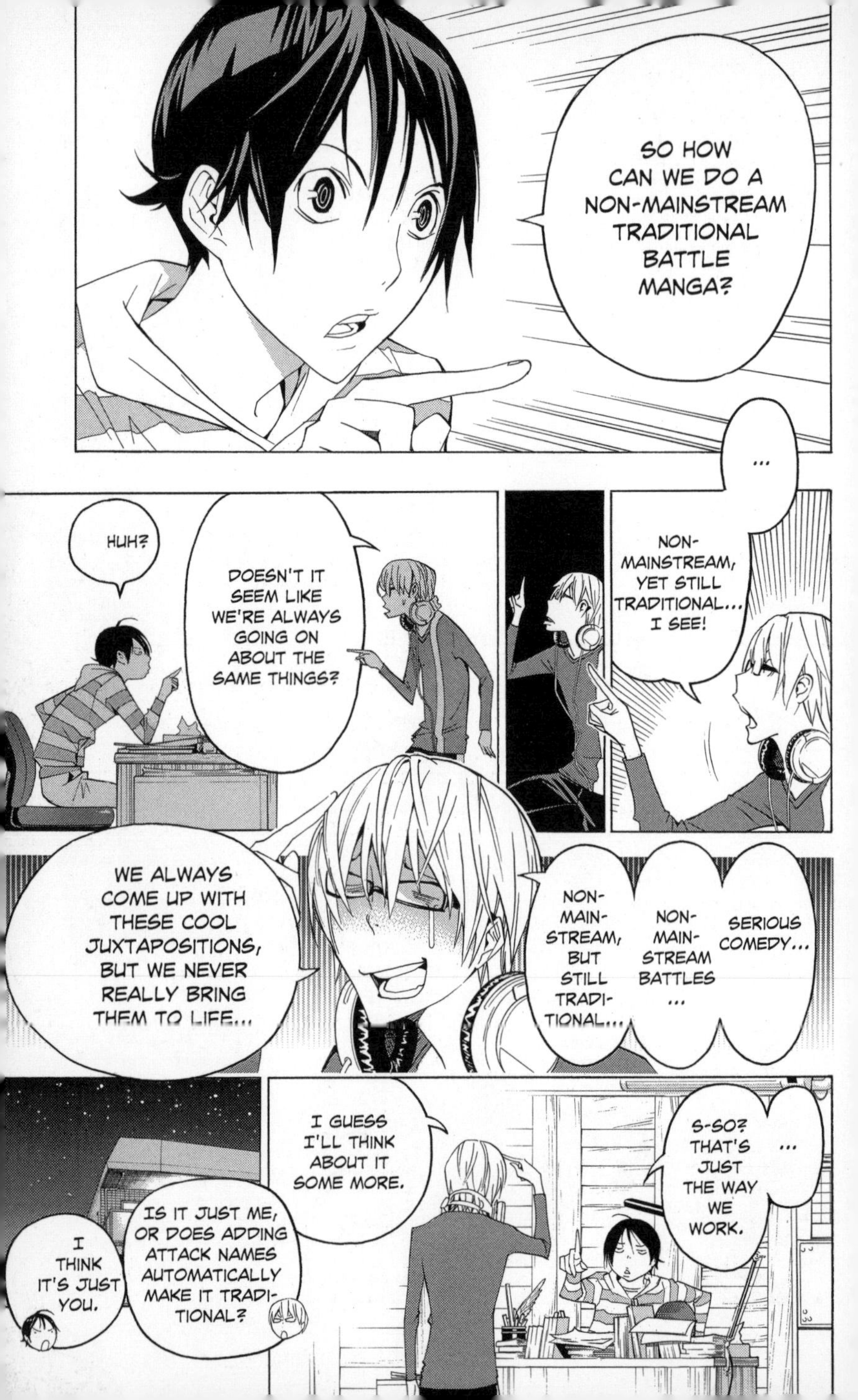
SO HOW CAN WE DO A NON-MAINSTREAM TRADITIONAL BATTLE MANGA?
...
NON-MAINSTREAM, YET STILL TRADITIONAL... I SEE!
DOESN'T IT SEEM LIKE WE'RE ALWAYS GOING ON ABOUT THE SAME THINGS?
HUH?
SERIOUS COMEDY...
NON-MAIN-STREAM BATTLES...
NON-MAIN-STREAM, BUT STILL TRADI-TIONAL...
WE ALWAYS COME UP WITH THESE COOL JUXTAPOSITIONS, BUT WE NEVER REALLY BRING THEM TO LIFE...
...
S-SO? THAT'S JUST THE WAY WE WORK.
I GUESS I'LL THINK ABOUT IT SOME MORE.
IS IT JUST ME, OR DOES ADDING ATTACK NAMES AUTOMATICALLY MAKE IT TRADI-TIONAL?
I THINK IT'S JUST YOU.

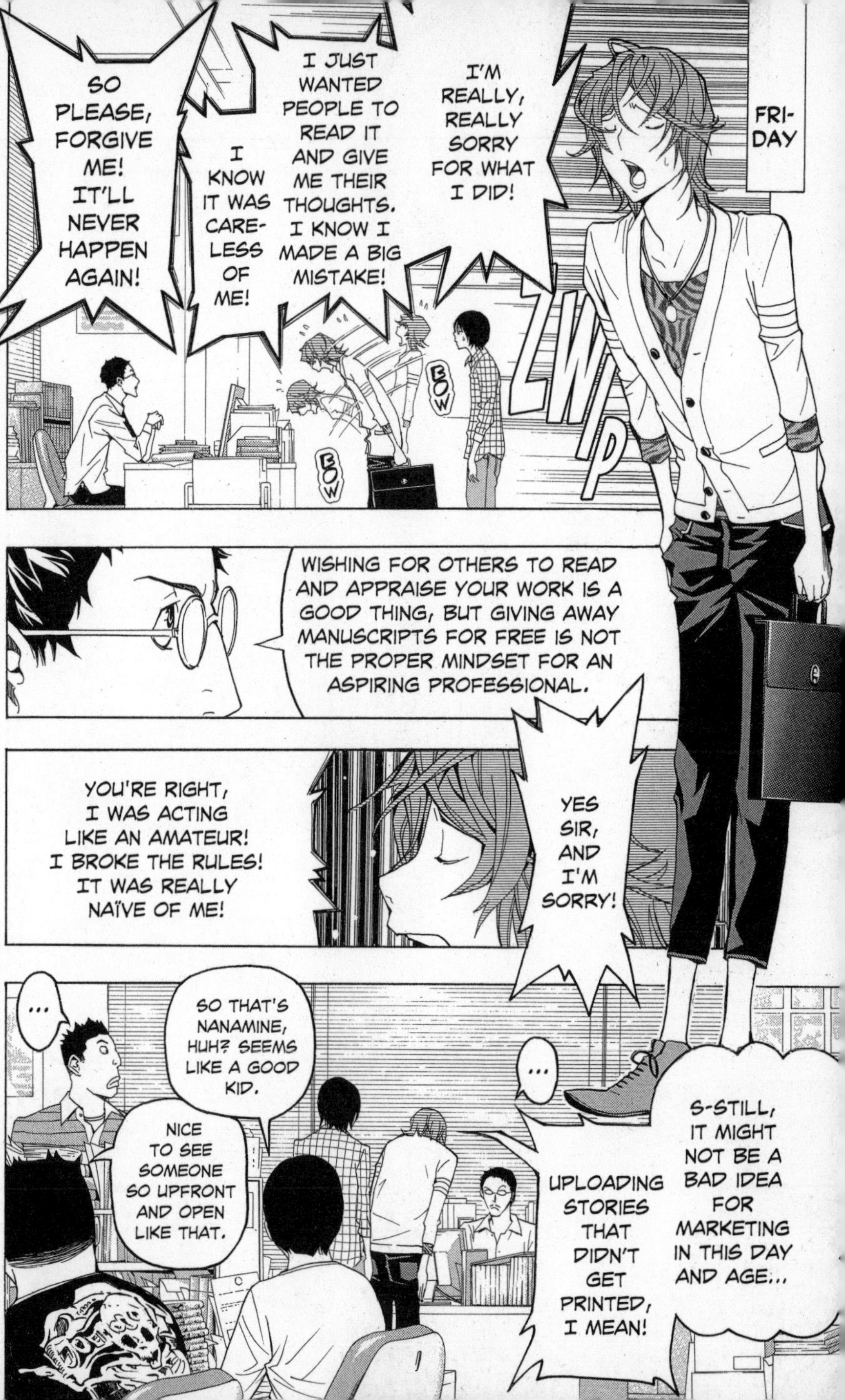
FRIDAY
I'M REALLY, REALLY SORRY FOR WHAT I DID!
I JUST WANTED PEOPLE TO READ IT AND GIVE ME THEIR THOUGHTS. I KNOW I MADE A BIG MISTAKE!
I KNOW IT WAS CARELESS OF ME!
SO PLEASE, FORGIVE ME! IT'LL NEVER HAPPEN AGAIN!
ZWIP
BOW
BOW
WISHING FOR OTHERS TO READ AND APPRAISE YOUR WORK IS A GOOD THING, BUT GIVING AWAY MANUSCRIPTS FOR FREE IS NOT THE PROPER MINDSET FOR AN ASPIRING PROFESSIONAL.
YES SIR, AND I'M SORRY!
YOU'RE RIGHT, I WAS ACTING LIKE AN AMATEUR! I BROKE THE RULES! IT WAS REALLY NAÏVE OF ME!
S-STILL, IT MIGHT NOT BE A BAD IDEA FOR MARKETING IN THIS DAY AND AGE...
UPLOADING STORIES THAT DIDN'T GET PRINTED, I MEAN!
...
SO THAT'S NANAMINE, HUH? SEEMS LIKE A GOOD KID.
NICE TO SEE SOMEONE SO UPFRONT AND OPEN LIKE THAT.
...

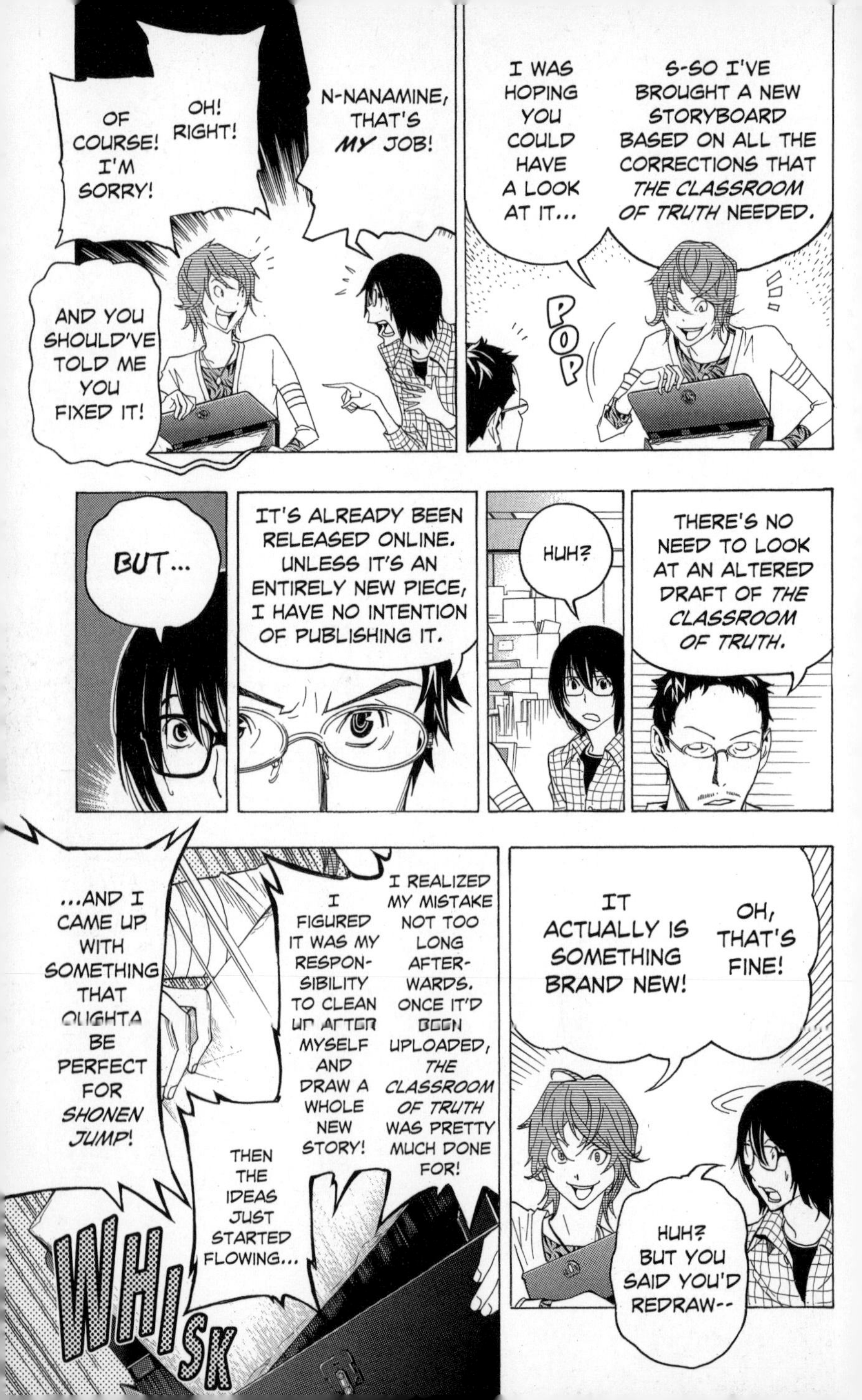
S-SO I'VE BROUGHT A NEW STORYBOARD BASED ON ALL THE CORRECTIONS THAT *THE CLASSROOM OF TRUTH* NEEDED.
I WAS HOPING YOU COULD HAVE A LOOK AT IT...
POP
N-NANAMINE, THAT'S *MY* JOB!
OH! RIGHT!
OF COURSE! I'M SORRY!
AND YOU SHOULD'VE TOLD ME YOU FIXED IT!
THERE'S NO NEED TO LOOK AT AN ALTERED DRAFT OF *THE CLASSROOM OF TRUTH.*
HUH?
IT'S ALREADY BEEN RELEASED ONLINE. UNLESS IT'S AN ENTIRELY NEW PIECE, I HAVE NO INTENTION OF PUBLISHING IT.
BUT...
OH, THAT'S FINE!
IT ACTUALLY IS SOMETHING BRAND NEW!
HUH? BUT YOU SAID YOU'D REDRAW--
I REALIZED MY MISTAKE NOT TOO LONG AFTERWARDS. ONCE IT'D BEEN UPLOADED, *THE CLASSROOM OF TRUTH* WAS PRETTY MUCH DONE FOR!
I FIGURED IT WAS MY RESPONSIBILITY TO CLEAN UP AFTER MYSELF AND DRAW A WHOLE NEW STORY!
THEN THE IDEAS JUST STARTED FLOWING...
...AND I CAME UP WITH SOMETHING THAT OUGHTA BE PERFECT FOR *SHONEN JUMP!*
WHISK

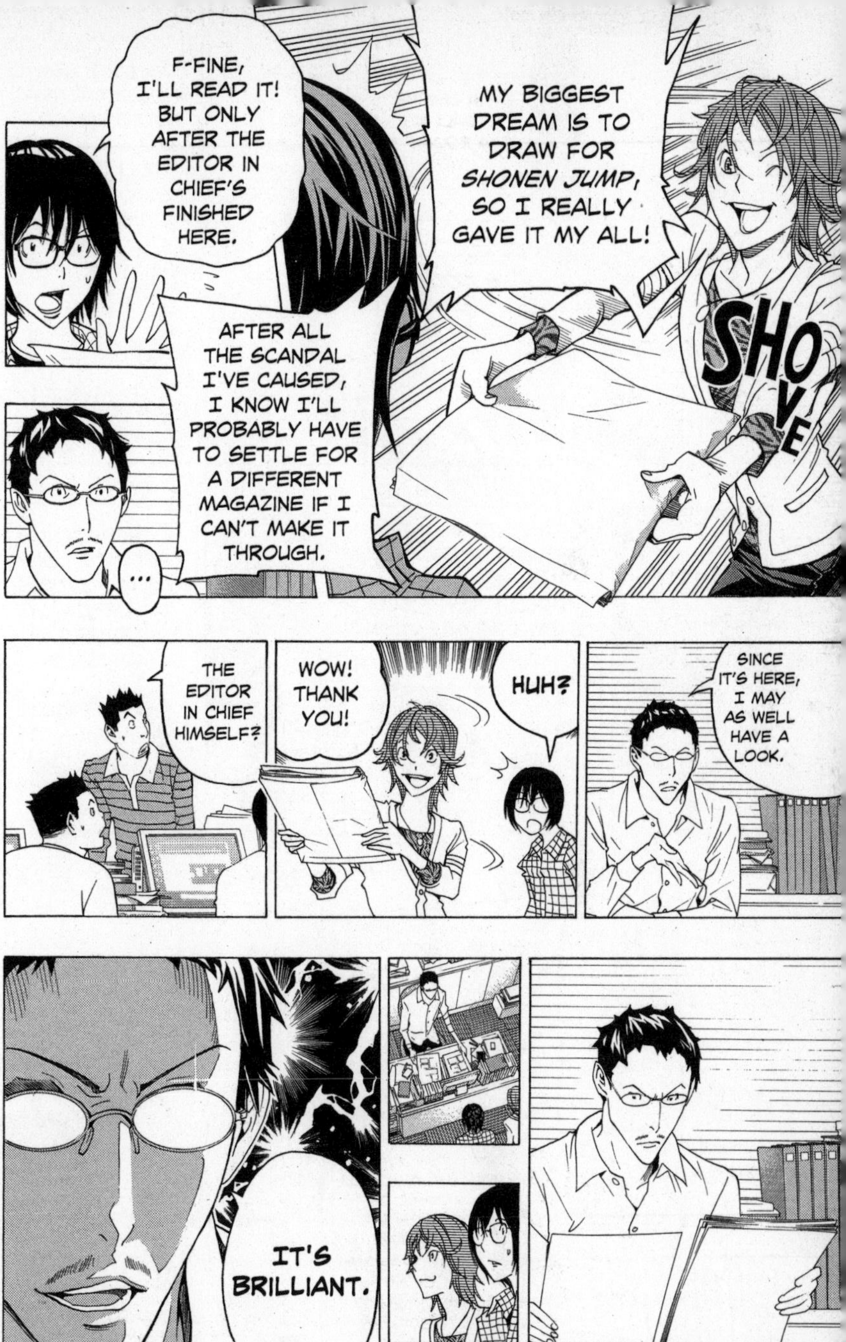
MY BIGGEST DREAM IS TO DRAW FOR *SHONEN JUMP*, SO I REALLY GAVE IT MY ALL!
SHOVE
AFTER ALL THE SCANDAL I'VE CAUSED, I KNOW I'LL PROBABLY HAVE TO SETTLE FOR A DIFFERENT MAGAZINE IF I CAN'T MAKE IT THROUGH.
F-FINE, I'LL READ IT! BUT ONLY AFTER THE EDITOR IN CHIEF'S FINISHED HERE.
...
SINCE IT'S HERE, I MAY AS WELL HAVE A LOOK.
HUH?
WOW! THANK YOU!
THE EDITOR IN CHIEF HIMSELF?
IT'S BRILLIANT.

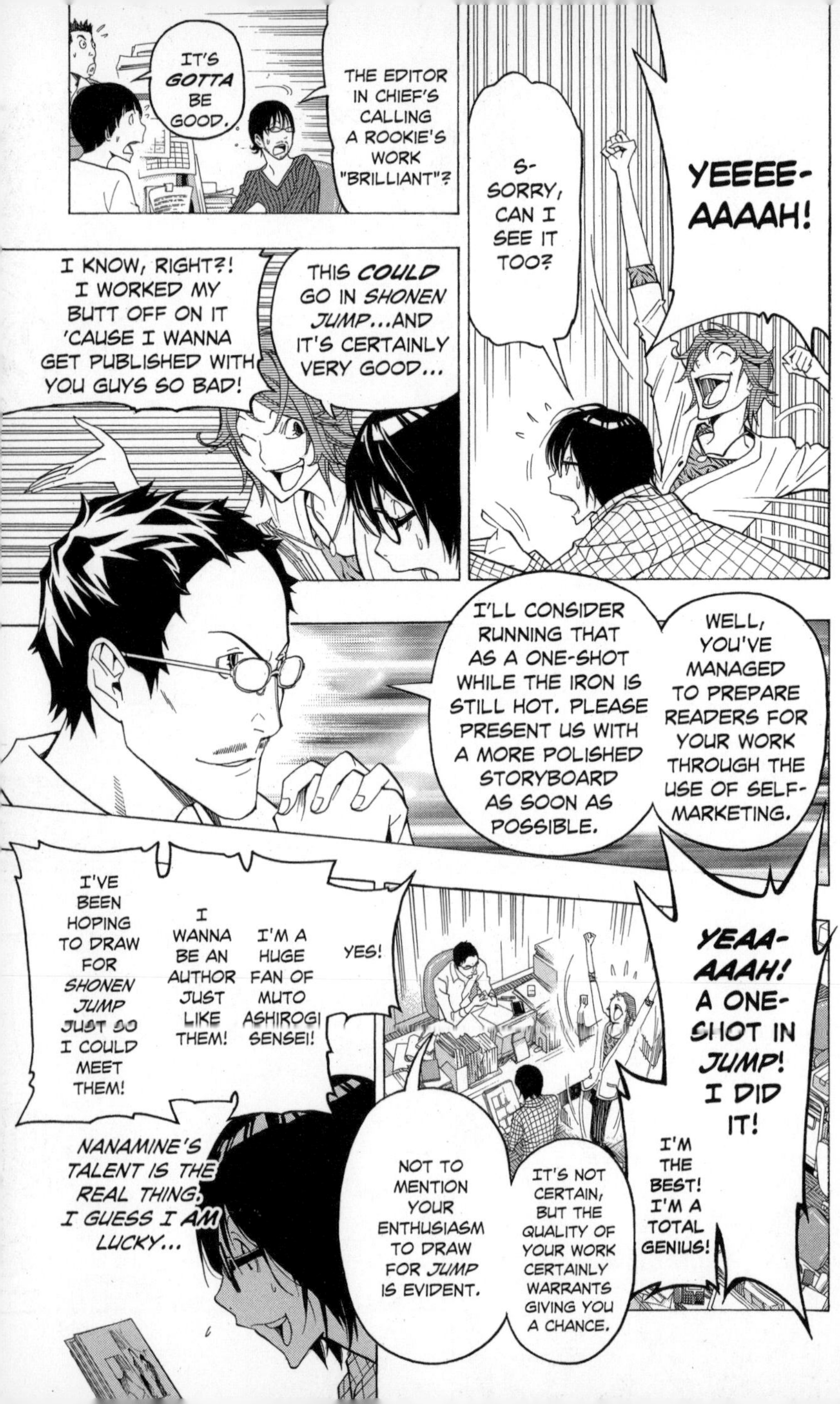
YEEEE-AAAAH!
S-SORRY, CAN I SEE IT TOO?
THE EDITOR IN CHIEF'S CALLING A ROOKIE'S WORK "BRILLIANT"?
IT'S *GOTTA* BE GOOD.
THIS *COULD* GO IN *SHONEN JUMP*...AND IT'S CERTAINLY VERY GOOD...
I KNOW, RIGHT?! I WORKED MY BUTT OFF ON IT 'CAUSE I WANNA GET PUBLISHED WITH YOU GUYS SO BAD!
WELL, YOU'VE MANAGED TO PREPARE READERS FOR YOUR WORK THROUGH THE USE OF SELF-MARKETING.
I'LL CONSIDER RUNNING THAT AS A ONE-SHOT WHILE THE IRON IS STILL HOT. PLEASE PRESENT US WITH A MORE POLISHED STORYBOARD AS SOON AS POSSIBLE.
YEAA-AAAH! A ONE-SHOT IN *JUMP*! I DID IT!
I'M THE BEST! I'M A TOTAL GENIUS!
IT'S NOT CERTAIN, BUT THE QUALITY OF YOUR WORK CERTAINLY WARRANTS GIVING YOU A CHANCE.
NOT TO MENTION YOUR ENTHUSIASM TO DRAW FOR *JUMP* IS EVIDENT.
YES!
I'M A HUGE FAN OF MUTO ASHIROGI SENSEI!
I WANNA BE AN AUTHOR JUST LIKE THEM!
I'VE BEEN HOPING TO DRAW FOR *SHONEN JUMP* JUST SO I COULD MEET THEM!
NANAMINE'S TALENT IS THE REAL THING. I GUESS I AM LUCKY...

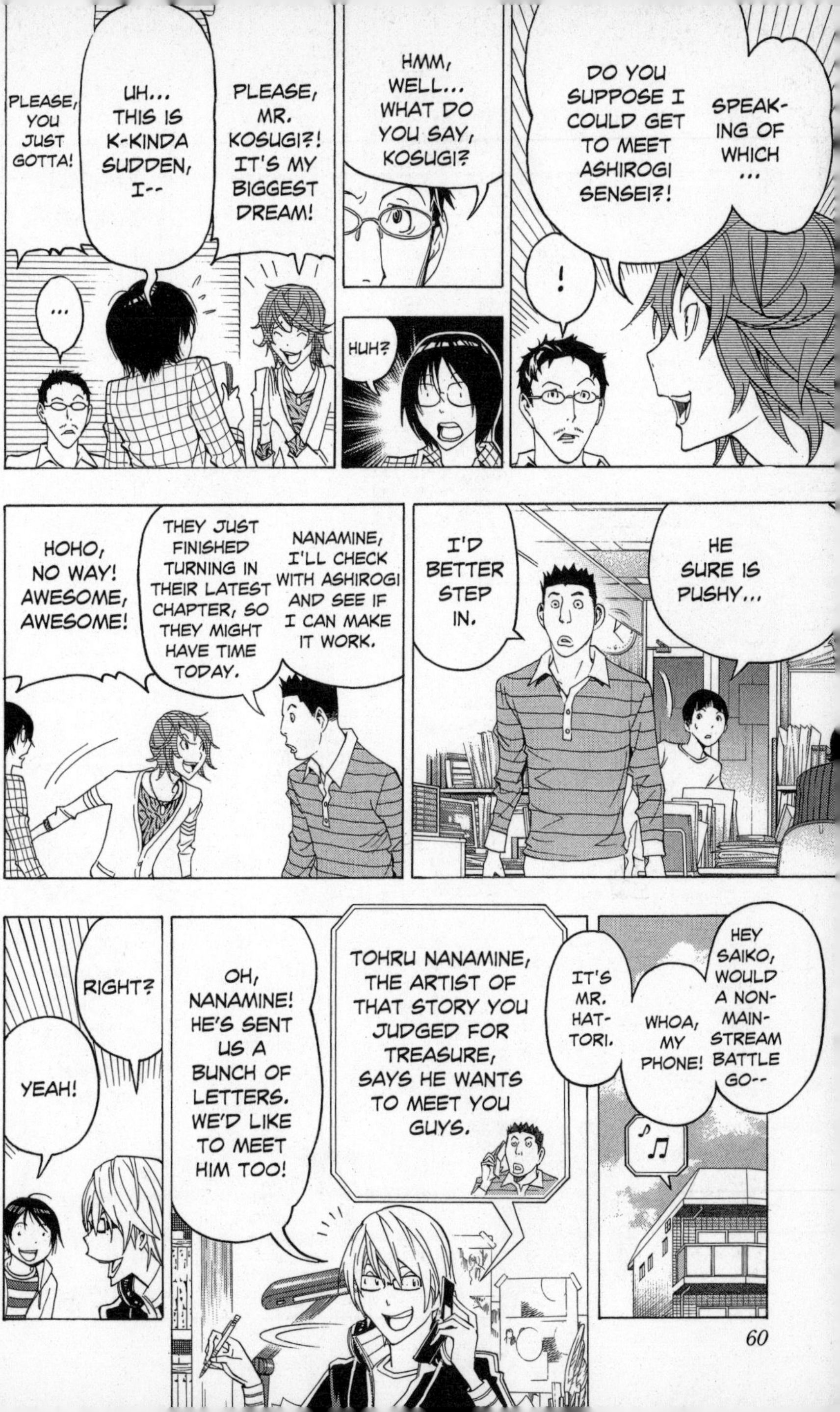
SPEAK-ING OF WHICH...
DO YOU SUPPOSE I COULD GET TO MEET ASHIROGI SENSEI?!
!
HMM, WELL... WHAT DO YOU SAY, KOSUGI?
HUH?
PLEASE, MR. KOSUGI?! IT'S MY BIGGEST DREAM!
UH... THIS IS K-KINDA SUDDEN, I--
PLEASE, YOU JUST GOTTA!
...
HE SURE IS PUSHY...
I'D BETTER STEP IN.
NANAMINE, I'LL CHECK WITH ASHIROGI AND SEE IF I CAN MAKE IT WORK.
THEY JUST FINISHED TURNING IN THEIR LATEST CHAPTER, SO THEY MIGHT HAVE TIME TODAY.
HOHO, NO WAY! AWESOME, AWESOME!
HEY SAIKO, WOULD A NON-MAINSTREAM BATTLE GO--
WHOA, MY PHONE!
IT'S MR. HAT-TORI.
♪♫
TOHRU NANAMINE, THE ARTIST OF THAT STORY YOU JUDGED FOR TREASURE, SAYS HE WANTS TO MEET YOU GUYS.
OH, NANAMINE! HE'S SENT US A BUNCH OF LETTERS. WE'D LIKE TO MEET HIM TOO!
RIGHT?
YEAH!

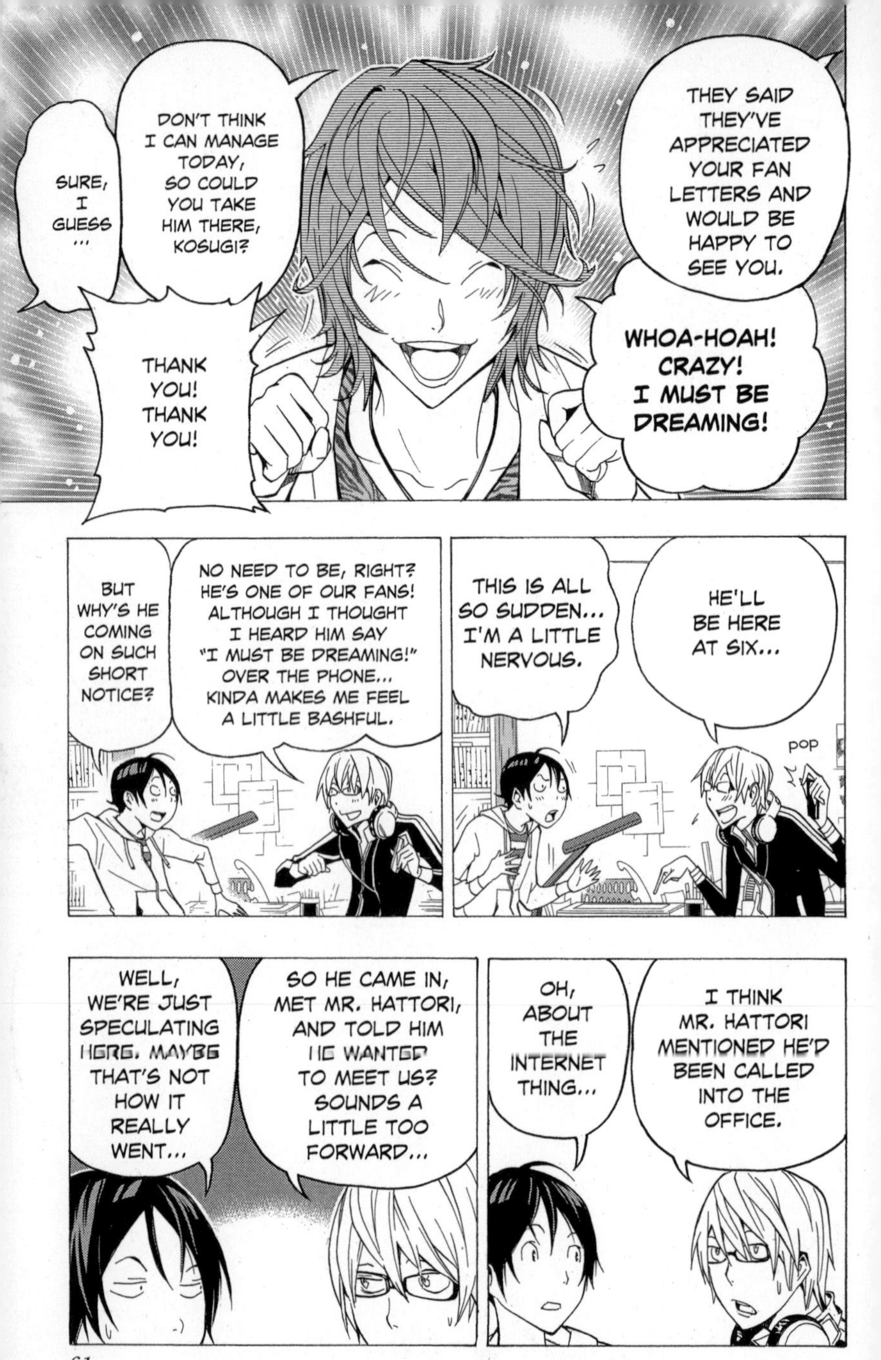
THEY SAID THEY'VE APPRECIATED YOUR FAN LETTERS AND WOULD BE HAPPY TO SEE YOU.
WHOA-HOAH! CRAZY! I MUST BE DREAMING!
DON'T THINK I CAN MANAGE TODAY, SO COULD YOU TAKE HIM THERE, KOSUGI?
SURE, I GUESS...
THANK YOU! THANK YOU!
HE'LL BE HERE AT SIX...
POP
THIS IS ALL SO SUDDEN... I'M A LITTLE NERVOUS.
NO NEED TO BE, RIGHT? HE'S ONE OF OUR FANS! ALTHOUGH I THOUGHT I HEARD HIM SAY "I MUST BE DREAMING!" OVER THE PHONE... KINDA MAKES ME FEEL A LITTLE BASHFUL.
BUT WHY'S HE COMING ON SUCH SHORT NOTICE?
I THINK MR. HATTORI MENTIONED HE'D BEEN CALLED INTO THE OFFICE.
OH, ABOUT THE INTERNET THING...
SO HE CAME IN, MET MR. HATTORI, AND TOLD HIM HE WANTED TO MEET US? SOUNDS A LITTLE TOO FORWARD...
WELL, WE'RE JUST SPECULATING HERE. MAYBE THAT'S NOT HOW IT REALLY WENT...

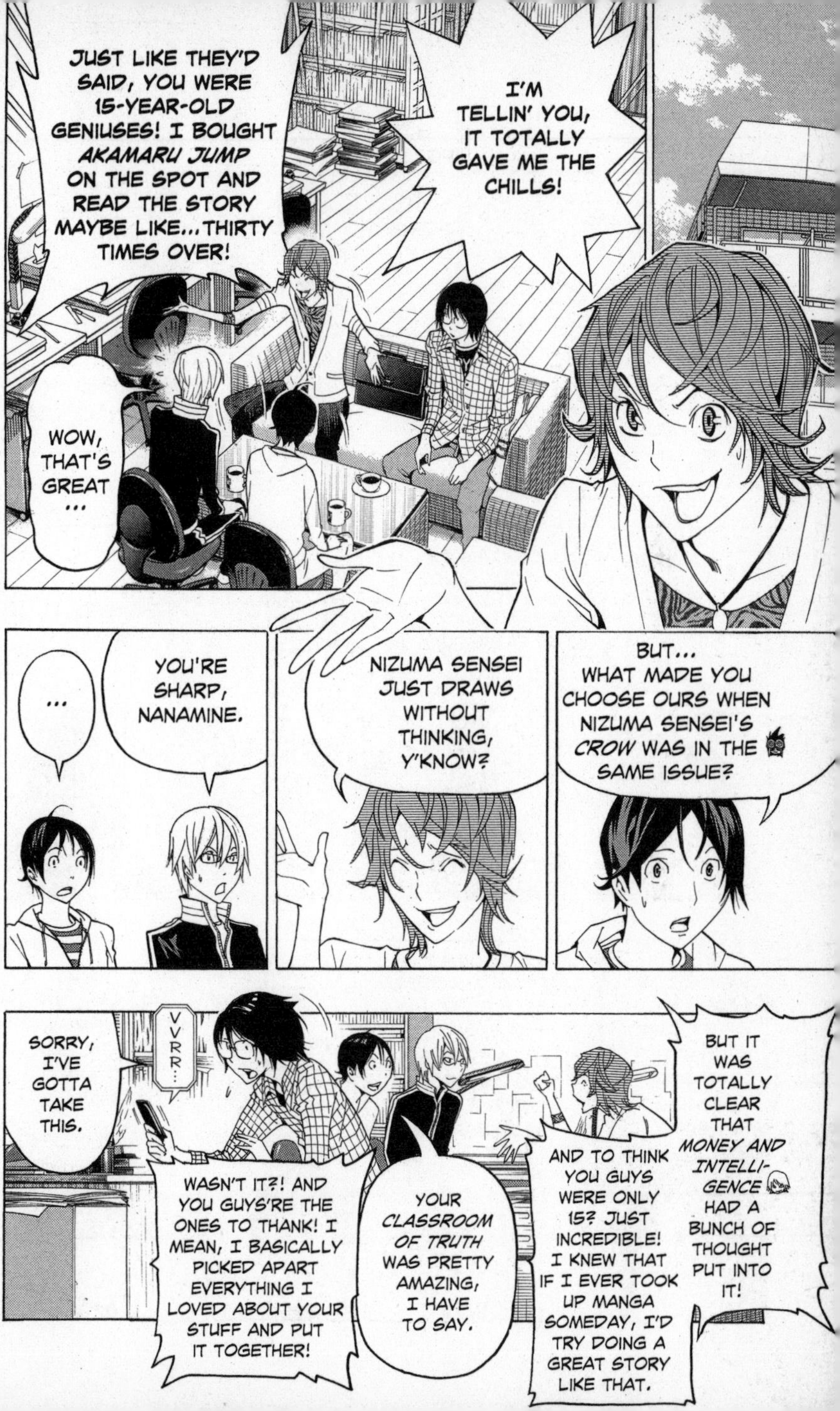

I'M TELLIN' YOU, IT TOTALLY GAVE ME THE CHILLS!
JUST LIKE THEY'D SAID, YOU WERE 15-YEAR-OLD GENIUSES! I BOUGHT AKAMARU JUMP ON THE SPOT AND READ THE STORY MAYBE LIKE... THIRTY TIMES OVER!
WOW, THAT'S GREAT ...
BUT... WHAT MADE YOU CHOOSE OURS WHEN NIZUMA SENSEI'S CROW WAS IN THE SAME ISSUE?
NIZUMA SENSEI JUST DRAWS WITHOUT THINKING, Y'KNOW?
YOU'RE SHARP, NANAMINE.
...
BUT IT WAS TOTALLY CLEAR THAT MONEY AND INTELLIGENCE HAD A BUNCH OF THOUGHT PUT INTO IT!
AND TO THINK YOU GUYS WERE ONLY 15? JUST INCREDIBLE! I KNEW THAT IF I EVER TOOK UP MANGA SOMEDAY, I'D TRY DOING A GREAT STORY LIKE THAT.
YOUR CLASSROOM OF TRUTH WAS PRETTY AMAZING, I HAVE TO SAY.
WASN'T IT?! AND YOU GUYS'RE THE ONES TO THANK! I MEAN, I BASICALLY PICKED APART EVERYTHING I LOVED ABOUT YOUR STUFF AND PUT IT TOGETHER!
VVRR...
SORRY, I'VE GOTTA TAKE THIS.

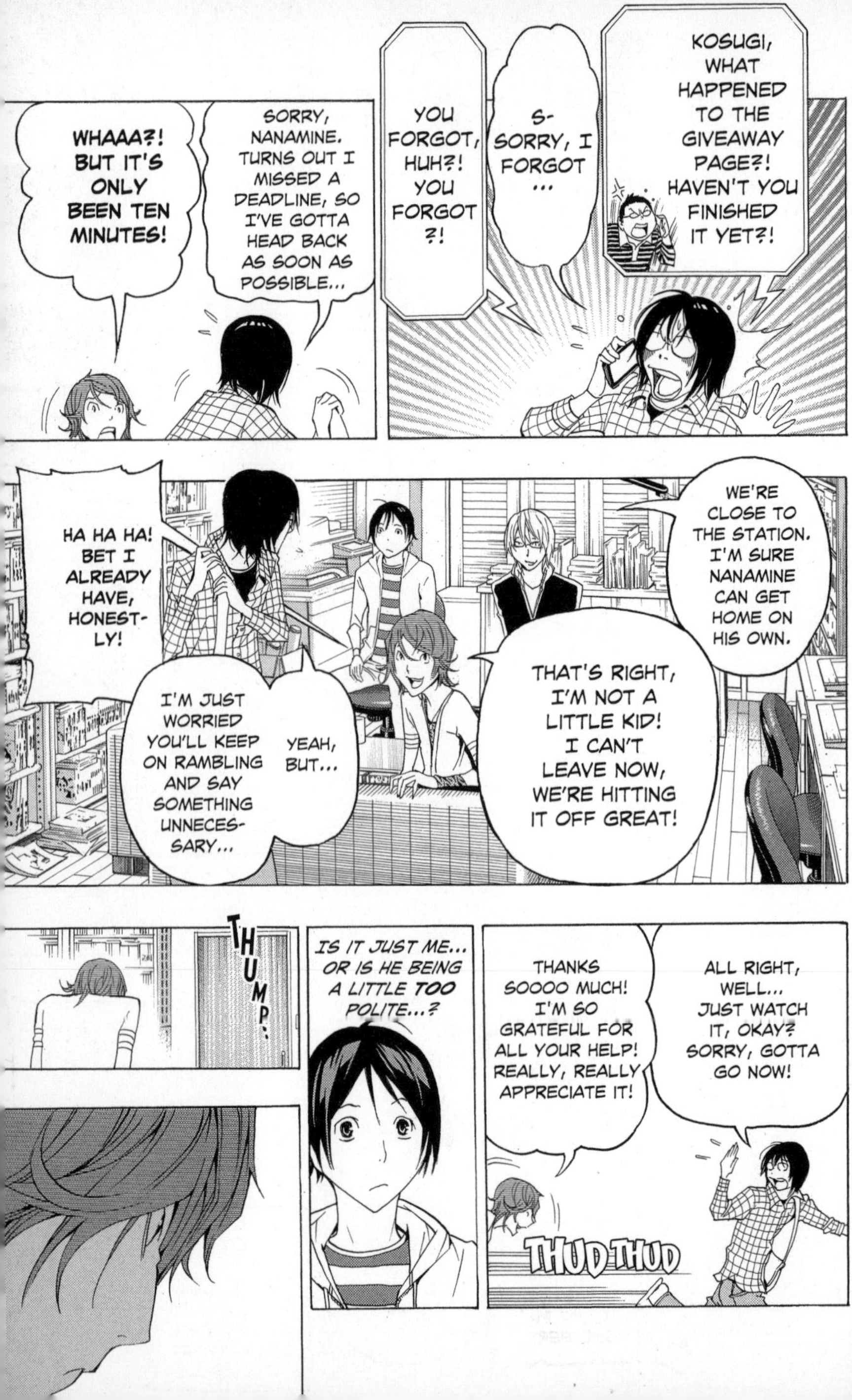
KOSUGI, WHAT HAPPENED TO THE GIVEAWAY PAGE?! HAVEN'T YOU FINISHED IT YET?!
S-SORRY, I FORGOT...
YOU FORGOT, HUH?! YOU FORGOT?!
SORRY, NANAMINE. TURNS OUT I MISSED A DEADLINE, SO I'VE GOTTA HEAD BACK AS SOON AS POSSIBLE...
WHAAA?! BUT IT'S ONLY BEEN TEN MINUTES!
WE'RE CLOSE TO THE STATION. I'M SURE NANAMINE CAN GET HOME ON HIS OWN.
THAT'S RIGHT, I'M NOT A LITTLE KID! I CAN'T LEAVE NOW, WE'RE HITTING IT OFF GREAT!
YEAH, BUT...
I'M JUST WORRIED YOU'LL KEEP ON RAMBLING AND SAY SOMETHING UNNECES-SARY...
HA HA HA! BET I ALREADY HAVE, HONEST-LY!
ALL RIGHT, WELL... JUST WATCH IT, OKAY? SORRY, GOTTA GO NOW!
THANKS SOOOO MUCH! I'M SO GRATEFUL FOR ALL YOUR HELP! REALLY, REALLY APPRECIATE IT!
THUD THUD
IS IT JUST ME... OR IS HE BEING A LITTLE TOO POLITE...?
THUMP...

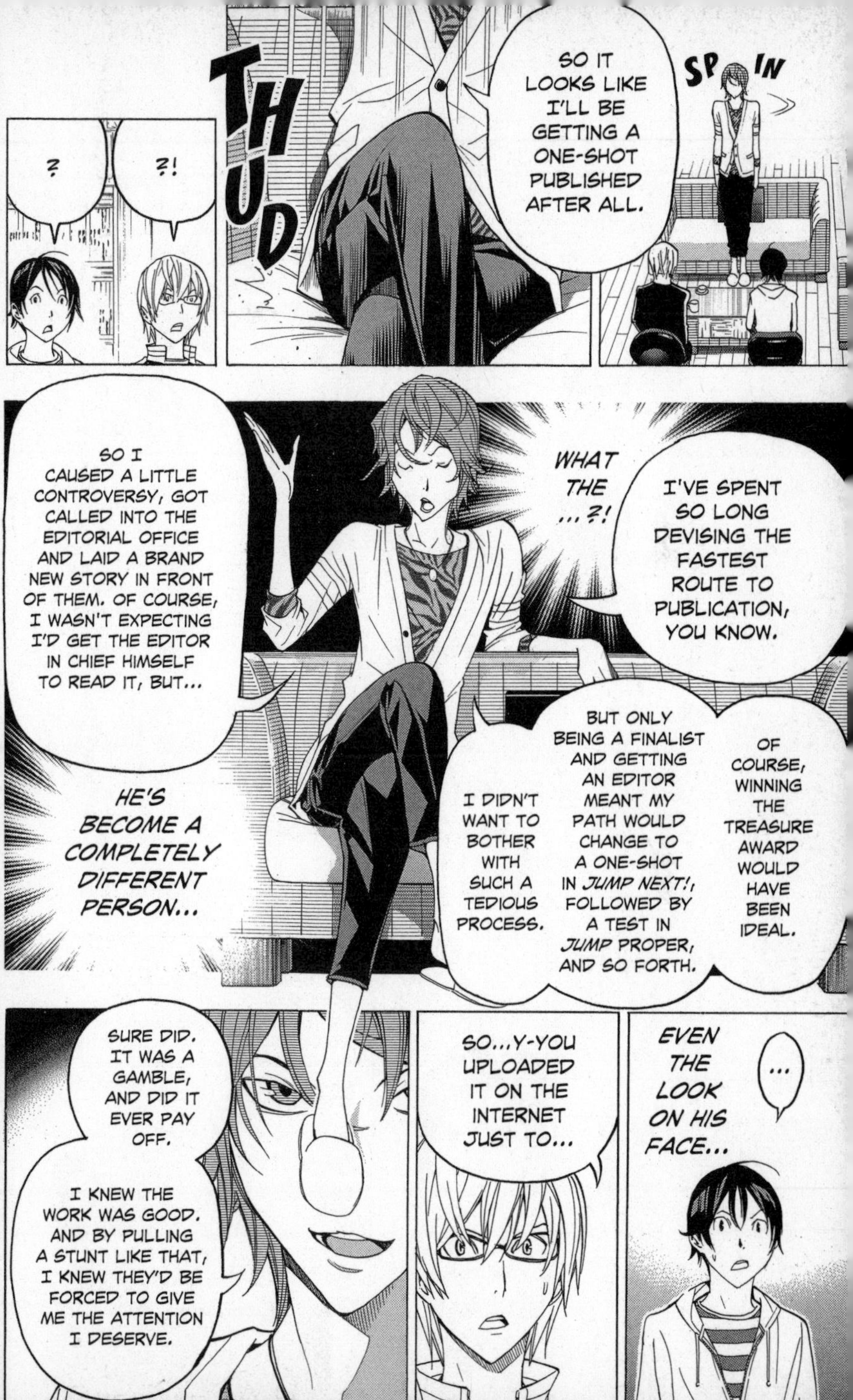
SPIN
THUD
SO IT LOOKS LIKE I'LL BE GETTING A ONE-SHOT PUBLISHED AFTER ALL.
?!
?
I'VE SPENT SO LONG DEVISING THE FASTEST ROUTE TO PUBLICATION, YOU KNOW.
WHAT THE ...?!
OF COURSE, WINNING THE TREASURE AWARD WOULD HAVE BEEN IDEAL.
BUT ONLY BEING A FINALIST AND GETTING AN EDITOR MEANT MY PATH WOULD CHANGE TO A ONE-SHOT IN JUMP NEXT!, FOLLOWED BY A TEST IN JUMP PROPER, AND SO FORTH.
I DIDN'T WANT TO BOTHER WITH SUCH A TEDIOUS PROCESS.
SO I CAUSED A LITTLE CONTROVERSY, GOT CALLED INTO THE EDITORIAL OFFICE AND LAID A BRAND NEW STORY IN FRONT OF THEM. OF COURSE, I WASN'T EXPECTING I'D GET THE EDITOR IN CHIEF HIMSELF TO READ IT, BUT...
HE'S BECOME A COMPLETELY DIFFERENT PERSON...
...
EVEN THE LOOK ON HIS FACE...
SO...Y-YOU UPLOADED IT ON THE INTERNET JUST TO...
SURE DID. IT WAS A GAMBLE, AND DID IT EVER PAY OFF.
I KNEW THE WORK WAS GOOD. AND BY PULLING A STUNT LIKE THAT, I KNEW THEY'D BE FORCED TO GIVE ME THE ATTENTION I DESERVE.

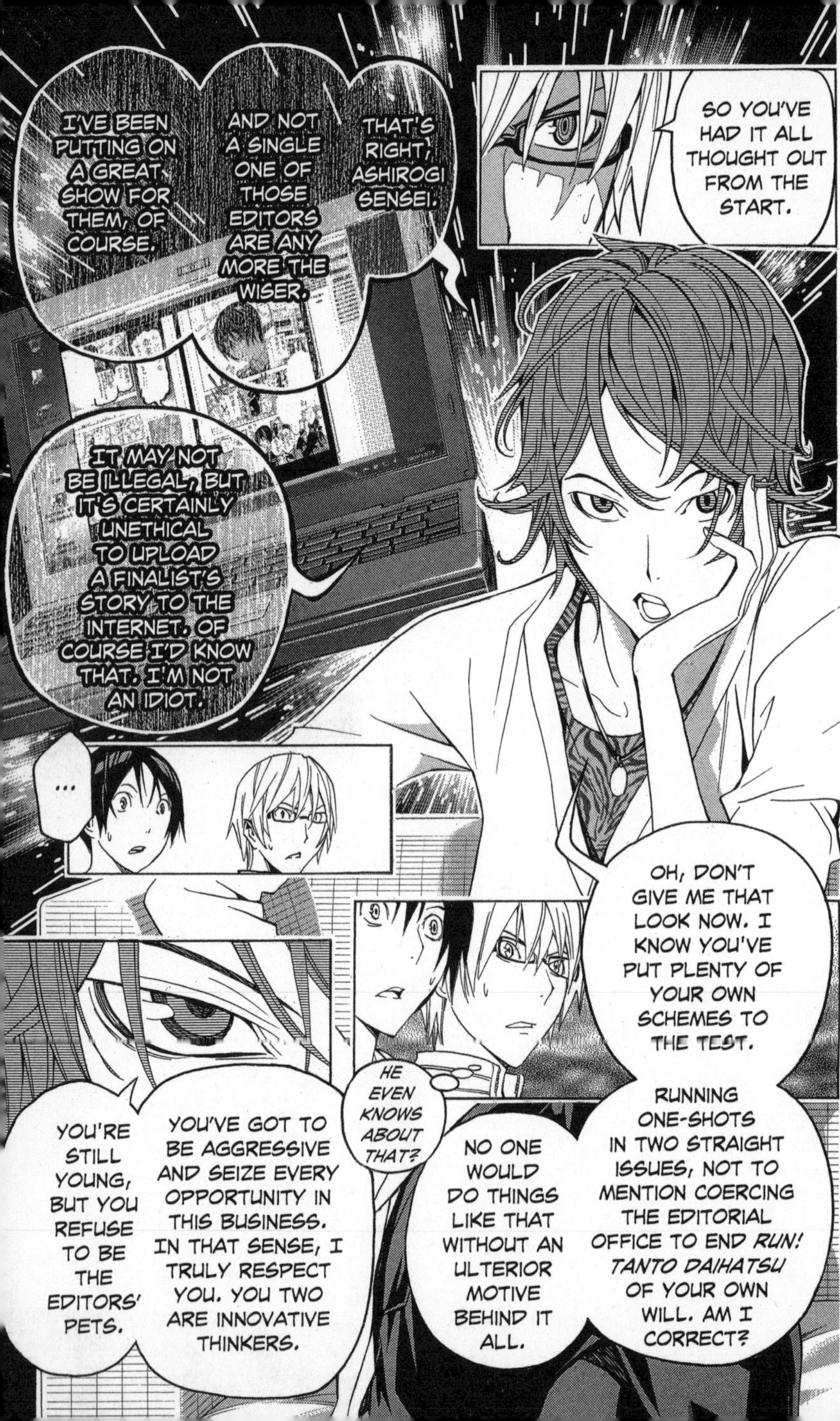
SO YOU'VE HAD IT ALL THOUGHT OUT FROM THE START.
THAT'S RIGHT, ASHIROGI SENSEI.
AND NOT A SINGLE ONE OF THOSE EDITORS ARE ANY MORE THE WISER.
I'VE BEEN PUTTING ON A GREAT SHOW FOR THEM, OF COURSE.
IT MAY NOT BE ILLEGAL, BUT IT'S CERTAINLY UNETHICAL TO UPLOAD A FINALIST'S STORY TO THE INTERNET. OF COURSE I'D KNOW THAT. I'M NOT AN IDIOT.
...
OH, DON'T GIVE ME THAT LOOK NOW. I KNOW YOU'VE PUT PLENTY OF YOUR OWN SCHEMES TO THE TEST.
RUNNING ONE-SHOTS IN TWO STRAIGHT ISSUES, NOT TO MENTION COERCING THE EDITORIAL OFFICE TO END *RUN! TANTO DAIHATSU* OF YOUR OWN WILL. AM I CORRECT?
NO ONE WOULD DO THINGS LIKE THAT WITHOUT AN ULTERIOR MOTIVE BEHIND IT ALL.
HE EVEN KNOWS ABOUT THAT?
YOU'VE GOT TO BE AGGRESSIVE AND SEIZE EVERY OPPORTUNITY IN THIS BUSINESS. IN THAT SENSE, I TRULY RESPECT YOU. YOU TWO ARE INNOVATIVE THINKERS.
YOU'RE STILL YOUNG, BUT YOU REFUSE TO BE THE EDITORS' PETS.

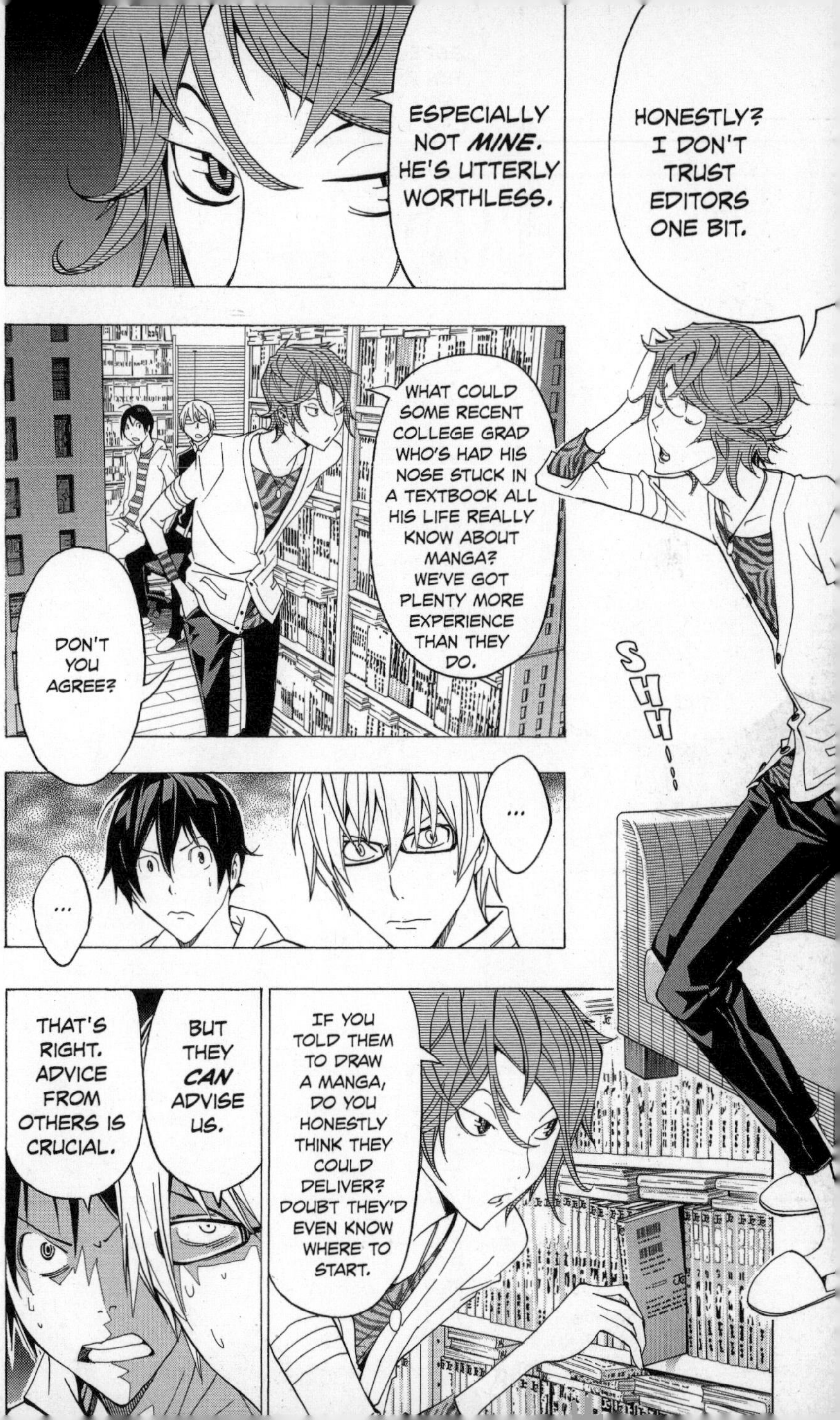
HONESTLY? I DON'T TRUST EDITORS ONE BIT.
ESPECIALLY NOT *MINE*. HE'S UTTERLY WORTHLESS.
SHH...
WHAT COULD SOME RECENT COLLEGE GRAD WHO'S HAD HIS NOSE STUCK IN A TEXTBOOK ALL HIS LIFE REALLY KNOW ABOUT MANGA? WE'VE GOT PLENTY MORE EXPERIENCE THAN THEY DO.
DON'T YOU AGREE?
...
...
IF YOU TOLD THEM TO DRAW A MANGA, DO YOU HONESTLY THINK THEY COULD DELIVER? DOUBT THEY'D EVEN KNOW WHERE TO START.
BUT THEY *CAN* ADVISE US.
THAT'S RIGHT. ADVICE FROM OTHERS IS CRUCIAL.

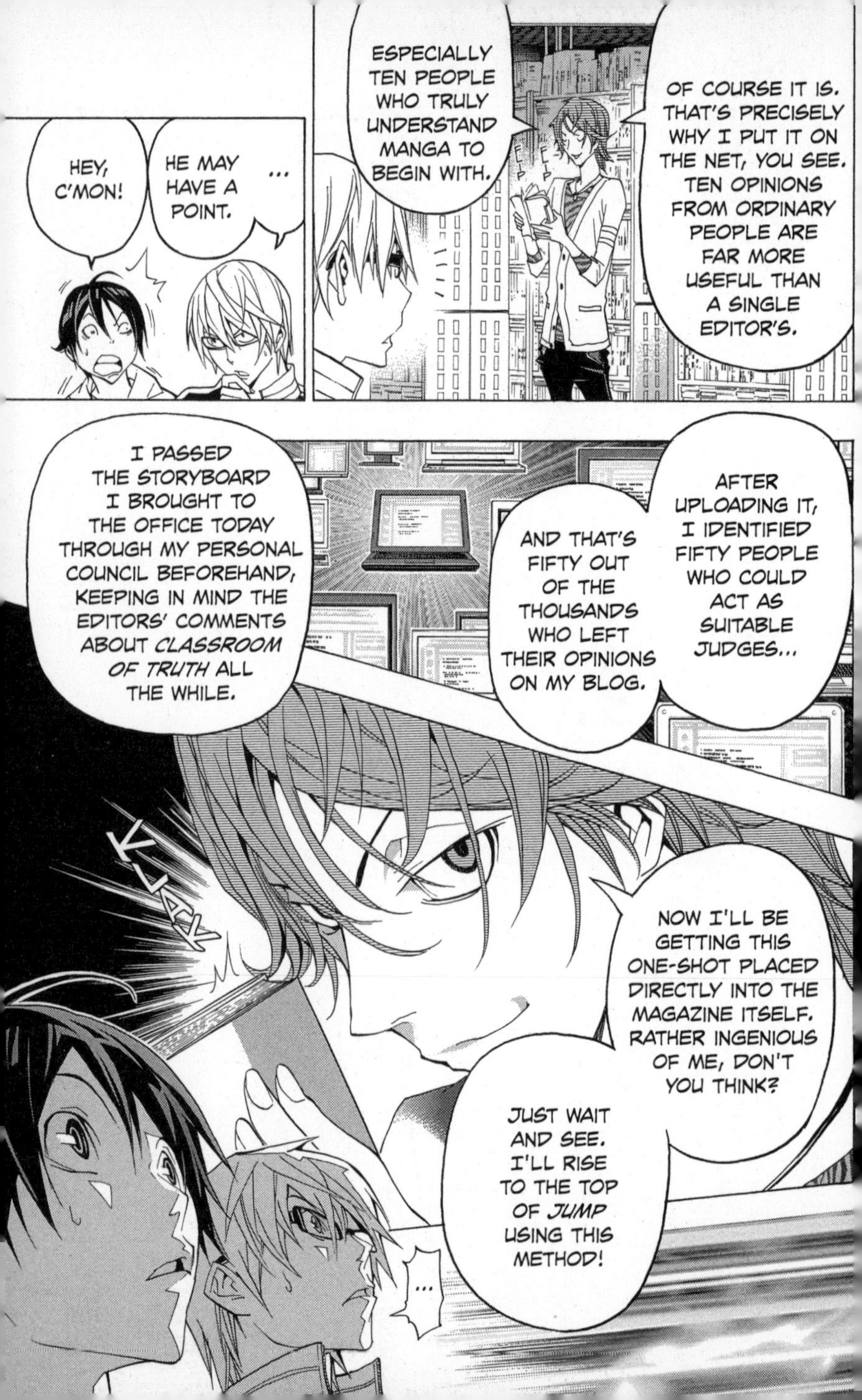
OF COURSE IT IS. THAT'S PRECISELY WHY I PUT IT ON THE NET, YOU SEE. TEN OPINIONS FROM ORDINARY PEOPLE ARE FAR MORE USEFUL THAN A SINGLE EDITOR'S.
ESPECIALLY TEN PEOPLE WHO TRULY UNDERSTAND MANGA TO BEGIN WITH.
...
HE MAY HAVE A POINT.
HEY, C'MON!
AFTER UPLOADING IT, I IDENTIFIED FIFTY PEOPLE WHO COULD ACT AS SUITABLE JUDGES...
AND THAT'S FIFTY OUT OF THE THOUSANDS WHO LEFT THEIR OPINIONS ON MY BLOG.
I PASSED THE STORYBOARD I BROUGHT TO THE OFFICE TODAY THROUGH MY PERSONAL COUNCIL BEFOREHAND, KEEPING IN MIND THE EDITORS' COMMENTS ABOUT *CLASSROOM OF TRUTH* ALL THE WHILE.
NOW I'LL BE GETTING THIS ONE-SHOT PLACED DIRECTLY INTO THE MAGAZINE ITSELF. RATHER INGENIOUS OF ME, DON'T YOU THINK?
KLACK
JUST WAIT AND SEE. I'LL RISE TO THE TOP OF *JUMP* USING THIS METHOD!
...

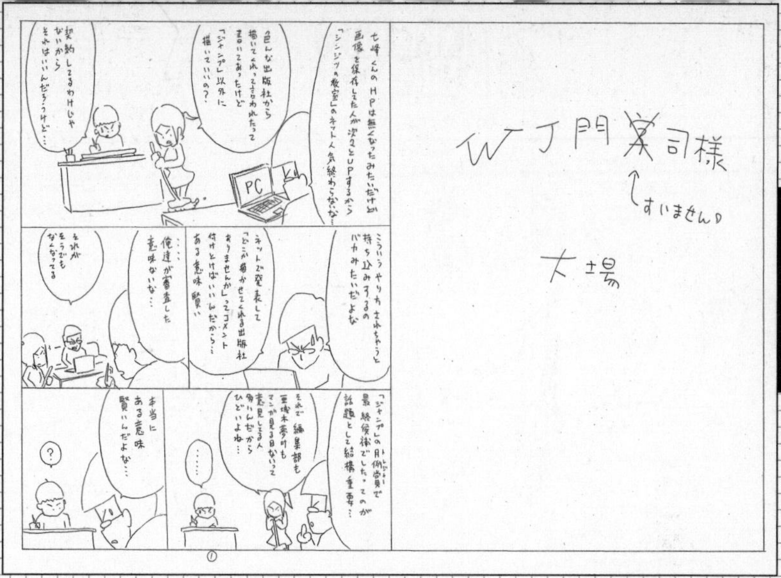
WJ門X司様
↑すいません。
大場
七峰くんのHPは無くなったみたいだけど画像を保存した人が次々とUPするから「シンジツの教室」のネット人気終わらないな…
色んな出版社から描いてくれって言われたってまいてあったけど「ジャンプ」以外に描いていいの?
契約してるわけじゃないからそれはいいんだろうけど…
こういうやり方されちゃうと持ち込みするのバカみたいだよな
ネットで発表して「どこか描かせてくれる出版社ありませんか」ってコメント付けとけばいいんだから…ある意味賢い
…俺達が審査した意味ないな…
それがそうでもなくなってる
「ジャンプ」の月例賞で最終候補でした、てのが話題として結構重要…
それで編集部も亜城木夢叶もさが見る目ないって意見してる人多いんだからひどいよね…
……
本当にある意味賢いんだよな…
?
OHBA'S STORYBOARD

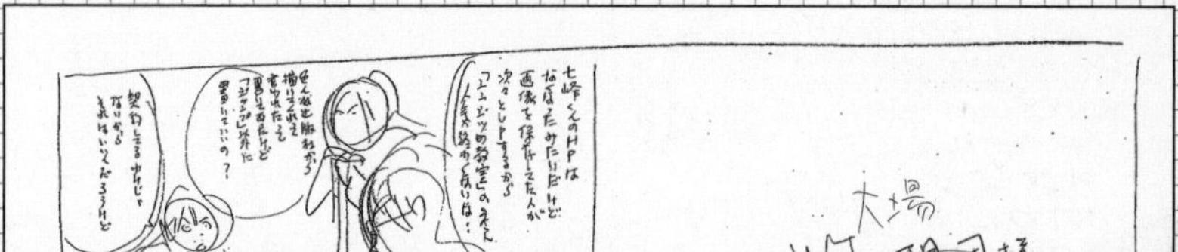
OBATA'S STORYBOARD

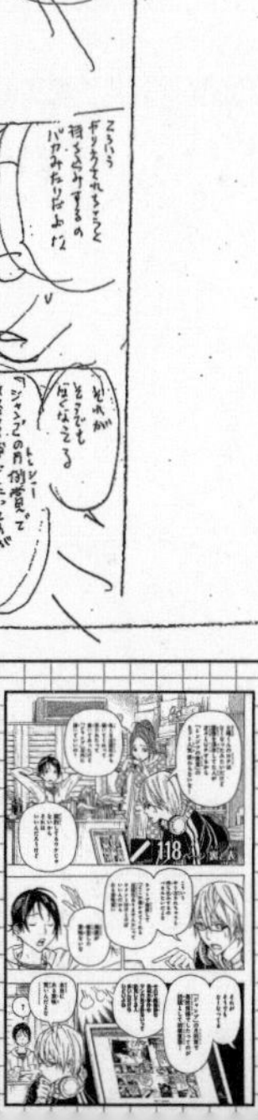
COMPLETE!

*CREATOR STORYBOARDS AND FINISHED PAGES IN JAPANESE

BAKUMAN。 vol.14

"Until the Final Draft Is Complete"

Chapter 118, pp. 20-21

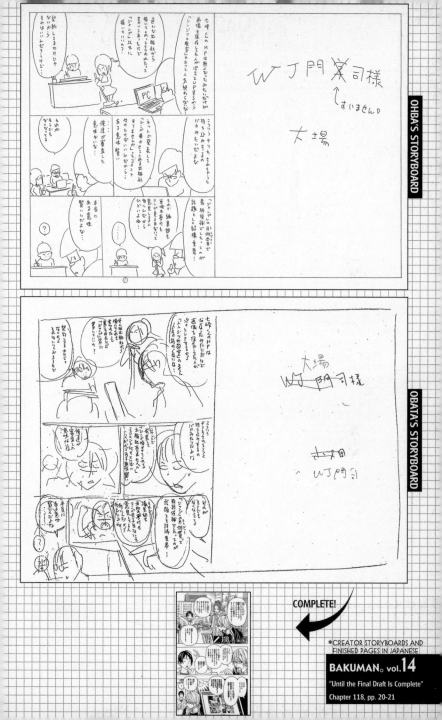

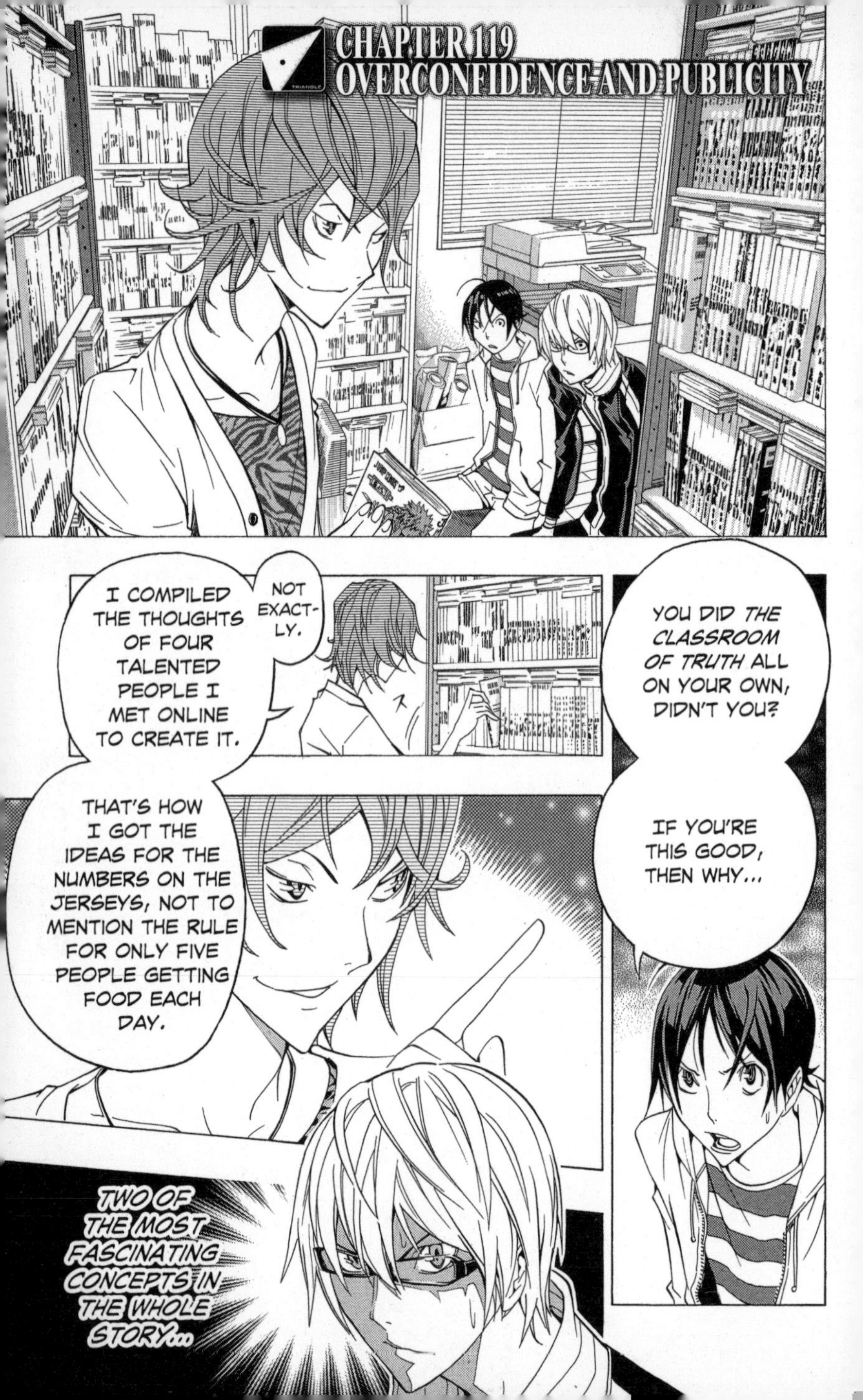
CHAPTER 119
OVERCONFIDENCE AND PUBLICITY
YOU DID THE CLASSROOM OF TRUTH ALL ON YOUR OWN, DIDN'T YOU?
IF YOU'RE THIS GOOD, THEN WHY...
NOT EXACTLY.
I COMPILED THE THOUGHTS OF FOUR TALENTED PEOPLE I MET ONLINE TO CREATE IT.
THAT'S HOW I GOT THE IDEAS FOR THE NUMBERS ON THE JERSEYS, NOT TO MENTION THE RULE FOR ONLY FIVE PEOPLE GETTING FOOD EACH DAY.
TWO OF THE MOST FASCINATING CONCEPTS IN THE WHOLE STORY...

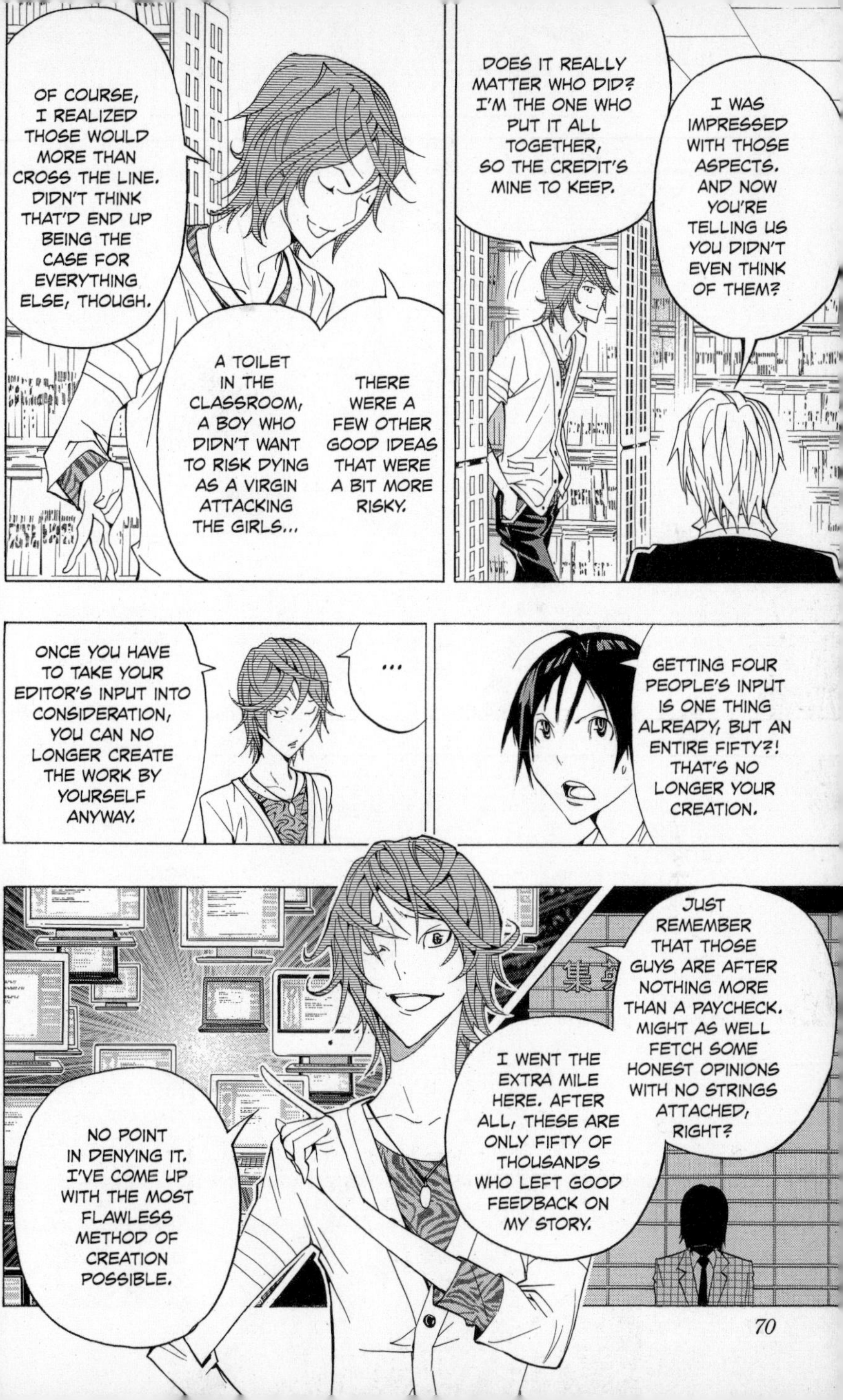
I WAS IMPRESSED WITH THOSE ASPECTS. AND NOW YOU'RE TELLING US YOU DIDN'T EVEN THINK OF THEM?
DOES IT REALLY MATTER WHO DID? I'M THE ONE WHO PUT IT ALL TOGETHER, SO THE CREDIT'S MINE TO KEEP.
THERE WERE A FEW OTHER GOOD IDEAS THAT WERE A BIT MORE RISKY.
A TOILET IN THE CLASSROOM, A BOY WHO DIDN'T WANT TO RISK DYING AS A VIRGIN ATTACKING THE GIRLS...
OF COURSE, I REALIZED THOSE WOULD MORE THAN CROSS THE LINE. DIDN'T THINK THAT'D END UP BEING THE CASE FOR EVERYTHING ELSE, THOUGH.
GETTING FOUR PEOPLE'S INPUT IS ONE THING ALREADY, BUT AN ENTIRE FIFTY?! THAT'S NO LONGER YOUR CREATION.
...
ONCE YOU HAVE TO TAKE YOUR EDITOR'S INPUT INTO CONSIDERATION, YOU CAN NO LONGER CREATE THE WORK BY YOURSELF ANYWAY.
JUST REMEMBER THAT THOSE GUYS ARE AFTER NOTHING MORE THAN A PAYCHECK. MIGHT AS WELL FETCH SOME HONEST OPINIONS WITH NO STRINGS ATTACHED, RIGHT?
I WENT THE EXTRA MILE HERE. AFTER ALL, THESE ARE ONLY FIFTY OF THOUSANDS WHO LEFT GOOD FEEDBACK ON MY STORY.
NO POINT IN DENYING IT. I'VE COME UP WITH THE MOST FLAWLESS METHOD OF CREATION POSSIBLE.

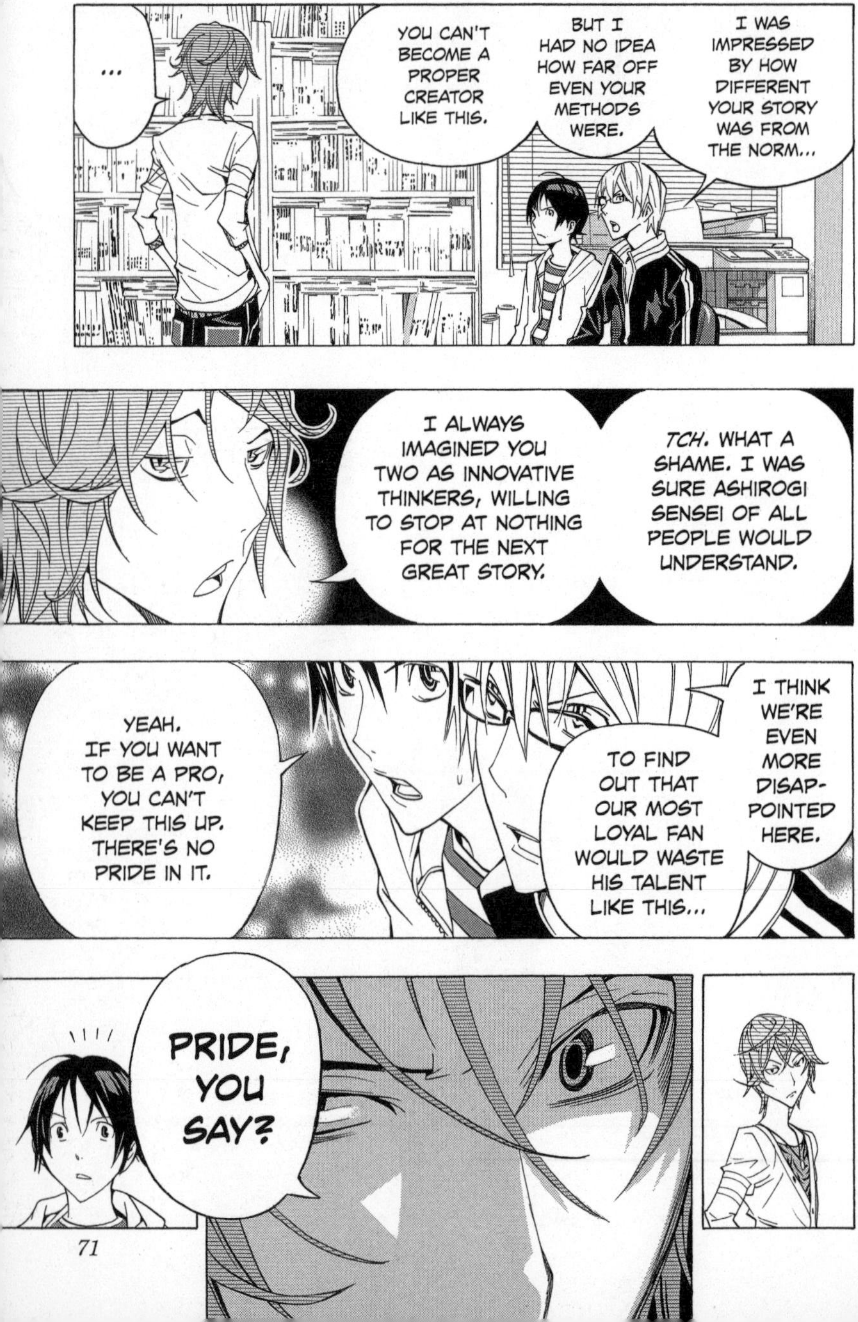

I WAS IMPRESSED BY HOW DIFFERENT YOUR STORY WAS FROM THE NORM...
BUT I HAD NO IDEA HOW FAR OFF EVEN YOUR METHODS WERE.
YOU CAN'T BECOME A PROPER CREATOR LIKE THIS.
...
TCH. WHAT A SHAME. I WAS SURE ASHIROGI SENSEI OF ALL PEOPLE WOULD UNDERSTAND.
I ALWAYS IMAGINED YOU TWO AS INNOVATIVE THINKERS, WILLING TO STOP AT NOTHING FOR THE NEXT GREAT STORY.
I THINK WE'RE EVEN MORE DISAP-POINTED HERE.
TO FIND OUT THAT OUR MOST LOYAL FAN WOULD WASTE HIS TALENT LIKE THIS...
YEAH. IF YOU WANT TO BE A PRO, YOU CAN'T KEEP THIS UP. THERE'S NO PRIDE IN IT.
PRIDE, YOU SAY?

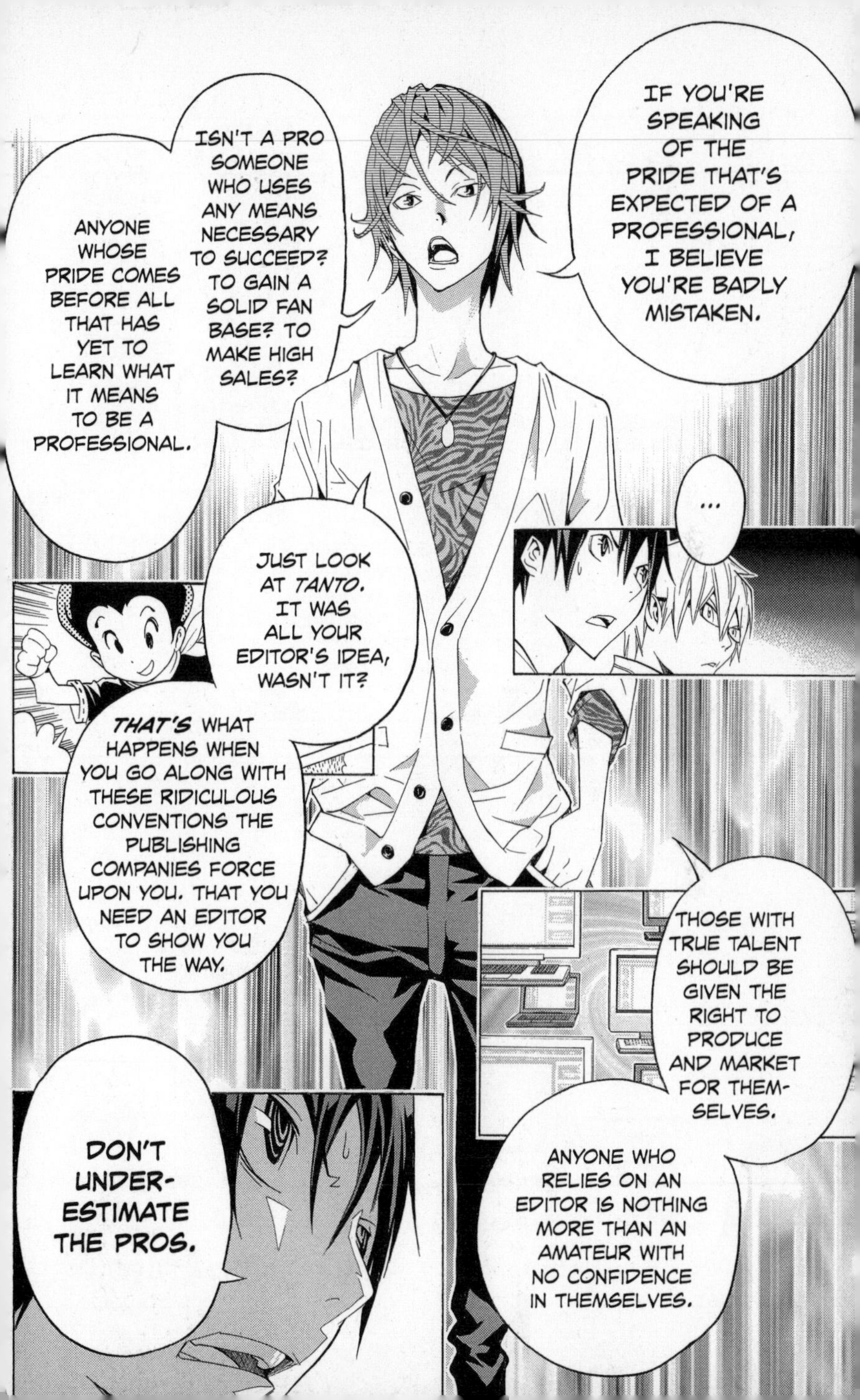
IF YOU'RE SPEAKING OF THE PRIDE THAT'S EXPECTED OF A PROFESSIONAL, I BELIEVE YOU'RE BADLY MISTAKEN.
ISN'T A PRO SOMEONE WHO USES ANY MEANS NECESSARY TO SUCCEED? TO GAIN A SOLID FAN BASE? TO MAKE HIGH SALES?
ANYONE WHOSE PRIDE COMES BEFORE ALL THAT HAS YET TO LEARN WHAT IT MEANS TO BE A PROFESSIONAL.
...
JUST LOOK AT *TANTO*. IT WAS ALL YOUR EDITOR'S IDEA, WASN'T IT?
THAT'S WHAT HAPPENS WHEN YOU GO ALONG WITH THESE RIDICULOUS CONVENTIONS THE PUBLISHING COMPANIES FORCE UPON YOU. THAT YOU NEED AN EDITOR TO SHOW YOU THE WAY.
THOSE WITH TRUE TALENT SHOULD BE GIVEN THE RIGHT TO PRODUCE AND MARKET FOR THEMSELVES.
ANYONE WHO RELIES ON AN EDITOR IS NOTHING MORE THAN AN AMATEUR WITH NO CONFIDENCE IN THEMSELVES.
DON'T UNDERESTIMATE THE PROS.

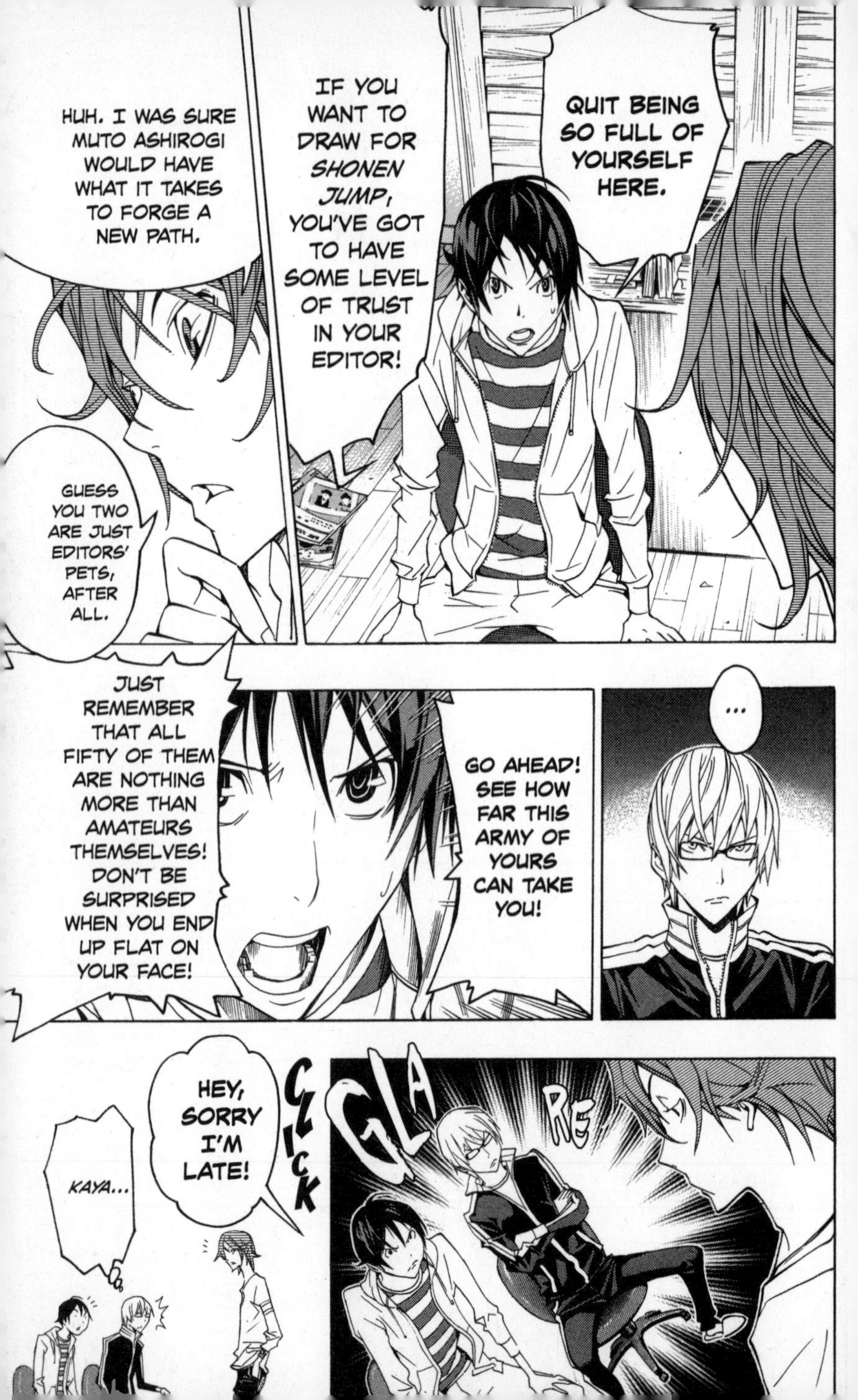
QUIT BEING SO FULL OF YOURSELF HERE.
IF YOU WANT TO DRAW FOR *SHONEN JUMP*, YOU'VE GOT TO HAVE SOME LEVEL OF TRUST IN YOUR EDITOR!
HUH. I WAS SURE MUTO ASHIROGI WOULD HAVE WHAT IT TAKES TO FORGE A NEW PATH.
GUESS YOU TWO ARE JUST EDITORS' PETS, AFTER ALL.
...
GO AHEAD! SEE HOW FAR THIS ARMY OF YOURS CAN TAKE YOU!
JUST REMEMBER THAT ALL FIFTY OF THEM ARE NOTHING MORE THAN AMATEURS THEMSELVES! DON'T BE SURPRISED WHEN YOU END UP FLAT ON YOUR FACE!
GLARE
CLICK
HEY, SORRY I'M LATE!
KAYA...

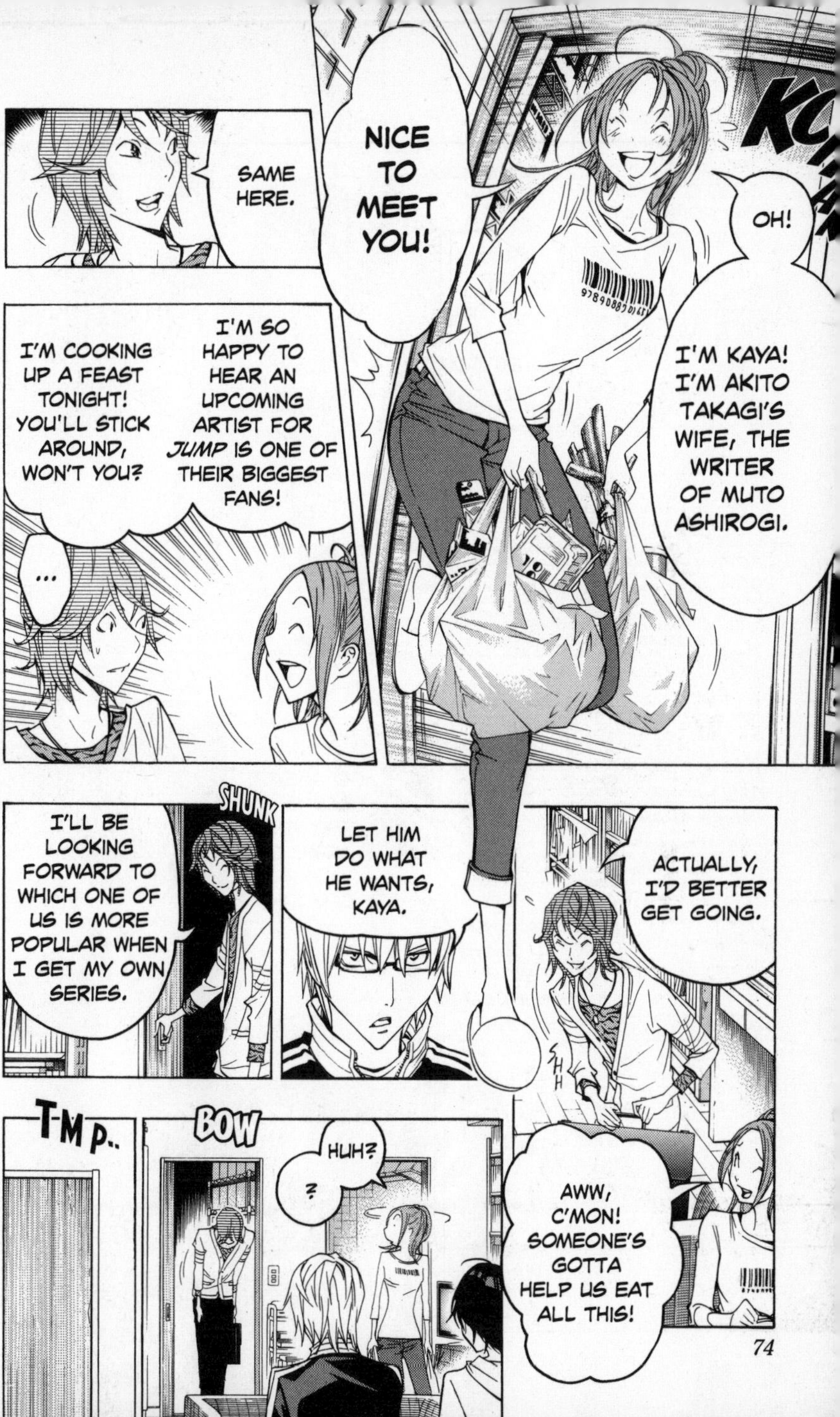
OH!
I'M KAYA! I'M AKITO TAKAGI'S WIFE, THE WRITER OF MUTO ASHIROGI.
NICE TO MEET YOU!
SAME HERE.
I'M SO HAPPY TO HEAR AN UPCOMING ARTIST FOR *JUMP* IS ONE OF THEIR BIGGEST FANS!
I'M COOKING UP A FEAST TONIGHT! YOU'LL STICK AROUND, WON'T YOU?
...
ACTUALLY, I'D BETTER GET GOING.
SHH
LET HIM DO WHAT HE WANTS, KAYA.
SHUNK
I'LL BE LOOKING FORWARD TO WHICH ONE OF US IS MORE POPULAR WHEN I GET MY OWN SERIES.
AWW, C'MON! SOMEONE'S GOTTA HELP US EAT ALL THIS!
HUH?
?
BOW
T-M P..

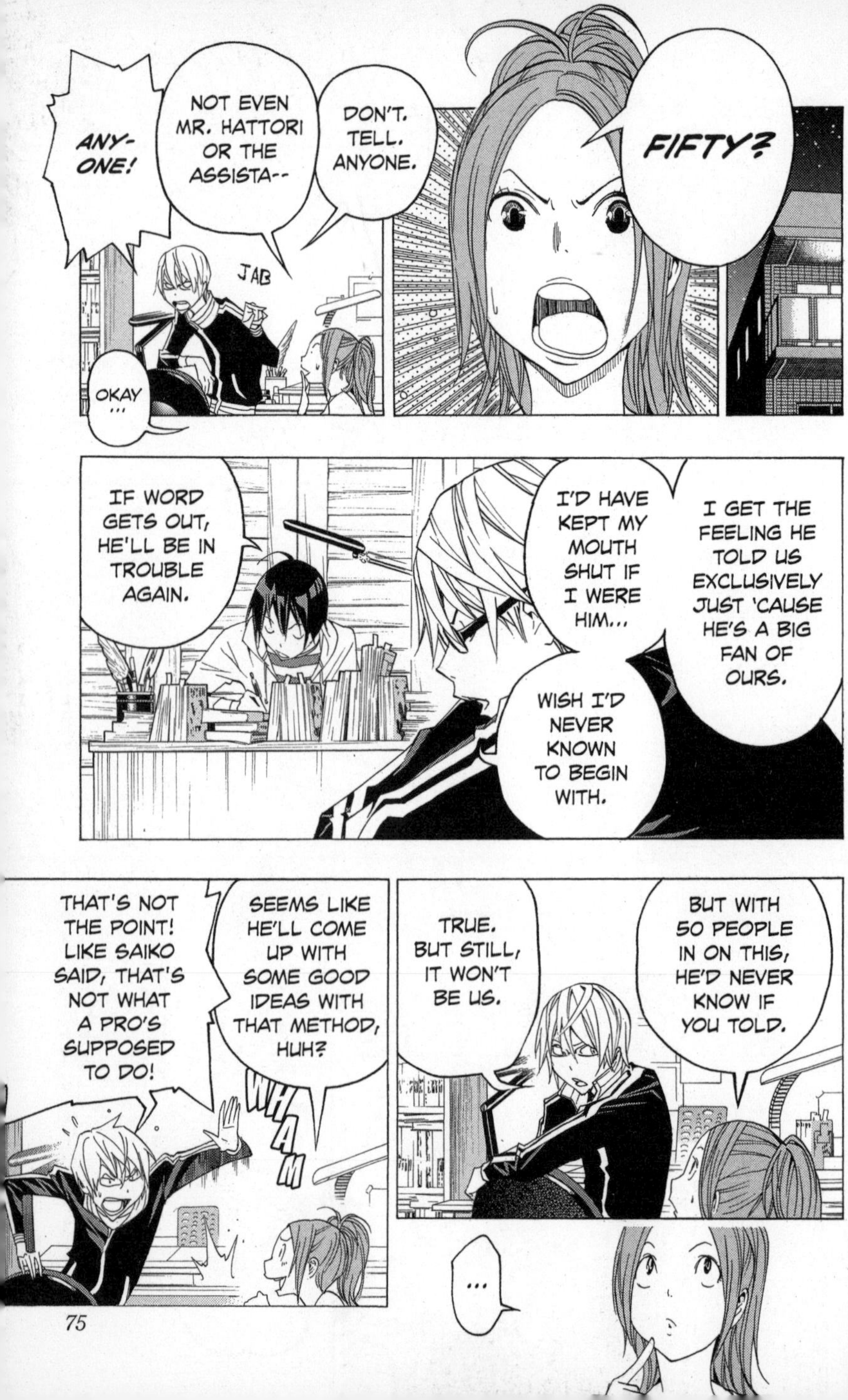
FIFTY?
DON'T. TELL. ANYONE.
NOT EVEN MR. HATTORI OR THE ASSISTA--
ANY-ONE!
JAB
OKAY...
I GET THE FEELING HE TOLD US EXCLUSIVELY JUST 'CAUSE HE'S A BIG FAN OF OURS.
I'D HAVE KEPT MY MOUTH SHUT IF I WERE HIM...
WISH I'D NEVER KNOWN TO BEGIN WITH.
IF WORD GETS OUT, HE'LL BE IN TROUBLE AGAIN.
BUT WITH 50 PEOPLE IN ON THIS, HE'D NEVER KNOW IF YOU TOLD.
TRUE. BUT STILL, IT WON'T BE US.
...
SEEMS LIKE HE'LL COME UP WITH SOME GOOD IDEAS WITH THAT METHOD, HUH?
THAT'S NOT THE POINT! LIKE SAIKO SAID, THAT'S NOT WHAT A PRO'S SUPPOSED TO DO!
WHAM

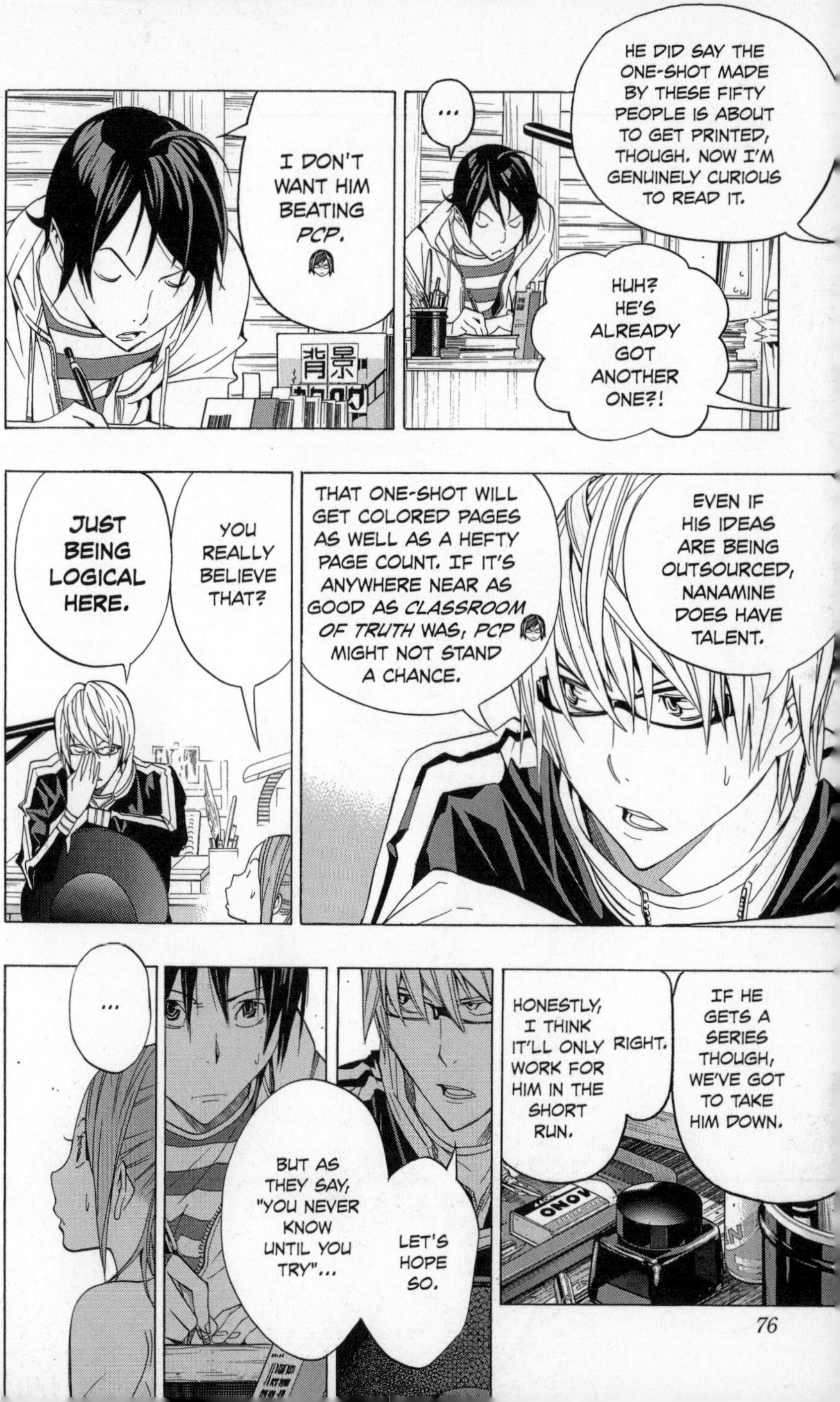

HE DID SAY THE ONE-SHOT MADE BY THESE FIFTY PEOPLE IS ABOUT TO GET PRINTED, THOUGH. NOW I'M GENUINELY CURIOUS TO READ IT.
...
HUH? HE'S ALREADY GOT ANOTHER ONE?!
I DON'T WANT HIM BEATING *PCP*.
EVEN IF HIS IDEAS ARE BEING OUTSOURCED, NANAMINE DOES HAVE TALENT.
THAT ONE-SHOT WILL GET COLORED PAGES AS WELL AS A HEFTY PAGE COUNT. IF IT'S ANYWHERE NEAR AS GOOD AS *CLASSROOM OF TRUTH* WAS, *PCP* MIGHT NOT STAND A CHANCE.
YOU REALLY BELIEVE THAT?
JUST BEING LOGICAL HERE.
IF HE GETS A SERIES THOUGH, WE'VE GOT TO TAKE HIM DOWN.
RIGHT.
HONESTLY, I THINK IT'LL ONLY WORK FOR HIM IN THE SHORT RUN.
BUT AS THEY SAY, "YOU NEVER KNOW UNTIL YOU TRY"...
LET'S HOPE SO.
...

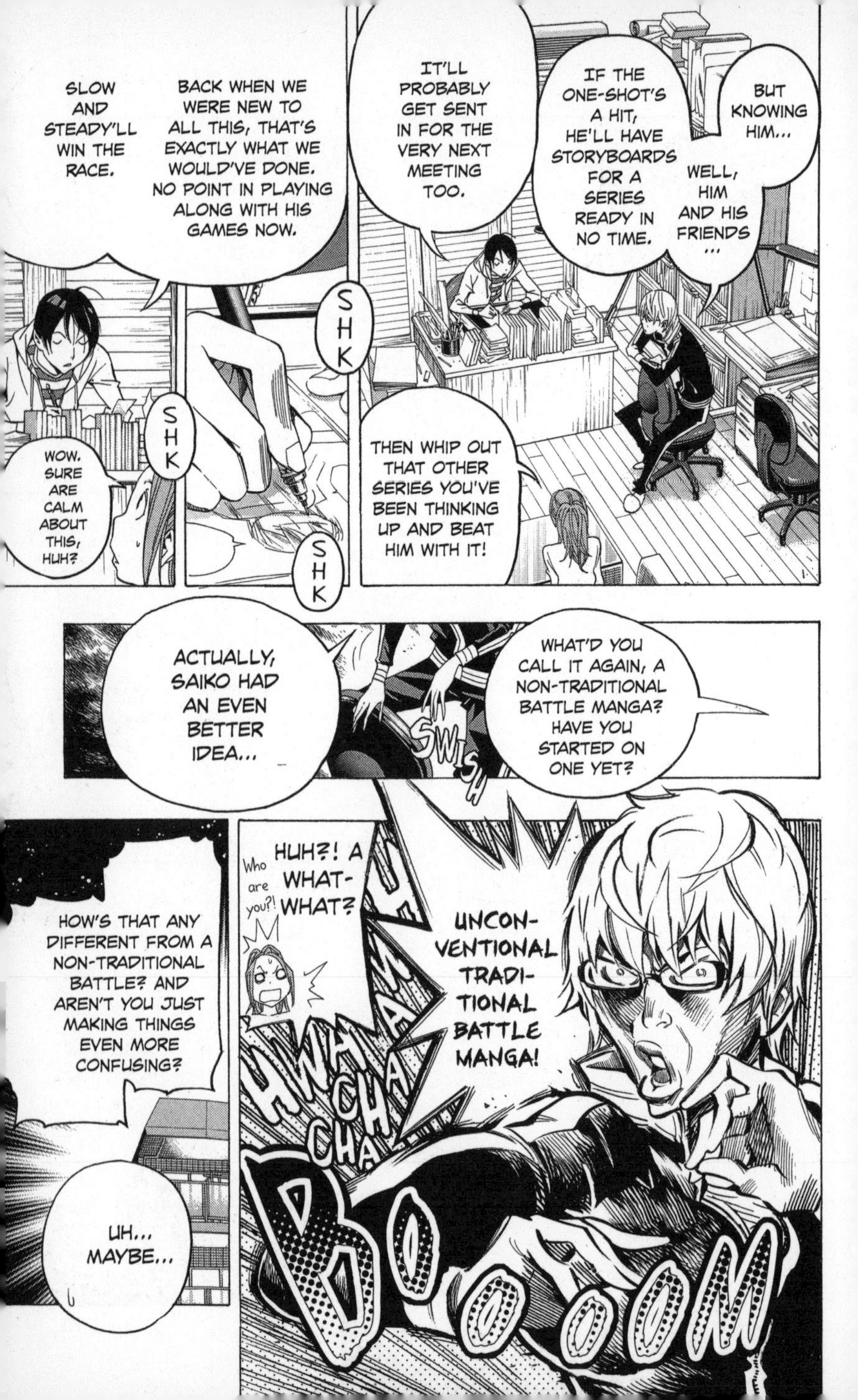

BUT KNOWING HIM...
WELL, HIM AND HIS FRIENDS...
IF THE ONE-SHOT'S A HIT, HE'LL HAVE STORYBOARDS FOR A SERIES READY IN NO TIME.
IT'LL PROBABLY GET SENT IN FOR THE VERY NEXT MEETING TOO.
THEN WHIP OUT THAT OTHER SERIES YOU'VE BEEN THINKING UP AND BEAT HIM WITH IT!
BACK WHEN WE WERE NEW TO ALL THIS, THAT'S EXACTLY WHAT WE WOULD'VE DONE. NO POINT IN PLAYING ALONG WITH HIS GAMES NOW.
SHK
SHK
SHK
SLOW AND STEADY'LL WIN THE RACE.
WOW. SURE ARE CALM ABOUT THIS, HUH?
WHAT'D YOU CALL IT AGAIN, A NON-TRADITIONAL BATTLE MANGA? HAVE YOU STARTED ON ONE YET?
SWISH
ACTUALLY, SAIKO HAD AN EVEN BETTER IDEA...
UNCON-VENTIONAL TRADI-TIONAL BATTLE MANGA!
WHACHACHA
BOOOOM
HUH?! A WHAT-WHAT?
Who are you?!
HOW'S THAT ANY DIFFERENT FROM A NON-TRADITIONAL BATTLE? AND AREN'T YOU JUST MAKING THINGS EVEN MORE CONFUSING?
UH... MAYBE...

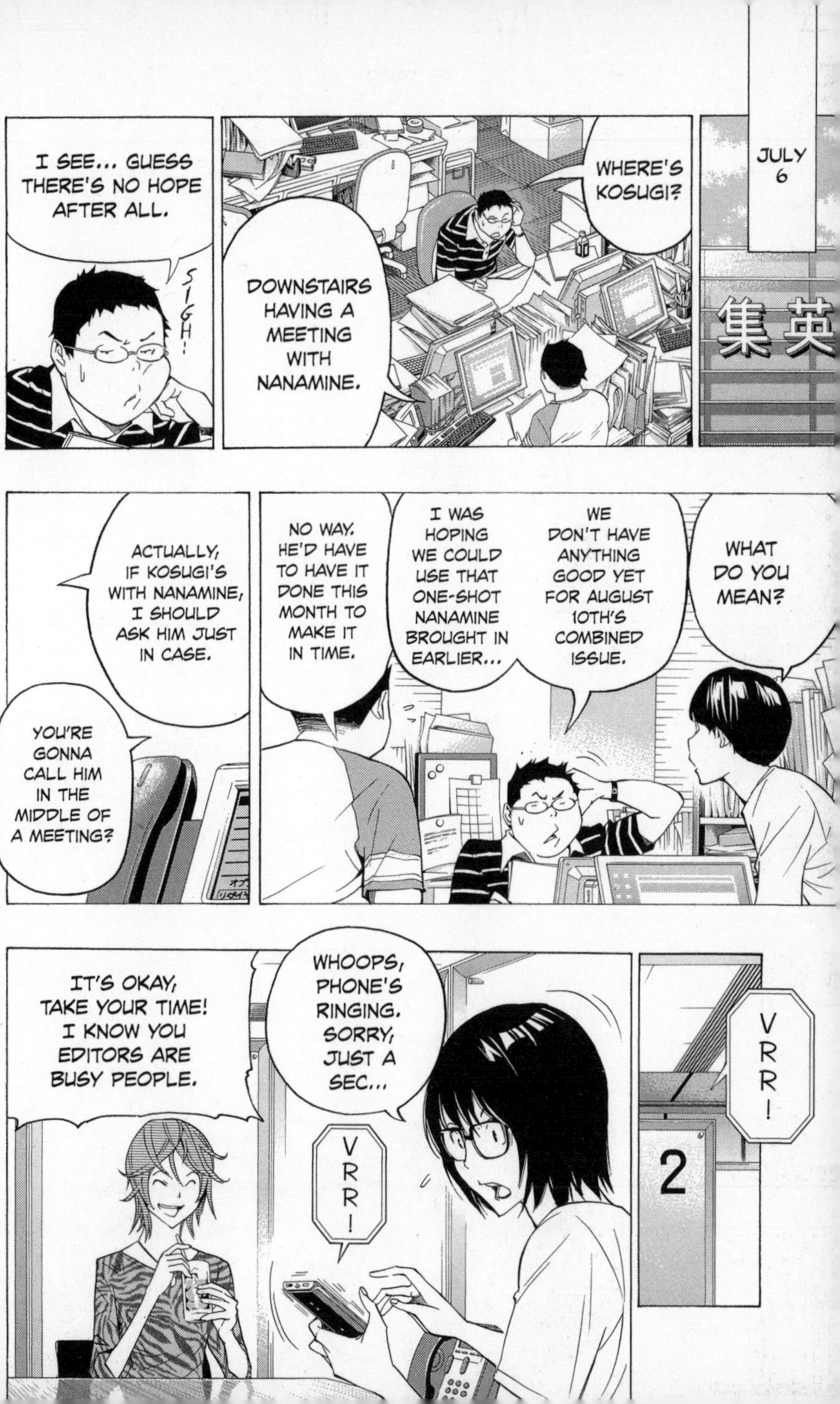
JULY 6
集英
WHERE'S KOSUGI?
DOWNSTAIRS HAVING A MEETING WITH NANAMINE.
I SEE... GUESS THERE'S NO HOPE AFTER ALL.
SIGH!
WHAT DO YOU MEAN?
WE DON'T HAVE ANYTHING GOOD YET FOR AUGUST 10TH'S COMBINED ISSUE.
I WAS HOPING WE COULD USE THAT ONE-SHOT NANAMINE BROUGHT IN EARLIER...
NO WAY. HE'D HAVE TO HAVE IT DONE THIS MONTH TO MAKE IT IN TIME.
ACTUALLY, IF KOSUGI'S WITH NANAMINE, I SHOULD ASK HIM JUST IN CASE.
YOU'RE GONNA CALL HIM IN THE MIDDLE OF A MEETING?
VRR!
2
VRR!
WHOOPS, PHONE'S RINGING. SORRY, JUST A SEC...
IT'S OKAY, TAKE YOUR TIME! I KNOW YOU EDITORS ARE BUSY PEOPLE.

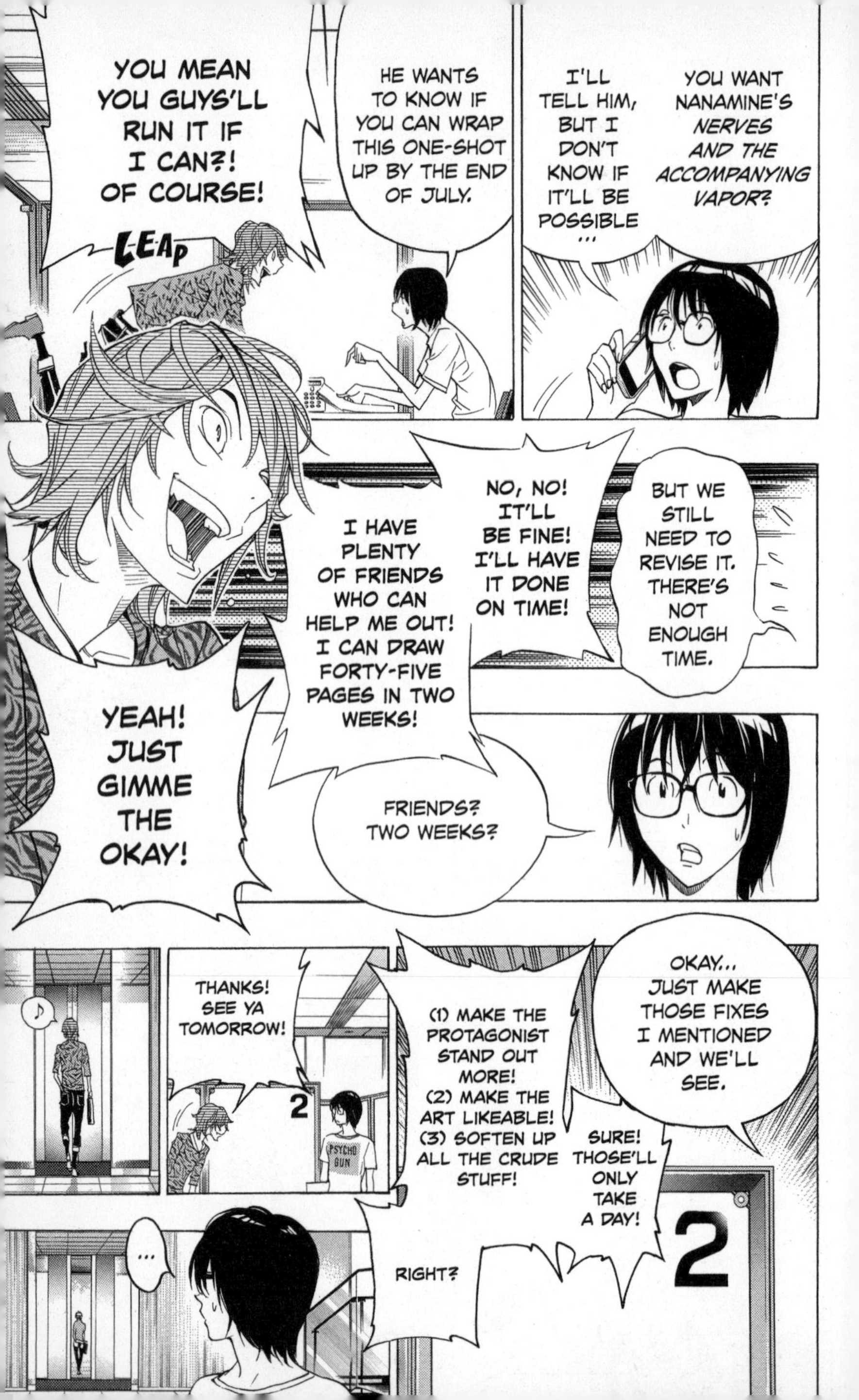
YOU WANT NANAMINE'S NERVES AND THE ACCOMPANYING VAPOR?
I'LL TELL HIM, BUT I DON'T KNOW IF IT'LL BE POSSIBLE...
HE WANTS TO KNOW IF YOU CAN WRAP THIS ONE-SHOT UP BY THE END OF JULY.
YOU MEAN YOU GUYS'LL RUN IT IF I CAN?! OF COURSE!
L-E-A-P
YEAH! JUST GIMME THE OKAY!
BUT WE STILL NEED TO REVISE IT. THERE'S NOT ENOUGH TIME.
NO, NO! IT'LL BE FINE! I'LL HAVE IT DONE ON TIME!
I HAVE PLENTY OF FRIENDS WHO CAN HELP ME OUT! I CAN DRAW FORTY-FIVE PAGES IN TWO WEEKS!
FRIENDS? TWO WEEKS?
OKAY... JUST MAKE THOSE FIXES I MENTIONED AND WE'LL SEE.
(1) MAKE THE PROTAGONIST STAND OUT MORE! (2) MAKE THE ART LIKEABLE! (3) SOFTEN UP ALL THE CRUDE STUFF!
SURE! THOSE'LL ONLY TAKE A DAY!
2
THANKS! SEE YA TOMORROW!
2
PSYCHO GUN
♪
...
RIGHT?

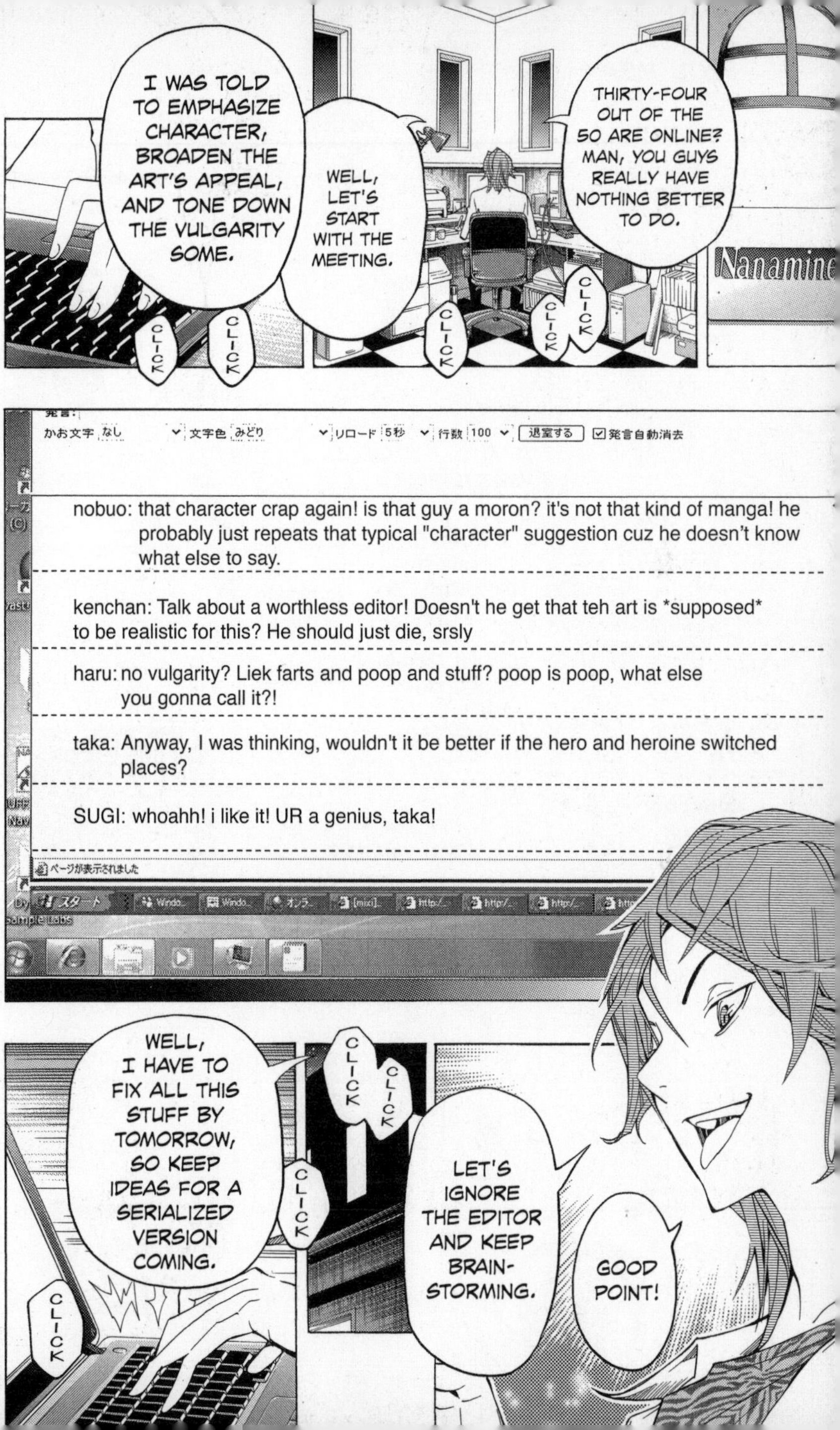
Nanamine
THIRTY-FOUR OUT OF THE 50 ARE ONLINE? MAN, YOU GUYS REALLY HAVE NOTHING BETTER TO DO.
CLICK
CLICK
WELL, LET'S START WITH THE MEETING.
CLICK
I WAS TOLD TO EMPHASIZE CHARACTER, BROADEN THE ART'S APPEAL, AND TONE DOWN THE VULGARITY SOME.
CLICK
CLICK
発言:
かお文字 なし 文字色 みどり リロード 5秒 行数 100 退室する 発言自動消去
nobuo: that character crap again! is that guy a moron? it's not that kind of manga! he probably just repeats that typical "character" suggestion cuz he doesn't know what else to say.
kenchan: Talk about a worthless editor! Doesn't he get that teh art is *supposed* to be realistic for this? He should just die, srsly
haru: no vulgarity? Liek farts and poop and stuff? poop is poop, what else you gonna call it?!
taka: Anyway, I was thinking, wouldn't it be better if the hero and heroine switched places?
SUGI: whoahh! i like it! UR a genius, taka!
ページが表示されました
スタート
LET'S IGNORE THE EDITOR AND KEEP BRAIN-STORMING.
GOOD POINT!
CLICK
CLICK
CLICK
WELL, I HAVE TO FIX ALL THIS STUFF BY TOMORROW, SO KEEP IDEAS FOR A SERIALIZED VERSION COMING.
CLICK

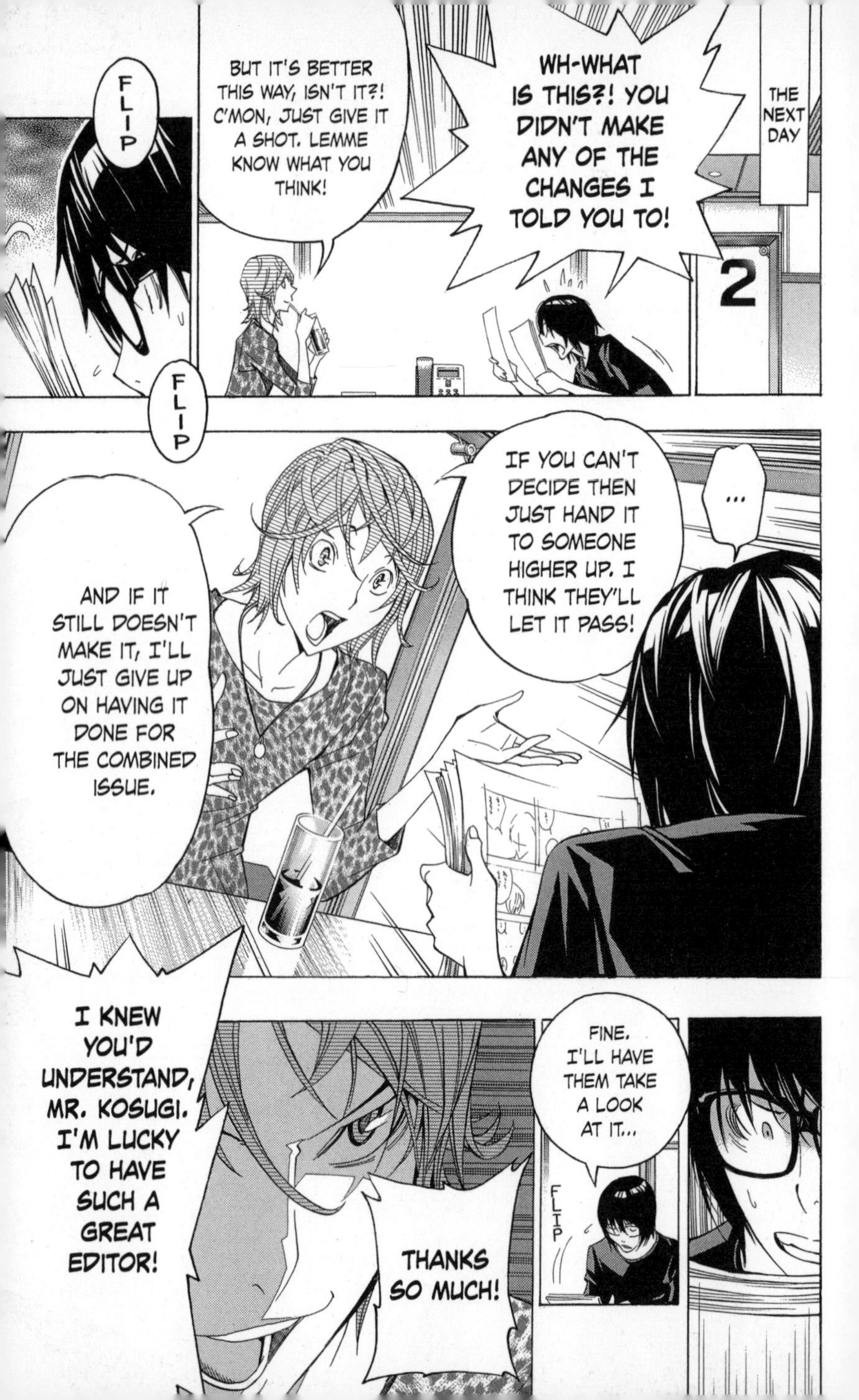
THE NEXT DAY
2
WH-WHAT IS THIS?! YOU DIDN'T MAKE ANY OF THE CHANGES I TOLD YOU TO!
BUT IT'S BETTER THIS WAY, ISN'T IT?! C'MON, JUST GIVE IT A SHOT. LEMME KNOW WHAT YOU THINK!
FLIP
FLIP
...
IF YOU CAN'T DECIDE THEN JUST HAND IT TO SOMEONE HIGHER UP. I THINK THEY'LL LET IT PASS!
AND IF IT STILL DOESN'T MAKE IT, I'LL JUST GIVE UP ON HAVING IT DONE FOR THE COMBINED ISSUE.
FINE. I'LL HAVE THEM TAKE A LOOK AT IT...
FLIP
I KNEW YOU'D UNDERSTAND, MR. KOSUGI. I'M LUCKY TO HAVE SUCH A GREAT EDITOR!
THANKS SO MUCH!

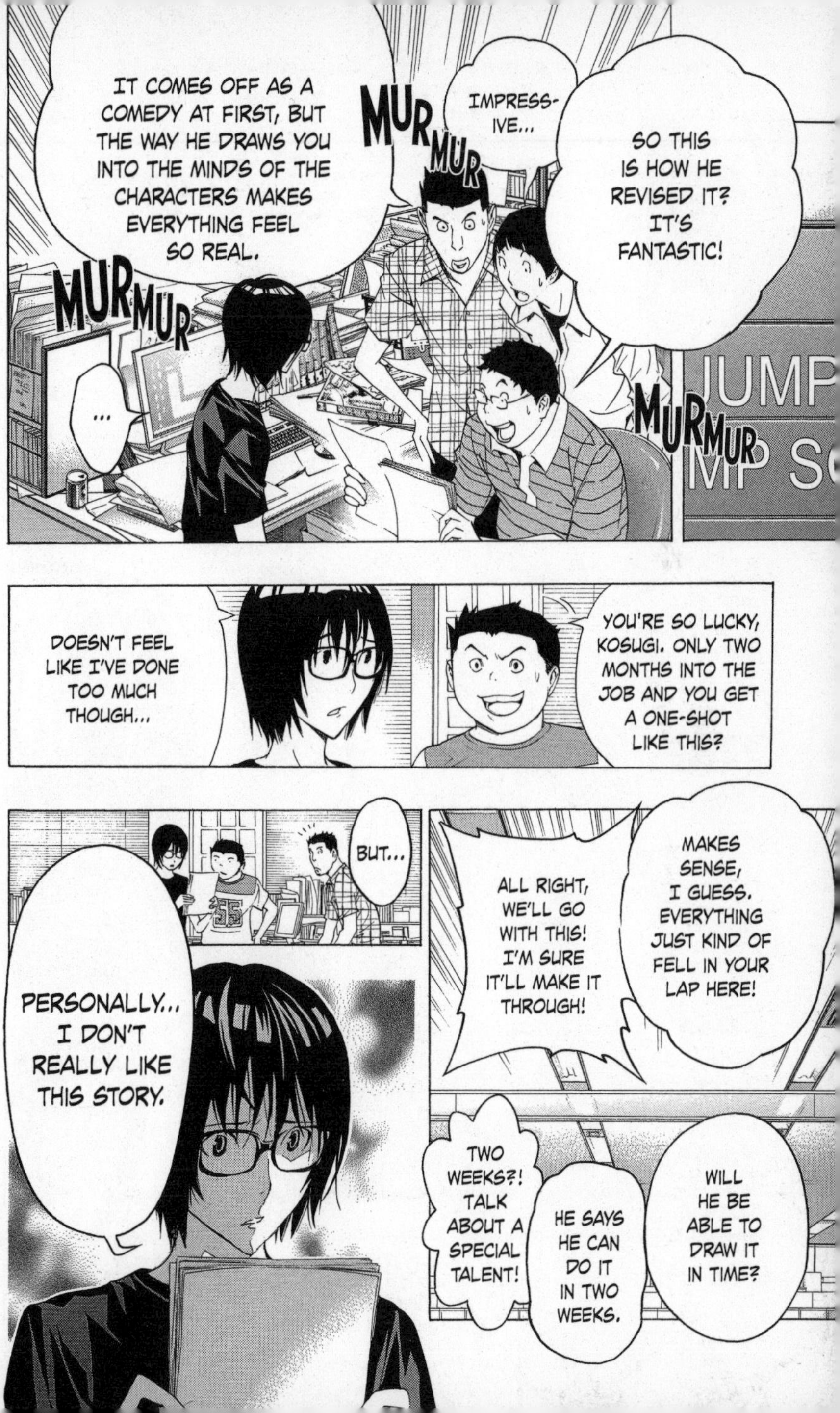
SO THIS IS HOW HE REVISED IT? IT'S FANTASTIC!
IMPRESS-IVE...
MURMUR
IT COMES OFF AS A COMEDY AT FIRST, BUT THE WAY HE DRAWS YOU INTO THE MINDS OF THE CHARACTERS MAKES EVERYTHING FEEL SO REAL.
JUMP
MURMUR
MURMUR
...
YOU'RE SO LUCKY, KOSUGI. ONLY TWO MONTHS INTO THE JOB AND YOU GET A ONE-SHOT LIKE THIS?
DOESN'T FEEL LIKE I'VE DONE TOO MUCH THOUGH...
MAKES SENSE, I GUESS. EVERYTHING JUST KIND OF FELL IN YOUR LAP HERE!
ALL RIGHT, WE'LL GO WITH THIS! I'M SURE IT'LL MAKE IT THROUGH!
WILL HE BE ABLE TO DRAW IT IN TIME?
HE SAYS HE CAN DO IT IN TWO WEEKS.
TWO WEEKS?! TALK ABOUT A SPECIAL TALENT!
BUT...
PERSONALLY... I DON'T REALLY LIKE THIS STORY.

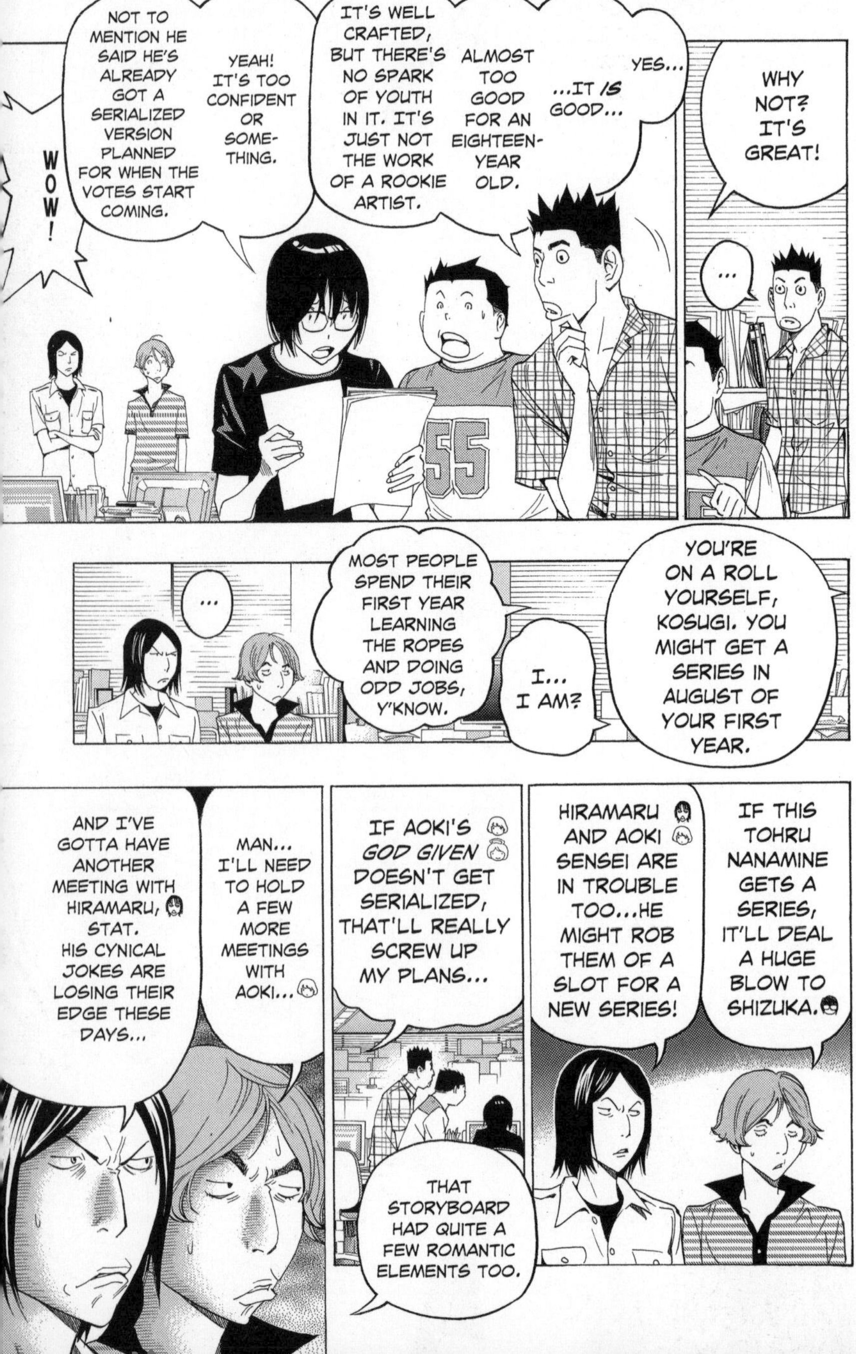
WHY NOT? IT'S GREAT!
...
YES...
...IT IS GOOD...
ALMOST TOO GOOD FOR AN EIGHTEEN-YEAR OLD.
IT'S WELL CRAFTED, BUT THERE'S NO SPARK OF YOUTH IN IT. IT'S JUST NOT THE WORK OF A ROOKIE ARTIST.
YEAH! IT'S TOO CONFIDENT OR SOME-THING.
NOT TO MENTION HE SAID HE'S ALREADY GOT A SERIALIZED VERSION PLANNED FOR WHEN THE VOTES START COMING.
WOW!
YOU'RE ON A ROLL YOURSELF, KOSUGI. YOU MIGHT GET A SERIES IN AUGUST OF YOUR FIRST YEAR.
I... I AM?
MOST PEOPLE SPEND THEIR FIRST YEAR LEARNING THE ROPES AND DOING ODD JOBS, Y'KNOW.
...
IF THIS TOHRU NANAMINE GETS A SERIES, IT'LL DEAL A HUGE BLOW TO SHIZUKA.
HIRAMARU AND AOKI SENSEI ARE IN TROUBLE TOO...HE MIGHT ROB THEM OF A SLOT FOR A NEW SERIES!
IF AOKI'S GOD GIVEN DOESN'T GET SERIALIZED, THAT'LL REALLY SCREW UP MY PLANS...
THAT STORYBOARD HAD QUITE A FEW ROMANTIC ELEMENTS TOO.
MAN... I'LL NEED TO HOLD A FEW MORE MEETINGS WITH AOKI...
AND I'VE GOTTA HAVE ANOTHER MEETING WITH HIRAMARU, STAT. HIS CYNICAL JOKES ARE LOSING THEIR EDGE THESE DAYS...

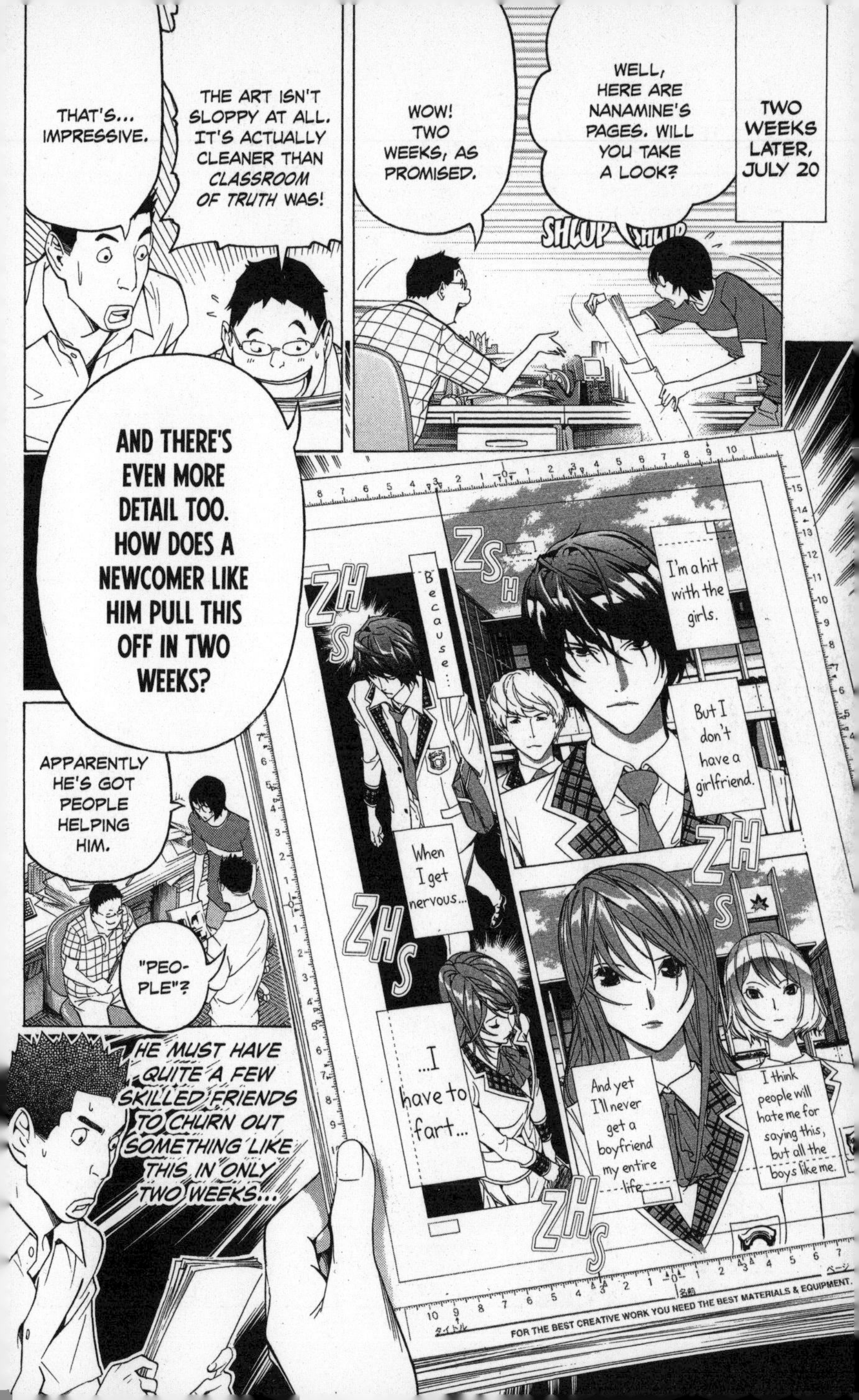
TWO WEEKS LATER, JULY 20
WELL, HERE ARE NANAMINE'S PAGES. WILL YOU TAKE A LOOK?
SHLUP SHLUP
WOW! TWO WEEKS, AS PROMISED.
THE ART ISN'T SLOPPY AT ALL. IT'S ACTUALLY CLEANER THAN CLASSROOM OF TRUTH WAS!
THAT'S... IMPRESSIVE.
AND THERE'S EVEN MORE DETAIL TOO. HOW DOES A NEWCOMER LIKE HIM PULL THIS OFF IN TWO WEEKS?
ZSH
I'm a hit with the girls.
But I don't have a girlfriend.
ZHS
Because...
When I get nervous...
...I have to fart...
ZHS
I think people will hate me for saying this, but all the boys like me.
And yet I'll never get a boyfriend my entire life.
ZHS
FOR THE BEST CREATIVE WORK YOU NEED THE BEST MATERIALS & EQUIPMENT.
APPARENTLY HE'S GOT PEOPLE HELPING HIM.
"PEO-PLE"?
HE MUST HAVE QUITE A FEW SKILLED FRIENDS TO CHURN OUT SOMETHING LIKE THIS IN ONLY TWO WEEKS...

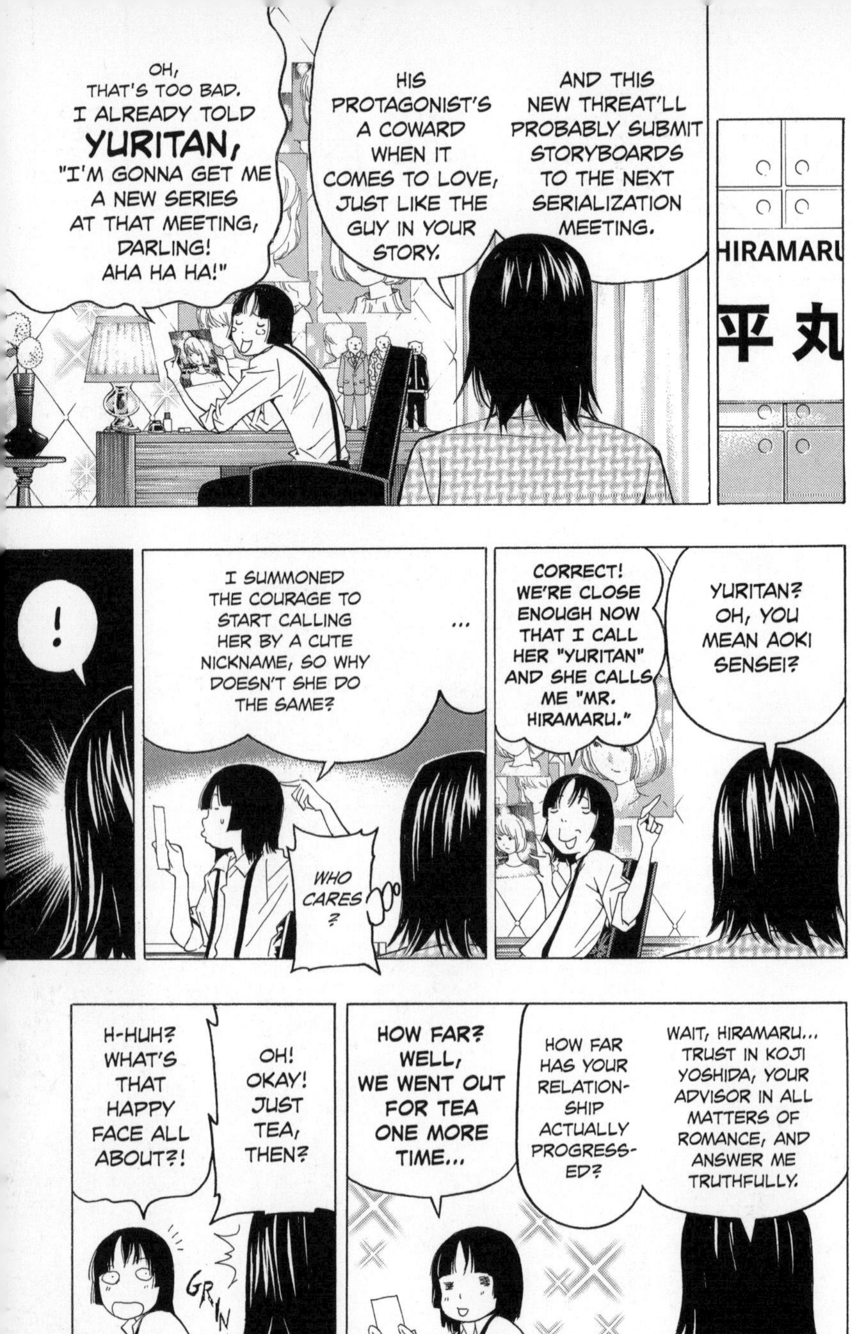
HIRAMARU
平丸
AND THIS NEW THREAT'LL PROBABLY SUBMIT STORYBOARDS TO THE NEXT SERIALIZATION MEETING.
HIS PROTAGONIST'S A COWARD WHEN IT COMES TO LOVE, JUST LIKE THE GUY IN YOUR STORY.
OH, THAT'S TOO BAD. I ALREADY TOLD YURITAN, "I'M GONNA GET ME A NEW SERIES AT THAT MEETING, DARLING! AHA HA HA!"
YURITAN? OH, YOU MEAN AOKI SENSEI?
CORRECT! WE'RE CLOSE ENOUGH NOW THAT I CALL HER "YURITAN" AND SHE CALLS ME "MR. HIRAMARU."
...
I SUMMONED THE COURAGE TO START CALLING HER BY A CUTE NICKNAME, SO WHY DOESN'T SHE DO THE SAME?
WHO CARES?
!
WAIT, HIRAMARU... TRUST IN KOJI YOSHIDA, YOUR ADVISOR IN ALL MATTERS OF ROMANCE, AND ANSWER ME TRUTHFULLY.
HOW FAR HAS YOUR RELATION-SHIP ACTUALLY PROGRESS-ED?
HOW FAR? WELL, WE WENT OUT FOR TEA ONE MORE TIME...
OH! OKAY! JUST TEA, THEN?
H-HUH? WHAT'S THAT HAPPY FACE ALL ABOUT?!
GRIN...

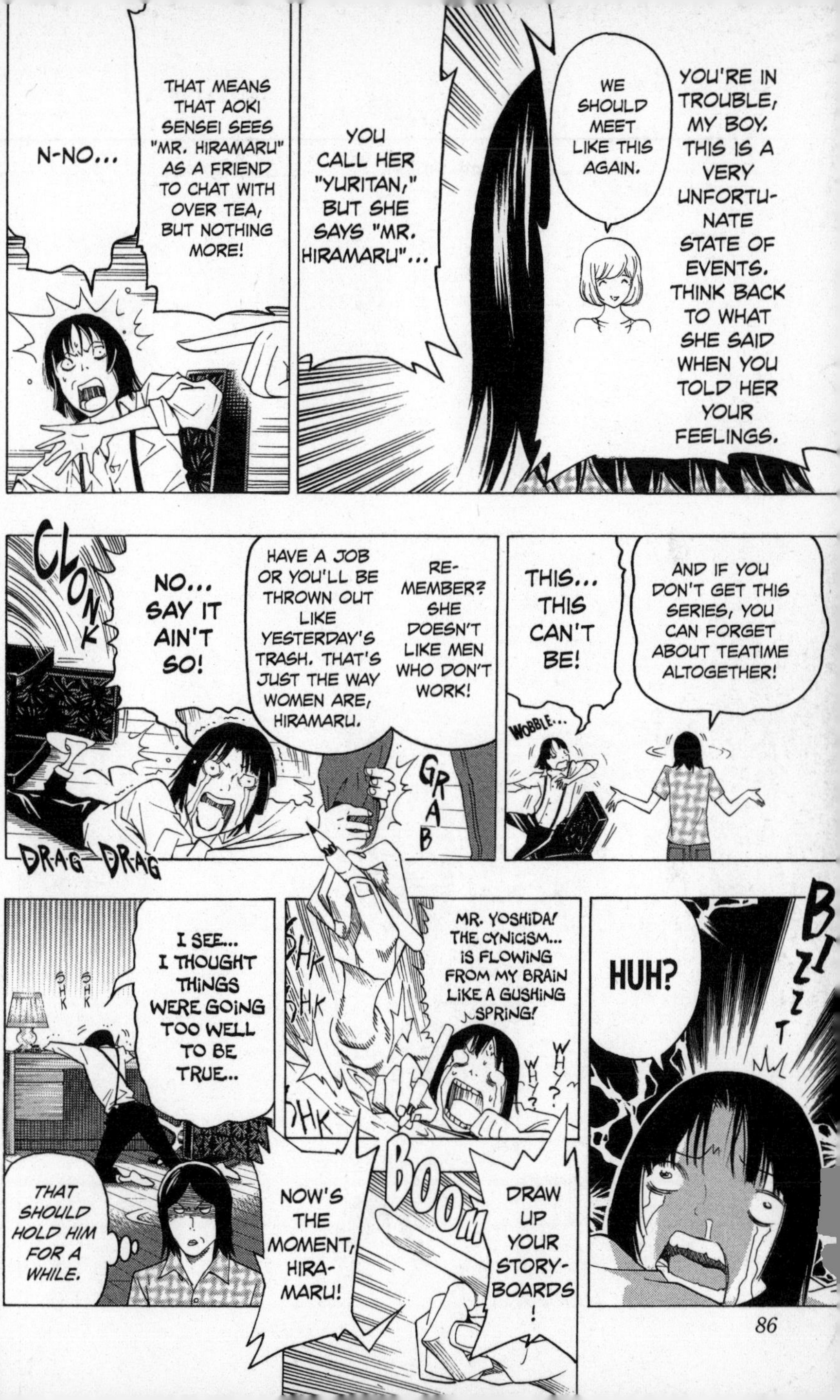
YOU'RE IN TROUBLE, MY BOY. THIS IS A VERY UNFORTUNATE STATE OF EVENTS. THINK BACK TO WHAT SHE SAID WHEN YOU TOLD HER YOUR FEELINGS.
WE SHOULD MEET LIKE THIS AGAIN.
YOU CALL HER "YURITAN," BUT SHE SAYS "MR. HIRAMARU"...
THAT MEANS THAT AOKI SENSEI SEES "MR. HIRAMARU" AS A FRIEND TO CHAT WITH OVER TEA, BUT NOTHING MORE!
N-NO...
AND IF YOU DON'T GET THIS SERIES, YOU CAN FORGET ABOUT TEATIME ALTOGETHER!
THIS... THIS CAN'T BE!
WOBBLE...
RE-MEMBER? SHE DOESN'T LIKE MEN WHO DON'T WORK!
HAVE A JOB OR YOU'LL BE THROWN OUT LIKE YESTERDAY'S TRASH. THAT'S JUST THE WAY WOMEN ARE, HIRAMARU.
GRAB
NO... SAY IT AIN'T SO!
CLONK
DRAG DRAG
BIZZT
HUH?
MR. YOSHIDA! THE CYNICISM... IS FLOWING FROM MY BRAIN LIKE A GUSHING SPRING!
WHY? WHY?
SHK SHK SHK
I SEE... I THOUGHT THINGS WERE GOING TOO WELL TO BE TRUE..
SHK SHK
DRAW UP YOUR STORYBOARDS!
BOOM
NOW'S THE MOMENT, HIRAMARU!
THAT SHOULD HOLD HIM FOR A WHILE.

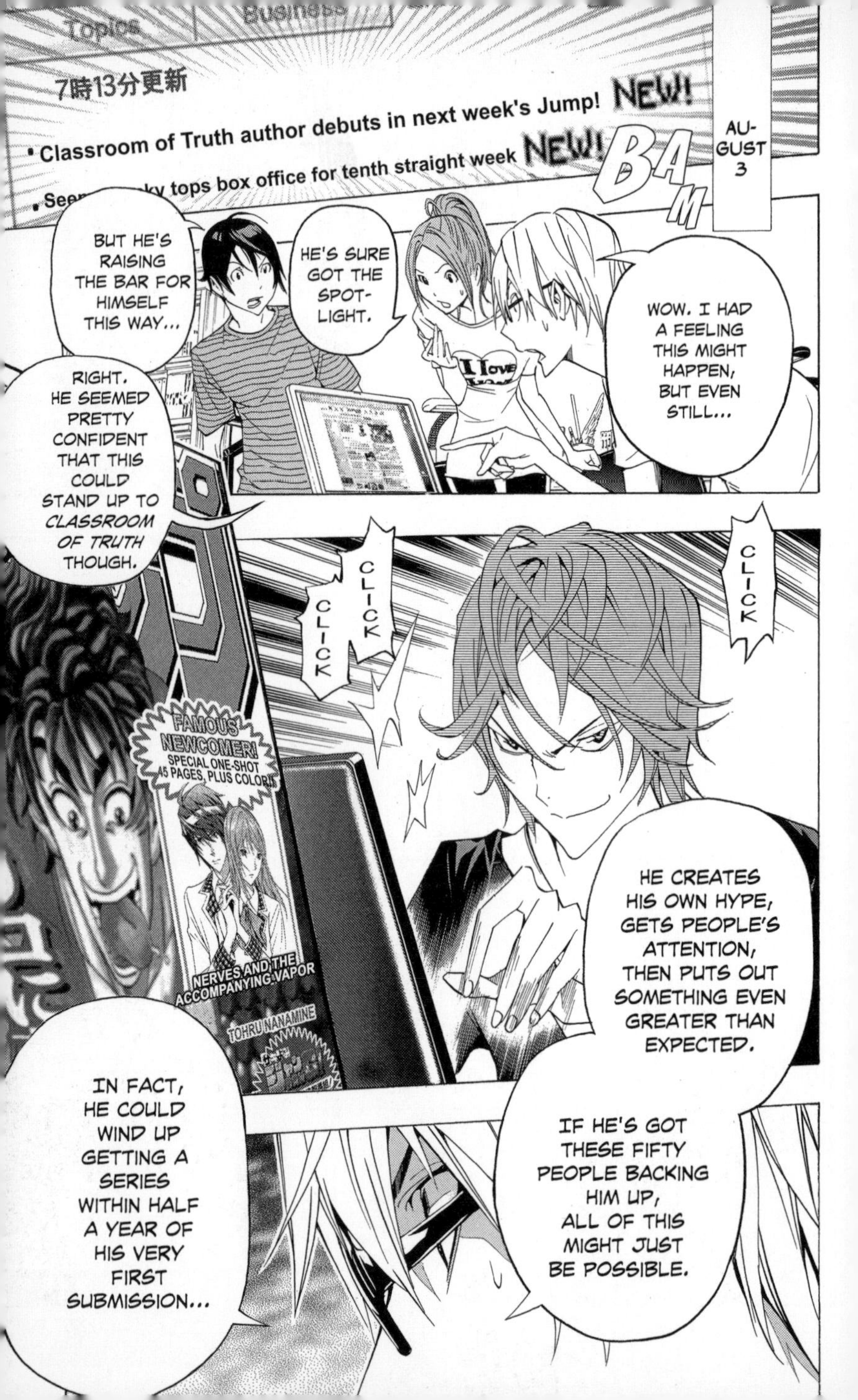

AUGUST 3
Topics
7時13分更新
• Classroom of Truth author debuts in next week's Jump! NEW!
tops box office for tenth straight week NEW!
BAM
WOW. I HAD A FEELING THIS MIGHT HAPPEN, BUT EVEN STILL...
HE'S SURE GOT THE SPOTLIGHT.
BUT HE'S RAISING THE BAR FOR HIMSELF THIS WAY...
RIGHT. HE SEEMED PRETTY CONFIDENT THAT THIS COULD STAND UP TO *CLASSROOM OF TRUTH* THOUGH.
CLICK
CLICK
CLICK
FAMOUS NEWCOMER! SPECIAL ONE-SHOT 45 PAGES, PLUS COLOR!
NERVES AND THE ACCOMPANYING VAPOR
TOHRU NANAMINE
HE CREATES HIS OWN HYPE, GETS PEOPLE'S ATTENTION, THEN PUTS OUT SOMETHING EVEN GREATER THAN EXPECTED.
IF HE'S GOT THESE FIFTY PEOPLE BACKING HIM UP, ALL OF THIS MIGHT JUST BE POSSIBLE.
IN FACT, HE COULD WIND UP GETTING A SERIES WITHIN HALF A YEAR OF HIS VERY FIRST SUBMISSION...

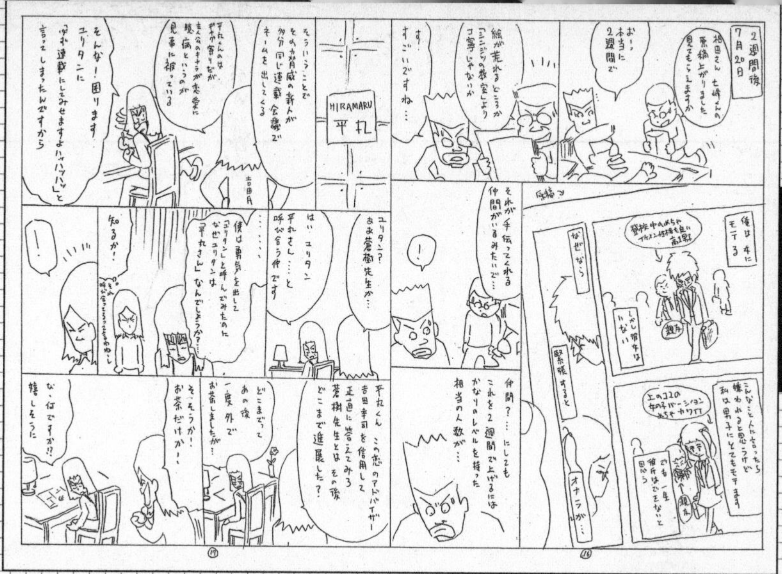
2週間後 7月20日
相田さん 七峰くんの原稿上がりました 見てもらえますか
お!本当に2週間で
絵が荒れるどころか『ミンジンの教室』より丁寧じゃないか
す、すごいですね…
原稿
俺は本当にモテる
なぜなら
緊張すると
オナラが…
こんなことになったら嫌われると思うけど 私は男子にとてもモテます
でも一生彼氏はできないと思う
それが手伝ってくれる仲間がいるみたいで…
!
仲間?…にしてもこれを2週間で上げるにはかなりのレベルを持った相当の人数が…
そういうことで その才能の新人が多分同じ連載会議でネームを出してくる
HIRAMARU
平丸
平丸さんのはギャグ寄りだが主人公のキャラが恋愛に臆病というのが見事に被っている
そんな!困ります ユリタンに「必ず連載にしてみせますよハハハッ」と言ってしまったんですから
ユリタン?ああ蒼樹先生か…
はい ユリタン 平丸さん…と呼び合う仲です
……
僕は勇気を出して「ユリタン」と呼んでみたのに なぜユリタンは「平丸さん」なんでしょうか?…
知るか!
!
平丸くん この恋のアドバイザー吉田幸司を信用して正直に答えてみろ 蒼樹先生とはその後どこまで進展した?
どこまでって あの後一度外でお茶しましたが…
そ…そうか!お茶だけか!
な…何ですか!?嬉しそうに

OHBA'S STORYBOARD

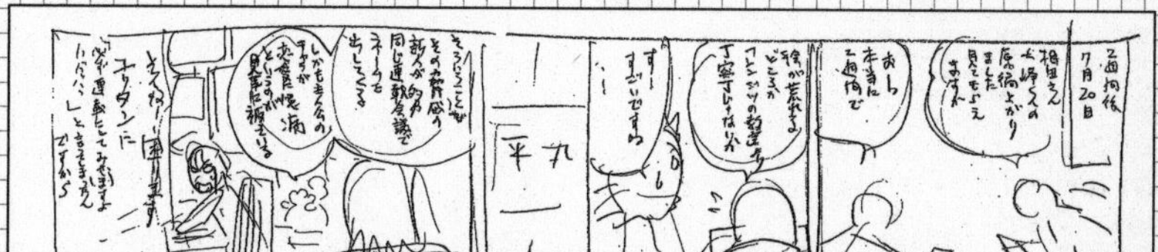

OBATA'S STORYBOARD

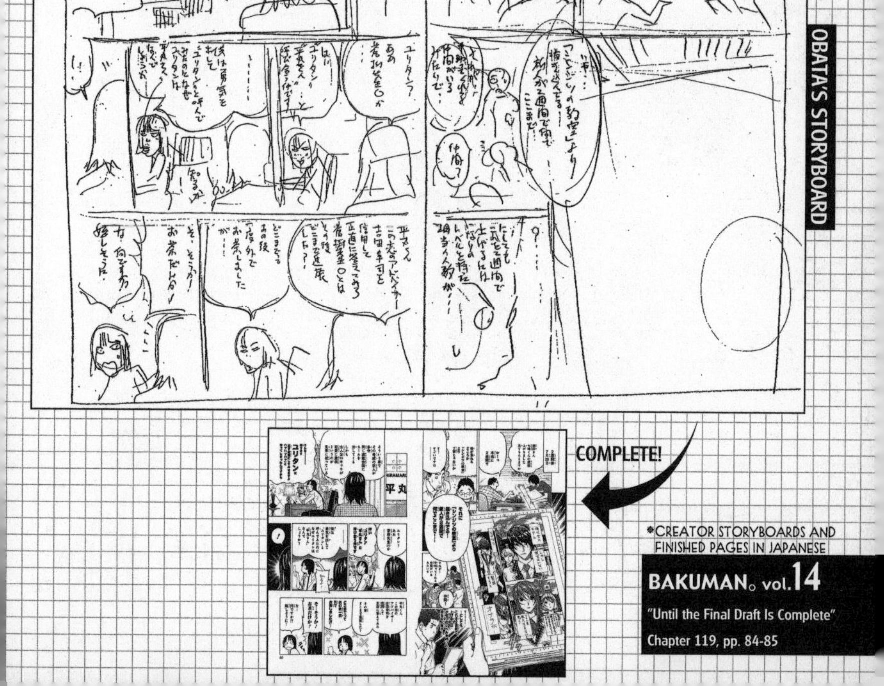

COMPLETE!

*CREATOR STORYBOARDS AND FINISHED PAGES IN JAPANESE

BAKUMAN。 vol.14

"Until the Final Draft Is Complete"

Chapter 119, pp. 84-85

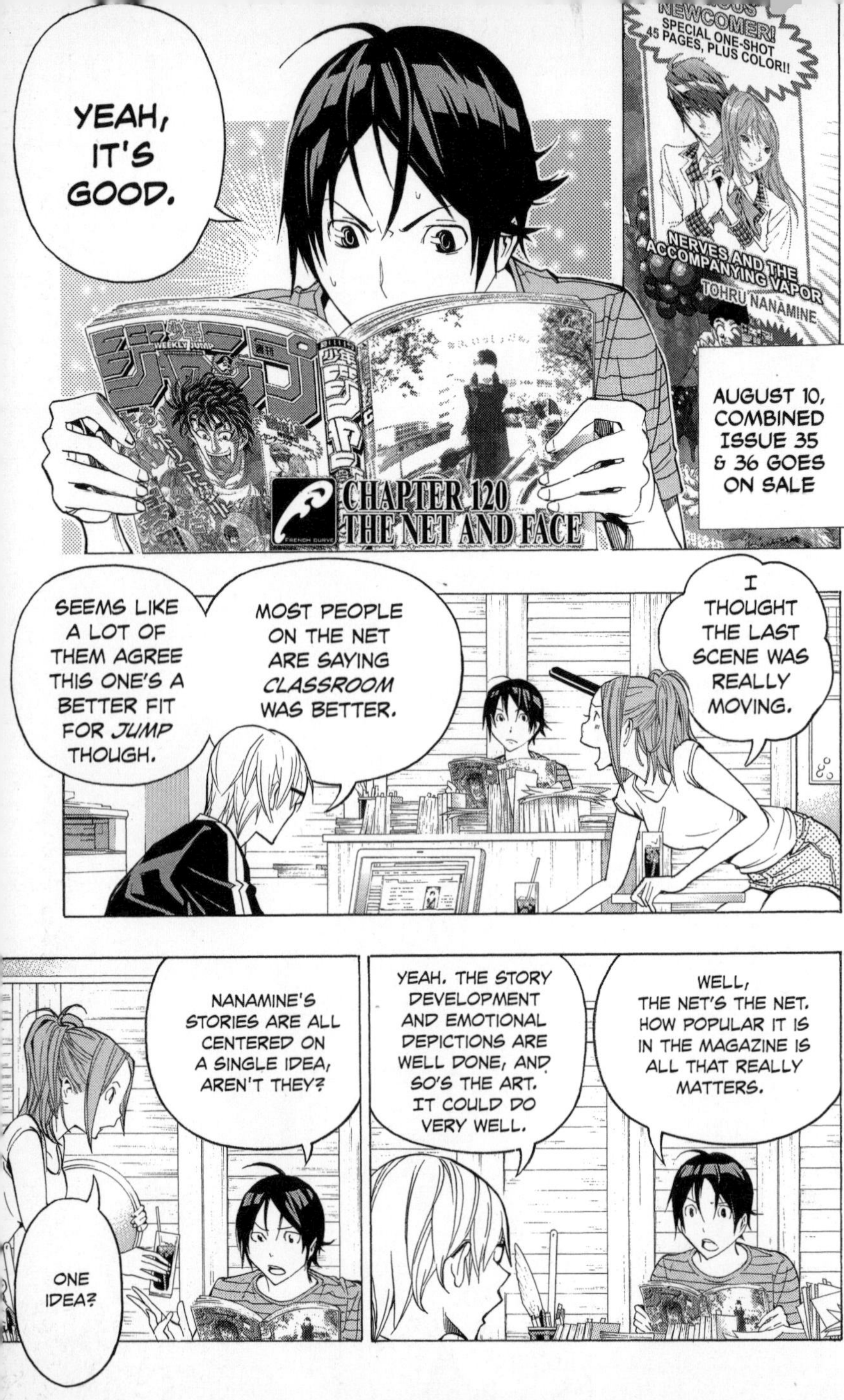
NEWCOMER!
SPECIAL ONE-SHOT
45 PAGES, PLUS COLOR!!
NERVES AND THE ACCOMPANYING VAPOR
TOHRU NANAMINE
AUGUST 10, COMBINED ISSUE 35 & 36 GOES ON SALE
CHAPTER 120
THE NET AND FACE
YEAH, IT'S GOOD.
I THOUGHT THE LAST SCENE WAS REALLY MOVING.
MOST PEOPLE ON THE NET ARE SAYING *CLASSROOM* WAS BETTER.
SEEMS LIKE A LOT OF THEM AGREE THIS ONE'S A BETTER FIT FOR *JUMP* THOUGH.
WELL, THE NET'S THE NET. HOW POPULAR IT IS IN THE MAGAZINE IS ALL THAT REALLY MATTERS.
YEAH. THE STORY DEVELOPMENT AND EMOTIONAL DEPICTIONS ARE WELL DONE, AND SO'S THE ART. IT COULD DO VERY WELL.
NANAMINE'S STORIES ARE ALL CENTERED ON A SINGLE IDEA, AREN'T THEY?
ONE IDEA?

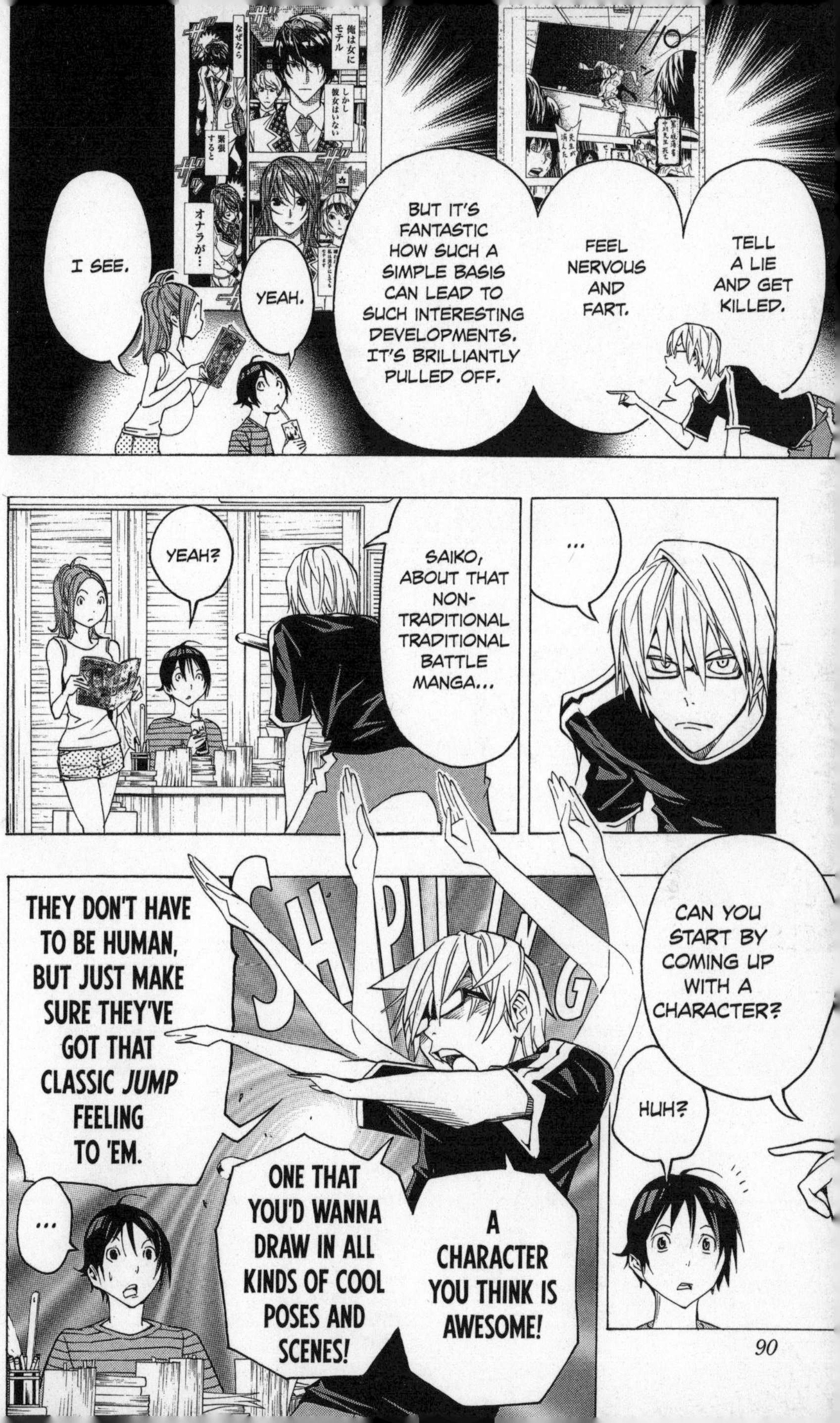
TELL A LIE AND GET KILLED.
FEEL NERVOUS AND FART.
BUT IT'S FANTASTIC HOW SUCH A SIMPLE BASIS CAN LEAD TO SUCH INTERESTING DEVELOPMENTS. IT'S BRILLIANTLY PULLED OFF.
俺は女にモテル
なぜなら
しかし彼女はいない
緊張すると
オナラが…
YEAH.
I SEE.
...
SAIKO, ABOUT THAT NON-TRADITIONAL TRADITIONAL BATTLE MANGA...
YEAH?
CAN YOU START BY COMING UP WITH A CHARACTER?
HUH?
THEY DON'T HAVE TO BE HUMAN, BUT JUST MAKE SURE THEY'VE GOT THAT CLASSIC *JUMP* FEELING TO 'EM.
A CHARACTER YOU THINK IS AWESOME!
ONE THAT YOU'D WANNA DRAW IN ALL KINDS OF COOL POSES AND SCENES!
...

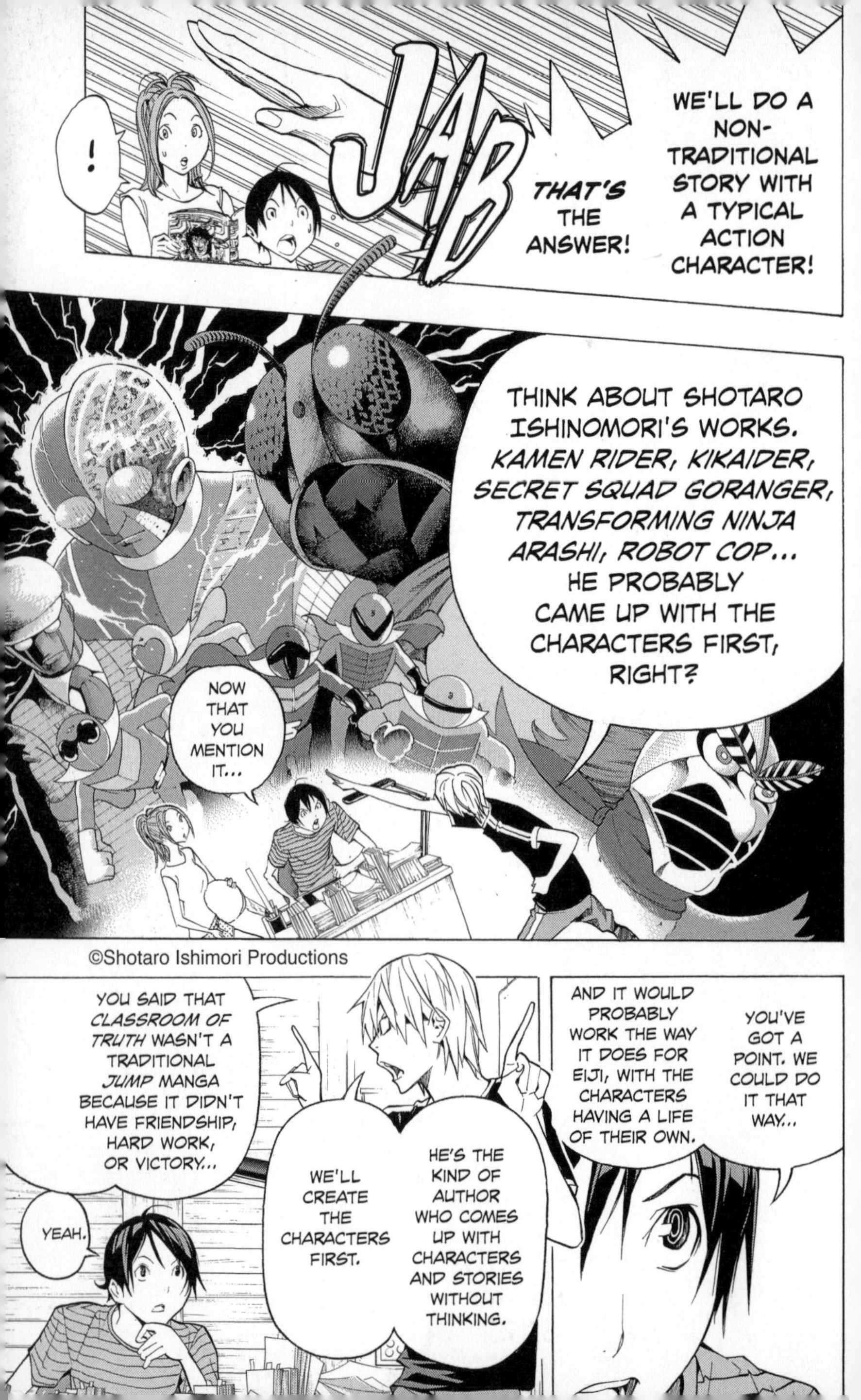
WE'LL DO A NON-TRADITIONAL STORY WITH A TYPICAL ACTION CHARACTER!
JAB
THAT'S THE ANSWER!
!
THINK ABOUT SHOTARO ISHINOMORI'S WORKS. *KAMEN RIDER, KIKAIDER, SECRET SQUAD GORANGER, TRANSFORMING NINJA ARASHI, ROBOT COP*... HE PROBABLY CAME UP WITH THE CHARACTERS FIRST, RIGHT?
NOW THAT YOU MENTION IT...
YOU SAID THAT *CLASSROOM OF TRUTH* WASN'T A TRADITIONAL *JUMP* MANGA BECAUSE IT DIDN'T HAVE FRIENDSHIP, HARD WORK, OR VICTORY...
YEAH.
HE'S THE KIND OF AUTHOR WHO COMES UP WITH CHARACTERS AND STORIES WITHOUT THINKING.
WE'LL CREATE THE CHARACTERS FIRST.
AND IT WOULD PROBABLY WORK THE WAY IT DOES FOR EIJI, WITH THE CHARACTERS HAVING A LIFE OF THEIR OWN.
YOU'VE GOT A POINT. WE COULD DO IT THAT WAY...

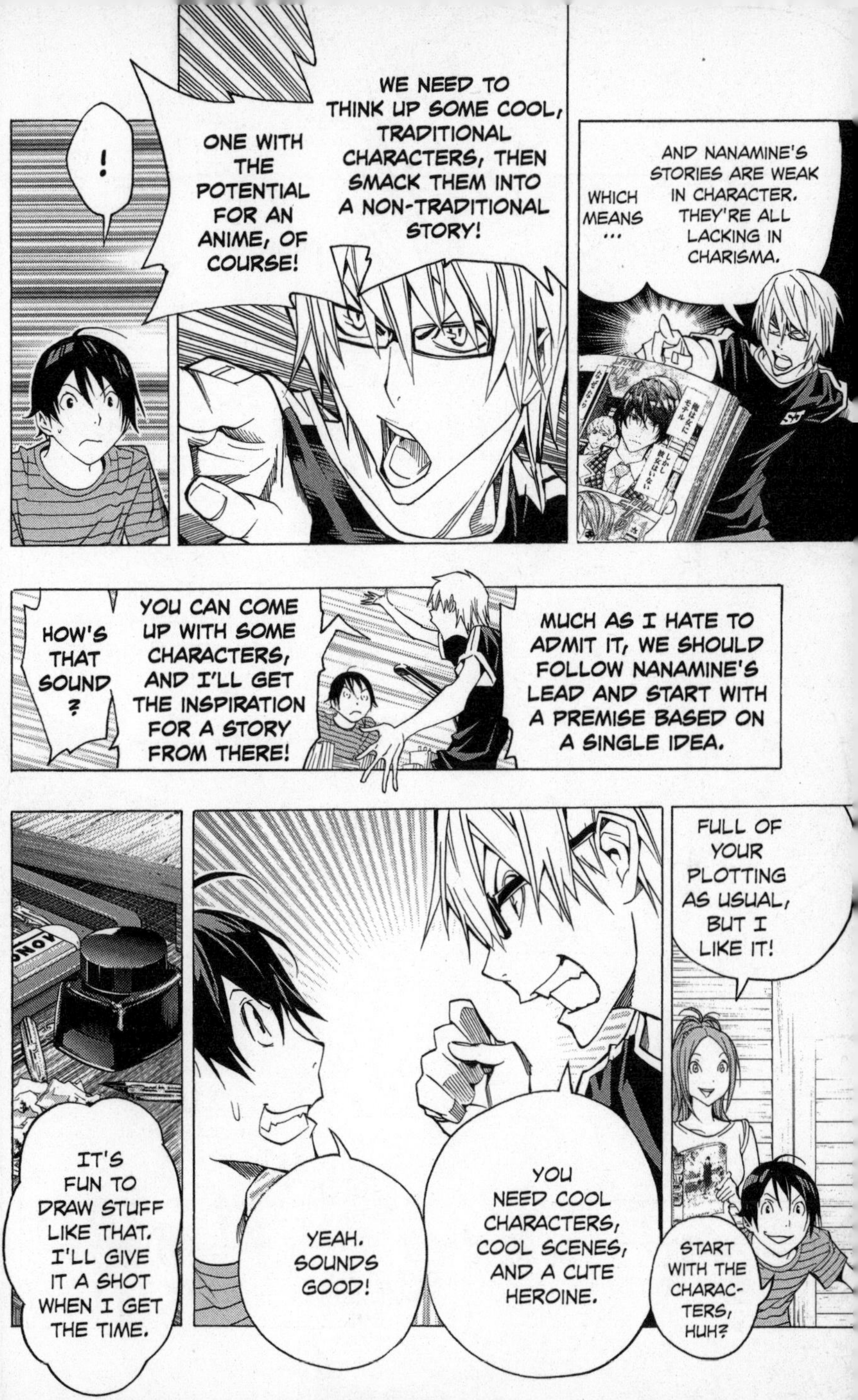
AND NANAMINE'S STORIES ARE WEAK IN CHARACTER. THEY'RE ALL LACKING IN CHARISMA.
WHICH MEANS...
WE NEED TO THINK UP SOME COOL, TRADITIONAL CHARACTERS, THEN SMACK THEM INTO A NON-TRADITIONAL STORY!
ONE WITH THE POTENTIAL FOR AN ANIME, OF COURSE!
!
MUCH AS I HATE TO ADMIT IT, WE SHOULD FOLLOW NANAMINE'S LEAD AND START WITH A PREMISE BASED ON A SINGLE IDEA.
YOU CAN COME UP WITH SOME CHARACTERS, AND I'LL GET THE INSPIRATION FOR A STORY FROM THERE!
HOW'S THAT SOUND?
FULL OF YOUR PLOTTING AS USUAL, BUT I LIKE IT!
START WITH THE CHARAC-TERS, HUH?
YOU NEED COOL CHARACTERS, COOL SCENES, AND A CUTE HEROINE.
YEAH. SOUNDS GOOD!
IT'S FUN TO DRAW STUFF LIKE THAT. I'LL GIVE IT A SHOT WHEN I GET THE TIME.

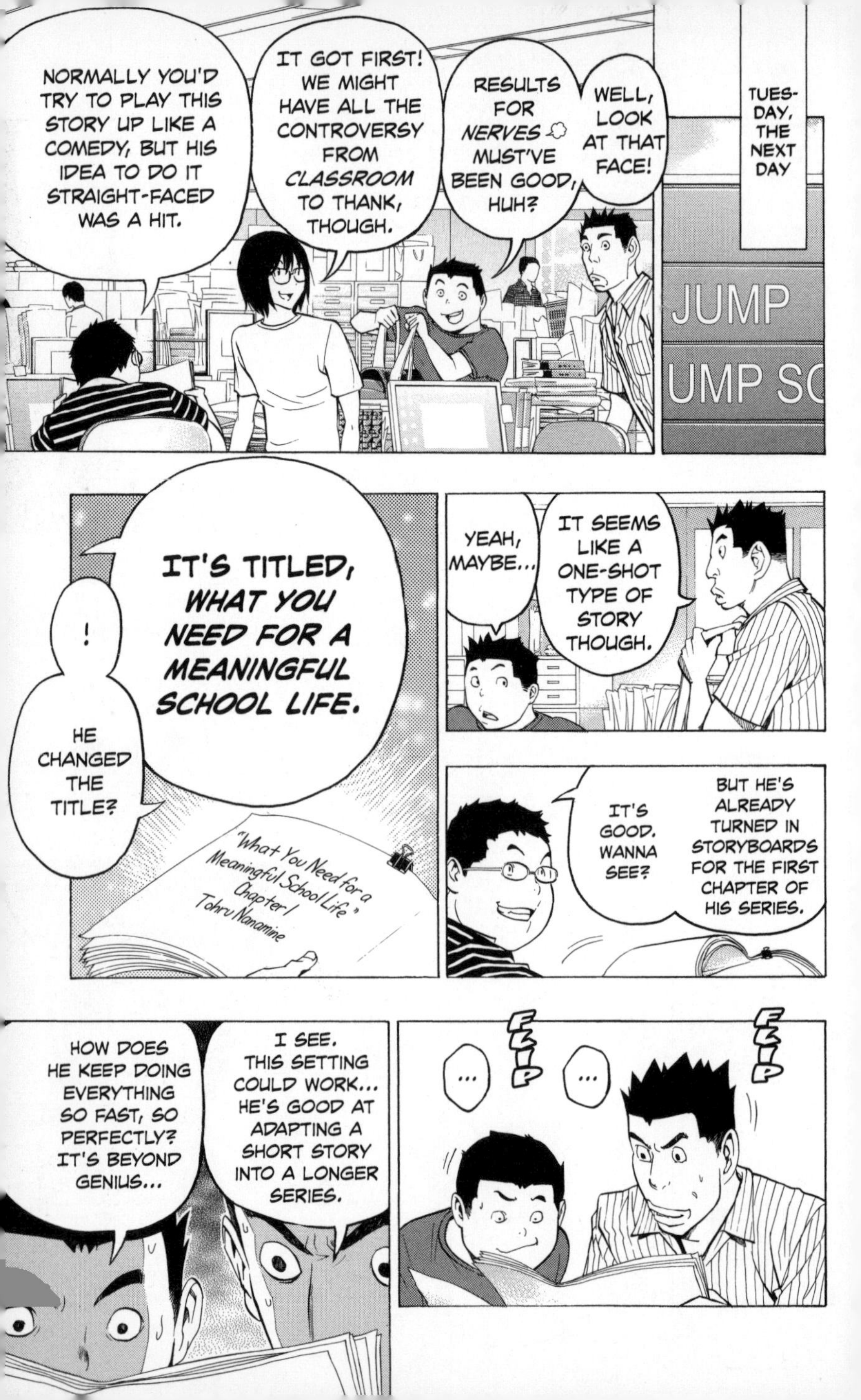
TUES-DAY, THE NEXT DAY
JUMP
WELL, LOOK AT THAT FACE!
RESULTS FOR NERVES MUST'VE BEEN GOOD, HUH?
IT GOT FIRST! WE MIGHT HAVE ALL THE CONTROVERSY FROM CLASSROOM TO THANK, THOUGH.
NORMALLY YOU'D TRY TO PLAY THIS STORY UP LIKE A COMEDY, BUT HIS IDEA TO DO IT STRAIGHT-FACED WAS A HIT.
IT SEEMS LIKE A ONE-SHOT TYPE OF STORY THOUGH.
YEAH, MAYBE...
BUT HE'S ALREADY TURNED IN STORYBOARDS FOR THE FIRST CHAPTER OF HIS SERIES.
IT'S GOOD. WANNA SEE?
IT'S TITLED, WHAT YOU NEED FOR A MEANINGFUL SCHOOL LIFE.
!
HE CHANGED THE TITLE?
"What You Need for a Meaningful School Life" Chapter 1 Tohru Nanamine
FLIP
...
FLIP
...
I SEE. THIS SETTING COULD WORK... HE'S GOOD AT ADAPTING A SHORT STORY INTO A LONGER SERIES.
HOW DOES HE KEEP DOING EVERYTHING SO FAST, SO PERFECTLY? IT'S BEYOND GENIUS...

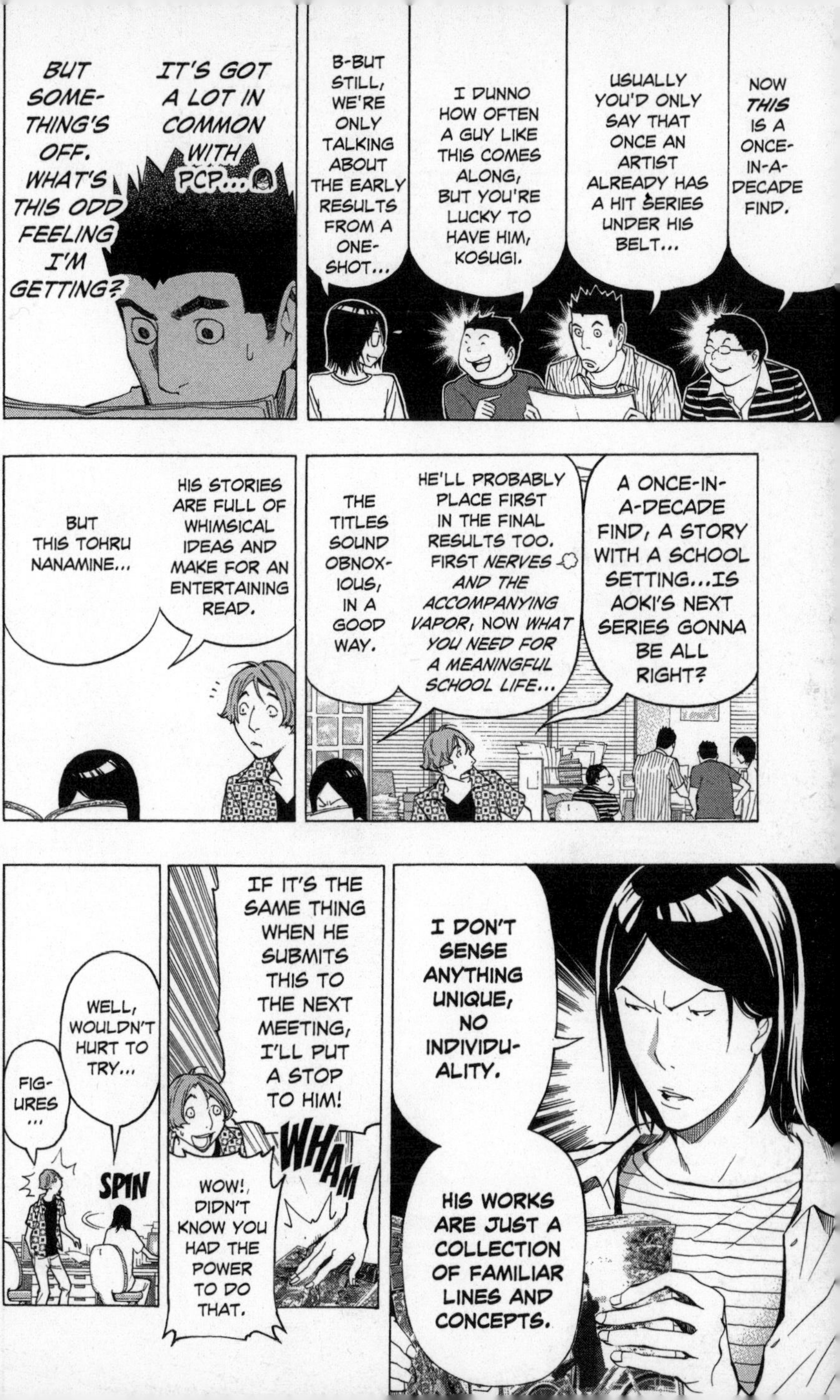

NOW *THIS* IS A ONCE-IN-A-DECADE FIND.
USUALLY YOU'D ONLY SAY THAT ONCE AN ARTIST ALREADY HAS A HIT SERIES UNDER HIS BELT...
I DUNNO HOW OFTEN A GUY LIKE THIS COMES ALONG, BUT YOU'RE LUCKY TO HAVE HIM, KOSUGI.
B-BUT STILL, WE'RE ONLY TALKING ABOUT THE EARLY RESULTS FROM A ONE-SHOT...
IT'S GOT A LOT IN COMMON WITH PCP...
BUT SOMETHING'S OFF. WHAT'S THIS ODD FEELING I'M GETTING?
A ONCE-IN-A-DECADE FIND, A STORY WITH A SCHOOL SETTING...IS AOKI'S NEXT SERIES GONNA BE ALL RIGHT?
HE'LL PROBABLY PLACE FIRST IN THE FINAL RESULTS TOO. FIRST *NERVES AND THE ACCOMPANYING VAPOR*, NOW *WHAT YOU NEED FOR A MEANINGFUL SCHOOL LIFE...*
THE TITLES SOUND OBNOXIOUS, IN A GOOD WAY.
HIS STORIES ARE FULL OF WHIMSICAL IDEAS AND MAKE FOR AN ENTERTAINING READ.
BUT THIS TOHRU NANAMINE...
I DON'T SENSE ANYTHING UNIQUE, NO INDIVIDUALITY.
HIS WORKS ARE JUST A COLLECTION OF FAMILIAR LINES AND CONCEPTS.
IF IT'S THE SAME THING WHEN HE SUBMITS THIS TO THE NEXT MEETING, I'LL PUT A STOP TO HIM!
WHAM
WOW! DIDN'T KNOW YOU HAD THE POWER TO DO THAT.
WELL, WOULDN'T HURT TO TRY...
FIGURES...
SPIN

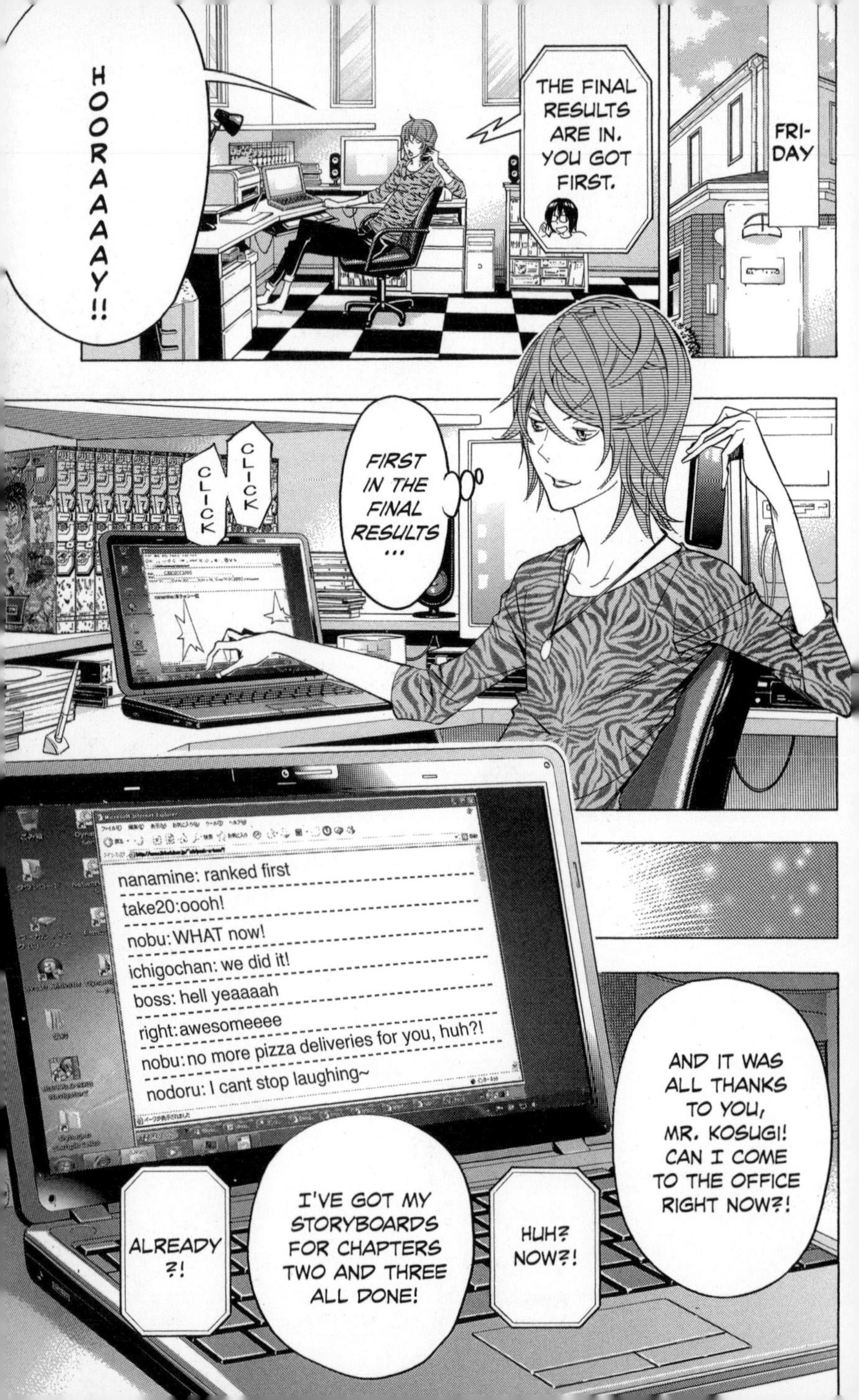
FRI-DAY
THE FINAL RESULTS ARE IN. YOU GOT FIRST.
HOORAAAAY!!
FIRST IN THE FINAL RESULTS...
CLICK
CLICK
nanamine: ranked first
take20:oooh!
nobu:WHAT now!
ichigochan: we did it!
boss: hell yeaaaah
right:awesomeeee
nobu:no more pizza deliveries for you, huh?!
nodoru: I cant stop laughing~
AND IT WAS ALL THANKS TO YOU, MR. KOSUGI! CAN I COME TO THE OFFICE RIGHT NOW?!
HUH? NOW?!
I'VE GOT MY STORYBOARDS FOR CHAPTERS TWO AND THREE ALL DONE!
ALREADY?!

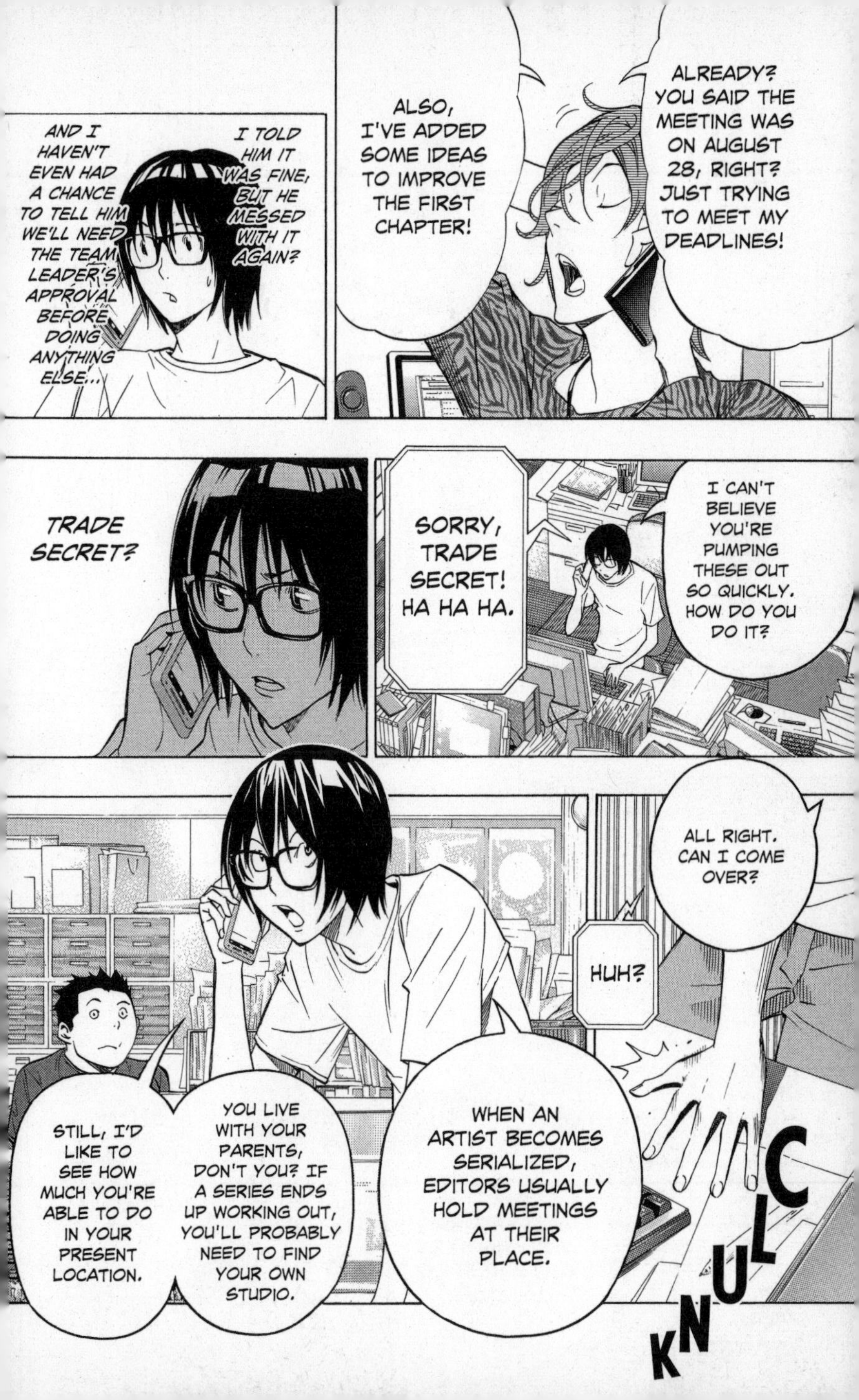

ALREADY? YOU SAID THE MEETING WAS ON AUGUST 28, RIGHT? JUST TRYING TO MEET MY DEADLINES!
ALSO, I'VE ADDED SOME IDEAS TO IMPROVE THE FIRST CHAPTER!
I TOLD HIM IT WAS FINE, BUT HE MESSED WITH IT AGAIN?
AND I HAVEN'T EVEN HAD A CHANCE TO TELL HIM WE'LL NEED THE TEAM LEADER'S APPROVAL BEFORE DOING ANYTHING ELSE...
I CAN'T BELIEVE YOU'RE PUMPING THESE OUT SO QUICKLY. HOW DO YOU DO IT?
SORRY, TRADE SECRET! HA HA HA.
TRADE SECRET?
ALL RIGHT. CAN I COME OVER?
HUH?
WHEN AN ARTIST BECOMES SERIALIZED, EDITORS USUALLY HOLD MEETINGS AT THEIR PLACE.
YOU LIVE WITH YOUR PARENTS, DON'T YOU? IF A SERIES ENDS UP WORKING OUT, YOU'LL PROBABLY NEED TO FIND YOUR OWN STUDIO.
STILL, I'D LIKE TO SEE HOW MUCH YOU'RE ABLE TO DO IN YOUR PRESENT LOCATION.
KNULC

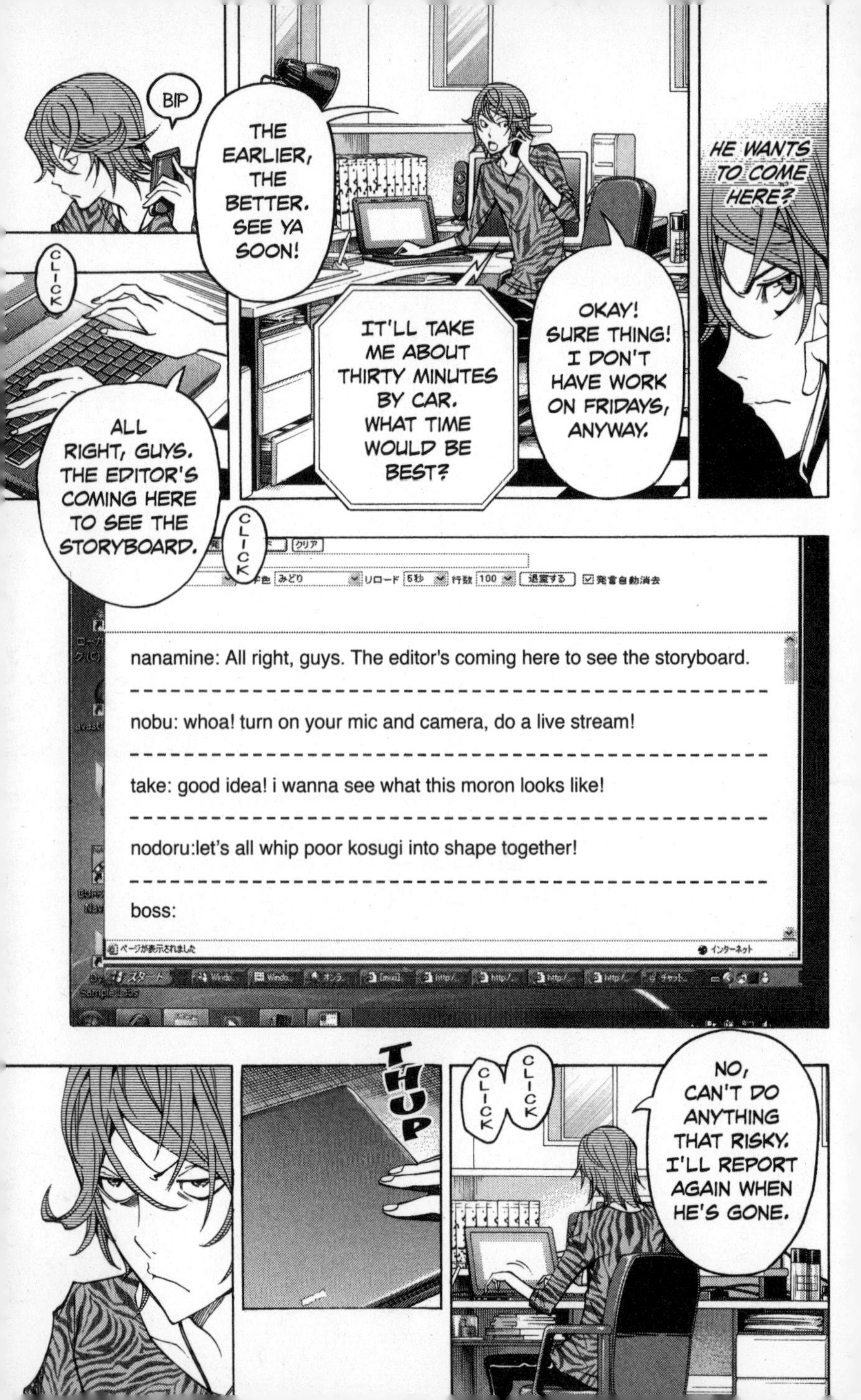
HE WANTS TO COME HERE?
OKAY! SURE THING! I DON'T HAVE WORK ON FRIDAYS, ANYWAY.
IT'LL TAKE ME ABOUT THIRTY MINUTES BY CAR. WHAT TIME WOULD BE BEST?
THE EARLIER, THE BETTER. SEE YA SOON!
BIP
CLICK
ALL RIGHT, GUYS. THE EDITOR'S COMING HERE TO SEE THE STORYBOARD.
CLICK
クリア
みどり
リロード 5秒 行数 100 退室する 発言自動消去
nanamine: All right, guys. The editor's coming here to see the storyboard.
nobu: whoa! turn on your mic and camera, do a live stream!
take: good idea! i wanna see what this moron looks like!
nodoru:let's all whip poor kosugi into shape together!
boss:
ページが表示されました
インターネット
スタート
NO, CAN'T DO ANYTHING THAT RISKY. I'LL REPORT AGAIN WHEN HE'S GONE.
CLICK
CLICK
THUP

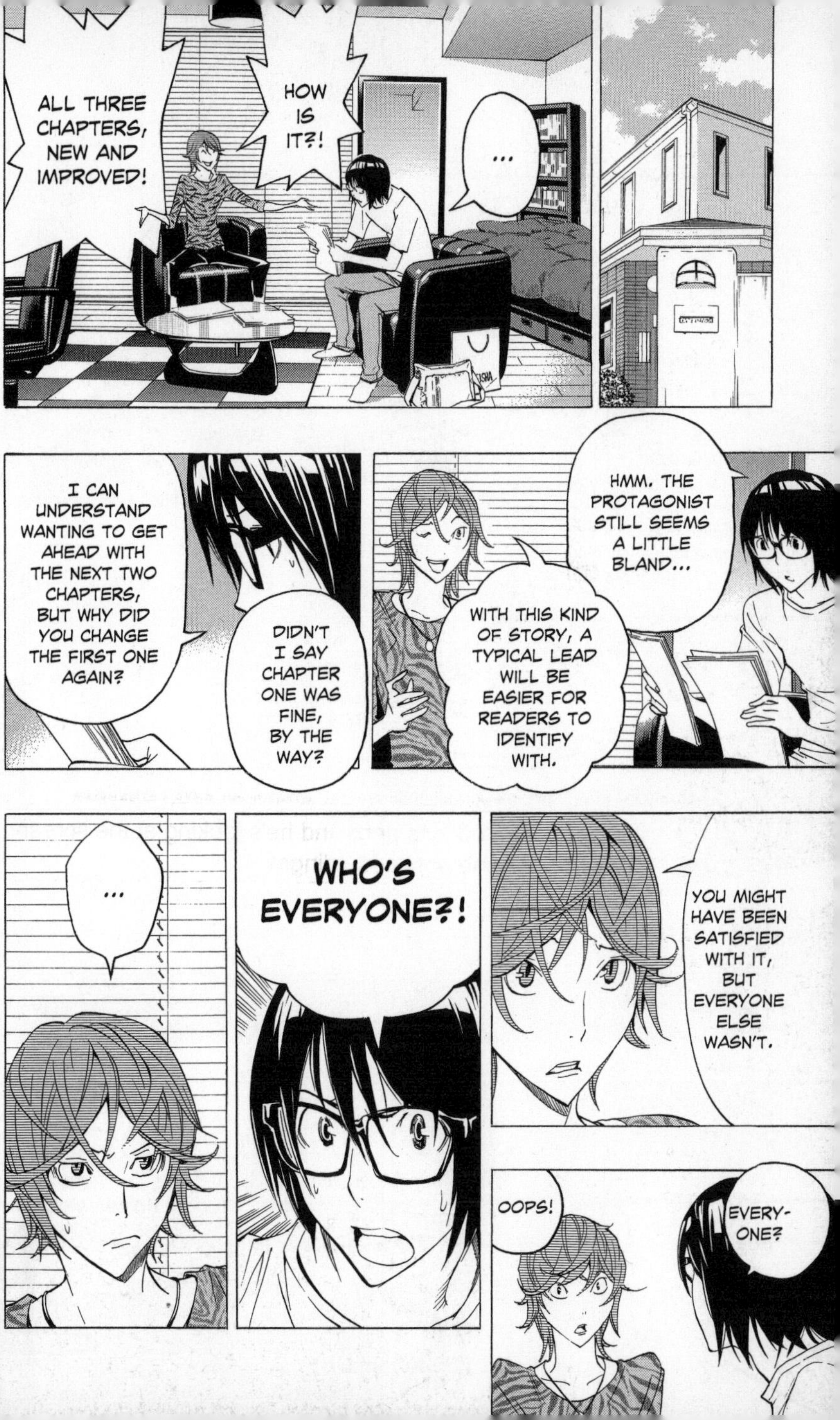
...
HOW IS IT?!
ALL THREE CHAPTERS, NEW AND IMPROVED!
HMM. THE PROTAGONIST STILL SEEMS A LITTLE BLAND...
WITH THIS KIND OF STORY, A TYPICAL LEAD WILL BE EASIER FOR READERS TO IDENTIFY WITH.
I CAN UNDERSTAND WANTING TO GET AHEAD WITH THE NEXT TWO CHAPTERS, BUT WHY DID YOU CHANGE THE FIRST ONE AGAIN?
DIDN'T I SAY CHAPTER ONE WAS FINE, BY THE WAY?
YOU MIGHT HAVE BEEN SATISFIED WITH IT, BUT EVERYONE ELSE WASN'T.
EVERY-ONE?
OOPS!
WHO'S EVERYONE?!
...

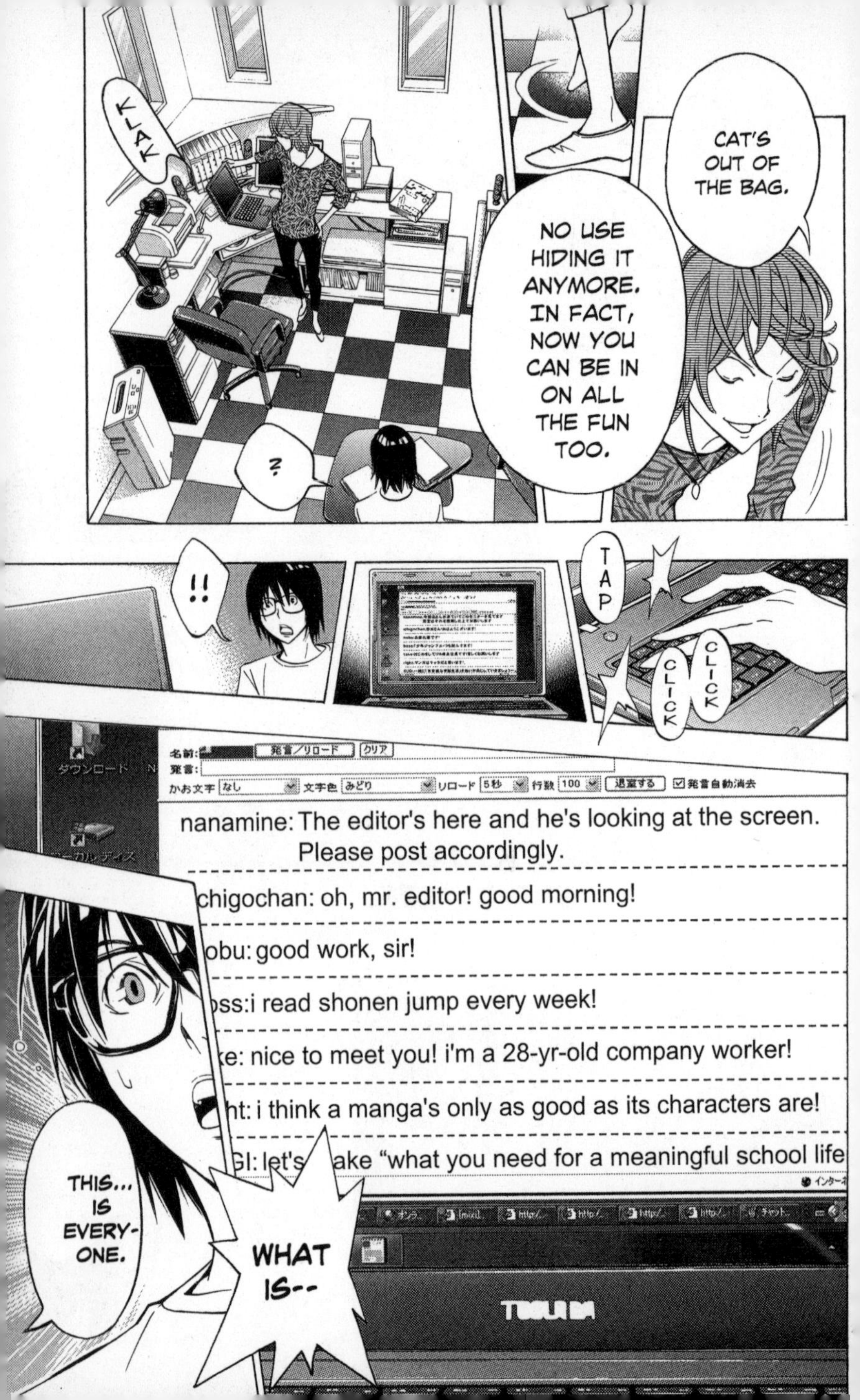
CAT'S OUT OF THE BAG.
NO USE HIDING IT ANYMORE. IN FACT, NOW YOU CAN BE IN ON ALL THE FUN TOO.
KLAK
?
TAP
CLICK
CLICK
!!
名前: 発言/リロード クリア
発言:
かお文字 なし 文字色 みどり リロード 5秒 行数 100 退室する 発言自動消去
nanamine: The editor's here and he's looking at the screen. Please post accordingly.
chigochan: oh, mr. editor! good morning!
obu: good work, sir!
ss:i read shonen jump every week!
ke: nice to meet you! i'm a 28-yr-old company worker!
ht: i think a manga's only as good as its characters are!
GI: let's ake “what you need for a meaningful school life
WHAT IS--
THIS... IS EVERYONE.

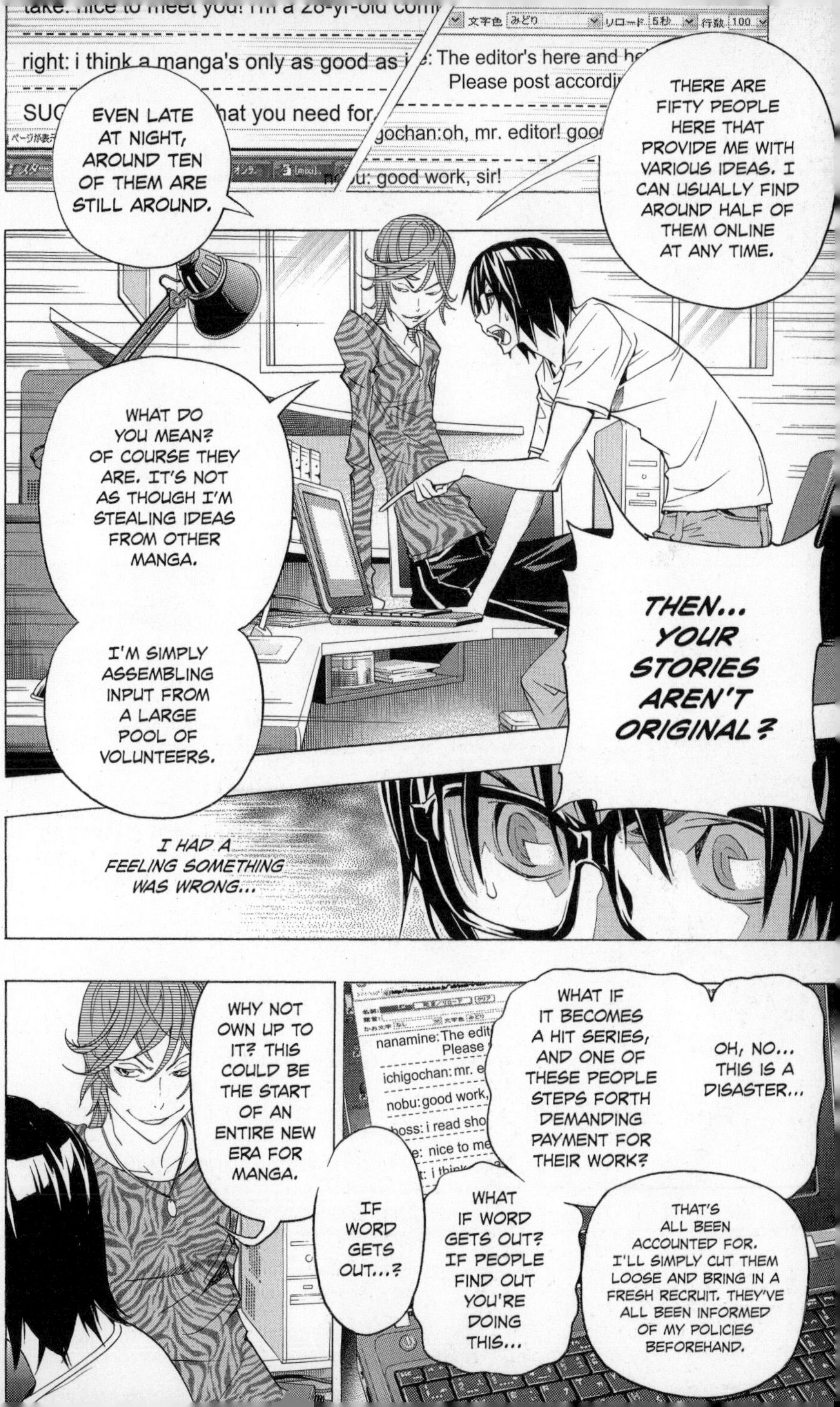

take: nice to meet you! i'm a 28-yr-old com
right: i think a manga's only as good as i
: The editor's here and he
Please post accordi
SUC
hat you need for
gochan:oh, mr. editor! goo
nobu: good work, sir!
THERE ARE FIFTY PEOPLE HERE THAT PROVIDE ME WITH VARIOUS IDEAS. I CAN USUALLY FIND AROUND HALF OF THEM ONLINE AT ANY TIME.
EVEN LATE AT NIGHT, AROUND TEN OF THEM ARE STILL AROUND.
THEN... YOUR STORIES AREN'T ORIGINAL?
WHAT DO YOU MEAN? OF COURSE THEY ARE. IT'S NOT AS THOUGH I'M STEALING IDEAS FROM OTHER MANGA.
I'M SIMPLY ASSEMBLING INPUT FROM A LARGE POOL OF VOLUNTEERS.
I HAD A FEELING SOMETHING WAS WRONG...
OH, NO... THIS IS A DISASTER...
WHAT IF IT BECOMES A HIT SERIES, AND ONE OF THESE PEOPLE STEPS FORTH DEMANDING PAYMENT FOR THEIR WORK?
THAT'S ALL BEEN ACCOUNTED FOR. I'LL SIMPLY CUT THEM LOOSE AND BRING IN A FRESH RECRUIT. THEY'VE ALL BEEN INFORMED OF MY POLICIES BEFOREHAND.
WHAT IF WORD GETS OUT? IF PEOPLE FIND OUT YOU'RE DOING THIS...
IF WORD GETS OUT...?
WHY NOT OWN UP TO IT? THIS COULD BE THE START OF AN ENTIRE NEW ERA FOR MANGA.

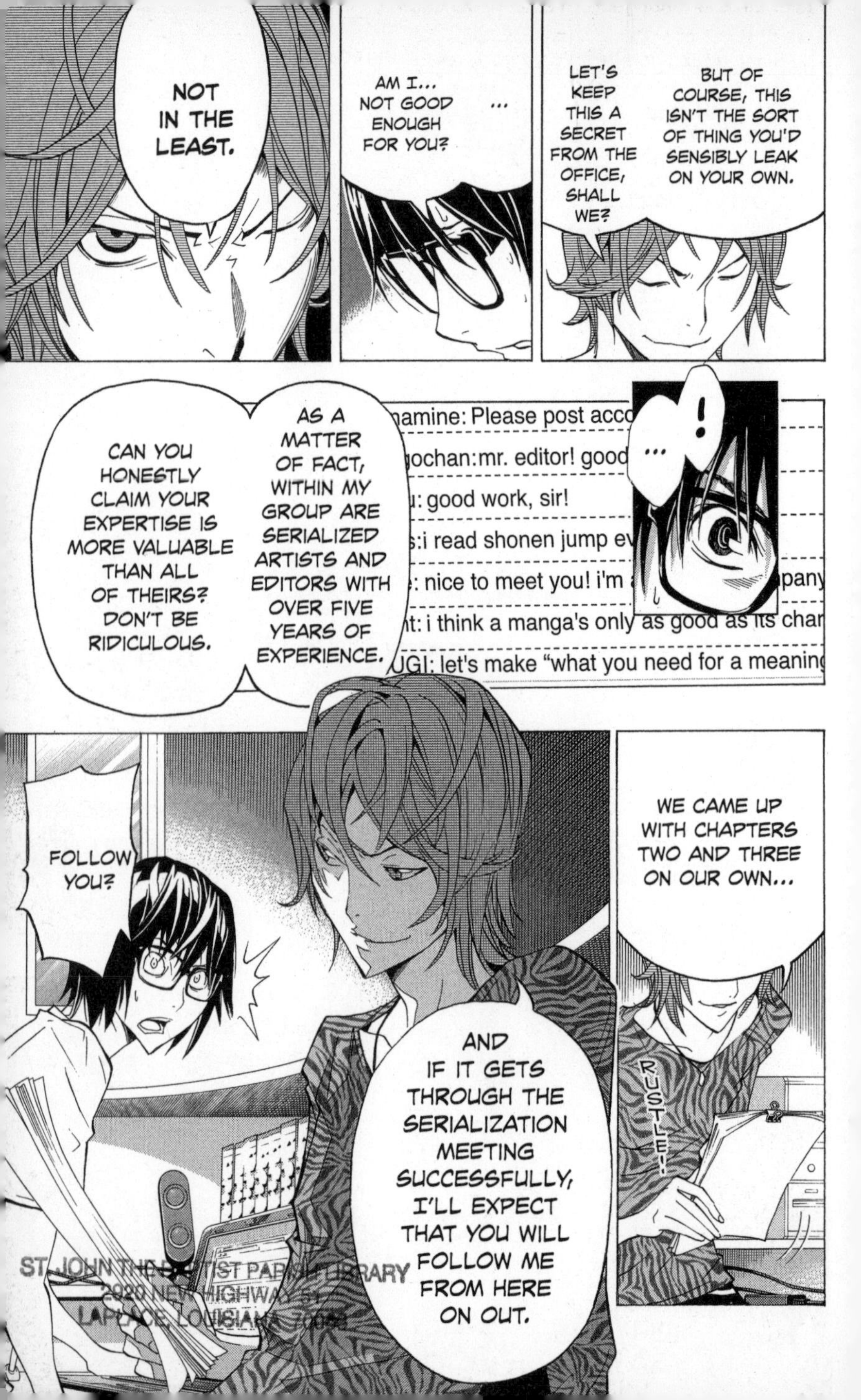
BUT OF COURSE, THIS ISN'T THE SORT OF THING YOU'D SENSIBLY LEAK ON YOUR OWN.
LET'S KEEP THIS A SECRET FROM THE OFFICE, SHALL WE?
...
AM I... NOT GOOD ENOUGH FOR YOU?
NOT IN THE LEAST.
!
...
amine: Please post acc
gochan:mr. editor! good
u: good work, sir!
s:i read shonen jump ev
: nice to meet you! i'm
pany
t: i think a manga's only as good as its char
UGI: let's make "what you need for a meanin
AS A MATTER OF FACT, WITHIN MY GROUP ARE SERIALIZED ARTISTS AND EDITORS WITH OVER FIVE YEARS OF EXPERIENCE.
CAN YOU HONESTLY CLAIM YOUR EXPERTISE IS MORE VALUABLE THAN ALL OF THEIRS? DON'T BE RIDICULOUS.
WE CAME UP WITH CHAPTERS TWO AND THREE ON OUR OWN...
RUSTLE!
AND IF IT GETS THROUGH THE SERIALIZATION MEETING SUCCESSFULLY, I'LL EXPECT THAT YOU WILL FOLLOW ME FROM HERE ON OUT.
FOLLOW YOU?

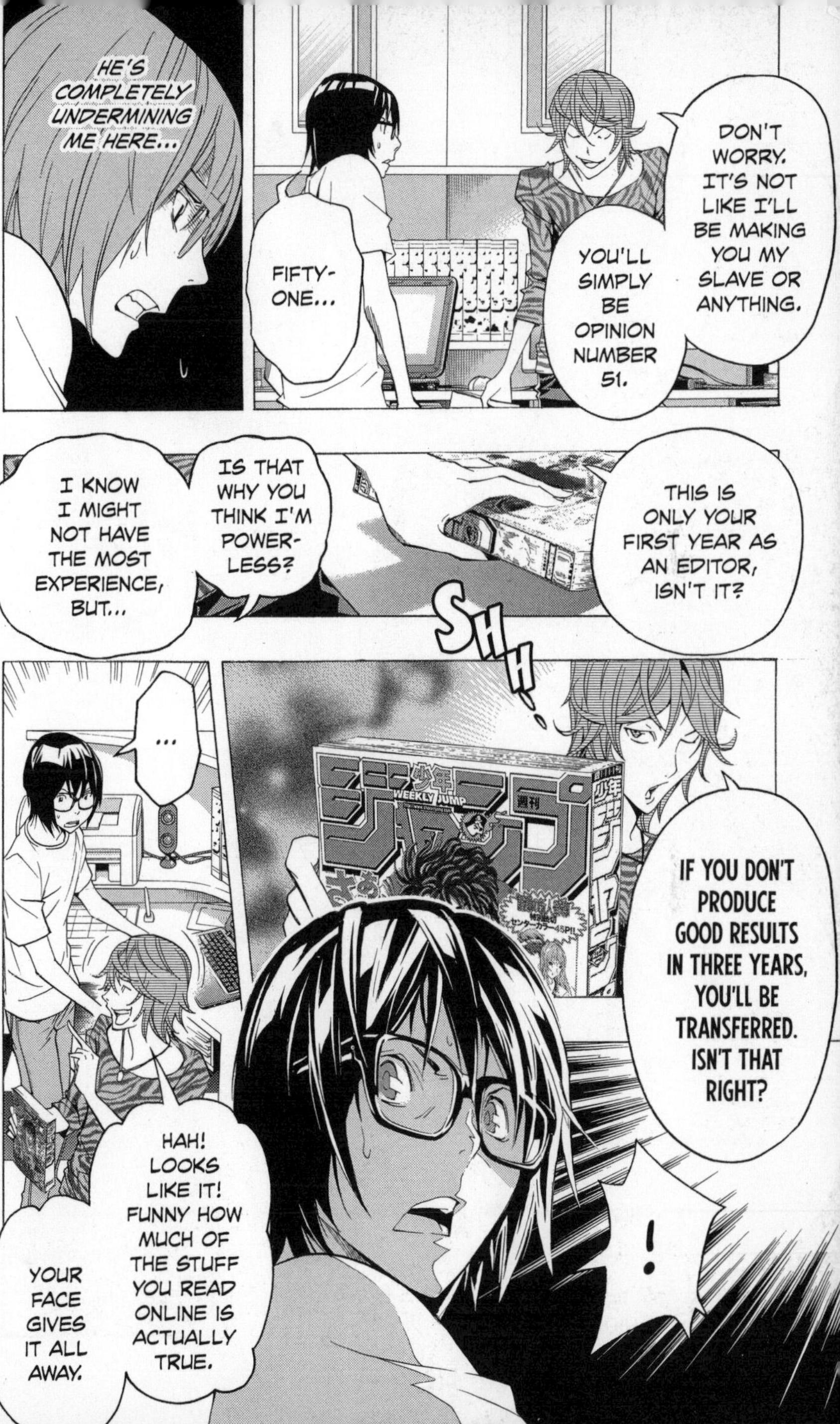
DON'T WORRY. IT'S NOT LIKE I'LL BE MAKING YOU MY SLAVE OR ANYTHING.
YOU'LL SIMPLY BE OPINION NUMBER 51.
FIFTY-ONE...
HE'S COMPLETELY UNDERMINING ME HERE...
THIS IS ONLY YOUR FIRST YEAR AS AN EDITOR, ISN'T IT?
IS THAT WHY YOU THINK I'M POWERLESS?
I KNOW I MIGHT NOT HAVE THE MOST EXPERIENCE, BUT...
SHH
WEEKLY JUMP
IF YOU DON'T PRODUCE GOOD RESULTS IN THREE YEARS, YOU'LL BE TRANSFERRED. ISN'T THAT RIGHT?
!
...
HAH! LOOKS LIKE IT! FUNNY HOW MUCH OF THE STUFF YOU READ ONLINE IS ACTUALLY TRUE.
YOUR FACE GIVES IT ALL AWAY.

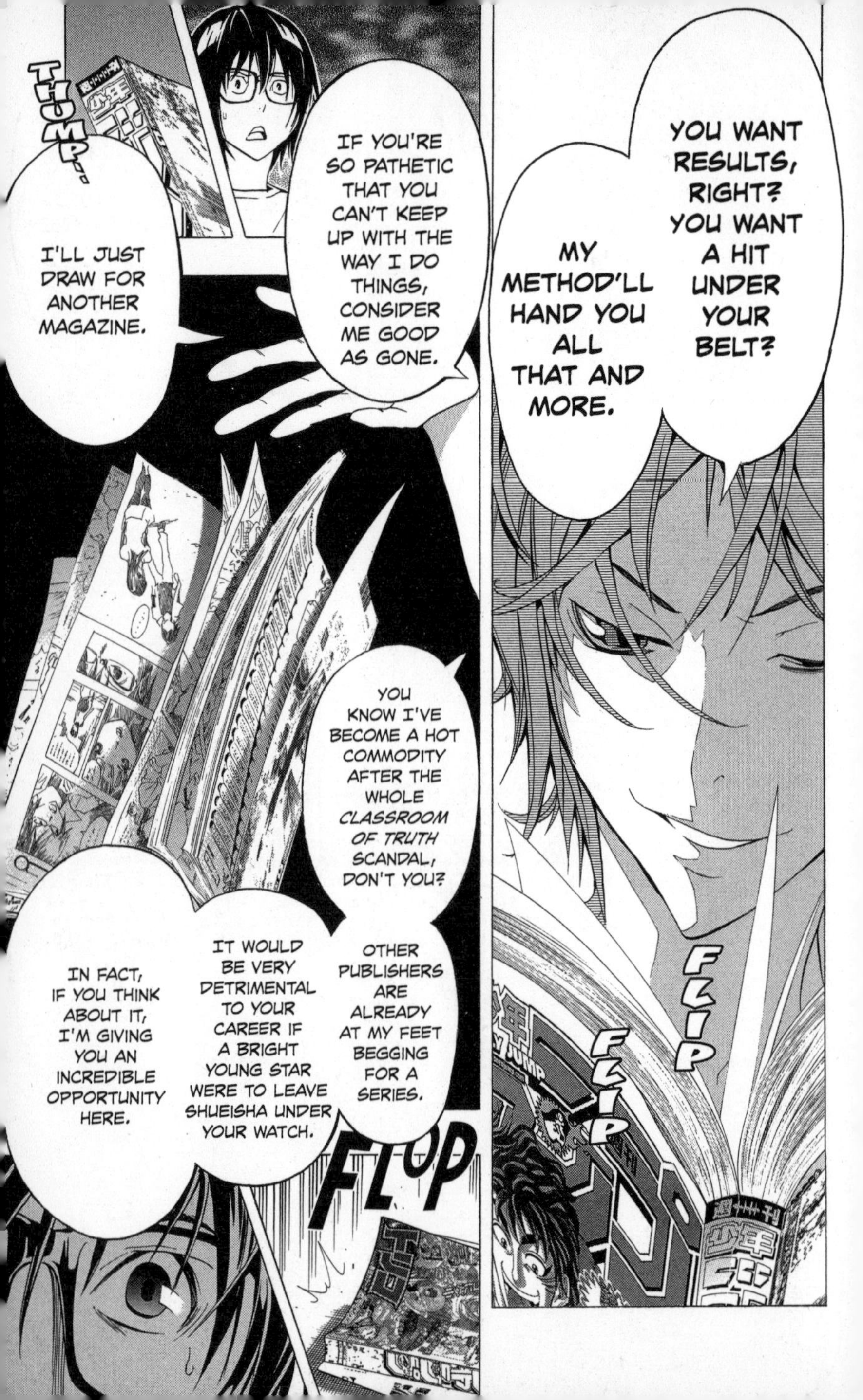
YOU WANT RESULTS, RIGHT? YOU WANT A HIT UNDER YOUR BELT?
MY METHOD'LL HAND YOU ALL THAT AND MORE.
FLIP
FLIP
IF YOU'RE SO PATHETIC THAT YOU CAN'T KEEP UP WITH THE WAY I DO THINGS, CONSIDER ME GOOD AS GONE.
THUMP...
I'LL JUST DRAW FOR ANOTHER MAGAZINE.
YOU KNOW I'VE BECOME A HOT COMMODITY AFTER THE WHOLE *CLASSROOM OF TRUTH* SCANDAL, DON'T YOU?
OTHER PUBLISHERS ARE ALREADY AT MY FEET BEGGING FOR A SERIES.
IT WOULD BE VERY DETRIMENTAL TO YOUR CAREER IF A BRIGHT YOUNG STAR WERE TO LEAVE SHUEISHA UNDER YOUR WATCH.
IN FACT, IF YOU THINK ABOUT IT, I'M GIVING YOU AN INCREDIBLE OPPORTUNITY HERE.
FLOP

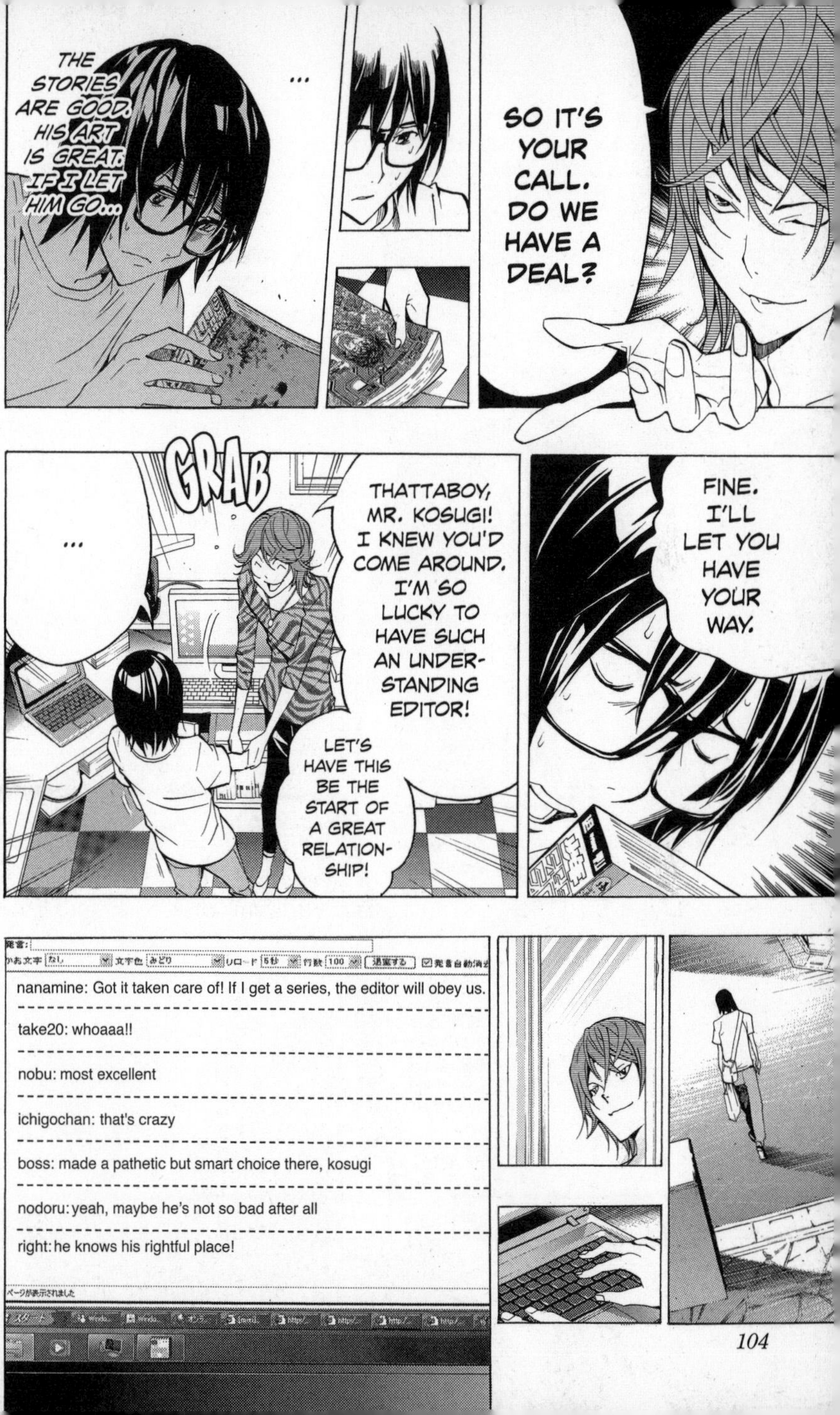
SO IT'S YOUR CALL. DO WE HAVE A DEAL?
...
THE STORIES ARE GOOD. HIS ART IS GREAT. IF I LET HIM GO...
FINE. I'LL LET YOU HAVE YOUR WAY.
GRAB
...
THATTABOY, MR. KOSUGI! I KNEW YOU'D COME AROUND. I'M SO LUCKY TO HAVE SUCH AN UNDER-STANDING EDITOR!
LET'S HAVE THIS BE THE START OF A GREAT RELATION-SHIP!
発言:
かお文字 なし 文字色 みどり リロード 5秒 行数 100 退室する
nanamine: Got it taken care of! If I get a series, the editor will obey us.
take20: whoaaa!!
nobu: most excellent
ichigochan: that's crazy
boss: made a pathetic but smart choice there, kosugi
nodoru: yeah, maybe he's not so bad after all
right: he knows his rightful place!
ページが表示されました
スタート

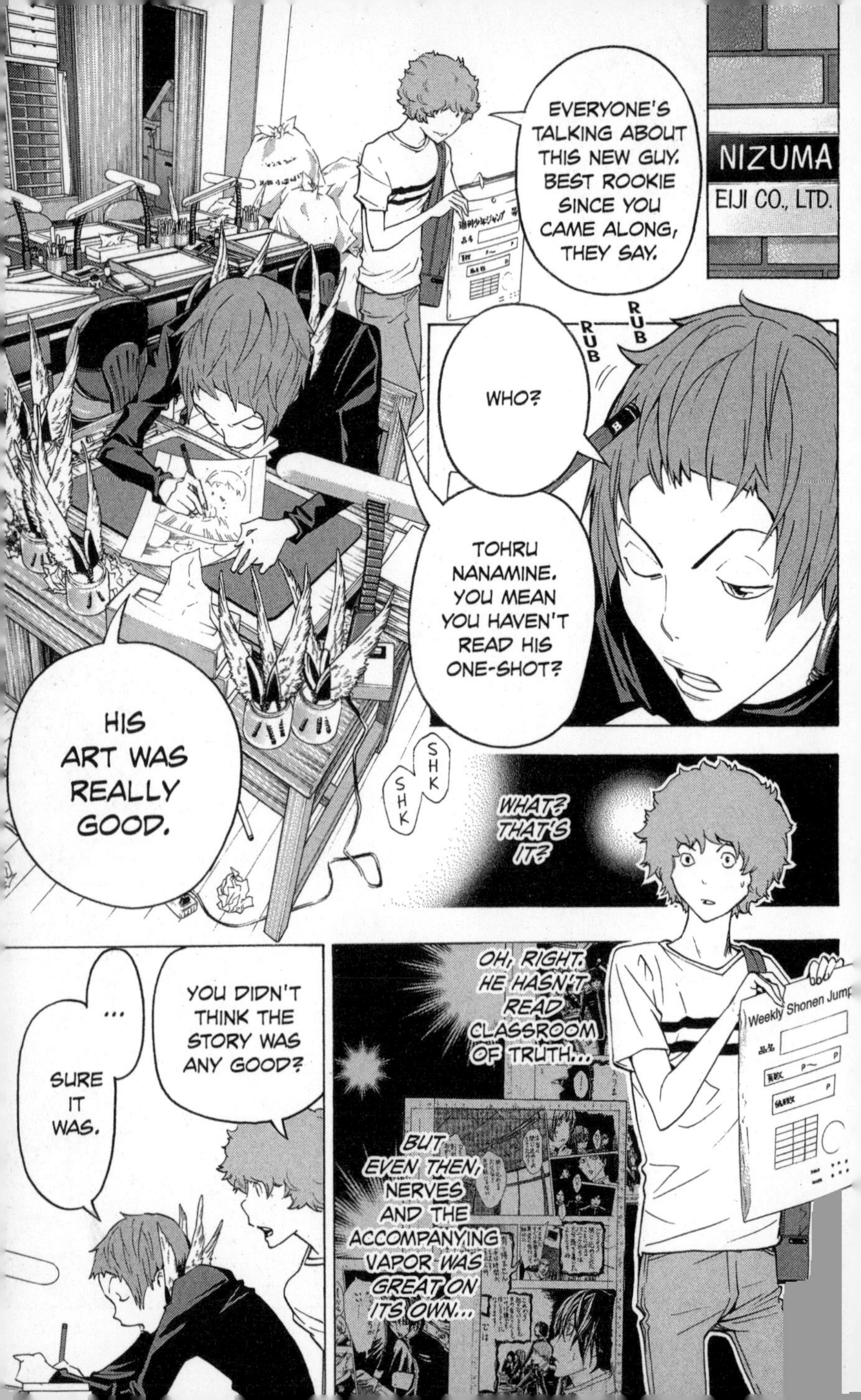

NIZUMA
EIJI CO., LTD.
EVERYONE'S TALKING ABOUT THIS NEW GUY. BEST ROOKIE SINCE YOU CAME ALONG, THEY SAY.
RUB RUB
WHO?
TOHRU NANAMINE. YOU MEAN YOU HAVEN'T READ HIS ONE-SHOT?
HIS ART WAS REALLY GOOD.
SHK SHK
WHAT? THAT'S IT?
OH, RIGHT. HE HASN'T READ CLASSROOM OF TRUTH...
Weekly Shonen Jump
BUT EVEN THEN, NERVES AND THE ACCOMPANYING VAPOR WAS GREAT ON ITS OWN...
YOU DIDN'T THINK THE STORY WAS ANY GOOD?
...
SURE IT WAS.

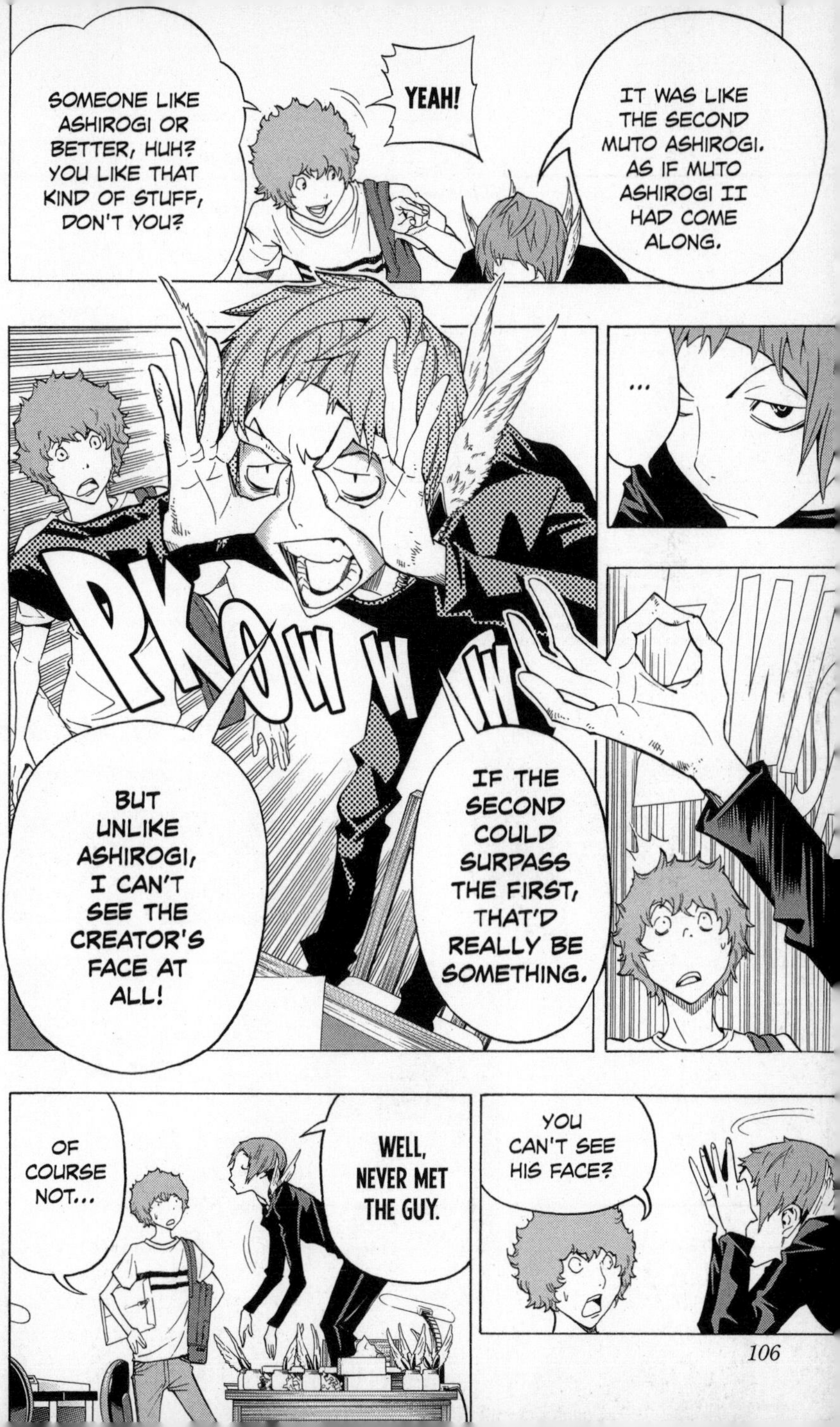
IT WAS LIKE THE SECOND MUTO ASHIROGI. AS IF MUTO ASHIROGI II HAD COME ALONG.
YEAH!
SOMEONE LIKE ASHIROGI OR BETTER, HUH? YOU LIKE THAT KIND OF STUFF, DON'T YOU?
...
IF THE SECOND COULD SURPASS THE FIRST, THAT'D REALLY BE SOMETHING.
PKOWWW
BUT UNLIKE ASHIROGI, I CAN'T SEE THE CREATOR'S FACE AT ALL!
YOU CAN'T SEE HIS FACE?
WELL, NEVER MET THE GUY.
OF COURSE NOT...

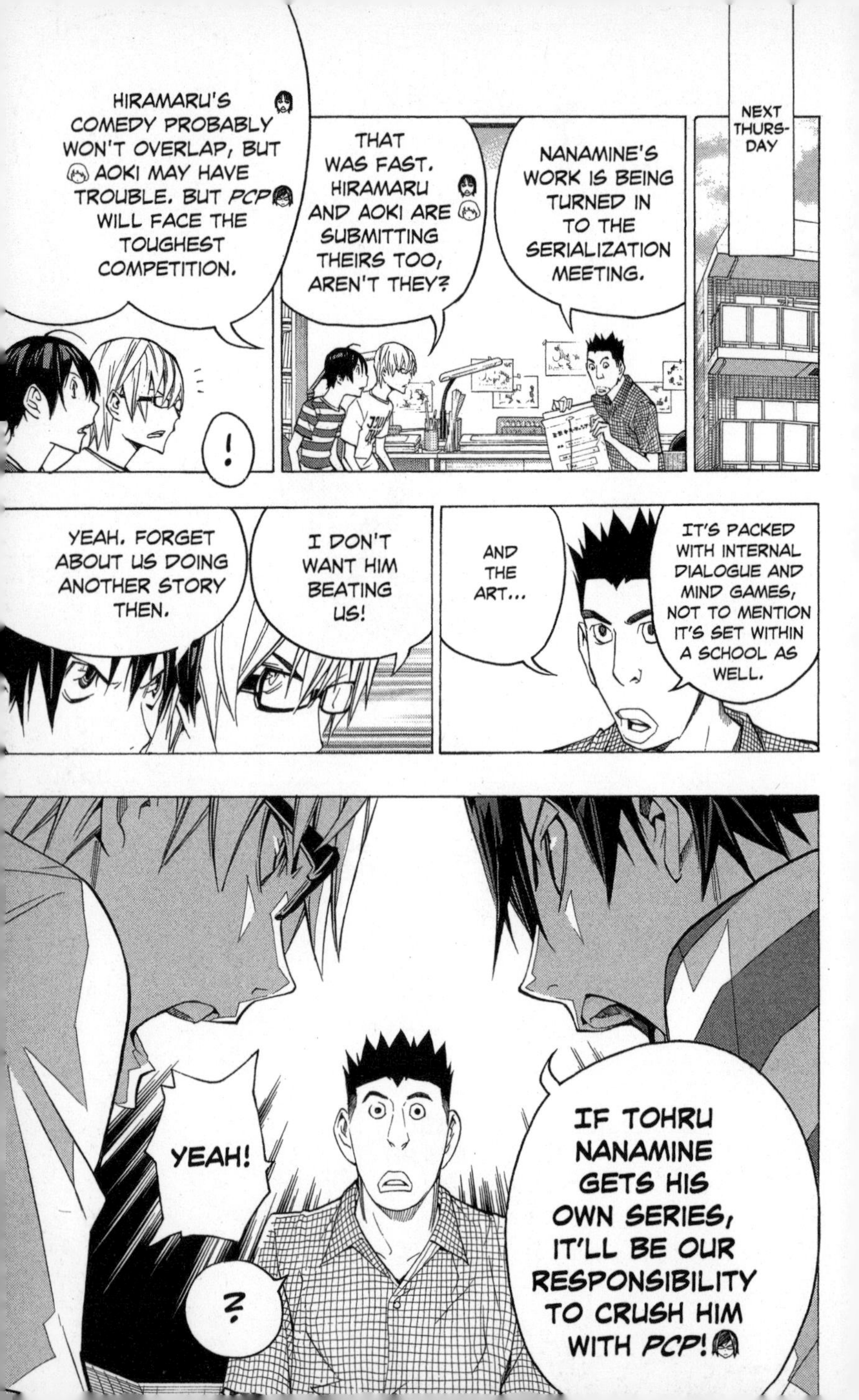
NEXT THURS-DAY
NANAMINE'S WORK IS BEING TURNED IN TO THE SERIALIZATION MEETING.
THAT WAS FAST. HIRAMARU AND AOKI ARE SUBMITTING THEIRS TOO, AREN'T THEY?
HIRAMARU'S COMEDY PROBABLY WON'T OVERLAP, BUT AOKI MAY HAVE TROUBLE. BUT *PCP* WILL FACE THE TOUGHEST COMPETITION.
!
IT'S PACKED WITH INTERNAL DIALOGUE AND MIND GAMES, NOT TO MENTION IT'S SET WITHIN A SCHOOL AS WELL.
AND THE ART...
I DON'T WANT HIM BEATING US!
YEAH. FORGET ABOUT US DOING ANOTHER STORY THEN.
IF TOHRU NANAMINE GETS HIS OWN SERIES, IT'LL BE OUR RESPONSIBILITY TO CRUSH HIM WITH *PCP*!
YEAH!
?

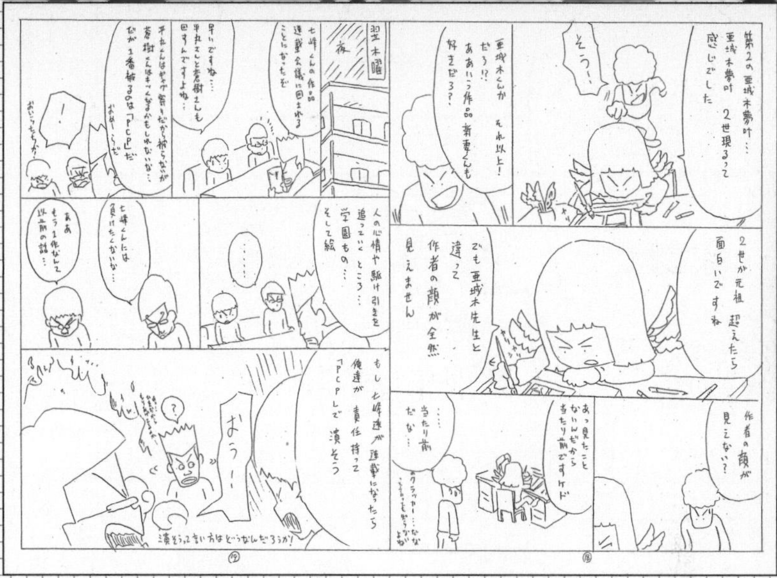

第2の亜城木夢叶…亜城木夢叶 2世現るって感じでした
そう…
亜城木くんがだろ!? それ以上! あぁいう作品 新妻くんも好きだろ?
2世が元祖超えたら面白いですね
でも亜城木先生と違って作者の顔が全然見えません
作者の顔が見えない?
あっ見たことないんだから当たり前ですケド
……当たり前だな…
翌木曜
夜
七峰くんの作品連載会議に回ることになったぞ
早いですね…平丸さんと蒼樹さんも回すんですよね…
だが1番怖るのは「PCP」だ
!
人の心情や駆け引きを追っていくところ…学園もの…そして絵
……
七峰くんには負けたくないな…
ああ もうネタ作なんて以前の話…
もし七峰達が連載になったら俺達が責任持って「PCP」で潰そう
?
おう!
潰そうって言い方はどうなんだろうか!

OHBA'S STORYBOARD

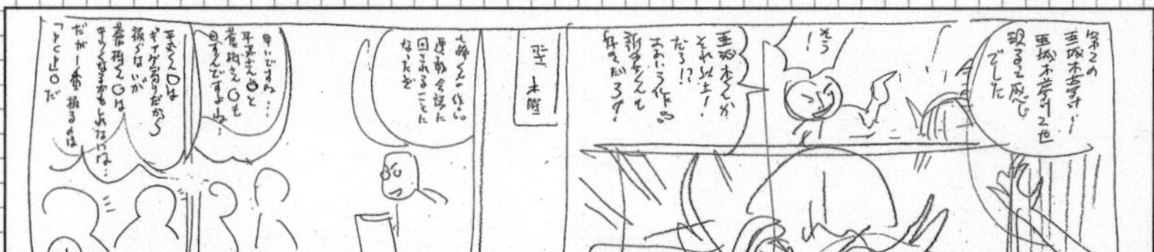

2世が元祖超えたら面白いですケド
でも亜城木先生と違って作者の顔が全然見えません
翌木曜
七峰くんの作品連載会議に回ることになったぞ
人の心情や駆け引きを追えてくところ
学園もの…
そして絵…
七峰くんには負けたくないな…
もし七峰達が連載になったら俺達が責任持って「PCP」で潰そう
おう
?

OBATA'S STORYBOARD

COMPLETE!

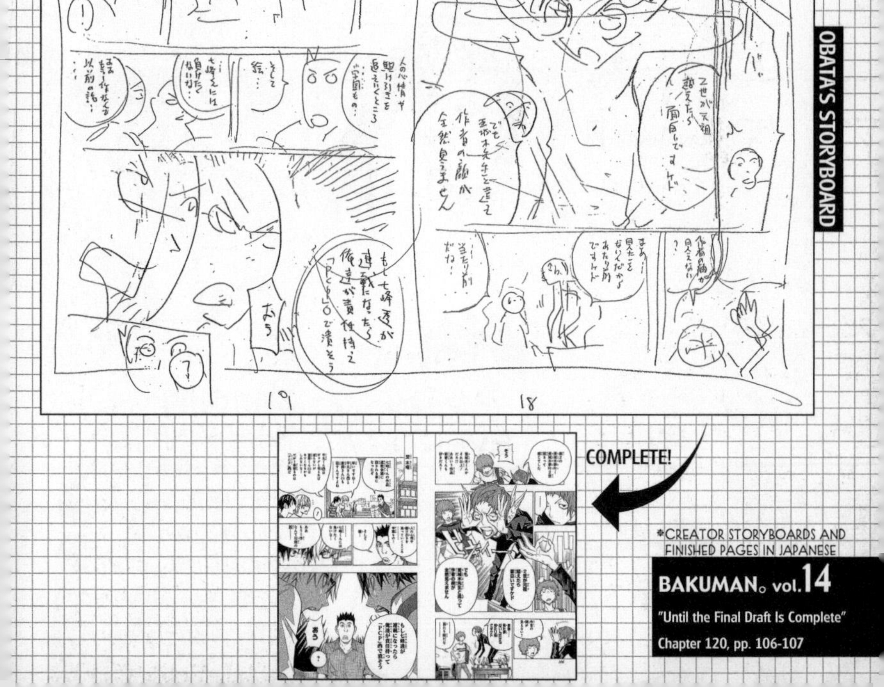

*CREATOR STORYBOARDS AND FINISHED PAGES IN JAPANESE

BAKUMAN。 vol.14

"Until the Final Draft Is Complete"

Chapter 120, pp. 106-107

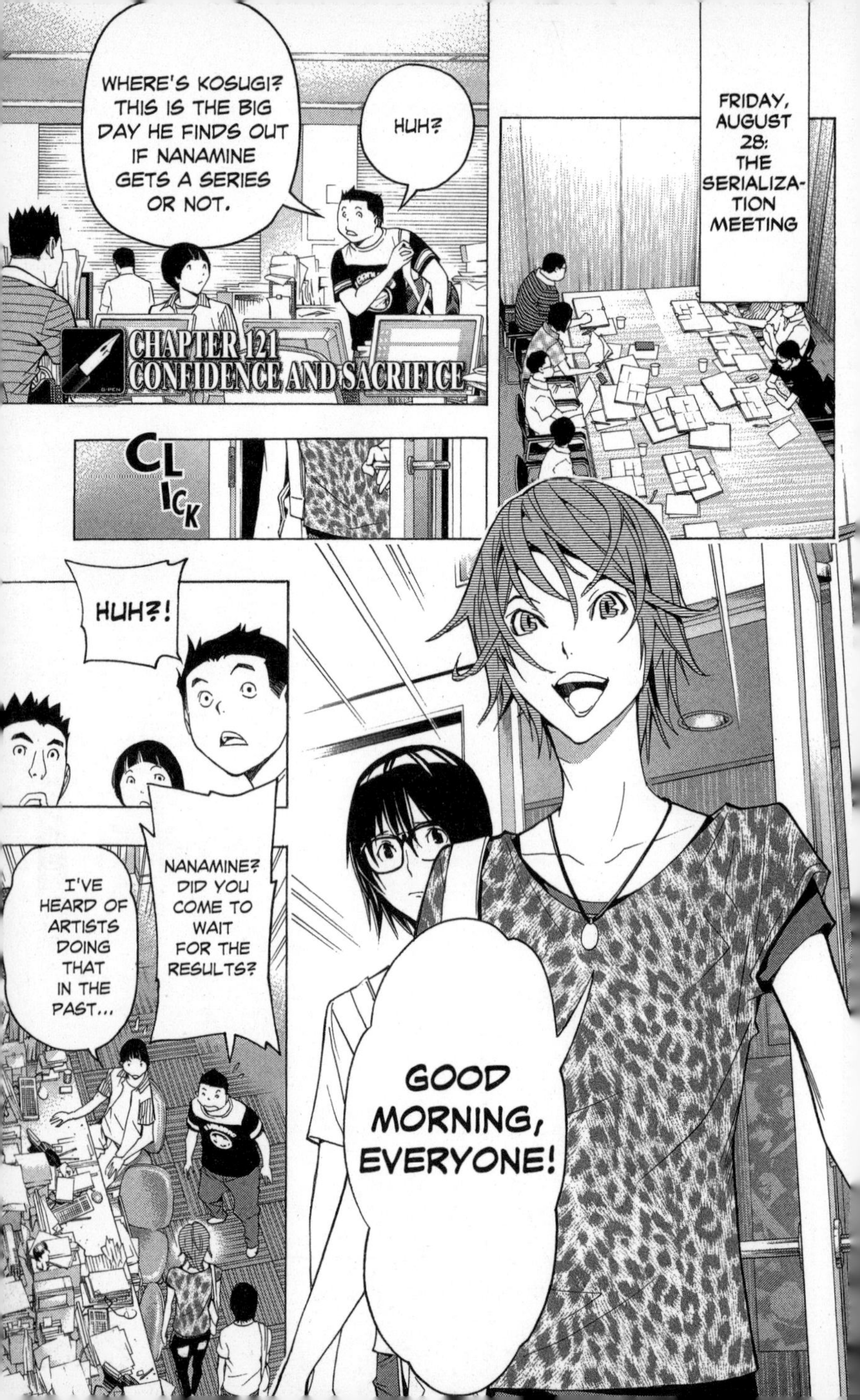
FRIDAY, AUGUST 28: THE SERIALIZATION MEETING
WHERE'S KOSUGI? THIS IS THE BIG DAY HE FINDS OUT IF NANAMINE GETS A SERIES OR NOT.
HUH?
CHAPTER 121 CONFIDENCE AND SACRIFICE
CLICK
GOOD MORNING, EVERYONE!
HUH?!
NANAMINE? DID YOU COME TO WAIT FOR THE RESULTS?
I'VE HEARD OF ARTISTS DOING THAT IN THE PAST...

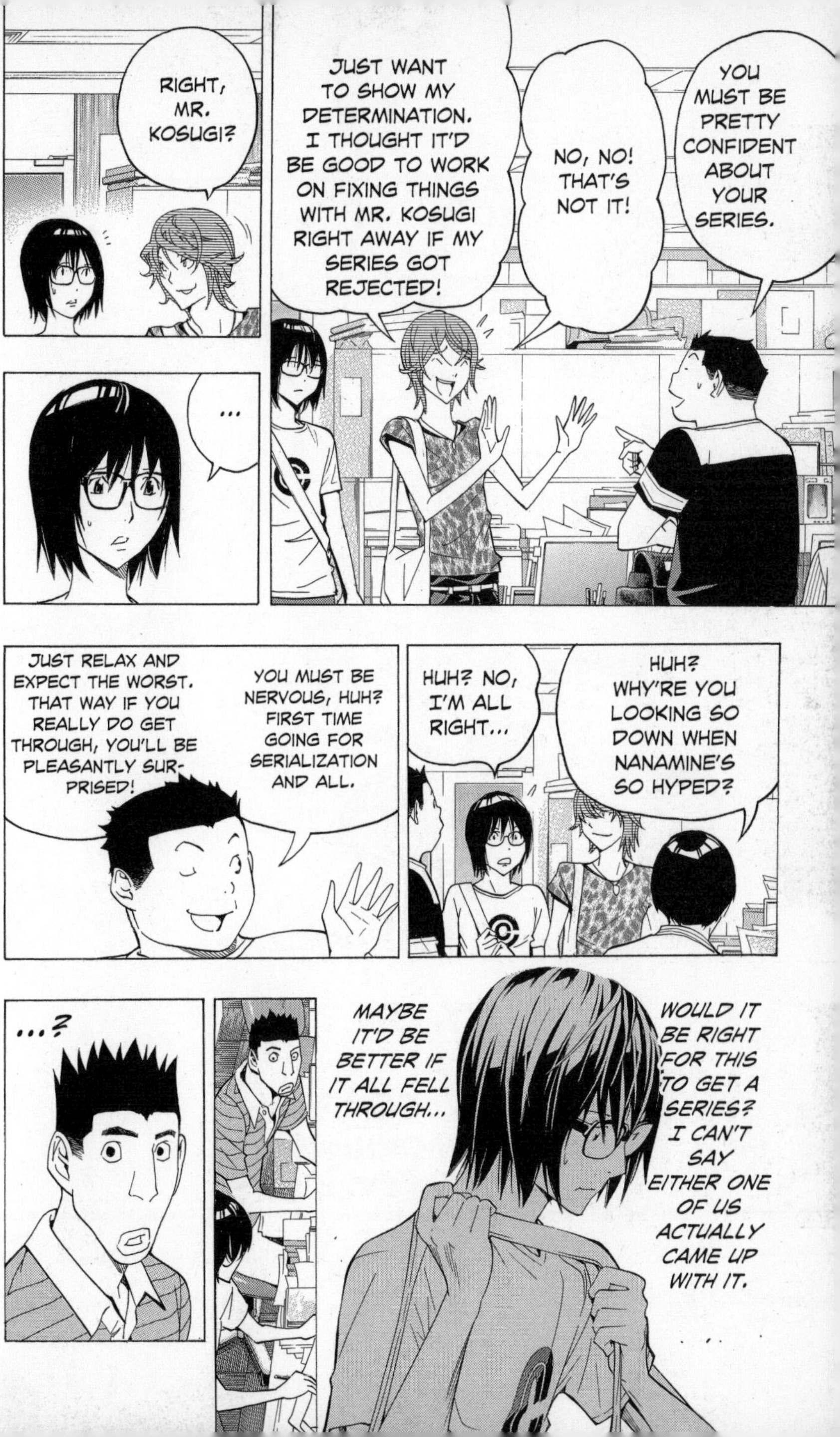
YOU MUST BE PRETTY CONFIDENT ABOUT YOUR SERIES.
NO, NO! THAT'S NOT IT!
JUST WANT TO SHOW MY DETERMINATION. I THOUGHT IT'D BE GOOD TO WORK ON FIXING THINGS WITH MR. KOSUGI RIGHT AWAY IF MY SERIES GOT REJECTED!
RIGHT, MR. KOSUGI?
...
HUH? WHY'RE YOU LOOKING SO DOWN WHEN NANAMINE'S SO HYPED?
HUH? NO, I'M ALL RIGHT...
YOU MUST BE NERVOUS, HUH? FIRST TIME GOING FOR SERIALIZATION AND ALL.
JUST RELAX AND EXPECT THE WORST. THAT WAY IF YOU REALLY DO GET THROUGH, YOU'LL BE PLEASANTLY SURPRISED!
WOULD IT BE RIGHT FOR THIS TO GET A SERIES? I CAN'T SAY EITHER ONE OF US ACTUALLY CAME UP WITH IT.
MAYBE IT'D BE BETTER IF IT ALL FELL THROUGH...
...?

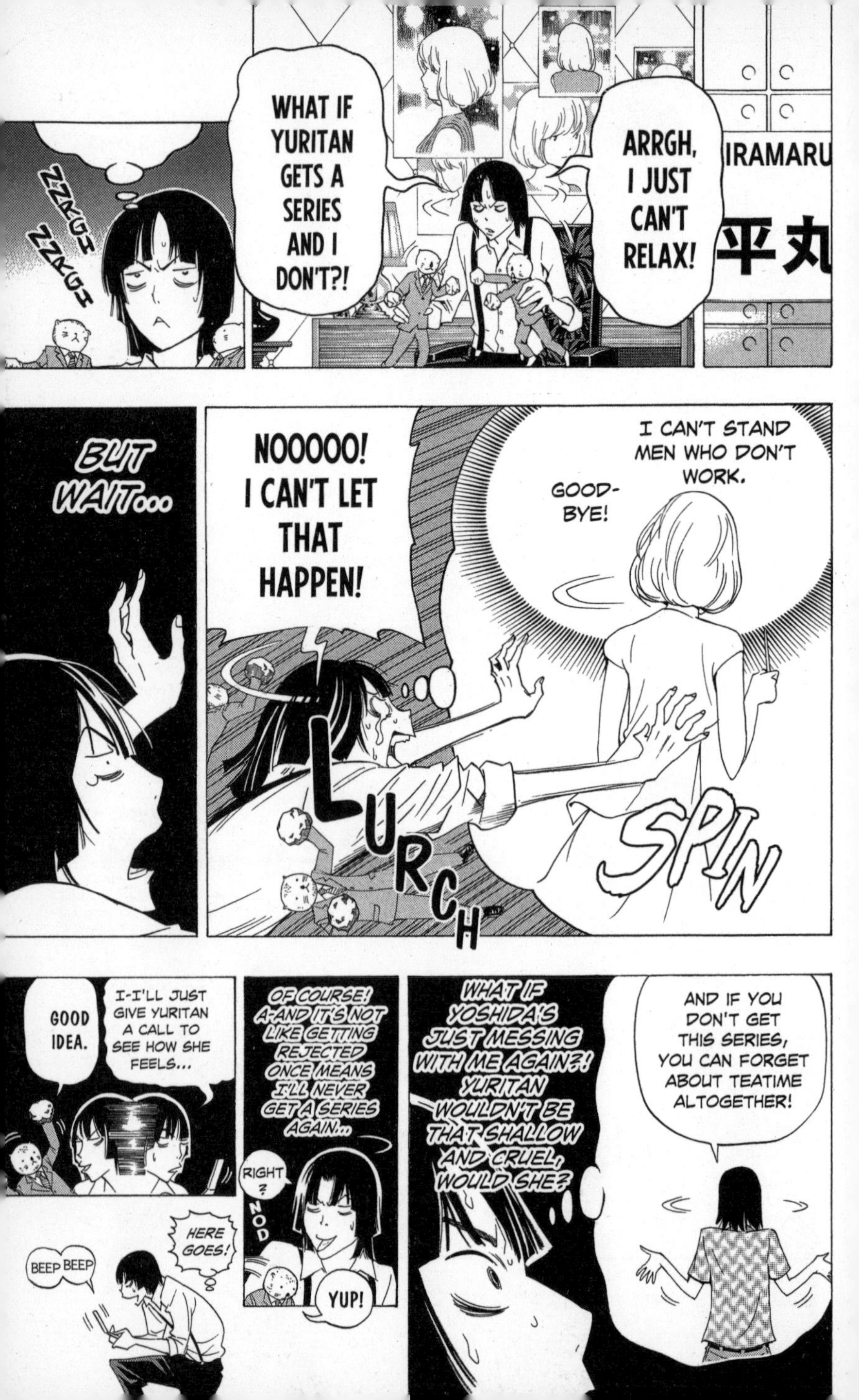
IRAMARU
平丸
ARRGH, I JUST CAN'T RELAX!
WHAT IF YURITAN GETS A SERIES AND I DON'T?!
ZZRGH ZZRGH
I CAN'T STAND MEN WHO DON'T WORK.
GOOD-BYE!
NOOOOO! I CAN'T LET THAT HAPPEN!
SPIN
LURCH
BUT WAIT...
AND IF YOU DON'T GET THIS SERIES, YOU CAN FORGET ABOUT TEATIME ALTOGETHER!
WHAT IF YOSHIDA'S JUST MESSING WITH ME AGAIN?! YURITAN WOULDN'T BE THAT SHALLOW AND CRUEL, WOULD SHE?
OF COURSE! A-AND IT'S NOT LIKE GETTING REJECTED ONCE MEANS I'LL NEVER GET A SERIES AGAIN...
RIGHT?
NOD
YUP!
I-I'LL JUST GIVE YURITAN A CALL TO SEE HOW SHE FEELS...
GOOD IDEA.
HERE GOES!
BEEP BEEP

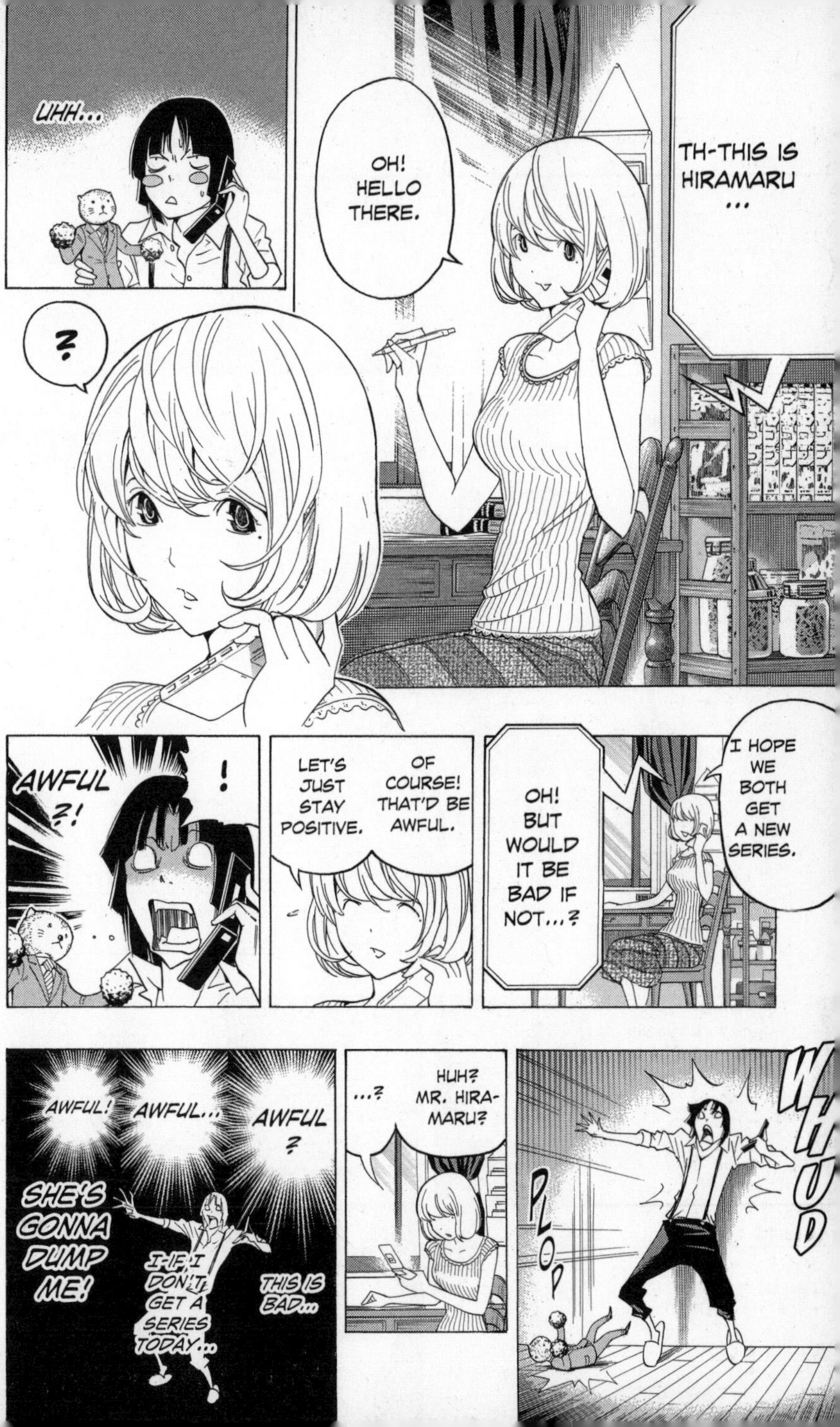
TH-THIS IS HIRAMARU ...
OH! HELLO THERE.
UHH...
?
I HOPE WE BOTH GET A NEW SERIES.
OH! BUT WOULD IT BE BAD IF NOT...?
OF COURSE! THAT'D BE AWFUL.
LET'S JUST STAY POSITIVE.
AWFUL ?!
!
WHUD
PLOP
HUH? MR. HIRA-MARU?
...?
AWFUL ?
AWFUL...
AWFUL!
THIS IS BAD...
I-IF I DON'T GET A SERIES TODAY...
SHE'S GONNA DUMP ME!

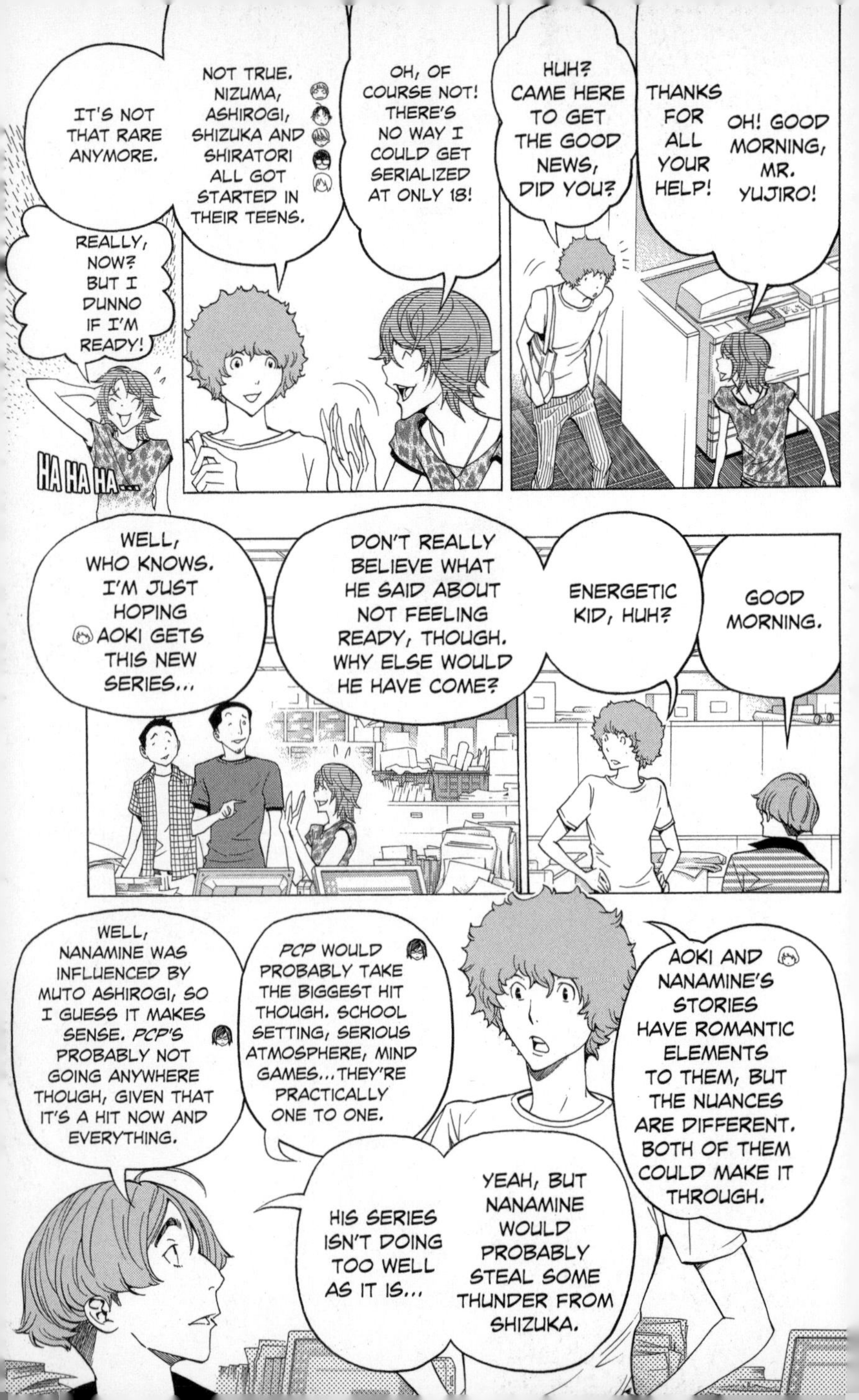
OH! GOOD MORNING, MR. YUJIRO!
THANKS FOR ALL YOUR HELP!
HUH? CAME HERE TO GET THE GOOD NEWS, DID YOU?
OH, OF COURSE NOT! THERE'S NO WAY I COULD GET SERIALIZED AT ONLY 18!
NOT TRUE. NIZUMA, ASHIROGI, SHIZUKA AND SHIRATORI ALL GOT STARTED IN THEIR TEENS.
IT'S NOT THAT RARE ANYMORE.
REALLY, NOW? BUT I DUNNO IF I'M READY!
HA HA HA...
GOOD MORNING.
ENERGETIC KID, HUH?
DON'T REALLY BELIEVE WHAT HE SAID ABOUT NOT FEELING READY, THOUGH. WHY ELSE WOULD HE HAVE COME?
WELL, WHO KNOWS. I'M JUST HOPING AOKI GETS THIS NEW SERIES...
AOKI AND NANAMINE'S STORIES HAVE ROMANTIC ELEMENTS TO THEM, BUT THE NUANCES ARE DIFFERENT. BOTH OF THEM COULD MAKE IT THROUGH.
YEAH, BUT NANAMINE WOULD PROBABLY STEAL SOME THUNDER FROM SHIZUKA.
HIS SERIES ISN'T DOING TOO WELL AS IT IS...
PCP WOULD PROBABLY TAKE THE BIGGEST HIT THOUGH. SCHOOL SETTING, SERIOUS ATMOSPHERE, MIND GAMES...THEY'RE PRACTICALLY ONE TO ONE.
WELL, NANAMINE WAS INFLUENCED BY MUTO ASHIROGI, SO I GUESS IT MAKES SENSE. *PCP*'S PROBABLY NOT GOING ANYWHERE THOUGH, GIVEN THAT IT'S A HIT NOW AND EVERYTHING.

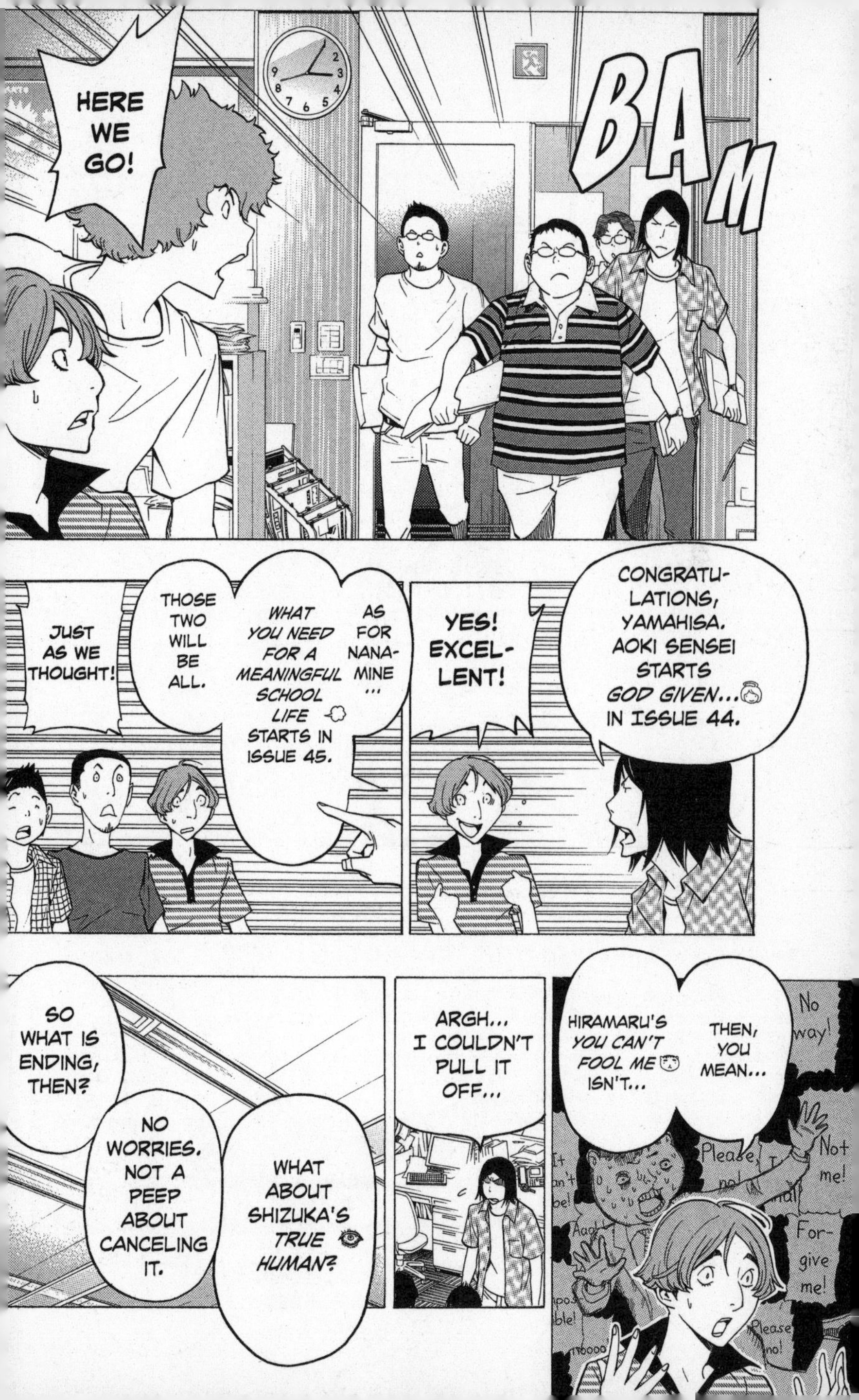
BAM
HERE WE GO!
CONGRATULATIONS, YAMAHISA. AOKI SENSEI STARTS *GOD GIVEN...* IN ISSUE 44.
YES! EXCELLENT!
AS FOR NANAMINE...
WHAT YOU NEED FOR A MEANINGFUL SCHOOL LIFE STARTS IN ISSUE 45.
THOSE TWO WILL BE ALL.
JUST AS WE THOUGHT!
No way!
THEN, YOU MEAN...
HIRAMARU'S *YOU CAN'T FOOL ME* ISN'T...
Not me!
Please, no!
Forgive me!
Please no!
ARGH... I COULDN'T PULL IT OFF...
WHAT ABOUT SHIZUKA'S *TRUE HUMAN?*
NO WORRIES. NOT A PEEP ABOUT CANCELING IT.
SO WHAT IS ENDING, THEN?

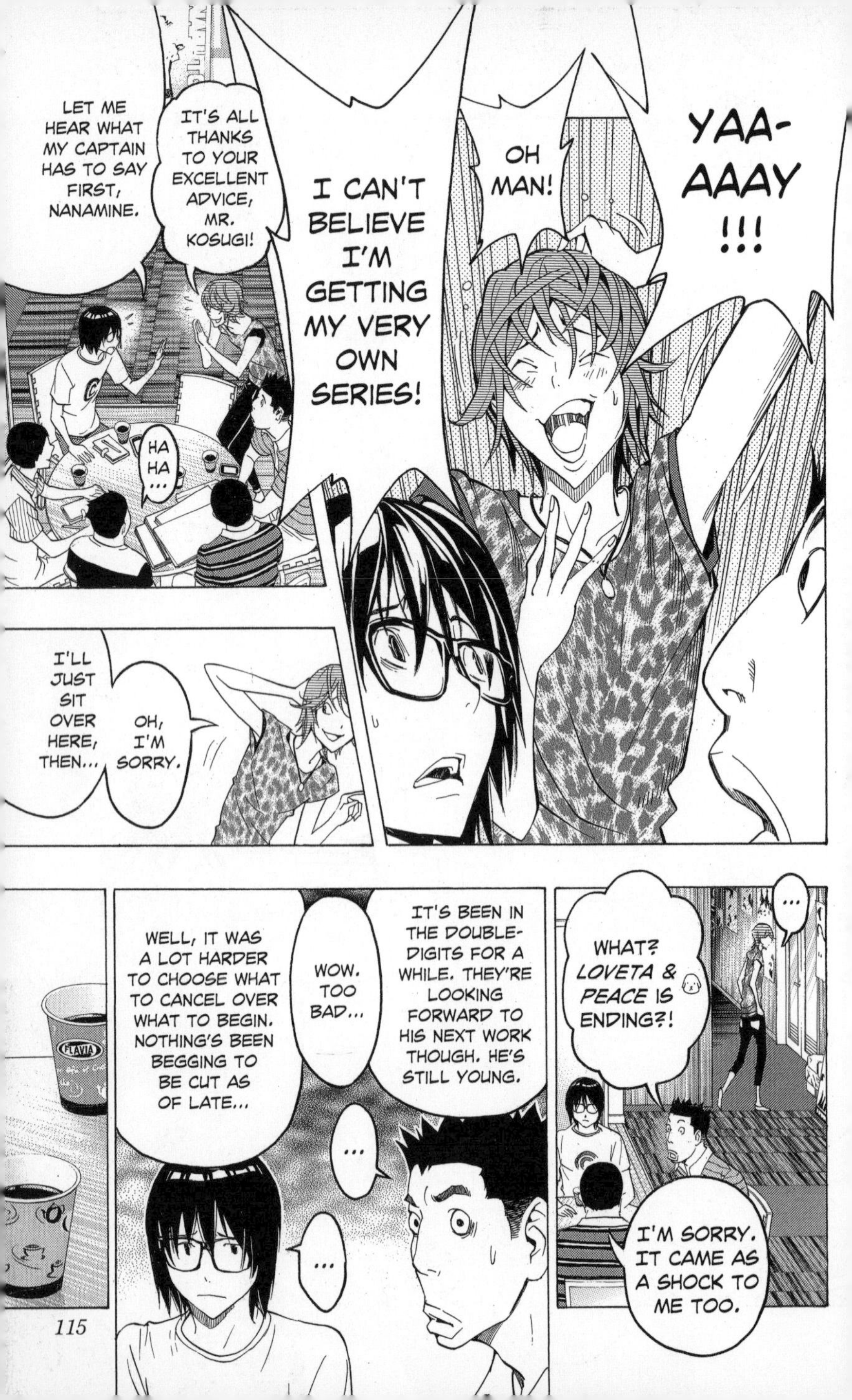
YAA-AAAY!!!
OH MAN!
I CAN'T BELIEVE I'M GETTING MY VERY OWN SERIES!
IT'S ALL THANKS TO YOUR EXCELLENT ADVICE, MR. KOSUGI!
LET ME HEAR WHAT MY CAPTAIN HAS TO SAY FIRST, NANAMINE.
HA HA...
OH, I'M SORRY.
I'LL JUST SIT OVER HERE, THEN...
...
WHAT? *LOVETA & PEACE* IS ENDING?!
I'M SORRY. IT CAME AS A SHOCK TO ME TOO.
IT'S BEEN IN THE DOUBLE-DIGITS FOR A WHILE. THEY'RE LOOKING FORWARD TO HIS NEXT WORK THOUGH. HE'S STILL YOUNG.
WOW. TOO BAD...
WELL, IT WAS A LOT HARDER TO CHOOSE WHAT TO CANCEL OVER WHAT TO BEGIN. NOTHING'S BEEN BEGGING TO BE CUT AS OF LATE...
...
...

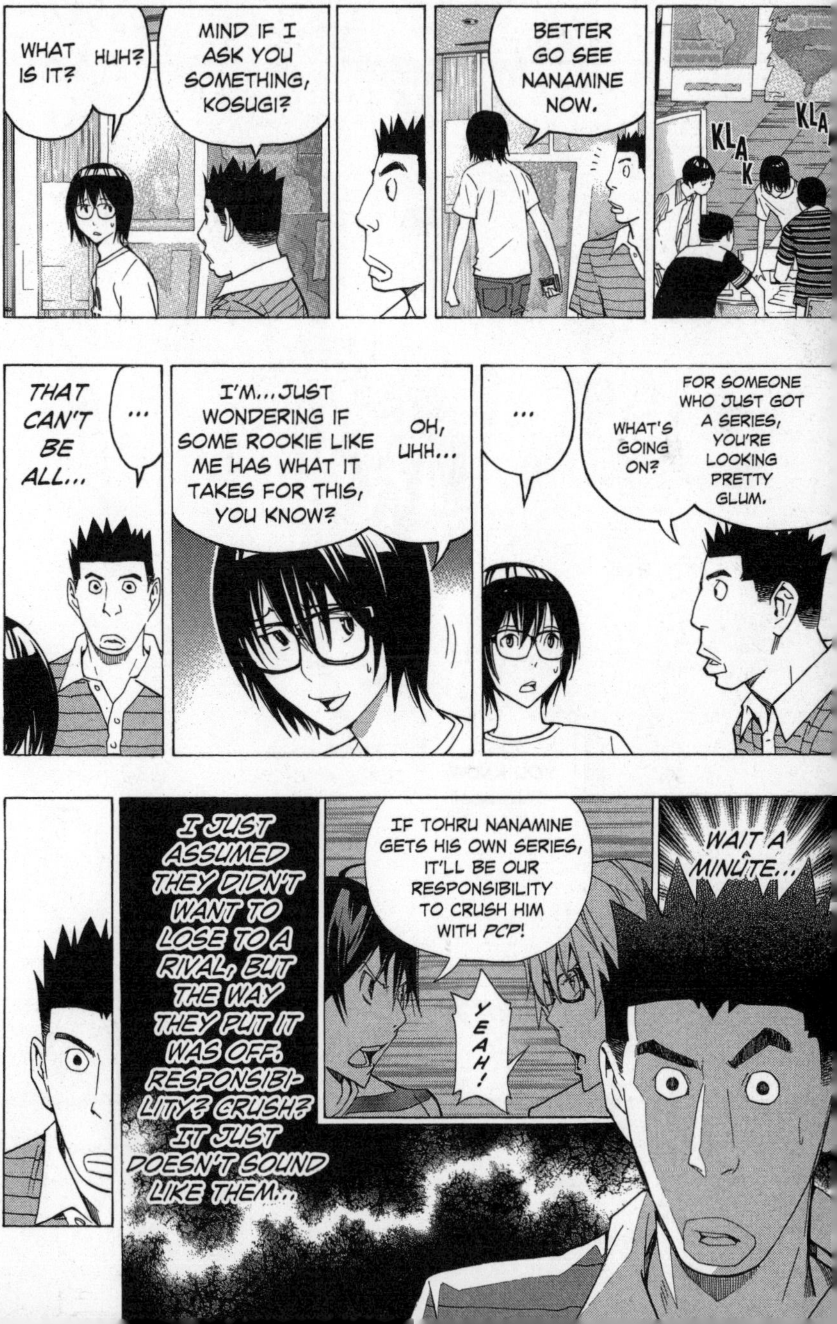
KLA
KLAK
BETTER GO SEE NANAMINE NOW.
MIND IF I ASK YOU SOMETHING, KOSUGI?
HUH?
WHAT IS IT?
FOR SOMEONE WHO JUST GOT A SERIES, YOU'RE LOOKING PRETTY GLUM.
WHAT'S GOING ON?
...
OH, UHH...
I'M...JUST WONDERING IF SOME ROOKIE LIKE ME HAS WHAT IT TAKES FOR THIS, YOU KNOW?
...
THAT CAN'T BE ALL...
WAIT A MINUTE...
IF TOHRU NANAMINE GETS HIS OWN SERIES, IT'LL BE OUR RESPONSIBILITY TO CRUSH HIM WITH PCP!
YEAH!
I JUST ASSUMED THEY DIDN'T WANT TO LOSE TO A RIVAL, BUT THE WAY THEY PUT IT WAS OFF. RESPONSIBILITY? CRUSH? IT JUST DOESN'T SOUND LIKE THEM...

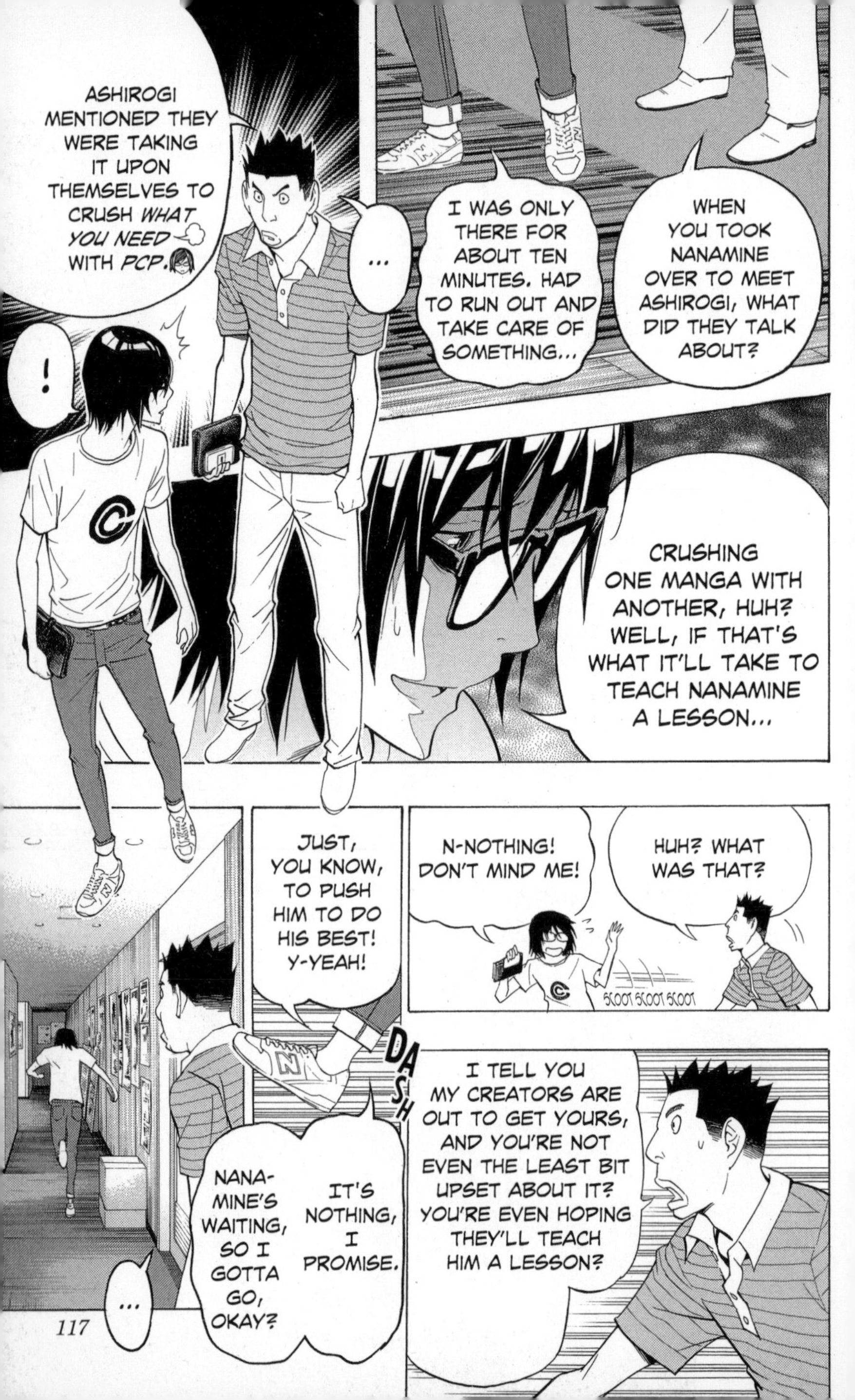
WHEN YOU TOOK NANAMINE OVER TO MEET ASHIROGI, WHAT DID THEY TALK ABOUT?
I WAS ONLY THERE FOR ABOUT TEN MINUTES. HAD TO RUN OUT AND TAKE CARE OF SOMETHING...
CRUSHING ONE MANGA WITH ANOTHER, HUH? WELL, IF THAT'S WHAT IT'LL TAKE TO TEACH NANAMINE A LESSON...
...
ASHIROGI MENTIONED THEY WERE TAKING IT UPON THEMSELVES TO CRUSH *WHAT YOU NEED* WITH *PCP*.
!
HUH? WHAT WAS THAT?
N-NOTHING! DON'T MIND ME!
SCOOT SCOOT SCOOT
JUST, YOU KNOW, TO PUSH HIM TO DO HIS BEST! Y-YEAH!
I TELL YOU MY CREATORS ARE OUT TO GET YOURS, AND YOU'RE NOT EVEN THE LEAST BIT UPSET ABOUT IT? YOU'RE EVEN HOPING THEY'LL TEACH HIM A LESSON?
DASH
IT'S NOTHING, I PROMISE.
NANA-MINE'S WAITING, SO I GOTTA GO, OKAY?
...

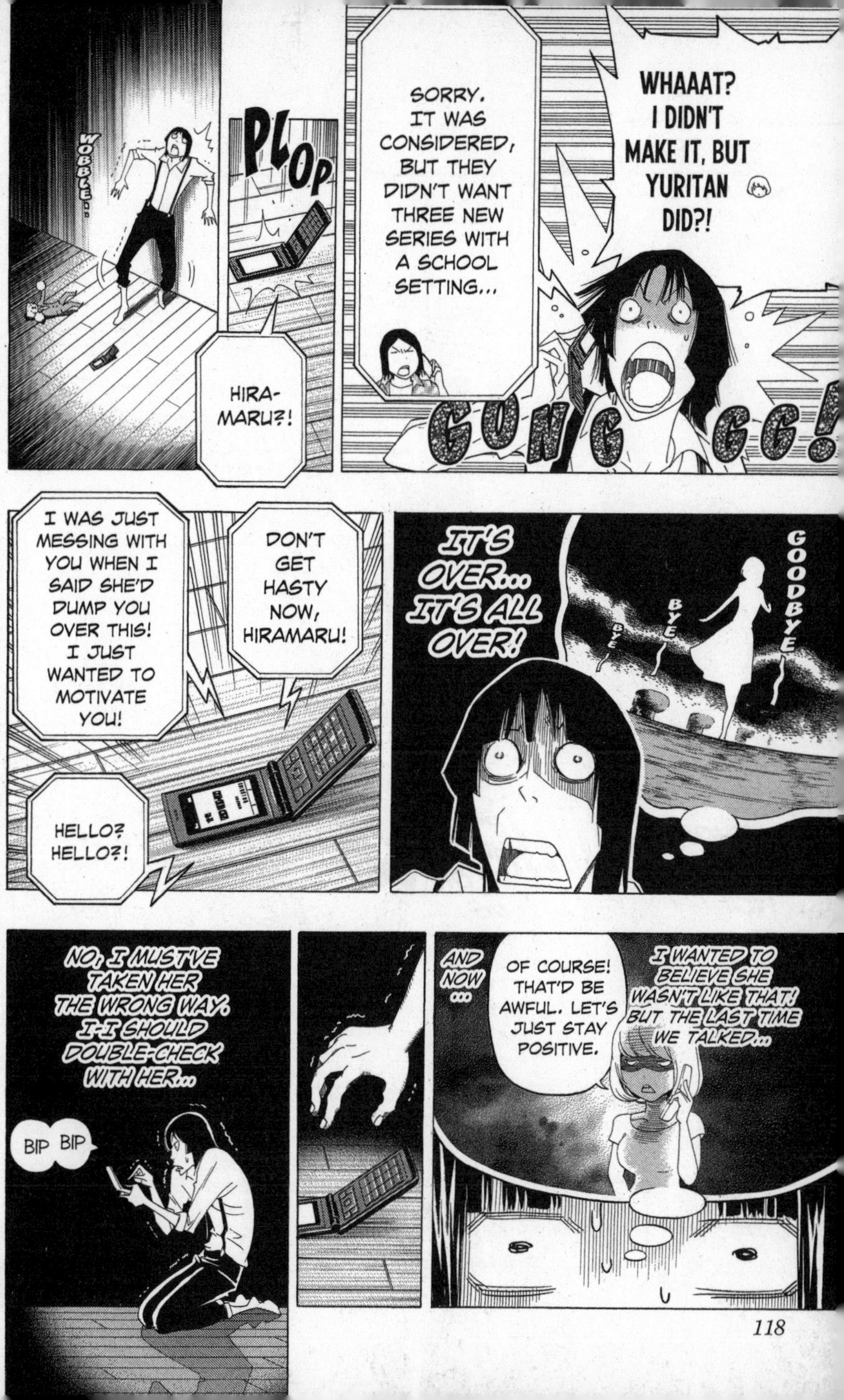
WHAAAT? I DIDN'T MAKE IT, BUT YURITAN DID?!
SORRY. IT WAS CONSIDERED, BUT THEY DIDN'T WANT THREE NEW SERIES WITH A SCHOOL SETTING...
GONGGG!
PLOP
HIRA-MARU?!
WOBBLE...
GOODBYE
BYE
BYE
IT'S OVER... IT'S ALL OVER!
DON'T GET HASTY NOW, HIRAMARU!
I WAS JUST MESSING WITH YOU WHEN I SAID SHE'D DUMP YOU OVER THIS! I JUST WANTED TO MOTIVATE YOU!
HELLO? HELLO?!
I WANTED TO BELIEVE SHE WASN'T LIKE THAT! BUT THE LAST TIME WE TALKED...
OF COURSE! THAT'D BE AWFUL. LET'S JUST STAY POSITIVE.
AND NOW...
NO, I MUST'VE TAKEN HER THE WRONG WAY. I-I SHOULD DOUBLE-CHECK WITH HER...
BIP BIP

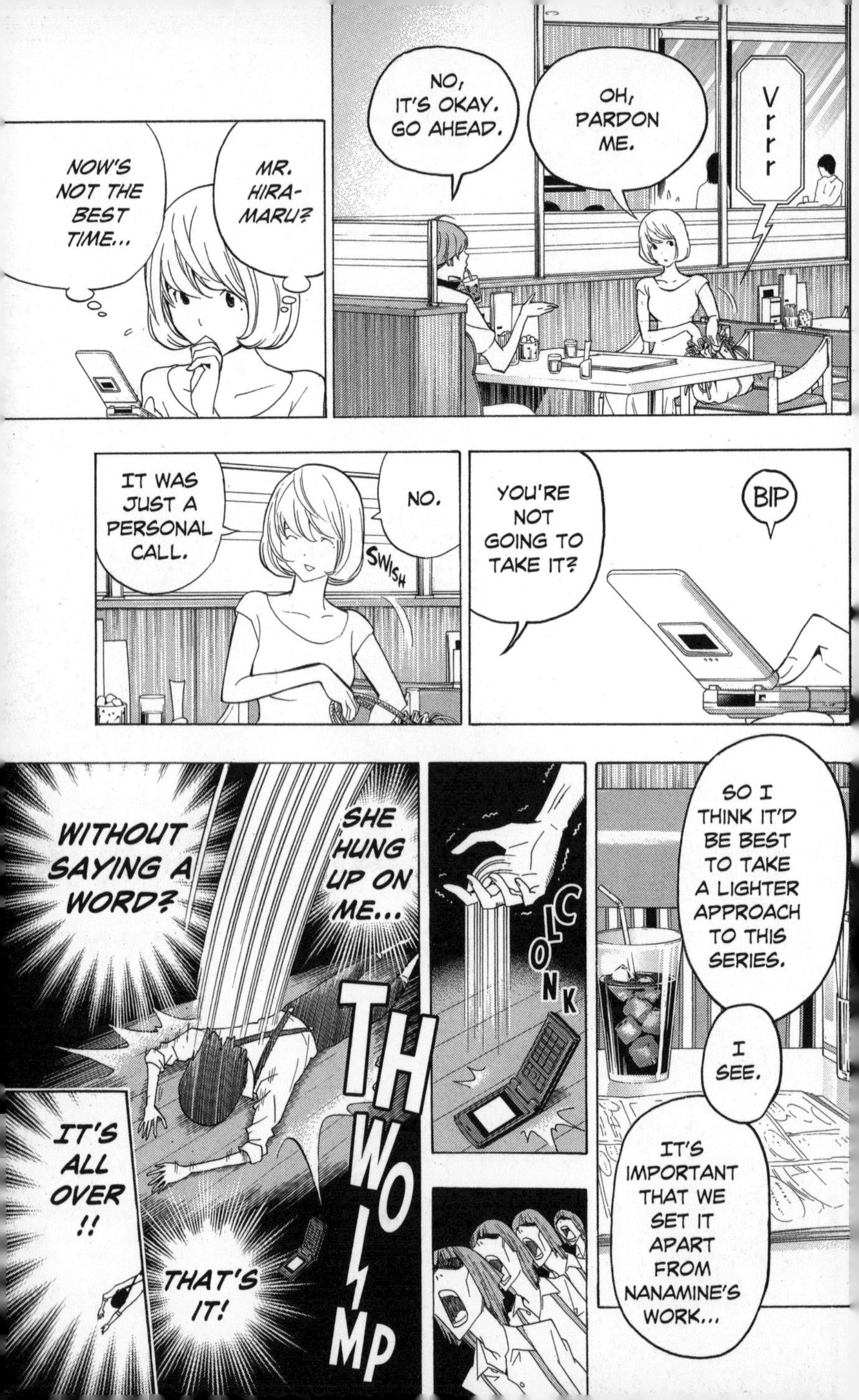
Vrrr
OH, PARDON ME.
NO, IT'S OKAY. GO AHEAD.
MR. HIRA-MARU?
NOW'S NOT THE BEST TIME...
BIP
YOU'RE NOT GOING TO TAKE IT?
NO.
SWISH
IT WAS JUST A PERSONAL CALL.
SO I THINK IT'D BE BEST TO TAKE A LIGHTER APPROACH TO THIS SERIES.
I SEE.
IT'S IMPORTANT THAT WE SET IT APART FROM NANAMINE'S WORK...
CLONK
SHE HUNG UP ON ME...
WITHOUT SAYING A WORD?
THWOMP
IT'S ALL OVER !!
THAT'S IT!

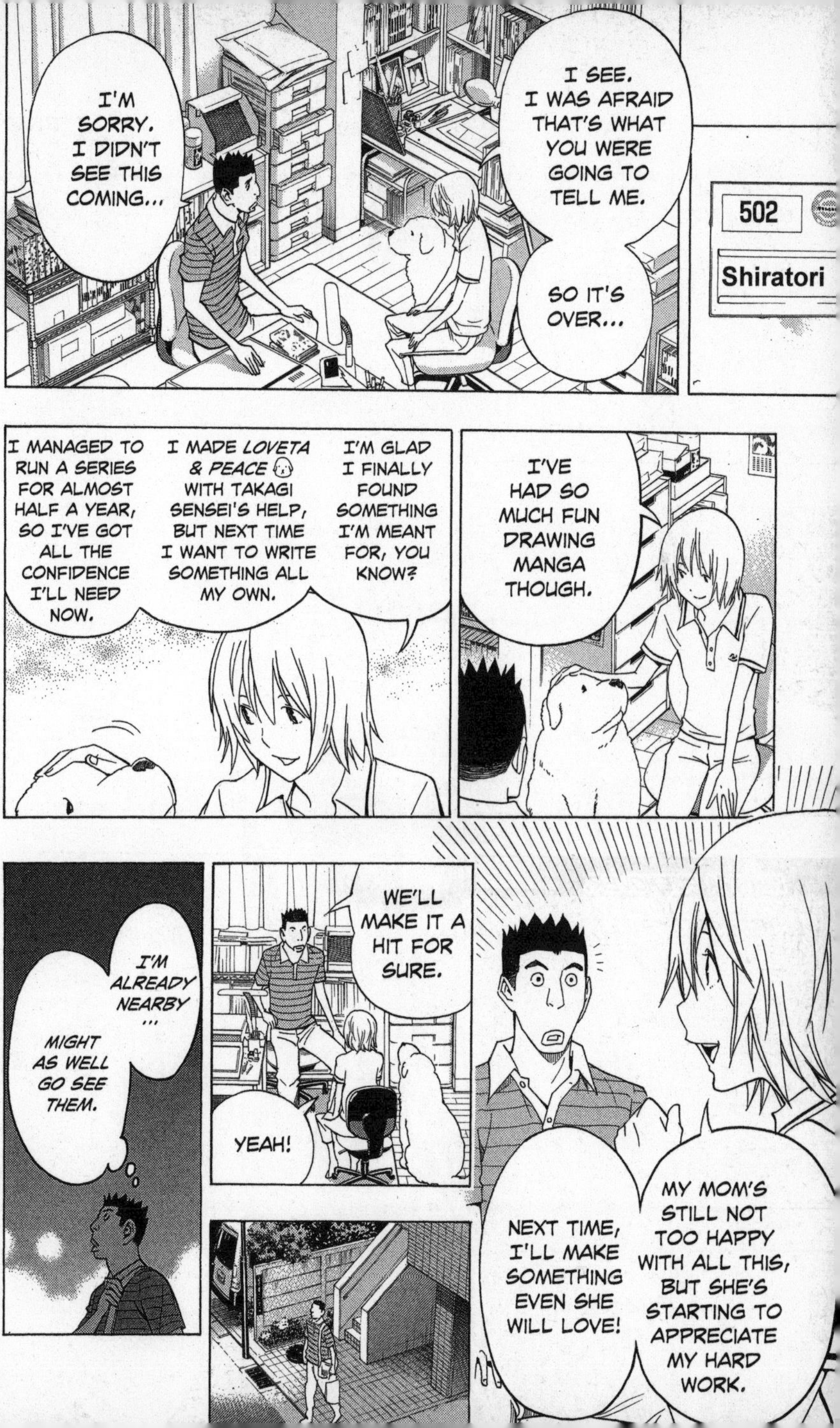
502
Shiratori
I SEE. I WAS AFRAID THAT'S WHAT YOU WERE GOING TO TELL ME.
SO IT'S OVER...
I'M SORRY. I DIDN'T SEE THIS COMING...
I'VE HAD SO MUCH FUN DRAWING MANGA THOUGH.
I MANAGED TO RUN A SERIES FOR ALMOST HALF A YEAR, SO I'VE GOT ALL THE CONFIDENCE I'LL NEED NOW. I MADE *LOVETA & PEACE* WITH TAKAGI SENSEI'S HELP, BUT NEXT TIME I WANT TO WRITE SOMETHING ALL MY OWN. I'M GLAD I FINALLY FOUND SOMETHING I'M MEANT FOR, YOU KNOW?
MY MOM'S STILL NOT TOO HAPPY WITH ALL THIS, BUT SHE'S STARTING TO APPRECIATE MY HARD WORK.
NEXT TIME, I'LL MAKE SOMETHING EVEN SHE WILL LOVE!
WE'LL MAKE IT A HIT FOR SURE.
YEAH!
I'M ALREADY NEARBY...
MIGHT AS WELL GO SEE THEM.

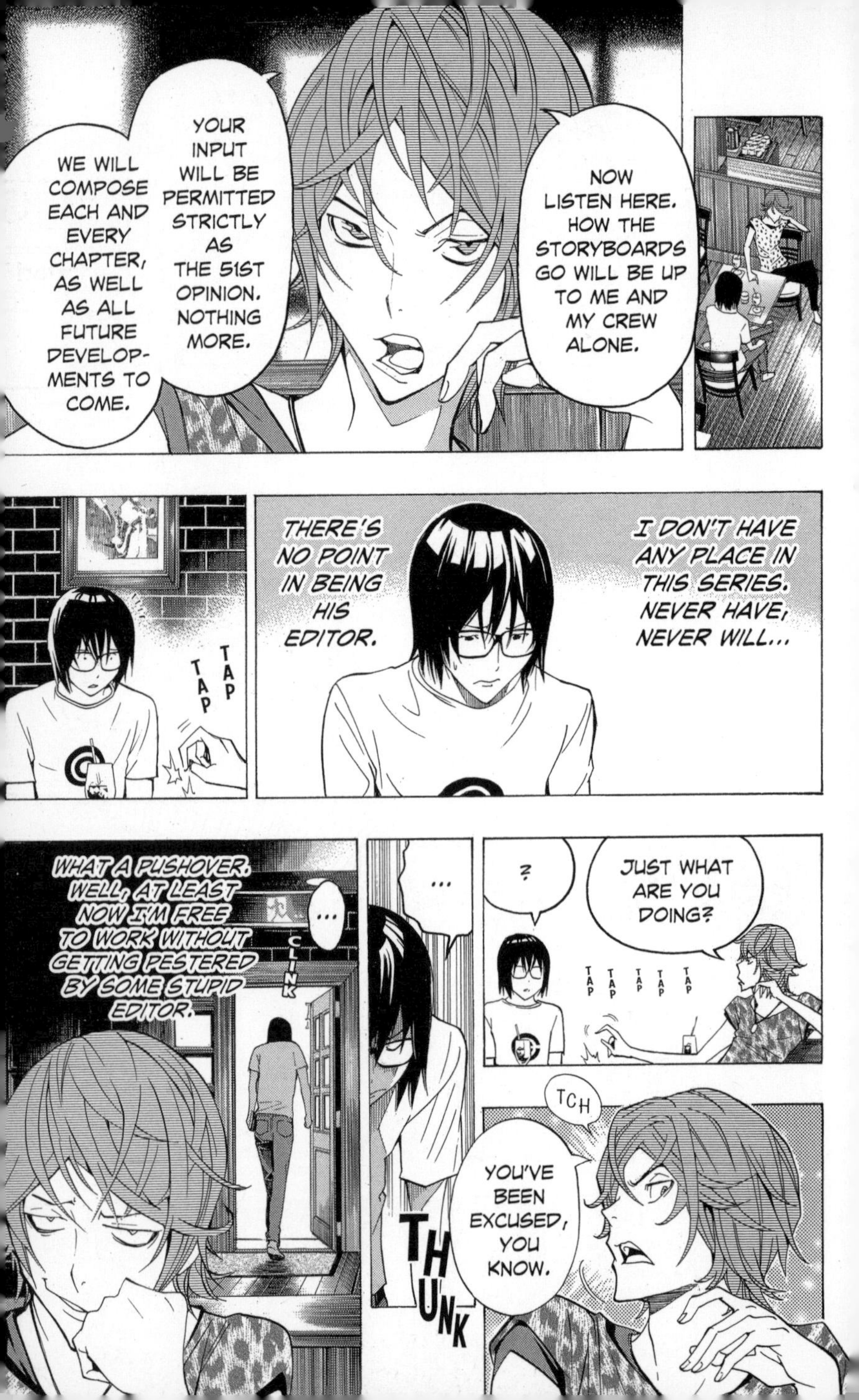
NOW LISTEN HERE. HOW THE STORYBOARDS GO WILL BE UP TO ME AND MY CREW ALONE.
YOUR INPUT WILL BE PERMITTED STRICTLY AS THE 51ST OPINION. NOTHING MORE.
WE WILL COMPOSE EACH AND EVERY CHAPTER, AS WELL AS ALL FUTURE DEVELOPMENTS TO COME.
I DON'T HAVE ANY PLACE IN THIS SERIES. NEVER HAVE, NEVER WILL...
THERE'S NO POINT IN BEING HIS EDITOR.
TAP TAP
JUST WHAT ARE YOU DOING?
?
TAP TAP TAP TAP TAP
TCH
YOU'VE BEEN EXCUSED, YOU KNOW.
...
THUNK
...
CLINK
WHAT A PUSHOVER. WELL, AT LEAST NOW I'M FREE TO WORK WITHOUT GETTING PESTERED BY SOME STUPID EDITOR.

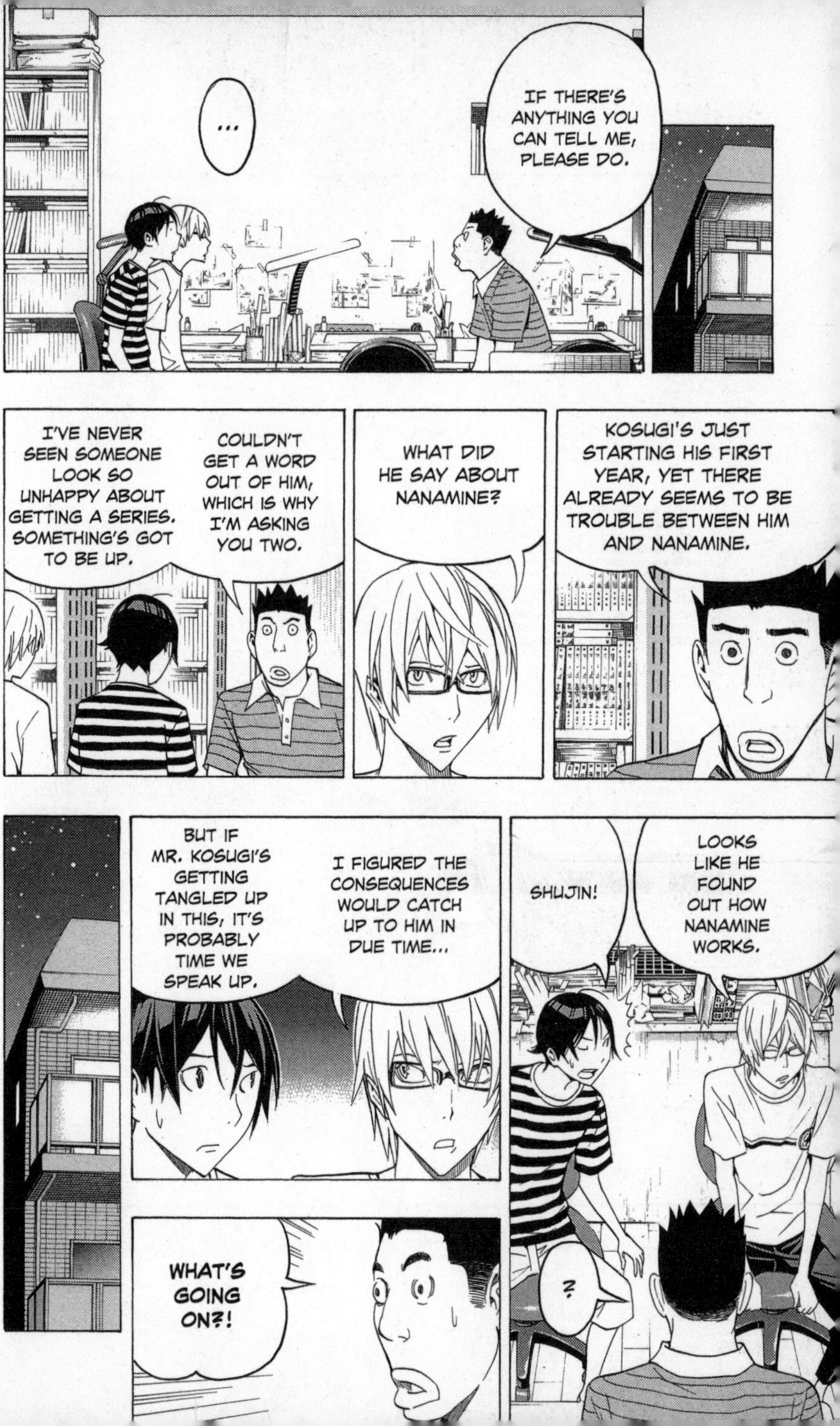
IF THERE'S ANYTHING YOU CAN TELL ME, PLEASE DO.
...
KOSUGI'S JUST STARTING HIS FIRST YEAR, YET THERE ALREADY SEEMS TO BE TROUBLE BETWEEN HIM AND NANAMINE.
WHAT DID HE SAY ABOUT NANAMINE?
COULDN'T GET A WORD OUT OF HIM, WHICH IS WHY I'M ASKING YOU TWO.
I'VE NEVER SEEN SOMEONE LOOK SO UNHAPPY ABOUT GETTING A SERIES. SOMETHING'S GOT TO BE UP.
LOOKS LIKE HE FOUND OUT HOW NANAMINE WORKS.
SHUJIN!
?
I FIGURED THE CONSEQUENCES WOULD CATCH UP TO HIM IN DUE TIME...
BUT IF MR. KOSUGI'S GETTING TANGLED UP IN THIS, IT'S PROBABLY TIME WE SPEAK UP.
WHAT'S GOING ON?!

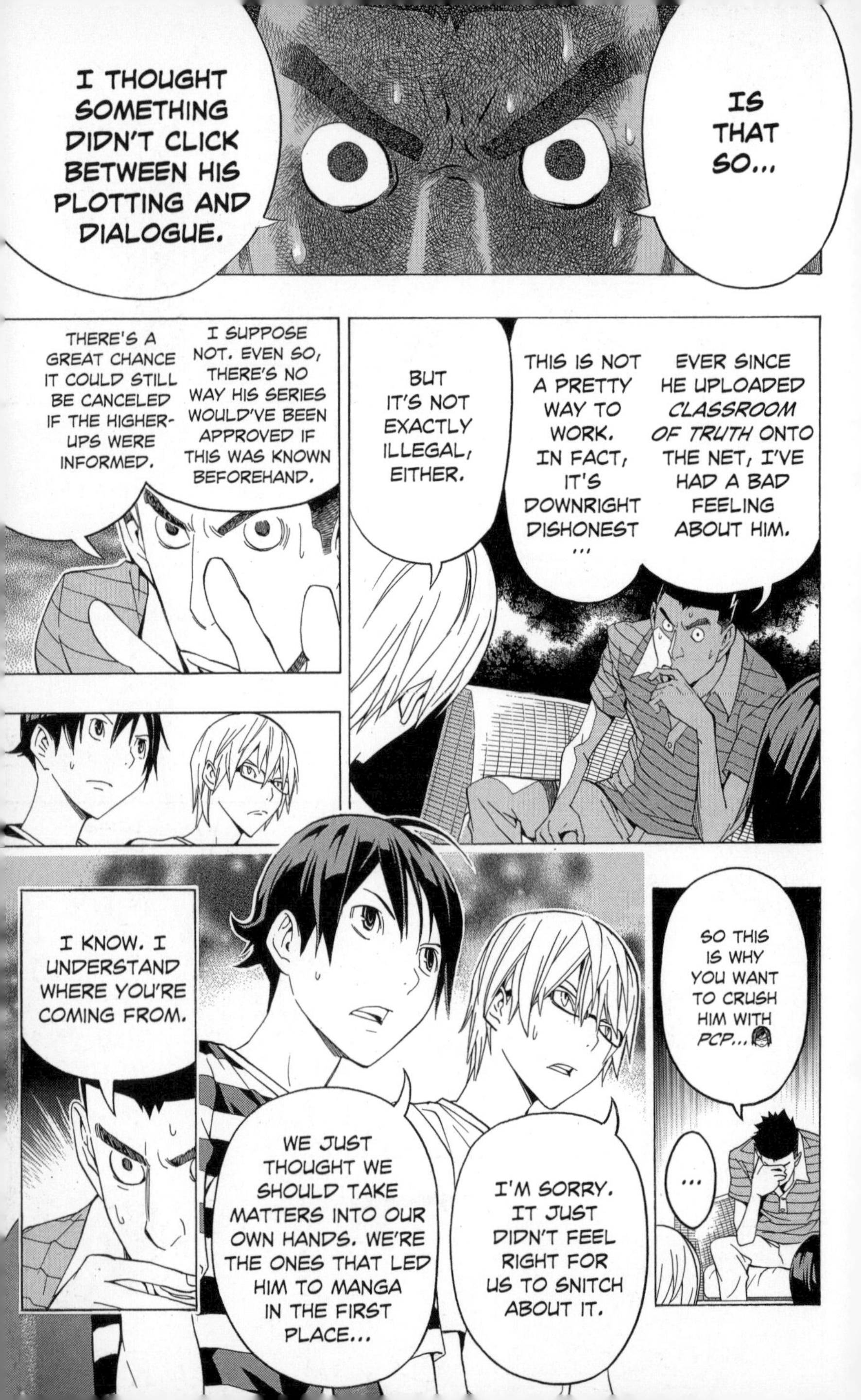
IS THAT SO...
I THOUGHT SOMETHING DIDN'T CLICK BETWEEN HIS PLOTTING AND DIALOGUE.
EVER SINCE HE UPLOADED *CLASSROOM OF TRUTH* ONTO THE NET, I'VE HAD A BAD FEELING ABOUT HIM.
THIS IS NOT A PRETTY WAY TO WORK. IN FACT, IT'S DOWNRIGHT DISHONEST...
BUT IT'S NOT EXACTLY ILLEGAL, EITHER.
I SUPPOSE NOT. EVEN SO, THERE'S NO WAY HIS SERIES WOULD'VE BEEN APPROVED IF THIS WAS KNOWN BEFOREHAND.
THERE'S A GREAT CHANCE IT COULD STILL BE CANCELED IF THE HIGHER-UPS WERE INFORMED.
SO THIS IS WHY YOU WANT TO CRUSH HIM WITH *PCP*...
...
I'M SORRY. IT JUST DIDN'T FEEL RIGHT FOR US TO SNITCH ABOUT IT.
WE JUST THOUGHT WE SHOULD TAKE MATTERS INTO OUR OWN HANDS. WE'RE THE ONES THAT LED HIM TO MANGA IN THE FIRST PLACE...
I KNOW. I UNDERSTAND WHERE YOU'RE COMING FROM.

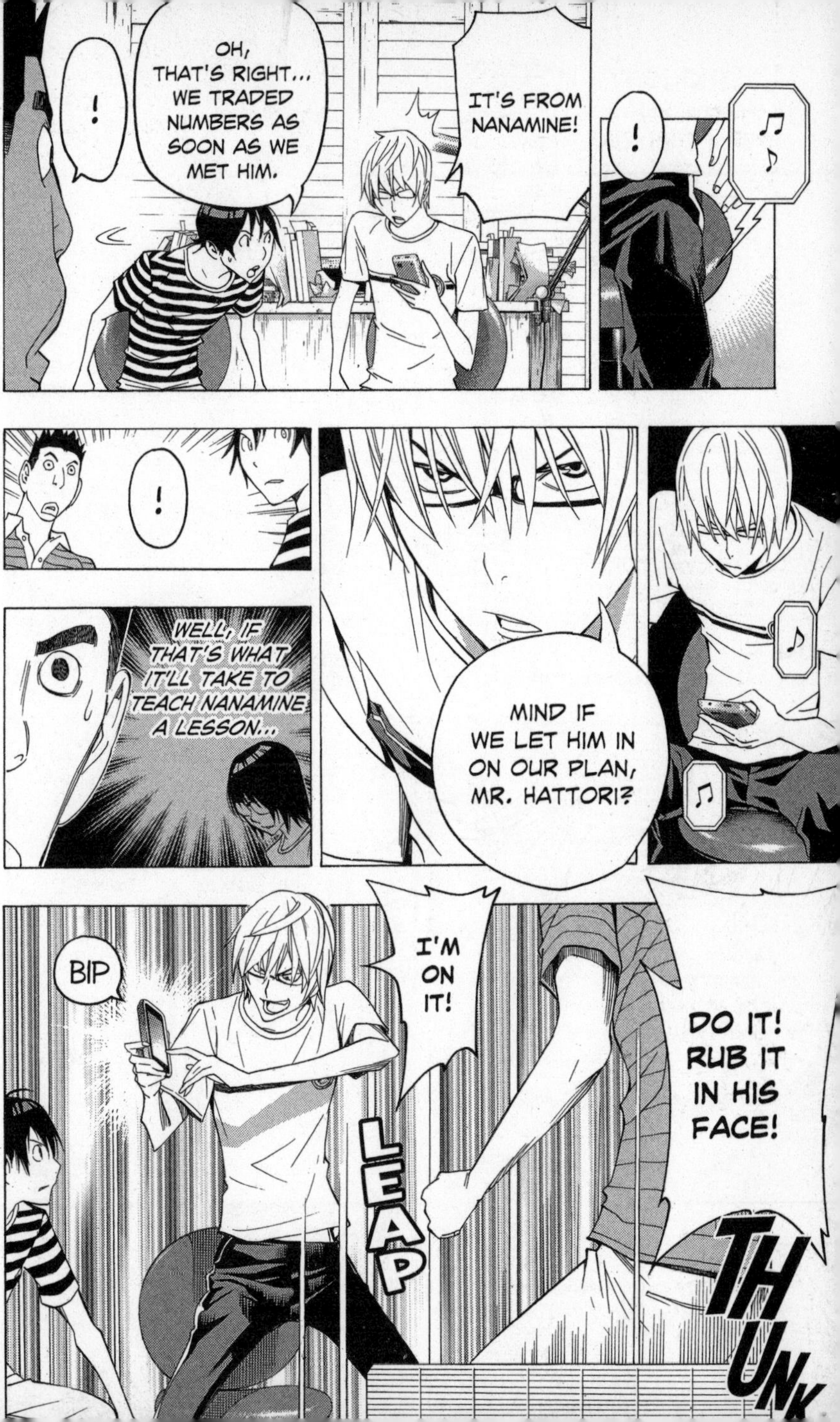
♫ ♪
!
IT'S FROM NANAMINE!
OH, THAT'S RIGHT... WE TRADED NUMBERS AS SOON AS WE MET HIM.
!
♪
♫
MIND IF WE LET HIM IN ON OUR PLAN, MR. HATTORI?
!
WELL, IF THAT'S WHAT IT'LL TAKE TO TEACH NANAMINE A LESSON...
DO IT! RUB IT IN HIS FACE!
THUNK
I'M ON IT!
LEAP
BIP

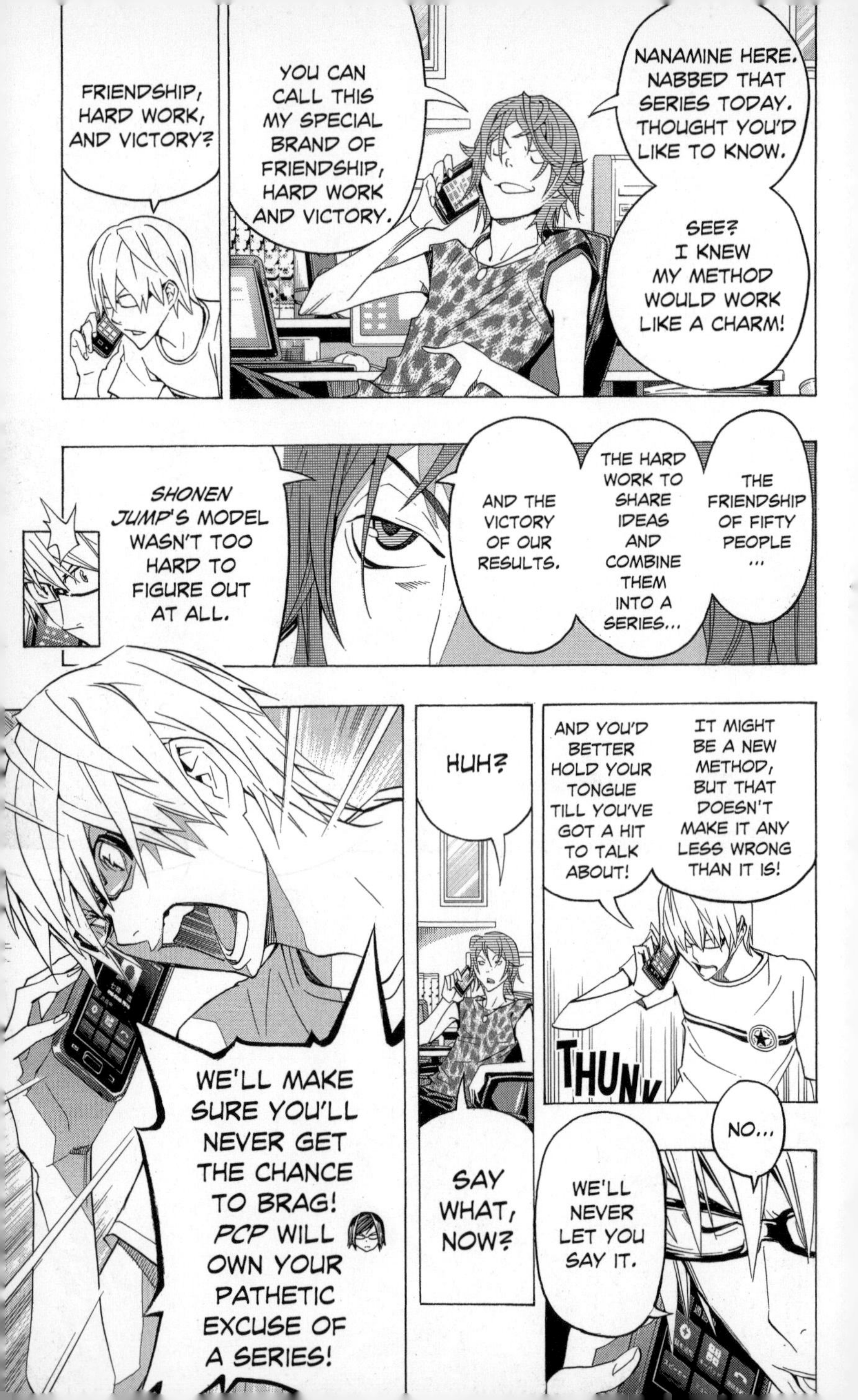
NANAMINE HERE. NABBED THAT SERIES TODAY. THOUGHT YOU'D LIKE TO KNOW.
SEE? I KNEW MY METHOD WOULD WORK LIKE A CHARM!
YOU CAN CALL THIS MY SPECIAL BRAND OF FRIENDSHIP, HARD WORK AND VICTORY.
FRIENDSHIP, HARD WORK, AND VICTORY?
THE FRIENDSHIP OF FIFTY PEOPLE...
THE HARD WORK TO SHARE IDEAS AND COMBINE THEM INTO A SERIES...
AND THE VICTORY OF OUR RESULTS.
SHONEN JUMP'S MODEL WASN'T TOO HARD TO FIGURE OUT AT ALL.
IT MIGHT BE A NEW METHOD, BUT THAT DOESN'T MAKE IT ANY LESS WRONG THAN IT IS!
AND YOU'D BETTER HOLD YOUR TONGUE TILL YOU'VE GOT A HIT TO TALK ABOUT!
THUNK
NO...
WE'LL NEVER LET YOU SAY IT.
HUH?
SAY WHAT, NOW?
WE'LL MAKE SURE YOU'LL NEVER GET THE CHANCE TO BRAG! *PCP* WILL OWN YOUR PATHETIC EXCUSE OF A SERIES!

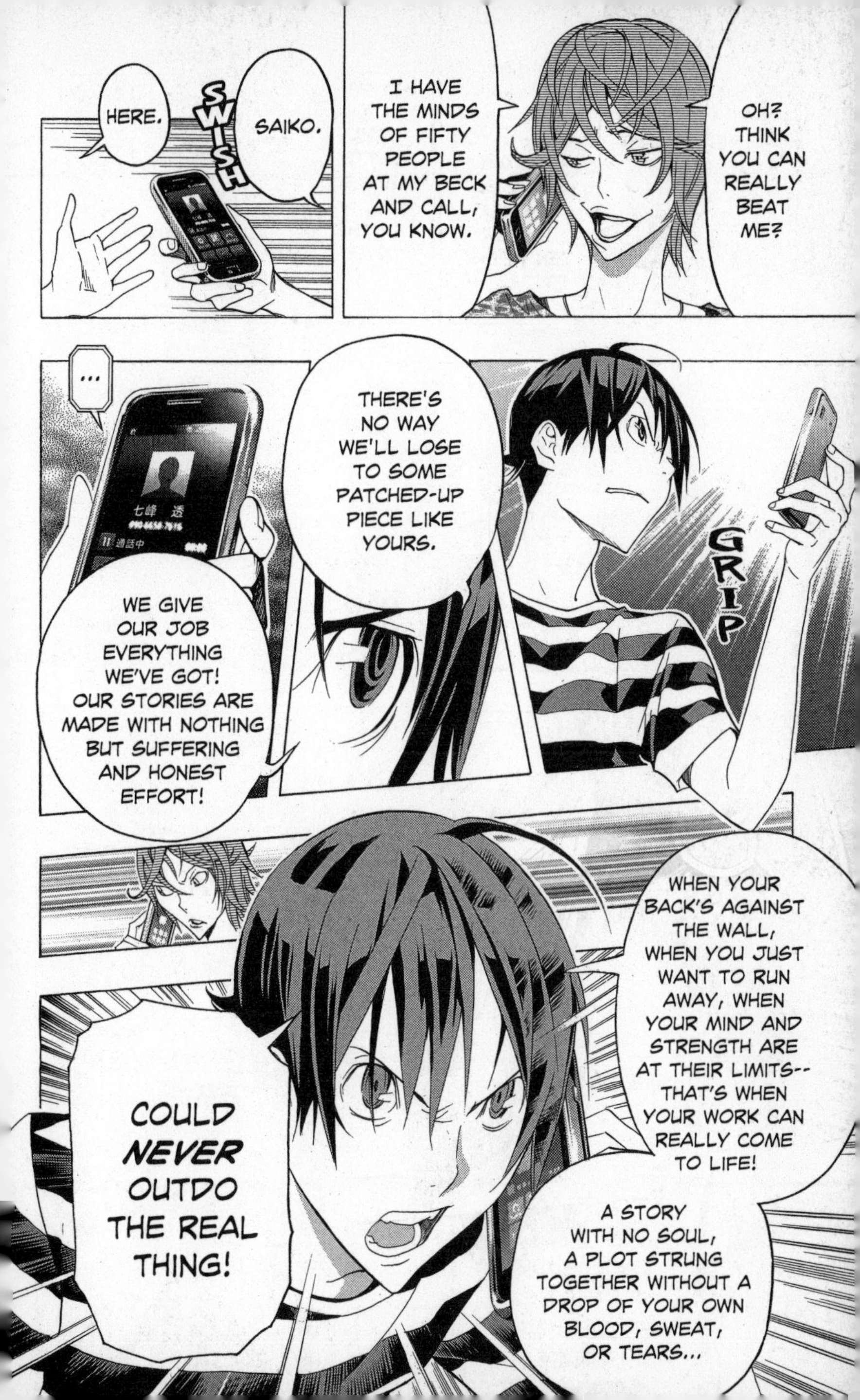
OH? THINK YOU CAN REALLY BEAT ME?
I HAVE THE MINDS OF FIFTY PEOPLE AT MY BECK AND CALL, YOU KNOW.
SAIKO.
SWISH
HERE.
GRIP
THERE'S NO WAY WE'LL LOSE TO SOME PATCHED-UP PIECE LIKE YOURS.
...
WE GIVE OUR JOB EVERYTHING WE'VE GOT! OUR STORIES ARE MADE WITH NOTHING BUT SUFFERING AND HONEST EFFORT!
WHEN YOUR BACK'S AGAINST THE WALL, WHEN YOU JUST WANT TO RUN AWAY, WHEN YOUR MIND AND STRENGTH ARE AT THEIR LIMITS--THAT'S WHEN YOUR WORK CAN REALLY COME TO LIFE!
A STORY WITH NO SOUL, A PLOT STRUNG TOGETHER WITHOUT A DROP OF YOUR OWN BLOOD, SWEAT, OR TEARS...
COULD *NEVER* OUTDO THE REAL THING!

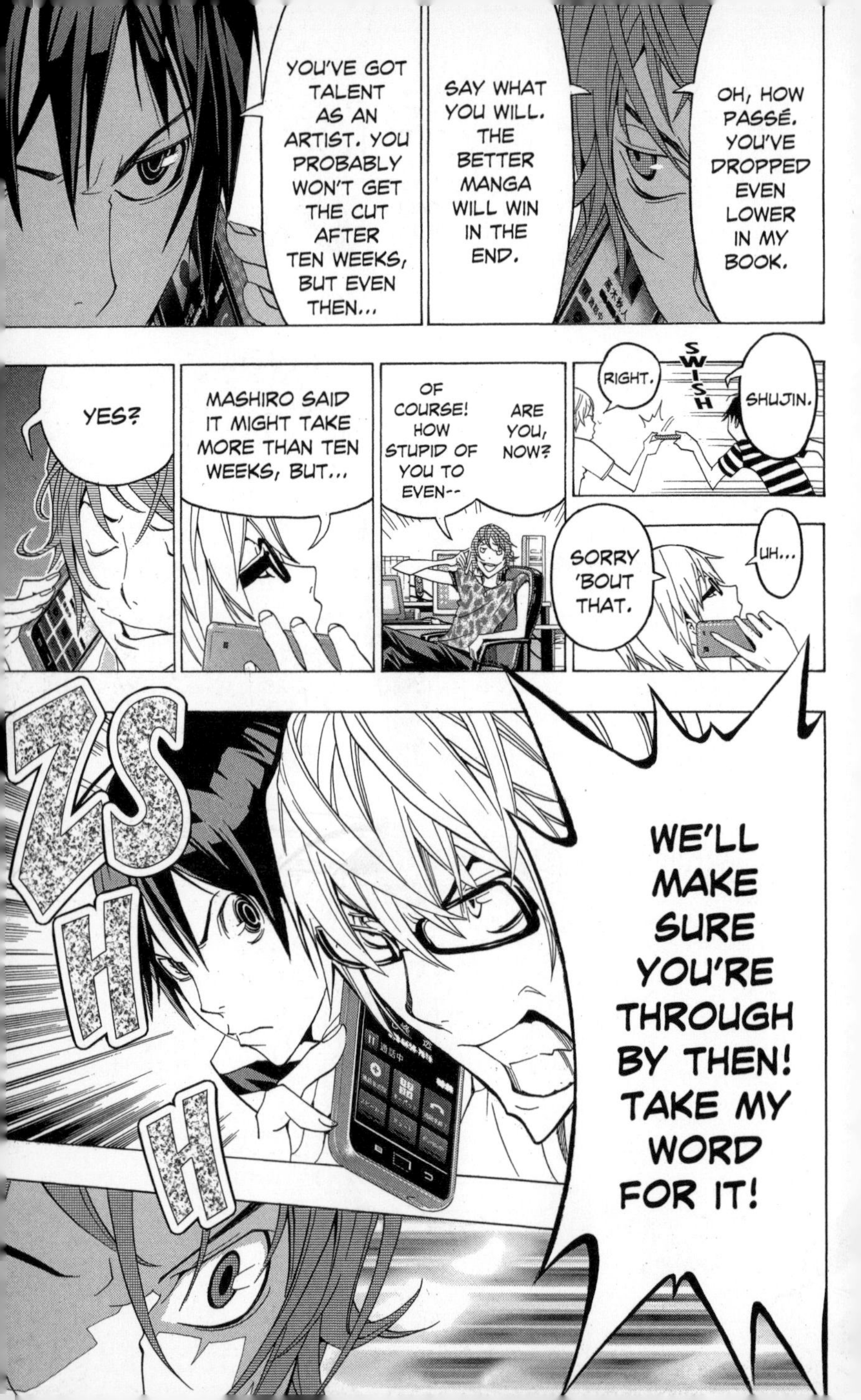
OH, HOW PASSÉ. YOU'VE DROPPED EVEN LOWER IN MY BOOK.
SAY WHAT YOU WILL. THE BETTER MANGA WILL WIN IN THE END.
YOU'VE GOT TALENT AS AN ARTIST. YOU PROBABLY WON'T GET THE CUT AFTER TEN WEEKS, BUT EVEN THEN...
SHUJIN.
SWISH
RIGHT.
UH...
SORRY 'BOUT THAT.
ARE YOU, NOW?
OF COURSE! HOW STUPID OF YOU TO EVEN--
MASHIRO SAID IT MIGHT TAKE MORE THAN TEN WEEKS, BUT...
YES?
WE'LL MAKE SURE YOU'RE THROUGH BY THEN! TAKE MY WORD FOR IT!
ZSSHH

OHBA'S STORYBOARD

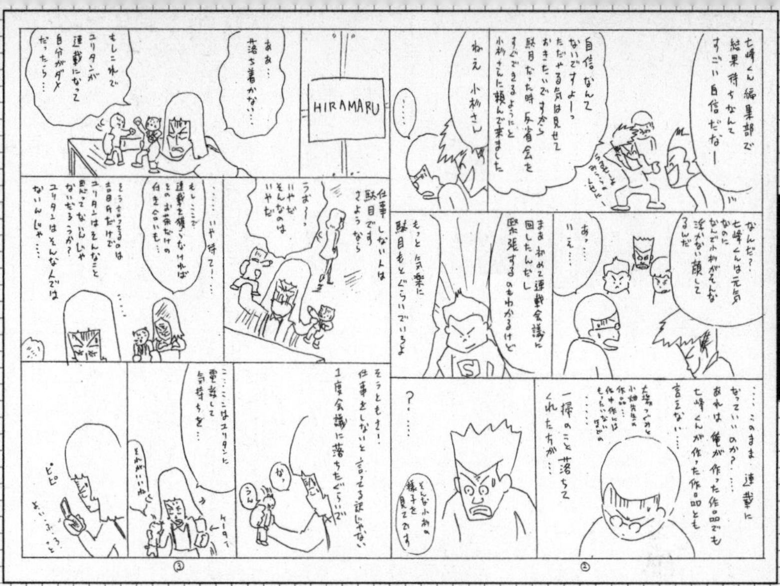

七峰くん編集部で結果待ちなんてすごい自信だなー
自信なんてないですよー。ただやる気は見せておきたいですから駄目だった時反省会をすぐできるようにと小杉さんに頼んで来ました
ねえ 小杉さん
……
なんだ？七峰くんは元気なのになんで小杉がそんな浮かない顔してるんだ
あっ…… いえ……
まぁ初めて連載会議に回したんだし緊張するのもわかるけど
もっと気楽に駄目もとぐらいでいろよ
……このまま連載になっていいのか？……おれは俺が作った作品でも七峰くんが作った作品とも言えない……
一掃のこと落ちてくれた方が……
？……
HIRAMARU
あぁ…落ち着かない……
もしこれでユリタンが連載になって自分がダメだったら……
仕事しないんは駄目です さようなら
うぅ～！いやだ そんなのはいやだ
……いや待て！……
もしここで連載を獲らなければそのお茶だけの付き合いも……
そうともさ！仕事をしないと言ってる訳じゃない 1度会議に落ちたぐらいで
な、
うん
ここ…ここはユリタンに電話して気持ちを……
ピピ
②
③

OBATA'S STORYBOARD

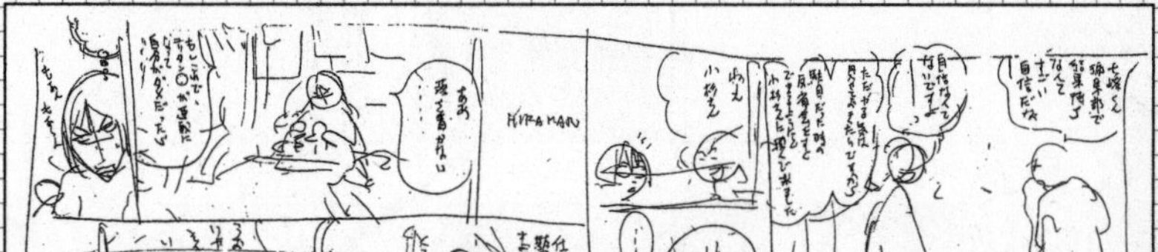

HIRAKAN

COMPLETE!

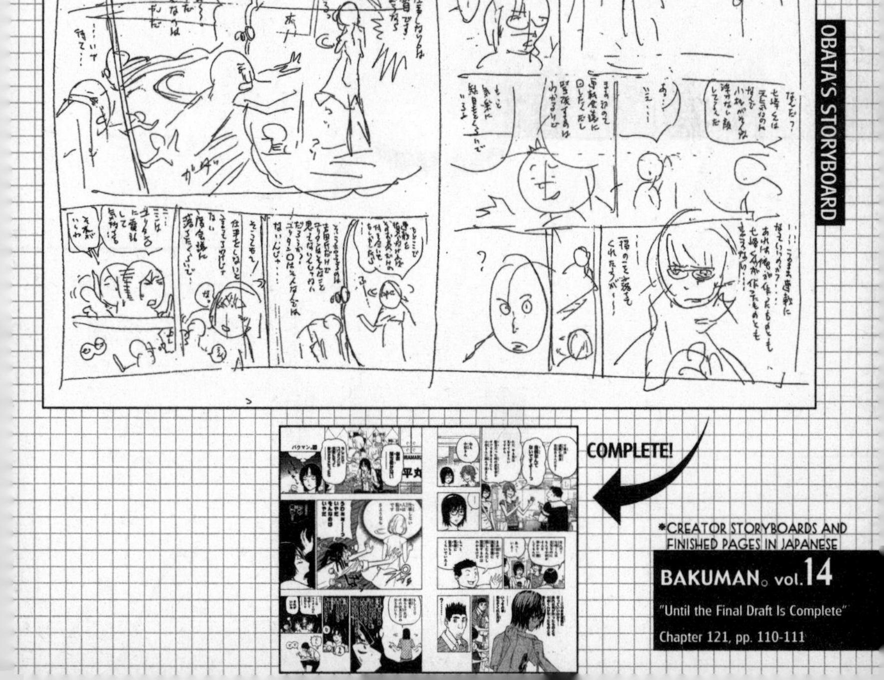

*CREATOR STORYBOARDS AND FINISHED PAGES IN JAPANESE

BAKUMAN。 vol.14

"Until the Final Draft Is Complete"

Chapter 121, pp. 110-111

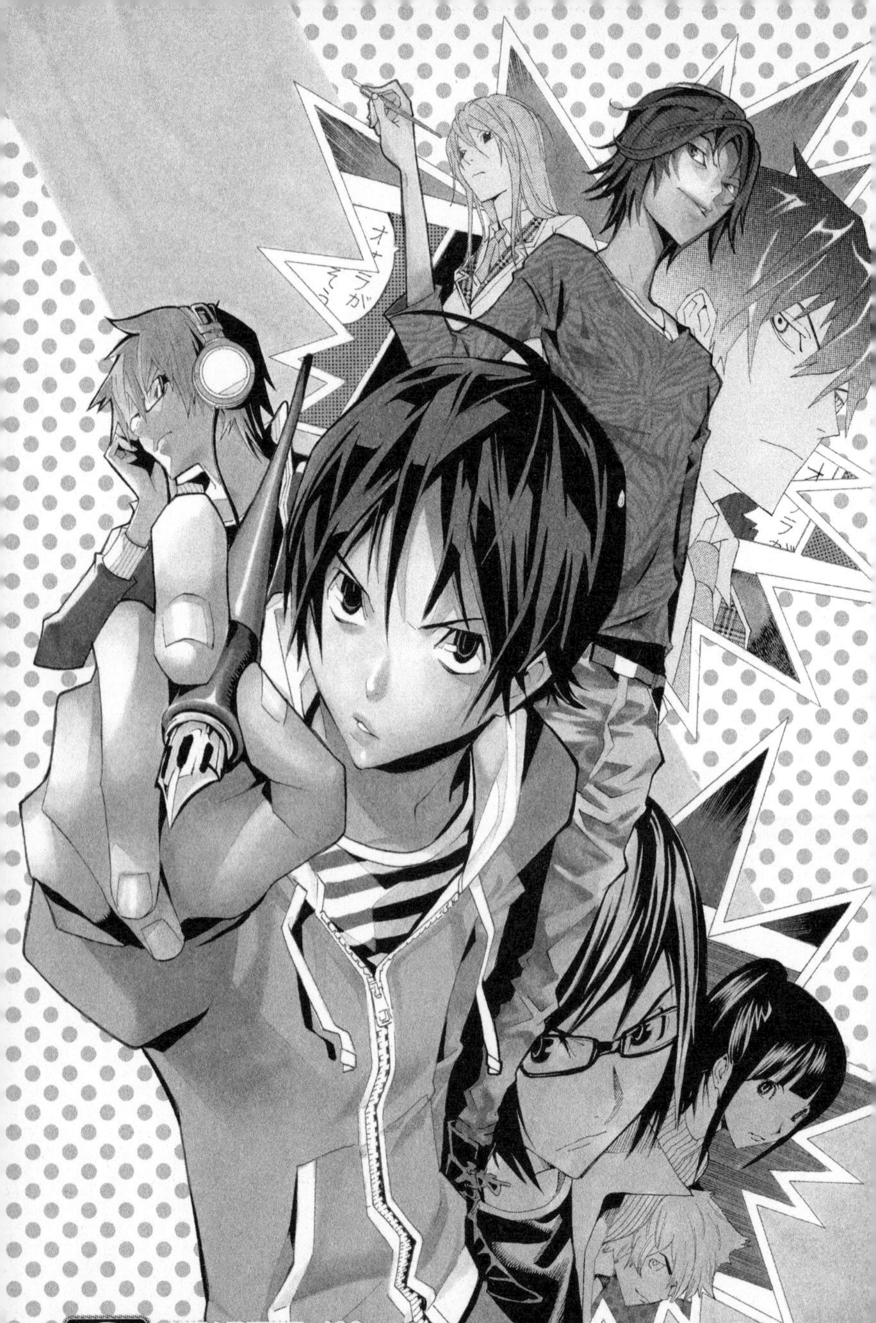

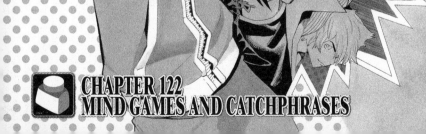

CHAPTER 122
MIND GAMES AND CATCHPHRASES

BAKUMAN。

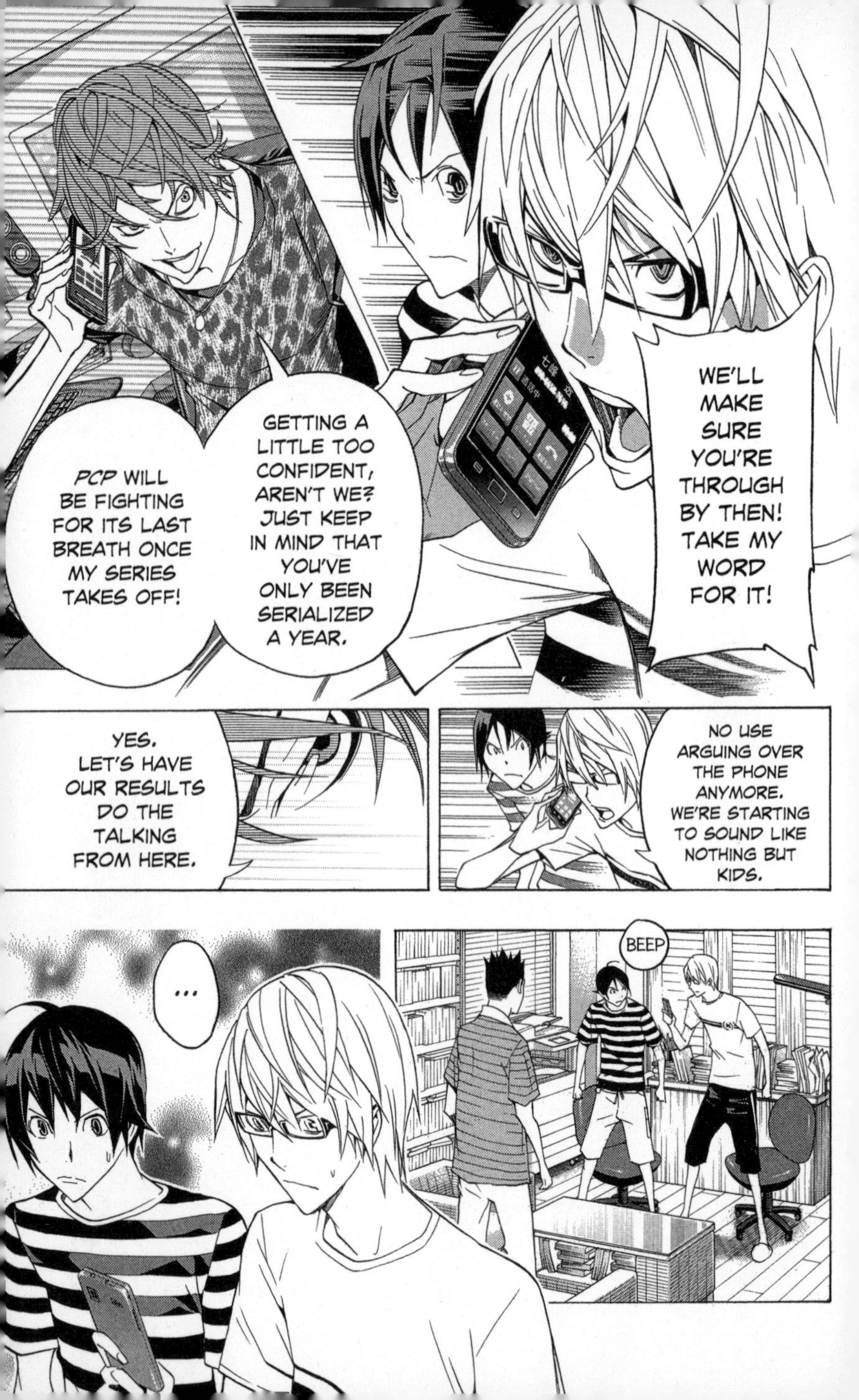
WE'LL MAKE SURE YOU'RE THROUGH BY THEN! TAKE MY WORD FOR IT!
GETTING A LITTLE TOO CONFIDENT, AREN'T WE? JUST KEEP IN MIND THAT YOU'VE ONLY BEEN SERIALIZED A YEAR.
PCP WILL BE FIGHTING FOR ITS LAST BREATH ONCE MY SERIES TAKES OFF!
NO USE ARGUING OVER THE PHONE ANYMORE. WE'RE STARTING TO SOUND LIKE NOTHING BUT KIDS.
YES. LET'S HAVE OUR RESULTS DO THE TALKING FROM HERE.
BEEP
...

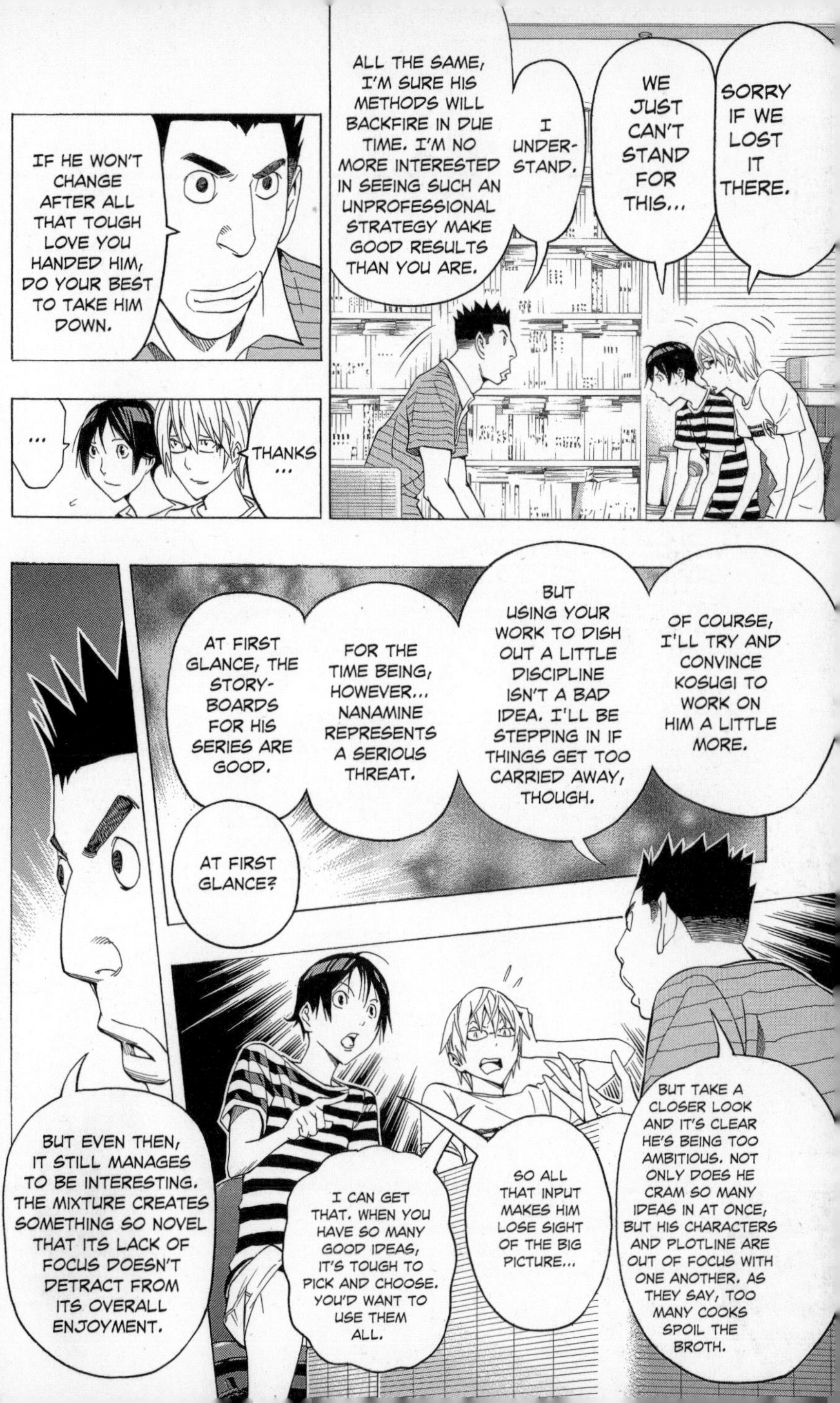

SORRY IF WE LOST IT THERE.
WE JUST CAN'T STAND FOR THIS...
I UNDERSTAND.
ALL THE SAME, I'M SURE HIS METHODS WILL BACKFIRE IN DUE TIME. I'M NO MORE INTERESTED IN SEEING SUCH AN UNPROFESSIONAL STRATEGY MAKE GOOD RESULTS THAN YOU ARE.
IF HE WON'T CHANGE AFTER ALL THAT TOUGH LOVE YOU HANDED HIM, DO YOUR BEST TO TAKE HIM DOWN.
THANKS...
...
OF COURSE, I'LL TRY AND CONVINCE KOSUGI TO WORK ON HIM A LITTLE MORE.
BUT USING YOUR WORK TO DISH OUT A LITTLE DISCIPLINE ISN'T A BAD IDEA. I'LL BE STEPPING IN IF THINGS GET TOO CARRIED AWAY, THOUGH.
FOR THE TIME BEING, HOWEVER... NANAMINE REPRESENTS A SERIOUS THREAT.
AT FIRST GLANCE, THE STORYBOARDS FOR HIS SERIES ARE GOOD.
AT FIRST GLANCE?
BUT TAKE A CLOSER LOOK AND IT'S CLEAR HE'S BEING TOO AMBITIOUS. NOT ONLY DOES HE CRAM SO MANY IDEAS IN AT ONCE, BUT HIS CHARACTERS AND PLOTLINE ARE OUT OF FOCUS WITH ONE ANOTHER. AS THEY SAY, TOO MANY COOKS SPOIL THE BROTH.
SO ALL THAT INPUT MAKES HIM LOSE SIGHT OF THE BIG PICTURE...
I CAN GET THAT. WHEN YOU HAVE SO MANY GOOD IDEAS, IT'S TOUGH TO PICK AND CHOOSE. YOU'D WANT TO USE THEM ALL.
BUT EVEN THEN, IT STILL MANAGES TO BE INTERESTING. THE MIXTURE CREATES SOMETHING SO NOVEL THAT ITS LACK OF FOCUS DOESN'T DETRACT FROM ITS OVERALL ENJOYMENT.

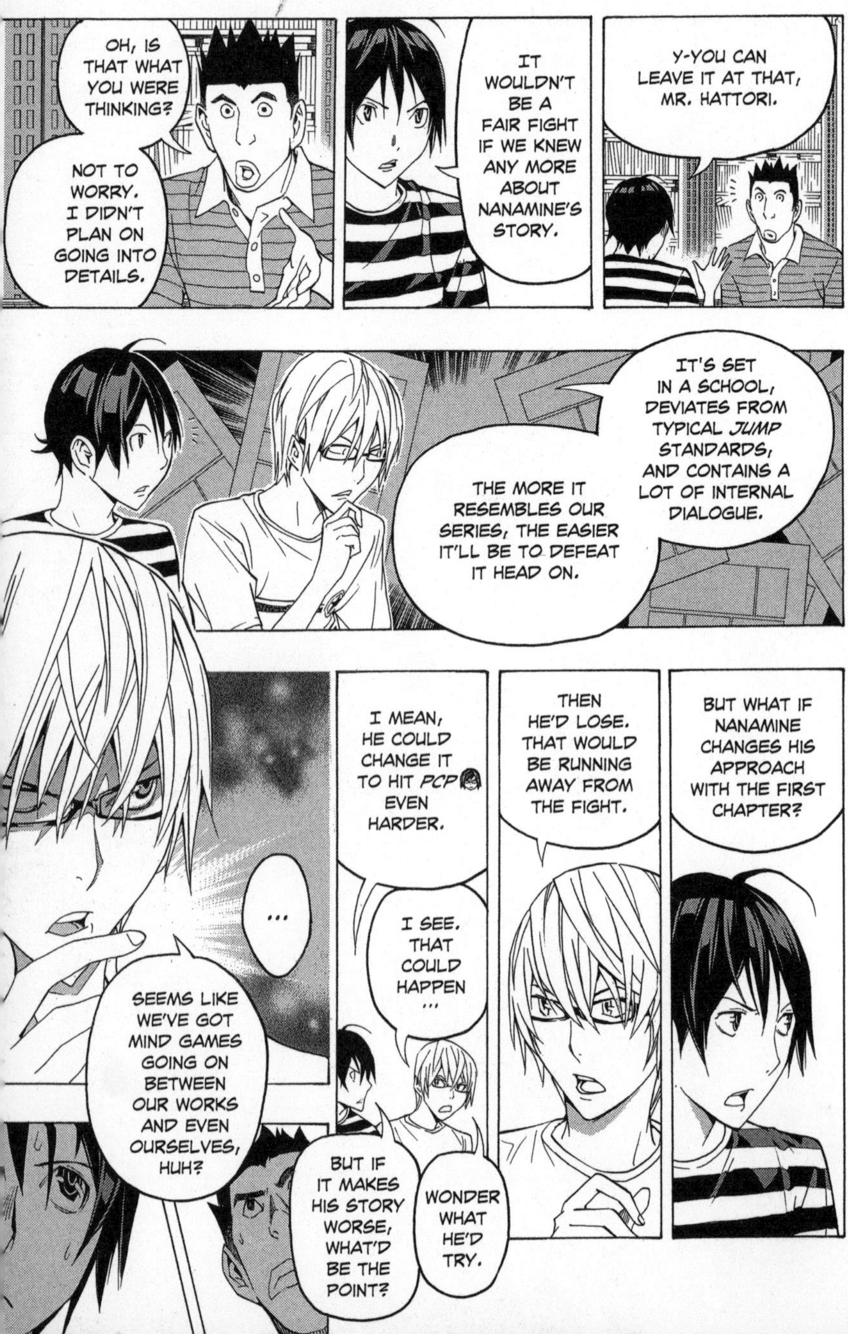
Y-YOU CAN LEAVE IT AT THAT, MR. HATTORI.
IT WOULDN'T BE A FAIR FIGHT IF WE KNEW ANY MORE ABOUT NANAMINE'S STORY.
OH, IS THAT WHAT YOU WERE THINKING?
NOT TO WORRY. I DIDN'T PLAN ON GOING INTO DETAILS.
IT'S SET IN A SCHOOL, DEVIATES FROM TYPICAL *JUMP* STANDARDS, AND CONTAINS A LOT OF INTERNAL DIALOGUE.
THE MORE IT RESEMBLES OUR SERIES, THE EASIER IT'LL BE TO DEFEAT IT HEAD ON.
BUT WHAT IF NANAMINE CHANGES HIS APPROACH WITH THE FIRST CHAPTER?
THEN HE'D LOSE. THAT WOULD BE RUNNING AWAY FROM THE FIGHT.
I MEAN, HE COULD CHANGE IT TO HIT *PCP* EVEN HARDER.
I SEE. THAT COULD HAPPEN...
WONDER WHAT HE'D TRY.
BUT IF IT MAKES HIS STORY WORSE, WHAT'D BE THE POINT?
...
SEEMS LIKE WE'VE GOT MIND GAMES GOING ON BETWEEN OUR WORKS AND EVEN OURSELVES, HUH?

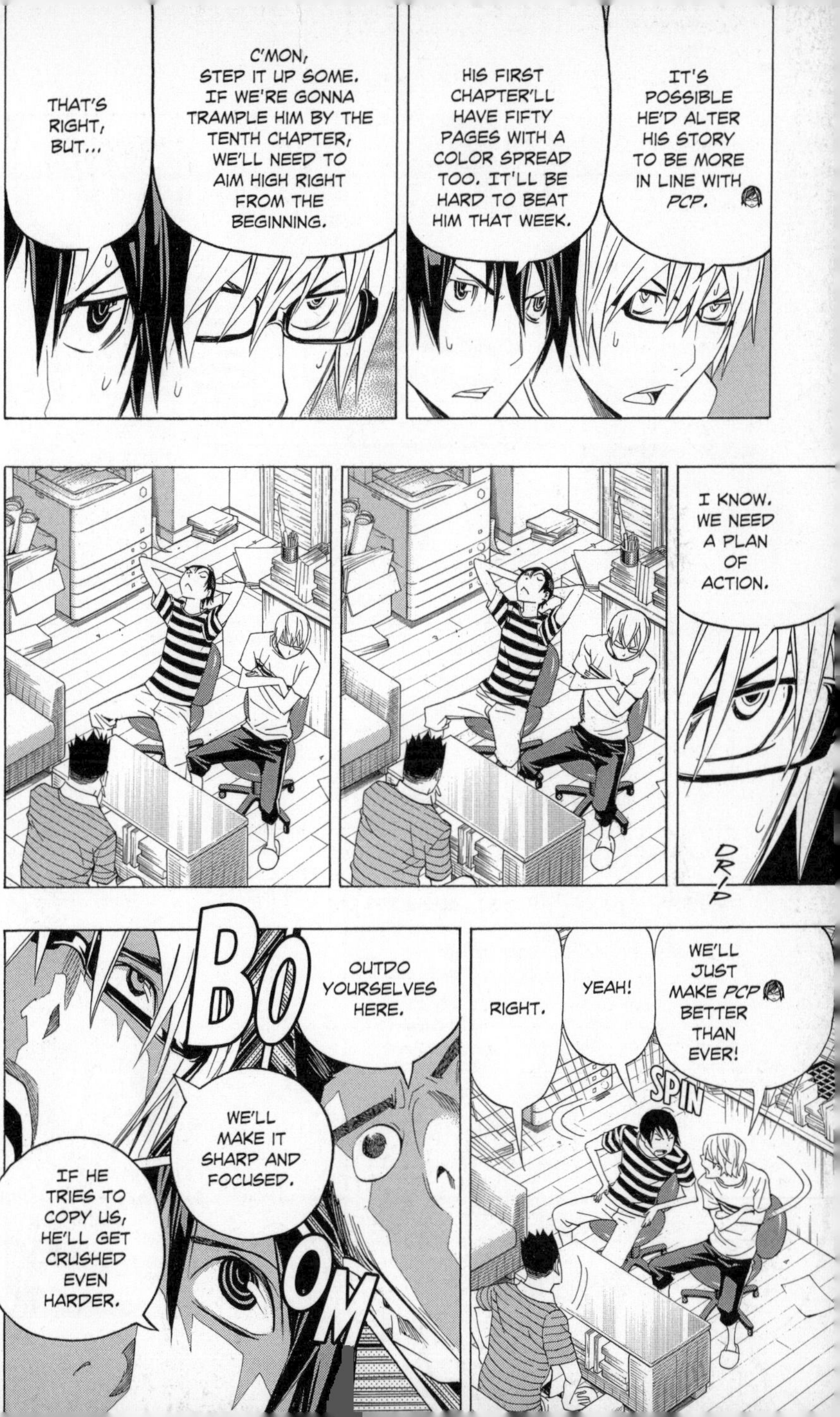
IT'S POSSIBLE HE'D ALTER HIS STORY TO BE MORE IN LINE WITH *PCP*.
HIS FIRST CHAPTER'LL HAVE FIFTY PAGES WITH A COLOR SPREAD TOO. IT'LL BE HARD TO BEAT HIM THAT WEEK.
C'MON, STEP IT UP SOME. IF WE'RE GONNA TRAMPLE HIM BY THE TENTH CHAPTER, WE'LL NEED TO AIM HIGH RIGHT FROM THE BEGINNING.
THAT'S RIGHT, BUT...
I KNOW. WE NEED A PLAN OF ACTION.
DRIP
WE'LL JUST MAKE *PCP* BETTER THAN EVER!
YEAH!
RIGHT.
SPIN
OUTDO YOURSELVES HERE.
BOOM
WE'LL MAKE IT SHARP AND FOCUSED.
IF HE TRIES TO COPY US, HE'LL GET CRUSHED EVEN HARDER.

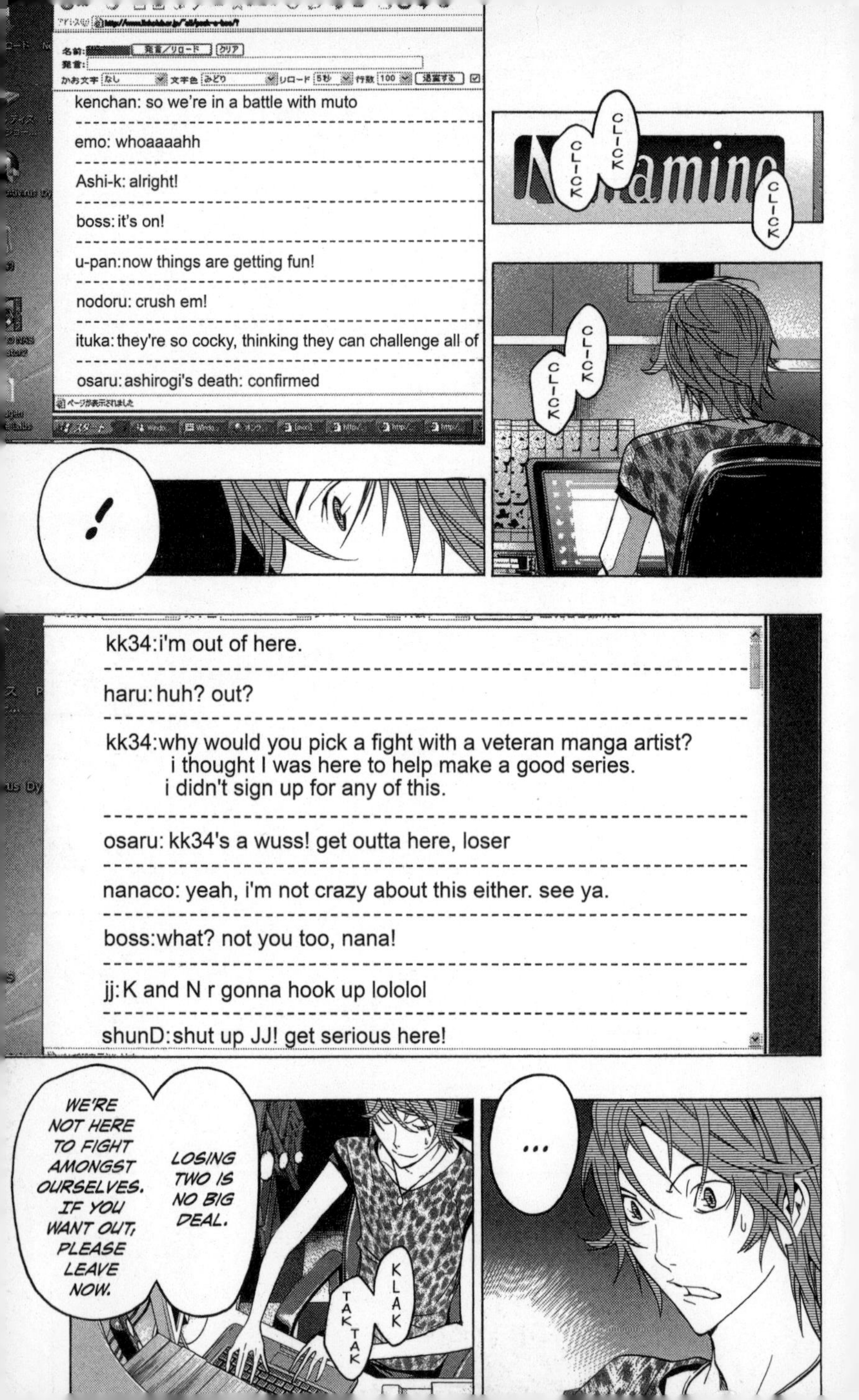

CLICK
CLICK
CLICK
CLICK
CLICK
kenchan: so we're in a battle with muto
emo: whoaaaahh
Ashi-k: alright!
boss: it's on!
u-pan: now things are getting fun!
nodoru: crush em!
ituka: they're so cocky, thinking they can challenge all of
osaru: ashirogi's death: confirmed
!
kk34: i'm out of here.
haru: huh? out?
kk34: why would you pick a fight with a veteran manga artist? i thought I was here to help make a good series. i didn't sign up for any of this.
osaru: kk34's a wuss! get outta here, loser
nanaco: yeah, i'm not crazy about this either. see ya.
boss: what? not you too, nana!
jj: K and N r gonna hook up lololol
shunD: shut up JJ! get serious here!
...
LOSING TWO IS NO BIG DEAL.
WE'RE NOT HERE TO FIGHT AMONGST OURSELVES. IF YOU WANT OUT, PLEASE LEAVE NOW.
KLAK
TAK TAK

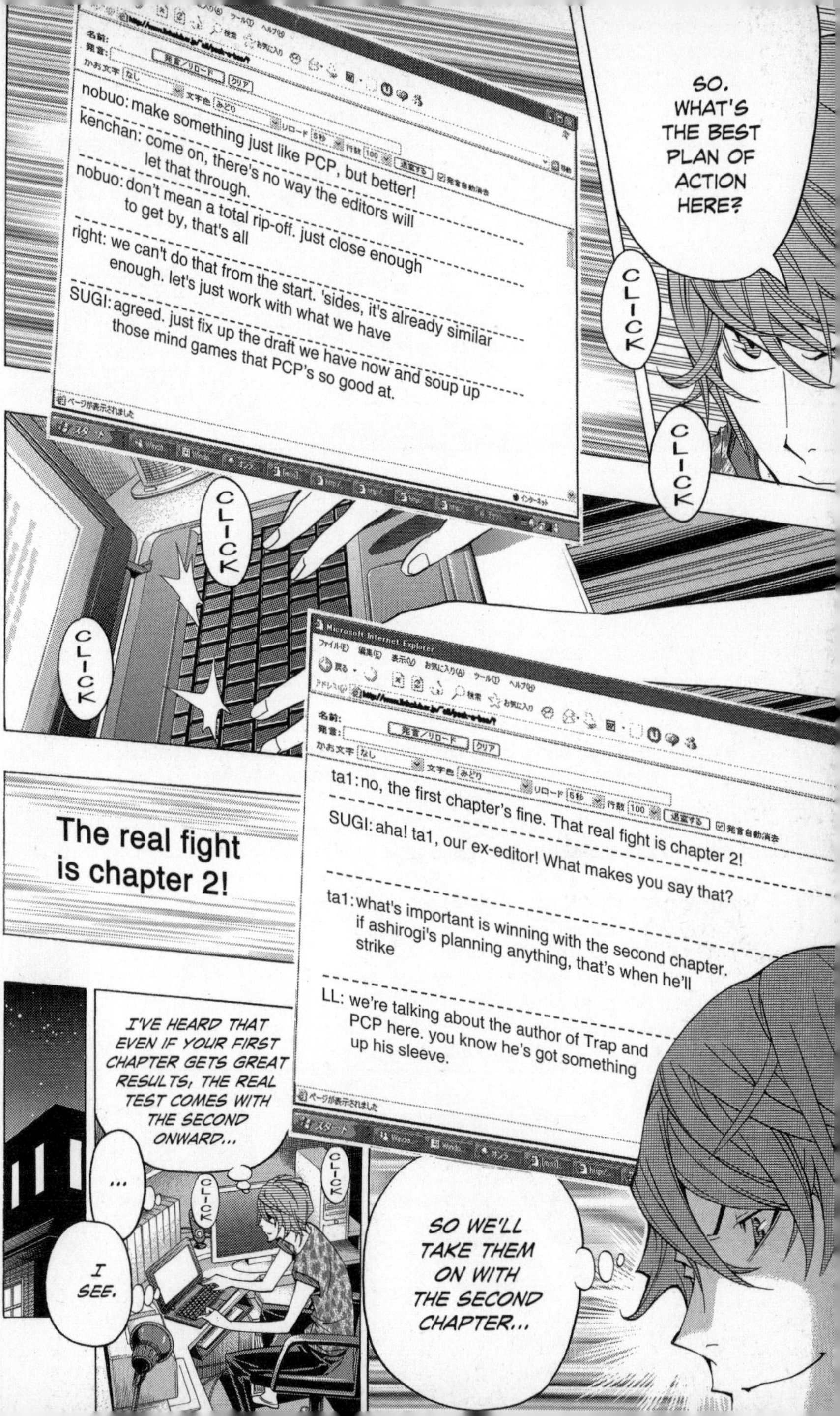
SO. WHAT'S THE BEST PLAN OF ACTION HERE?
CLICK
CLICK
名前:
発言:
発言／リロード
クリア
かお文字 なし
文字色 みどり
nobuo: make something just like PCP, but better!
kenchan: come on, there's no way the editors will let that through.
nobuo: don't mean a total rip-off. just close enough to get by, that's all
right: we can't do that from the start. 'sides, it's already similar enough. let's just work with what we have
SUGI: agreed. just fix up the draft we have now and soup up those mind games that PCP's so good at.
ページが表示されました
CLICK
CLICK
Microsoft Internet Explorer
名前:
発言:
発言／リロード
クリア
かお文字 なし
文字色 みどり
リロード 5秒
行数 100
退室する
発言自動消去
ta1: no, the first chapter's fine. That real fight is chapter 2!
SUGI: aha! ta1, our ex-editor! What makes you say that?
ta1: what's important is winning with the second chapter. if ashirogi's planning anything, that's when he'll strike
LL: we're talking about the author of Trap and PCP here. you know he's got something up his sleeve.
ページが表示されました
The real fight is chapter 2!
SO WE'LL TAKE THEM ON WITH THE SECOND CHAPTER...
I'VE HEARD THAT EVEN IF YOUR FIRST CHAPTER GETS GREAT RESULTS, THE REAL TEST COMES WITH THE SECOND ONWARD...
...
CLICK
CLICK
I SEE.

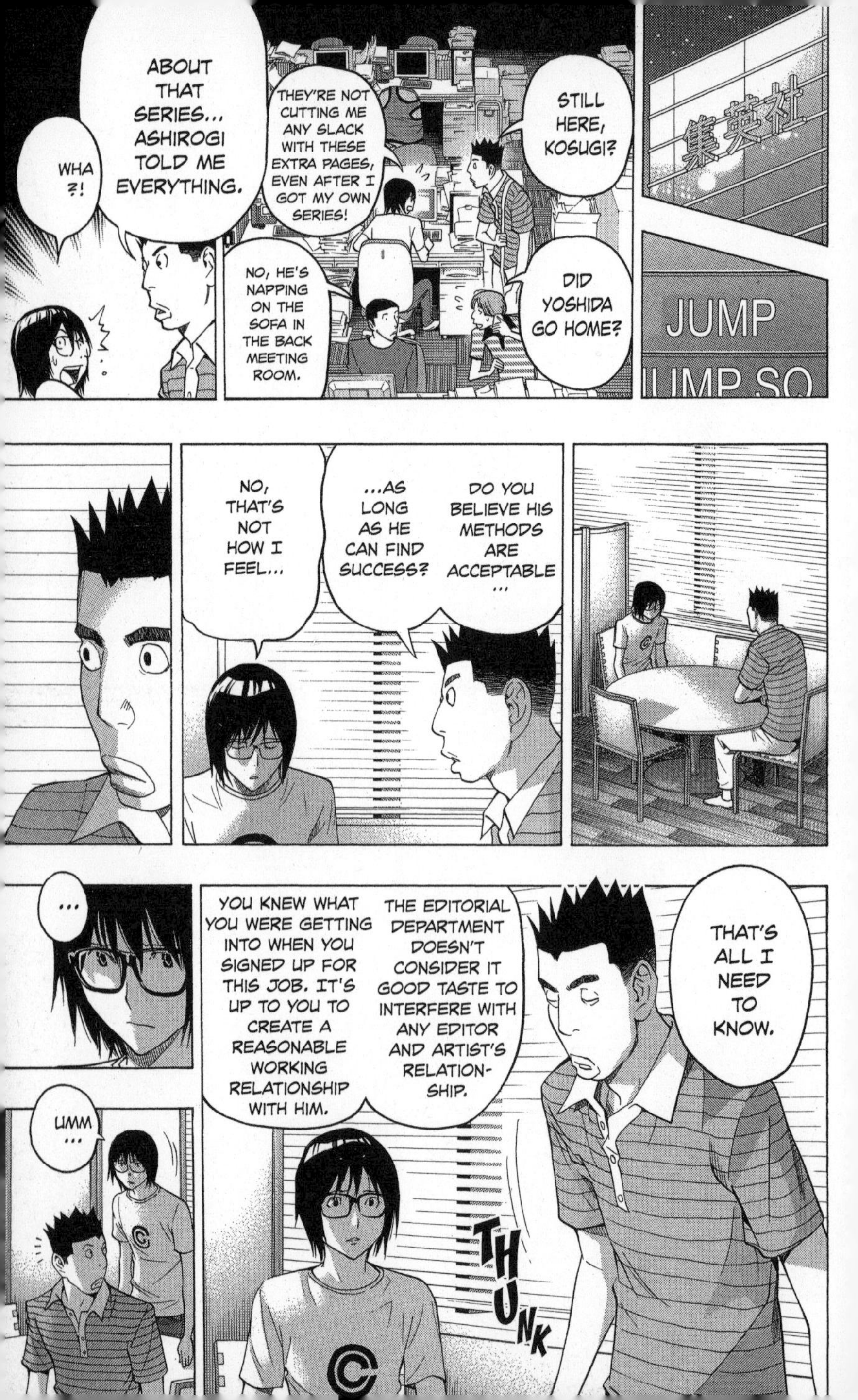
集英社
JUMP
STILL HERE, KOSUGI?
THEY'RE NOT CUTTING ME ANY SLACK WITH THESE EXTRA PAGES, EVEN AFTER I GOT MY OWN SERIES!
DID YOSHIDA GO HOME?
NO, HE'S NAPPING ON THE SOFA IN THE BACK MEETING ROOM.
ABOUT THAT SERIES... ASHIROGI TOLD ME EVERYTHING.
WHA?!
DO YOU BELIEVE HIS METHODS ARE ACCEPTABLE...
...AS LONG AS HE CAN FIND SUCCESS?
NO, THAT'S NOT HOW I FEEL...
THAT'S ALL I NEED TO KNOW.
THE EDITORIAL DEPARTMENT DOESN'T CONSIDER IT GOOD TASTE TO INTERFERE WITH ANY EDITOR AND ARTIST'S RELATIONSHIP.
YOU KNEW WHAT YOU WERE GETTING INTO WHEN YOU SIGNED UP FOR THIS JOB. IT'S UP TO YOU TO CREATE A REASONABLE WORKING RELATIONSHIP WITH HIM.
THUNK
...
UMM...

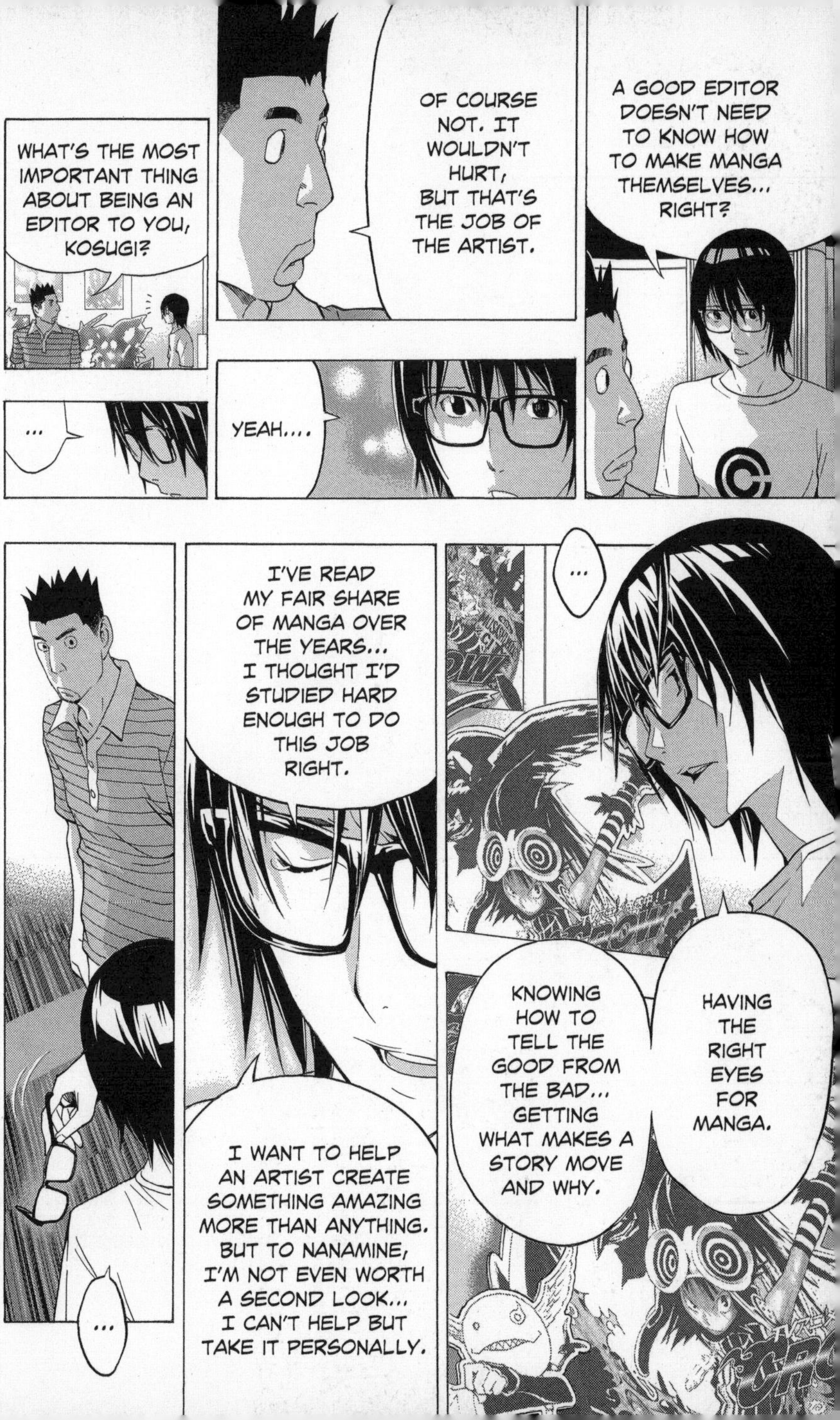
A GOOD EDITOR DOESN'T NEED TO KNOW HOW TO MAKE MANGA THEMSELVES... RIGHT?
OF COURSE NOT. IT WOULDN'T HURT, BUT THAT'S THE JOB OF THE ARTIST.
WHAT'S THE MOST IMPORTANT THING ABOUT BEING AN EDITOR TO YOU, KOSUGI?
YEAH....
...
...
HAVING THE RIGHT EYES FOR MANGA.
KNOWING HOW TO TELL THE GOOD FROM THE BAD... GETTING WHAT MAKES A STORY MOVE AND WHY.
I'VE READ MY FAIR SHARE OF MANGA OVER THE YEARS... I THOUGHT I'D STUDIED HARD ENOUGH TO DO THIS JOB RIGHT.
I WANT TO HELP AN ARTIST CREATE SOMETHING AMAZING MORE THAN ANYTHING. BUT TO NANAMINE, I'M NOT EVEN WORTH A SECOND LOOK... I CAN'T HELP BUT TAKE IT PERSONALLY.
...

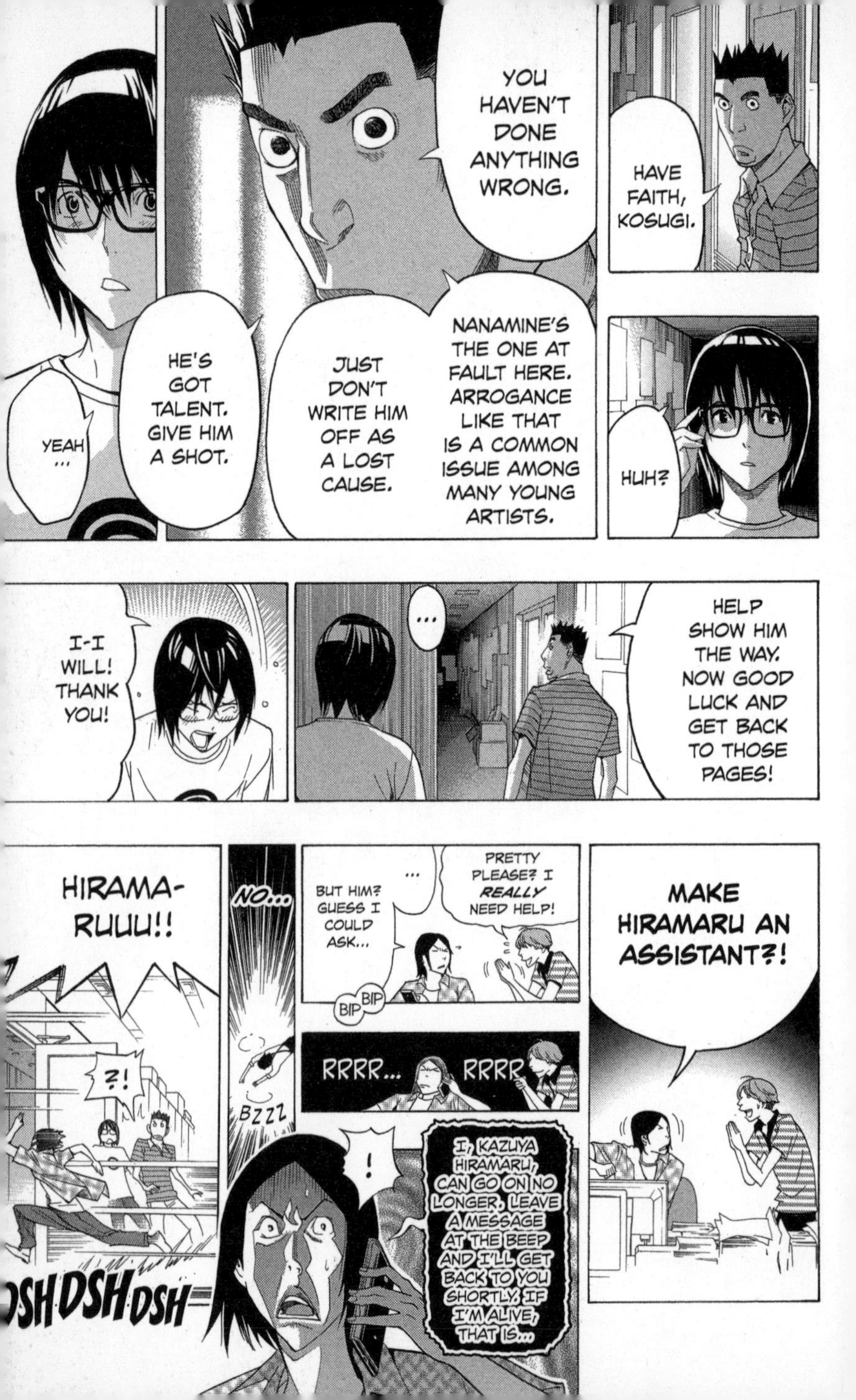

HAVE FAITH, KOSUGI.
HUH?
YOU HAVEN'T DONE ANYTHING WRONG.
NANAMINE'S THE ONE AT FAULT HERE. ARROGANCE LIKE THAT IS A COMMON ISSUE AMONG MANY YOUNG ARTISTS.
JUST DON'T WRITE HIM OFF AS A LOST CAUSE.
HE'S GOT TALENT. GIVE HIM A SHOT.
YEAH...
HELP SHOW HIM THE WAY. NOW GOOD LUCK AND GET BACK TO THOSE PAGES!
...
I-I WILL! THANK YOU!
MAKE HIRAMARU AN ASSISTANT?!
PRETTY PLEASE? I REALLY NEED HELP!
...
BUT HIM? GUESS I COULD ASK...
BIP BIP
RRRR... RRRR
!
I, KAZUYA HIRAMARU, CAN GO ON NO LONGER. LEAVE A MESSAGE AT THE BEEP AND I'LL GET BACK TO YOU SHORTLY. IF I'M ALIVE, THAT IS...
NO...
BZZZ
HIRAMA-RUUU!!
?!
DSH DSH DSH

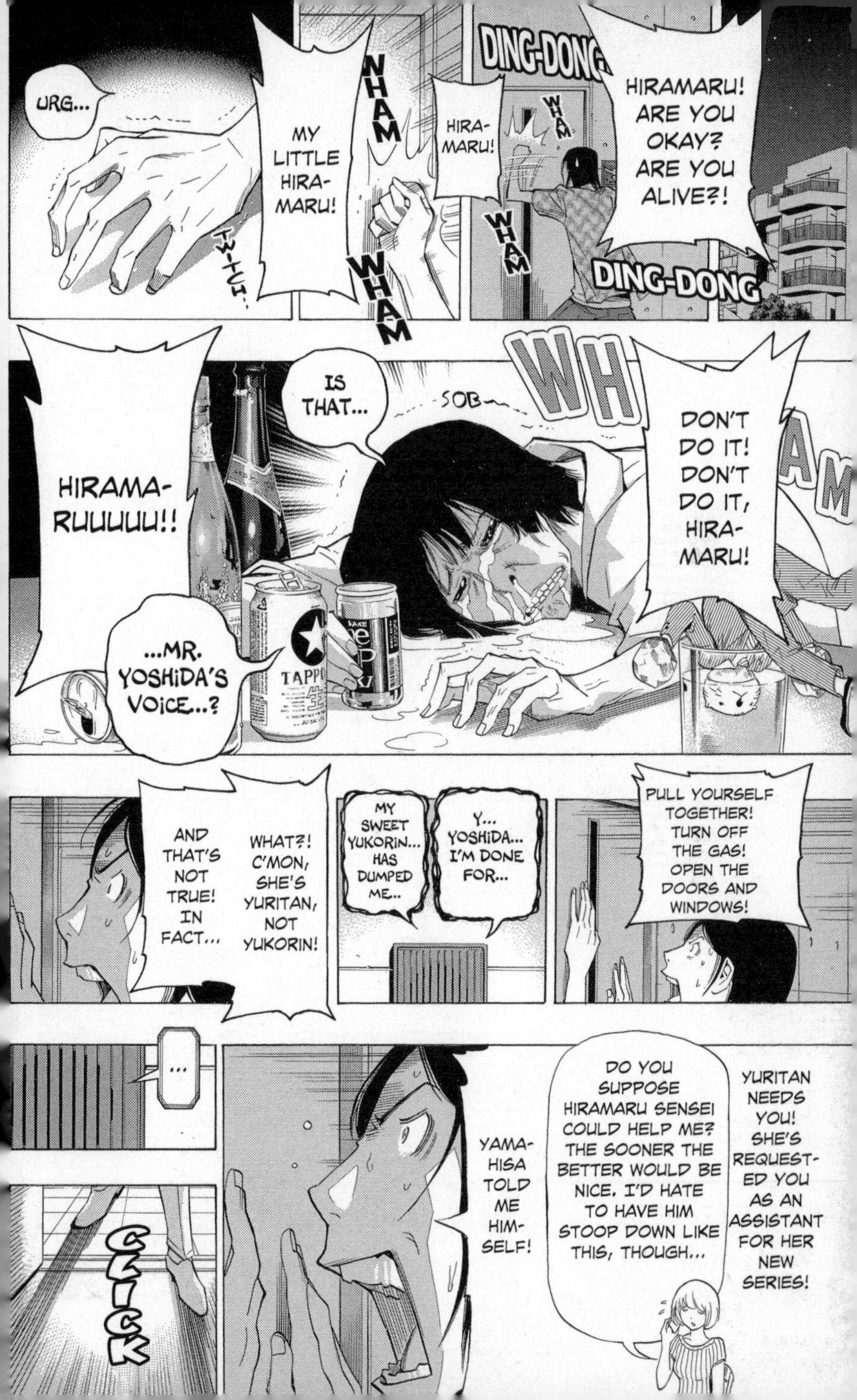
DING-DONG
HIRAMARU! ARE YOU OKAY? ARE YOU ALIVE?!
WHAM
WHAM
HIRA-MARU!
DING-DONG
MY LITTLE HIRA-MARU!
WHAM
WHAM
URG...
TWITCH
DON'T DO IT! DON'T DO IT, HIRA-MARU!
WHAM
SOB
IS THAT...
HIRAMA-RUUUUU!!
...MR. YOSHIDA'S VOICE...?
PULL YOURSELF TOGETHER! TURN OFF THE GAS! OPEN THE DOORS AND WINDOWS!
Y... YOSHIDA... I'M DONE FOR...
MY SWEET YUKORIN... HAS DUMPED ME..
WHAT?! C'MON, SHE'S YURITAN, NOT YUKORIN!
AND THAT'S NOT TRUE! IN FACT...
YURITAN NEEDS YOU! SHE'S REQUEST-ED YOU AS AN ASSISTANT FOR HER NEW SERIES!
DO YOU SUPPOSE HIRAMARU SENSEI COULD HELP ME? THE SOONER THE BETTER WOULD BE NICE. I'D HATE TO HAVE HIM STOOP DOWN LIKE THIS, THOUGH...
YAMA-HISA TOLD ME HIM-SELF!
...
CLICK

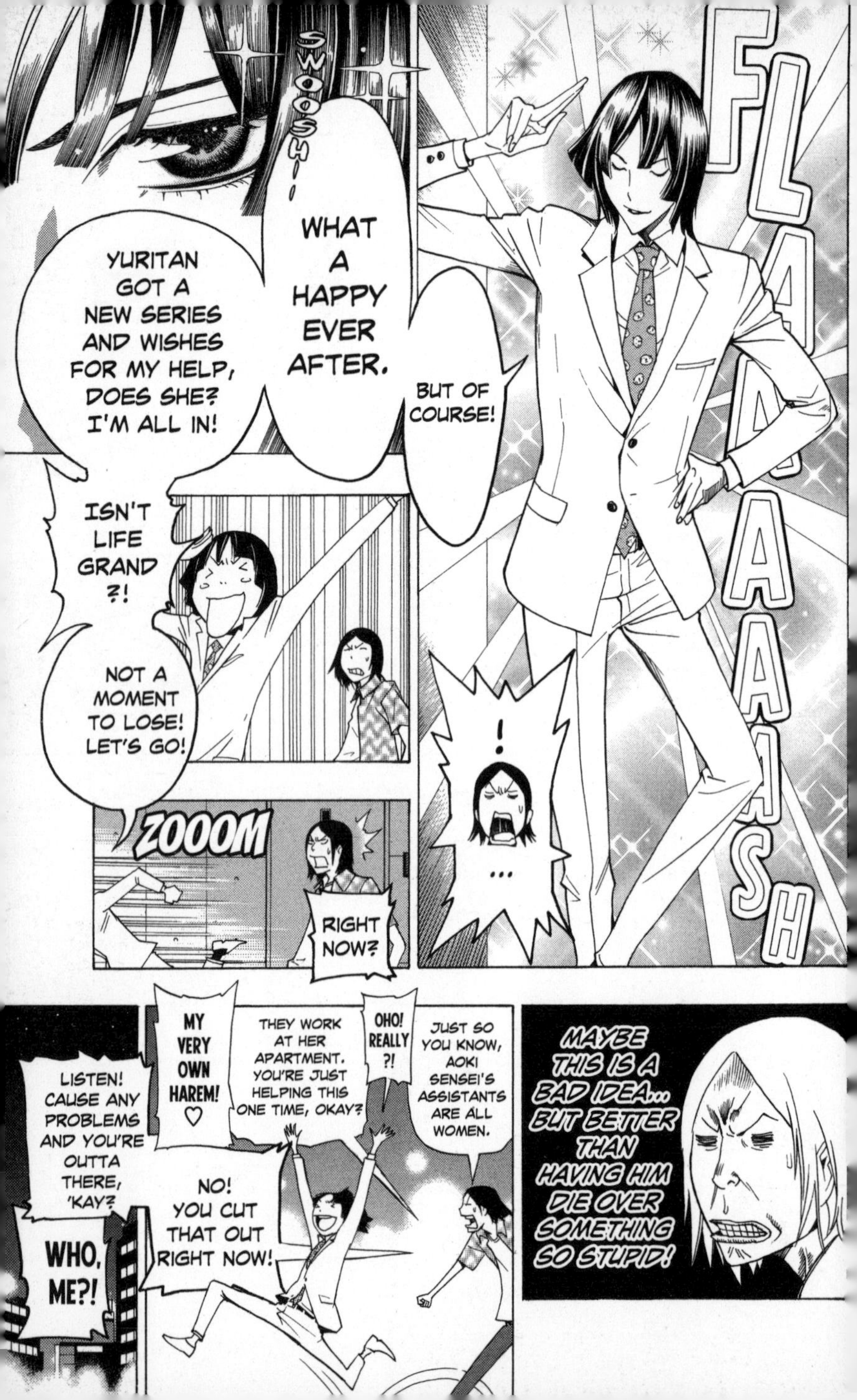
FLAAAAASH
BUT OF COURSE!
!
...
SWOOSH!!
WHAT A HAPPY EVER AFTER.
YURITAN GOT A NEW SERIES AND WISHES FOR MY HELP, DOES SHE? I'M ALL IN!
ISN'T LIFE GRAND?!
NOT A MOMENT TO LOSE! LET'S GO!
ZOOOM
RIGHT NOW?
MAYBE THIS IS A BAD IDEA... BUT BETTER THAN HAVING HIM DIE OVER SOMETHING SO STUPID!
JUST SO YOU KNOW, AOKI SENSEI'S ASSISTANTS ARE ALL WOMEN.
OHO! REALLY?!
THEY WORK AT HER APARTMENT. YOU'RE JUST HELPING THIS ONE TIME, OKAY?
MY VERY OWN HAREM! ♡
LISTEN! CAUSE ANY PROBLEMS AND YOU'RE OUTTA THERE, 'KAY?
NO! YOU CUT THAT OUT RIGHT NOW!
WHO, ME?!

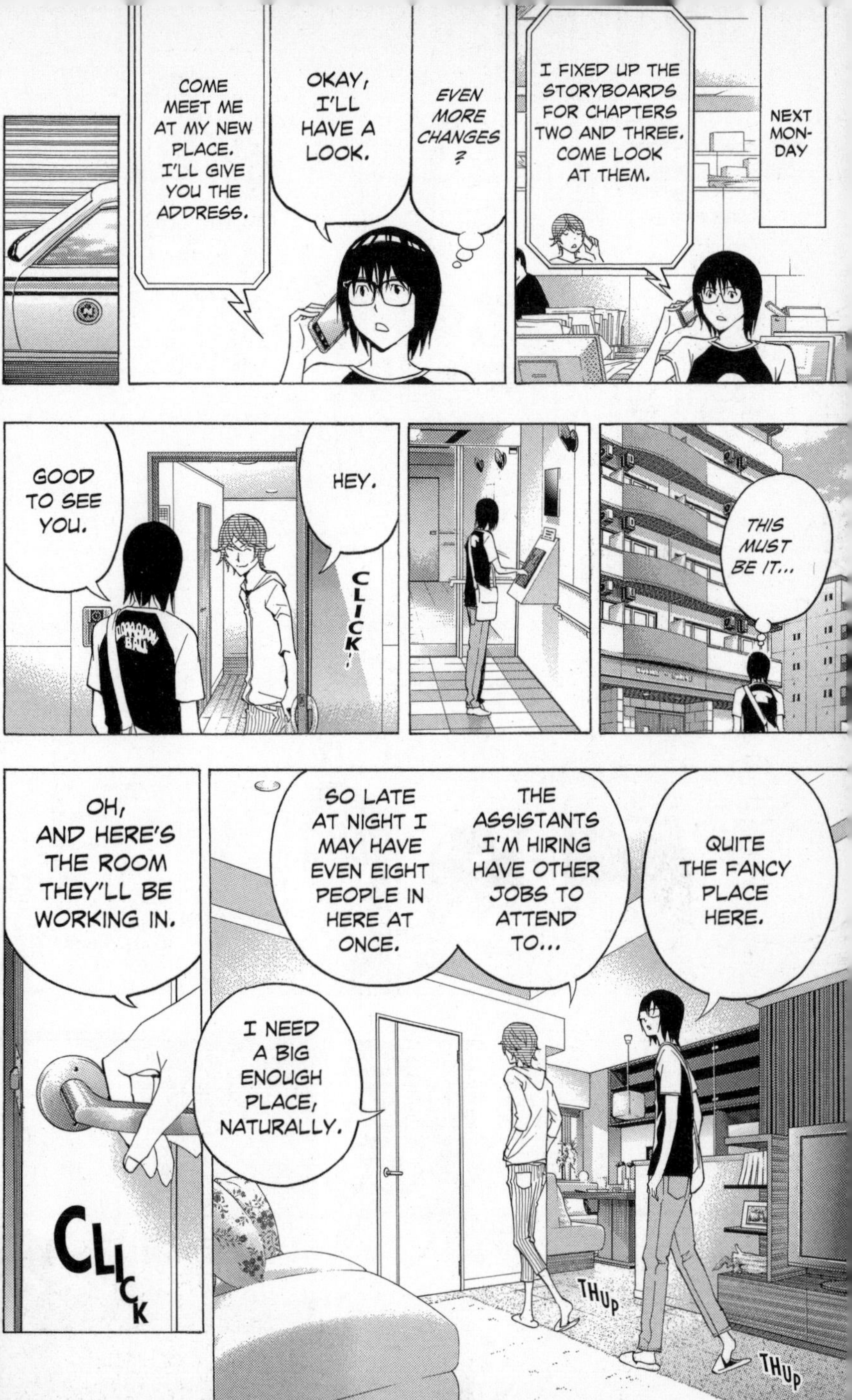
NEXT MONDAY
I FIXED UP THE STORYBOARDS FOR CHAPTERS TWO AND THREE. COME LOOK AT THEM.
EVEN MORE CHANGES?
OKAY, I'LL HAVE A LOOK.
COME MEET ME AT MY NEW PLACE. I'LL GIVE YOU THE ADDRESS.
THIS MUST BE IT...
HEY.
CLICK!
GOOD TO SEE YOU.
QUITE THE FANCY PLACE HERE.
THE ASSISTANTS I'M HIRING HAVE OTHER JOBS TO ATTEND TO...
SO LATE AT NIGHT I MAY HAVE EVEN EIGHT PEOPLE IN HERE AT ONCE.
I NEED A BIG ENOUGH PLACE, NATURALLY.
THUP
THUP
OH, AND HERE'S THE ROOM THEY'LL BE WORKING IN.
CLICK

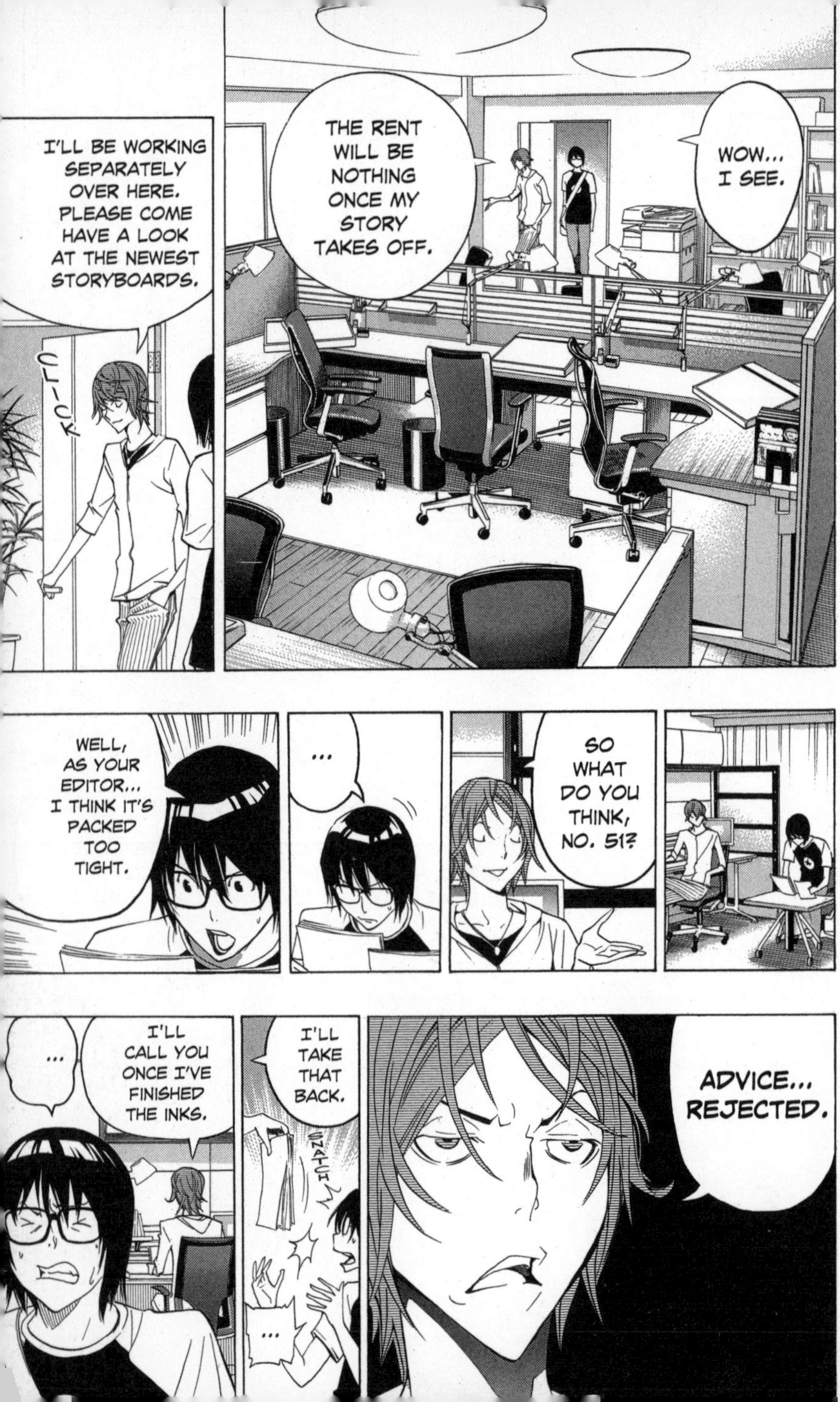
WOW... I SEE.
THE RENT WILL BE NOTHING ONCE MY STORY TAKES OFF.
I'LL BE WORKING SEPARATELY OVER HERE. PLEASE COME HAVE A LOOK AT THE NEWEST STORYBOARDS.
CLICK
SO WHAT DO YOU THINK, NO. 51?
...
WELL, AS YOUR EDITOR... I THINK IT'S PACKED TOO TIGHT.
ADVICE... REJECTED.
I'LL TAKE THAT BACK.
SNATCH
...
I'LL CALL YOU ONCE I'VE FINISHED THE INKS.
...

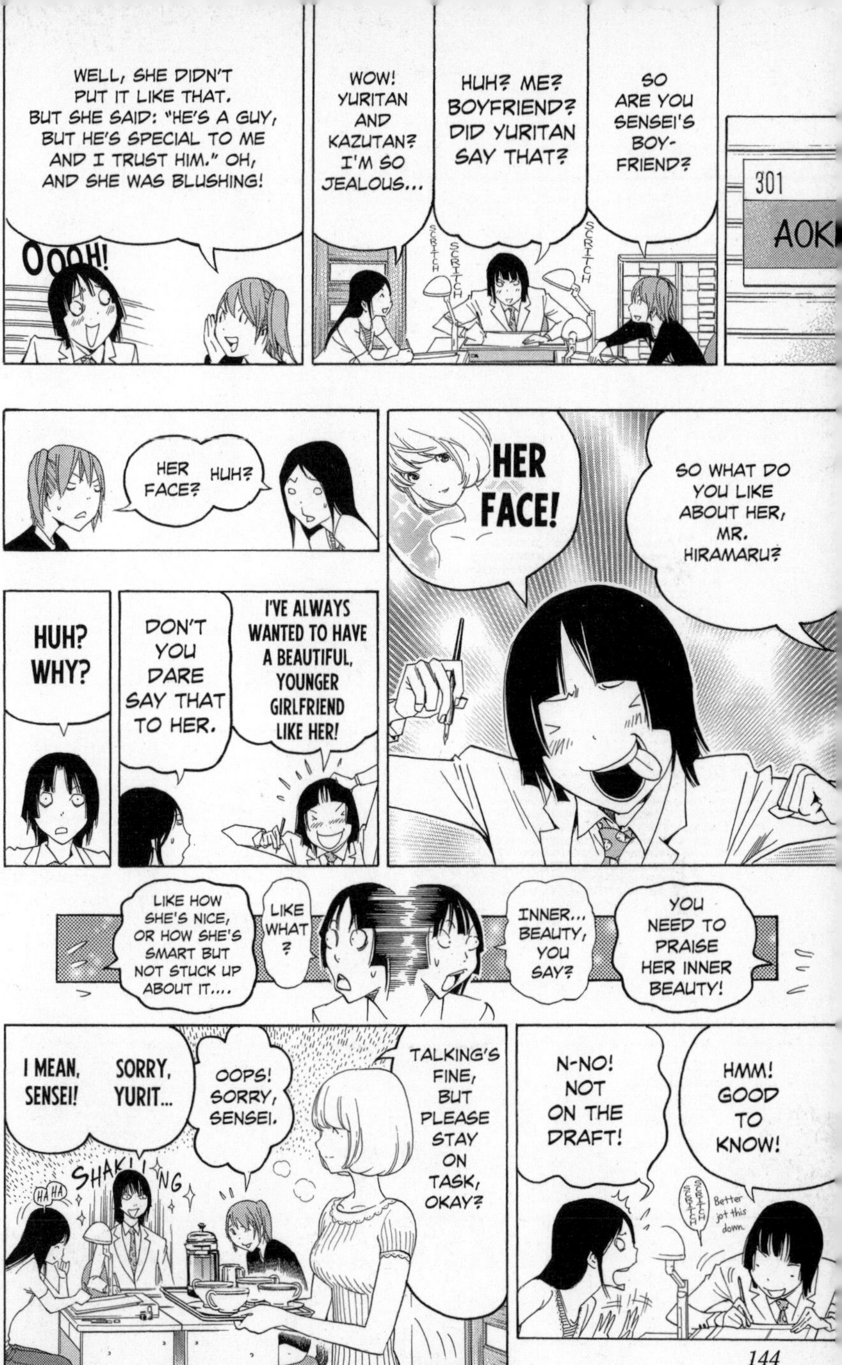
301
AOK
SO ARE YOU SENSEI'S BOY-FRIEND?
SCRITCH
HUH? ME? BOYFRIEND? DID YURITAN SAY THAT?
SCRITCH SCRITCH
WOW! YURITAN AND KAZUTAN? I'M SO JEALOUS...
WELL, SHE DIDN'T PUT IT LIKE THAT. BUT SHE SAID: "HE'S A GUY, BUT HE'S SPECIAL TO ME AND I TRUST HIM." OH, AND SHE WAS BLUSHING!
OOOH!
SO WHAT DO YOU LIKE ABOUT HER, MR. HIRAMARU?
HER FACE!
HER FACE? HUH?
I'VE ALWAYS WANTED TO HAVE A BEAUTIFUL, YOUNGER GIRLFRIEND LIKE HER!
DON'T YOU DARE SAY THAT TO HER.
HUH? WHY?
YOU NEED TO PRAISE HER INNER BEAUTY!
INNER... BEAUTY, YOU SAY?
LIKE WHAT?
LIKE HOW SHE'S NICE, OR HOW SHE'S SMART BUT NOT STUCK UP ABOUT IT....
HMM! GOOD TO KNOW!
SCRITCH SCRITCH
Better jot this down.
N-NO! NOT ON THE DRAFT!
TALKING'S FINE, BUT PLEASE STAY ON TASK, OKAY?
OOPS! SORRY, SENSEI.
SORRY, YURIT...
I MEAN, SENSEI!
SHAKING
HA HA
THUP THUP

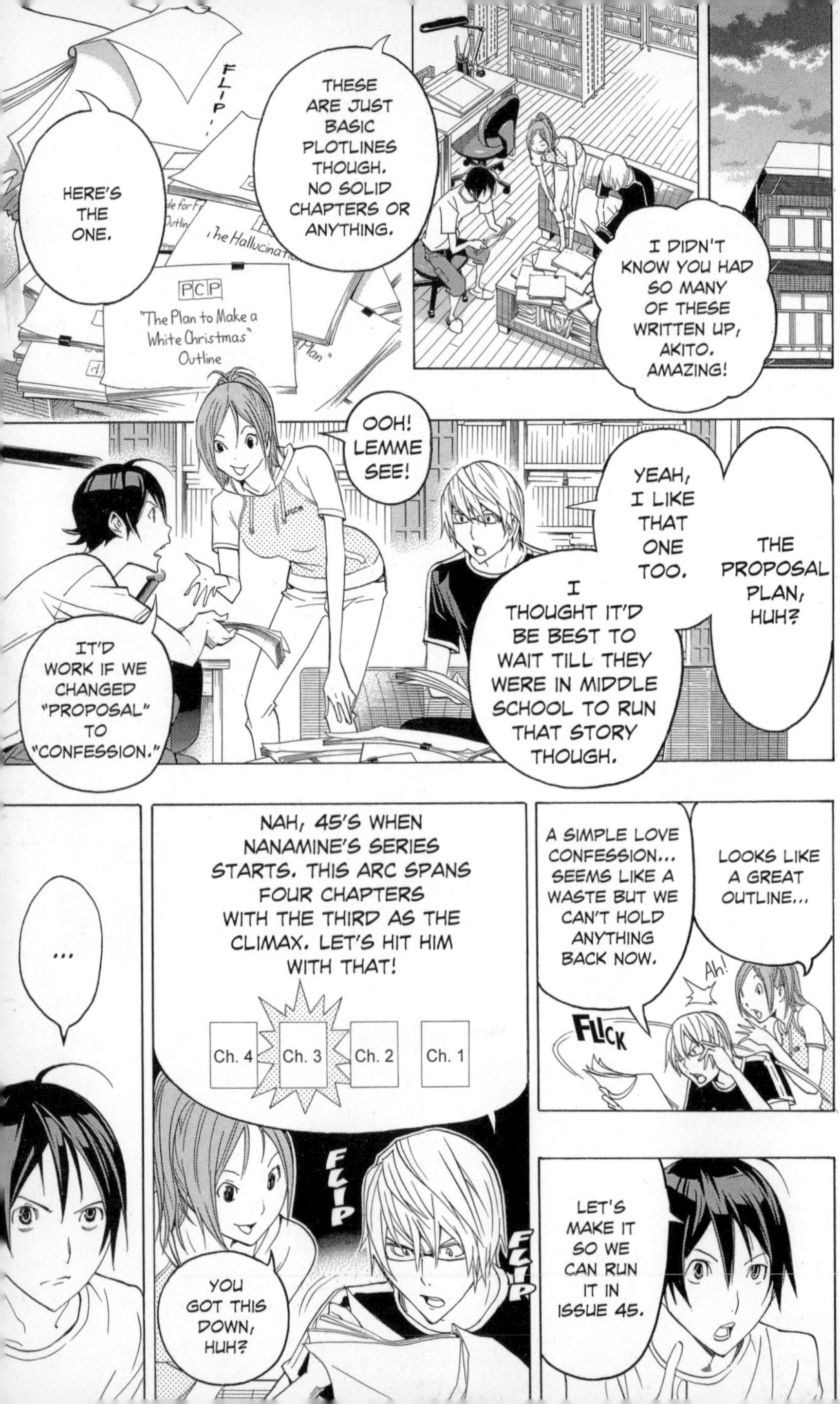
I DIDN'T KNOW YOU HAD SO MANY OF THESE WRITTEN UP, AKITO. AMAZING!
THESE ARE JUST BASIC PLOTLINES THOUGH. NO SOLID CHAPTERS OR ANYTHING.
FLIP
HERE'S THE ONE.
PCP
"The Plan to Make a White Christmas" Outline
THE PROPOSAL PLAN, HUH?
YEAH, I LIKE THAT ONE TOO.
OOH! LEMME SEE!
I THOUGHT IT'D BE BEST TO WAIT TILL THEY WERE IN MIDDLE SCHOOL TO RUN THAT STORY THOUGH.
IT'D WORK IF WE CHANGED "PROPOSAL" TO "CONFESSION."
LOOKS LIKE A GREAT OUTLINE...
A SIMPLE LOVE CONFESSION... SEEMS LIKE A WASTE BUT WE CAN'T HOLD ANYTHING BACK NOW.
Ah!
FLICK
LET'S MAKE IT SO WE CAN RUN IT IN ISSUE 45.
NAH, 45'S WHEN NANAMINE'S SERIES STARTS. THIS ARC SPANS FOUR CHAPTERS WITH THE THIRD AS THE CLIMAX. LET'S HIT HIM WITH THAT!
Ch. 1
Ch. 2
Ch. 3
Ch. 4
FLIP
FLIP
YOU GOT THIS DOWN, HUH?
...

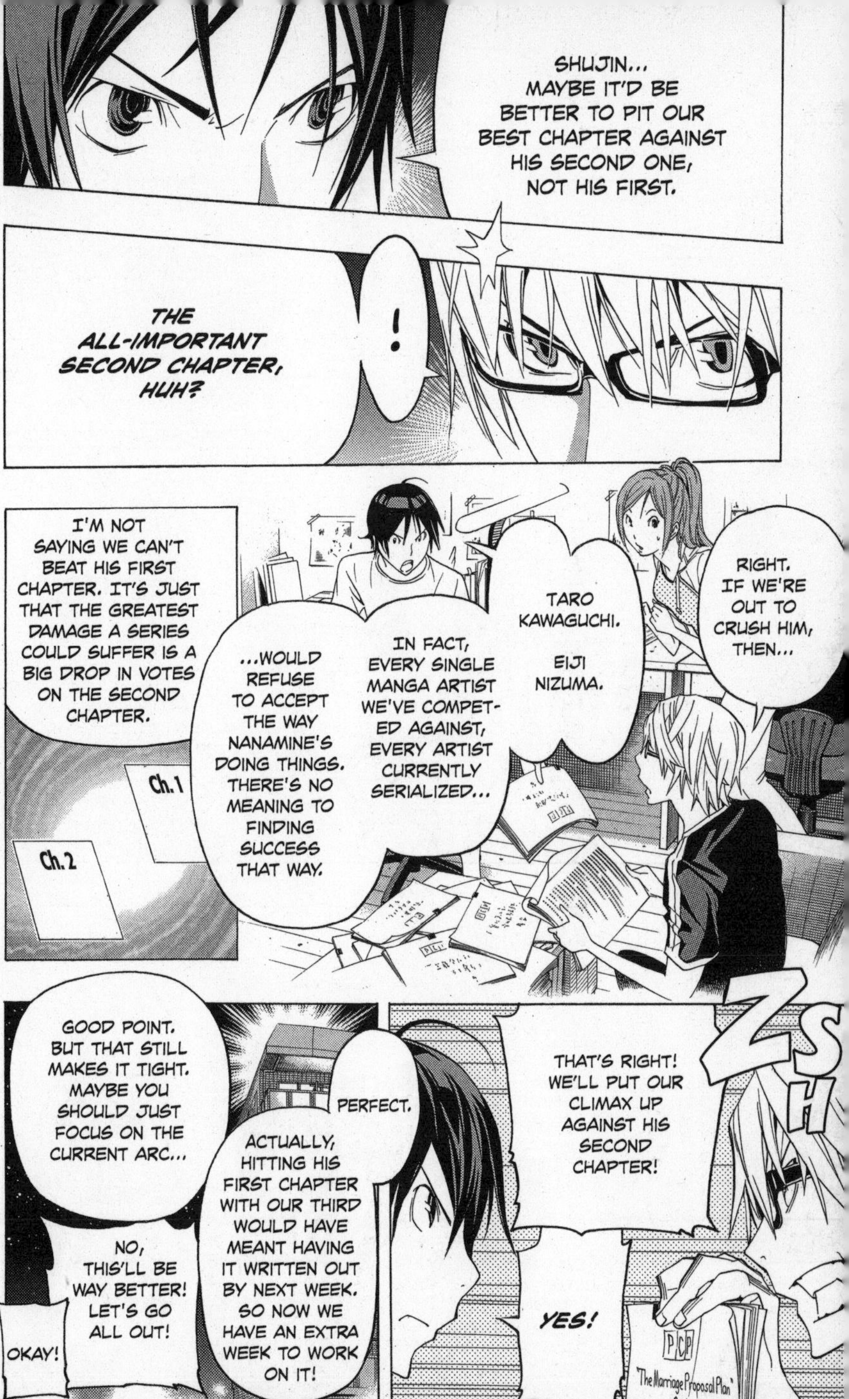
SHUJIN... MAYBE IT'D BE BETTER TO PIT OUR BEST CHAPTER AGAINST HIS SECOND ONE, NOT HIS FIRST.
!
THE ALL-IMPORTANT SECOND CHAPTER, HUH?
RIGHT. IF WE'RE OUT TO CRUSH HIM, THEN...
TARO KAWAGUCHI.
EIJI NIZUMA.
IN FACT, EVERY SINGLE MANGA ARTIST WE'VE COMPETED AGAINST, EVERY ARTIST CURRENTLY SERIALIZED...
...WOULD REFUSE TO ACCEPT THE WAY NANAMINE'S DOING THINGS. THERE'S NO MEANING TO FINDING SUCCESS THAT WAY.
I'M NOT SAYING WE CAN'T BEAT HIS FIRST CHAPTER. IT'S JUST THAT THE GREATEST DAMAGE A SERIES COULD SUFFER IS A BIG DROP IN VOTES ON THE SECOND CHAPTER.
Ch.1
Ch.2
ZSH
THAT'S RIGHT! WE'LL PUT OUR CLIMAX UP AGAINST HIS SECOND CHAPTER!
YES!
PCP
"The Marriage Proposal Plan"
Outline
PERFECT.
ACTUALLY, HITTING HIS FIRST CHAPTER WITH OUR THIRD WOULD HAVE MEANT HAVING IT WRITTEN OUT BY NEXT WEEK. SO NOW WE HAVE AN EXTRA WEEK TO WORK ON IT!
GOOD POINT. BUT THAT STILL MAKES IT TIGHT. MAYBE YOU SHOULD JUST FOCUS ON THE CURRENT ARC...
NO, THIS'LL BE WAY BETTER! LET'S GO ALL OUT!
OKAY!

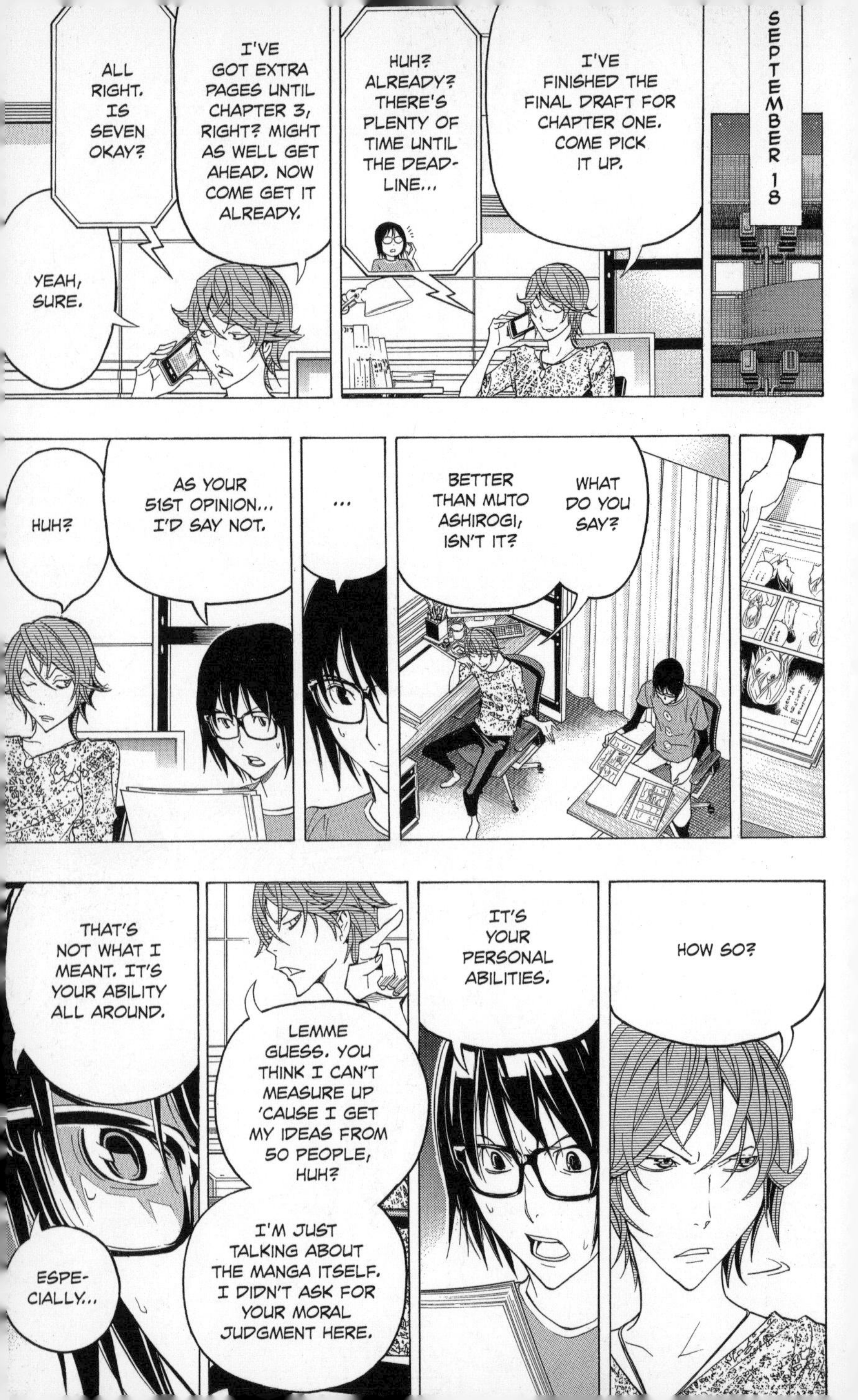
SEPTEMBER 18
I'VE FINISHED THE FINAL DRAFT FOR CHAPTER ONE. COME PICK IT UP.
HUH? ALREADY? THERE'S PLENTY OF TIME UNTIL THE DEAD-LINE...
I'VE GOT EXTRA PAGES UNTIL CHAPTER 3, RIGHT? MIGHT AS WELL GET AHEAD. NOW COME GET IT ALREADY.
ALL RIGHT. IS SEVEN OKAY?
YEAH, SURE.
WHAT DO YOU SAY?
BETTER THAN MUTO ASHIROGI, ISN'T IT?
...
AS YOUR 51ST OPINION... I'D SAY NOT.
HUH?
HOW SO?
IT'S YOUR PERSONAL ABILITIES.
LEMME GUESS. YOU THINK I CAN'T MEASURE UP 'CAUSE I GET MY IDEAS FROM 50 PEOPLE, HUH?
I'M JUST TALKING ABOUT THE MANGA ITSELF. I DIDN'T ASK FOR YOUR MORAL JUDGMENT HERE.
THAT'S NOT WHAT I MEANT. IT'S YOUR ABILITY ALL AROUND.
ESPE-CIALLY...

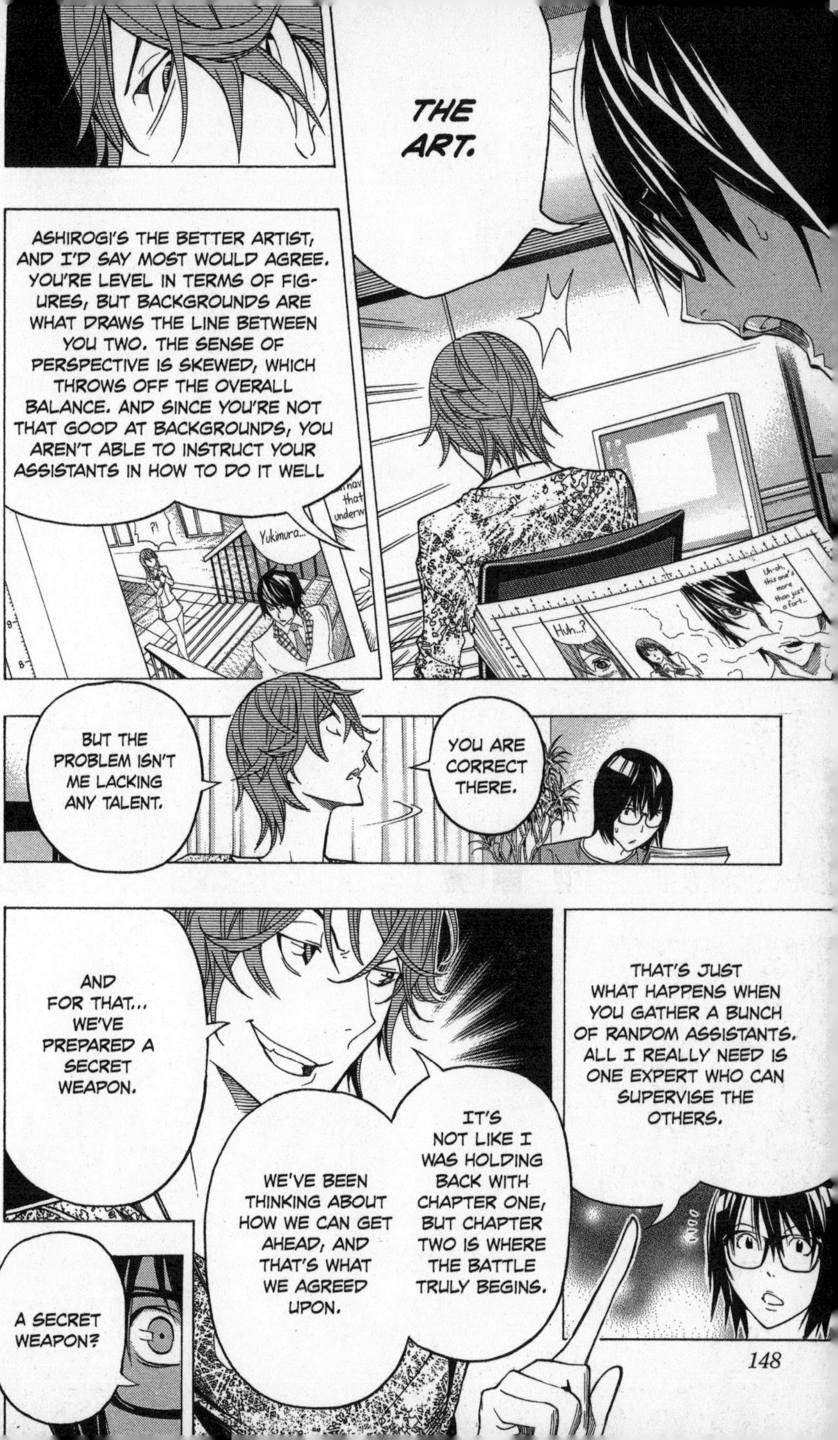
THE ART.
Uh-oh, this one's more than a fart...
Huh..?
ASHIROGI'S THE BETTER ARTIST, AND I'D SAY MOST WOULD AGREE. YOU'RE LEVEL IN TERMS OF FIGURES, BUT BACKGROUNDS ARE WHAT DRAWS THE LINE BETWEEN YOU TWO. THE SENSE OF PERSPECTIVE IS SKEWED, WHICH THROWS OFF THE OVERALL BALANCE. AND SINCE YOU'RE NOT THAT GOOD AT BACKGROUNDS, YOU AREN'T ABLE TO INSTRUCT YOUR ASSISTANTS IN HOW TO DO IT WELL
Yukimura...
?!
YOU ARE CORRECT THERE.
BUT THE PROBLEM ISN'T ME LACKING ANY TALENT.
THAT'S JUST WHAT HAPPENS WHEN YOU GATHER A BUNCH OF RANDOM ASSISTANTS. ALL I REALLY NEED IS ONE EXPERT WHO CAN SUPERVISE THE OTHERS.
AND FOR THAT... WE'VE PREPARED A SECRET WEAPON.
IT'S NOT LIKE I WAS HOLDING BACK WITH CHAPTER ONE, BUT CHAPTER TWO IS WHERE THE BATTLE TRULY BEGINS.
WE'VE BEEN THINKING ABOUT HOW WE CAN GET AHEAD, AND THAT'S WHAT WE AGREED UPON.
A SECRET WEAPON?

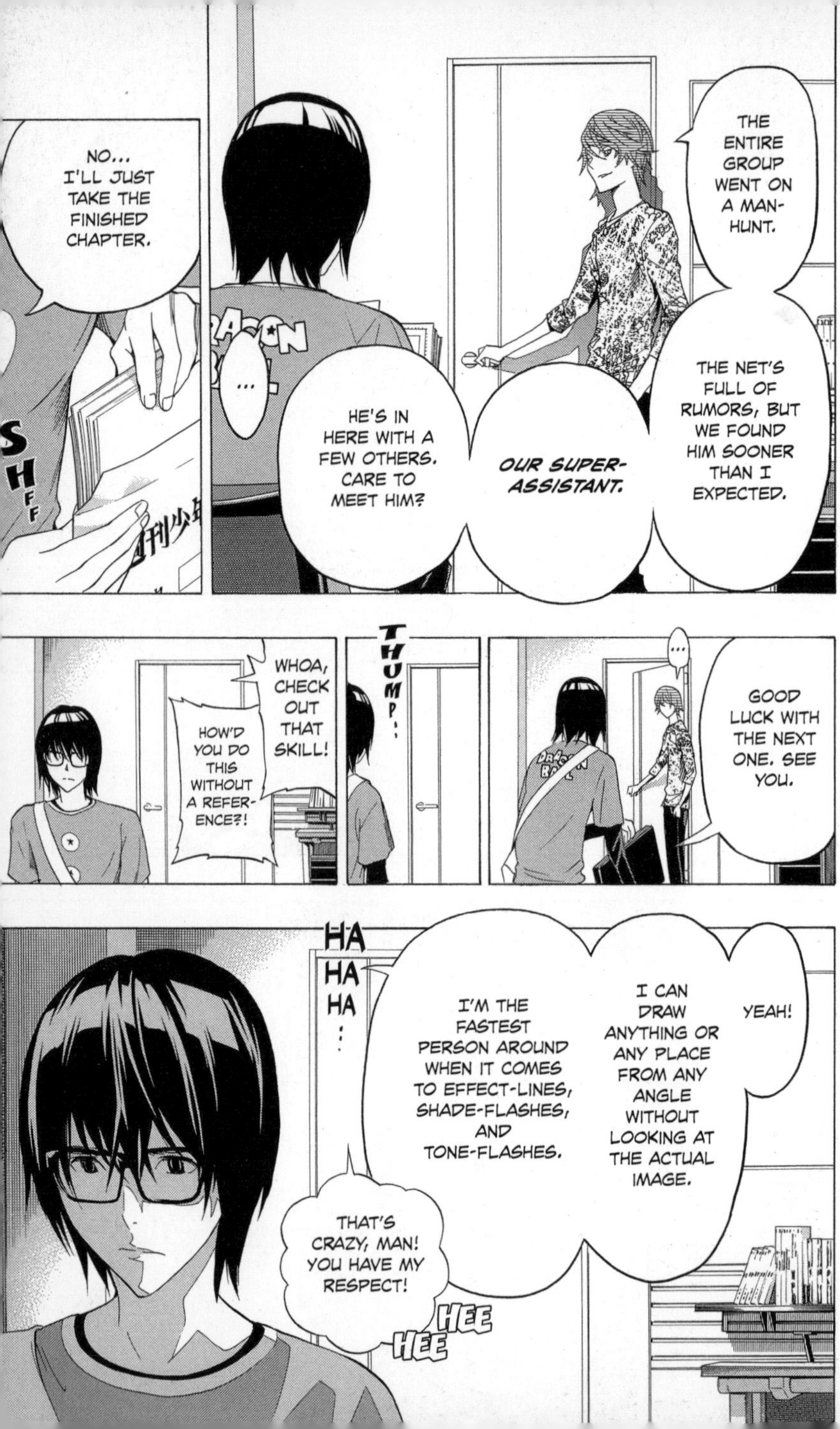
THE ENTIRE GROUP WENT ON A MAN-HUNT.
THE NET'S FULL OF RUMORS, BUT WE FOUND HIM SOONER THAN I EXPECTED.
OUR SUPER-ASSISTANT.
HE'S IN HERE WITH A FEW OTHERS. CARE TO MEET HIM?
...
NO... I'LL JUST TAKE THE FINISHED CHAPTER.
SHFF
...
GOOD LUCK WITH THE NEXT ONE. SEE YOU.
THUMP!!
WHOA, CHECK OUT THAT SKILL!
HOW'D YOU DO THIS WITHOUT A REFERENCE?!
YEAH!
I CAN DRAW ANYTHING OR ANY PLACE FROM ANY ANGLE WITHOUT LOOKING AT THE ACTUAL IMAGE.
I'M THE FASTEST PERSON AROUND WHEN IT COMES TO EFFECT-LINES, SHADE-FLASHES, AND TONE-FLASHES.
HA HA HA...
THAT'S CRAZY, MAN! YOU HAVE MY RESPECT!
HEE HEE

OHBA'S STORYBOARD

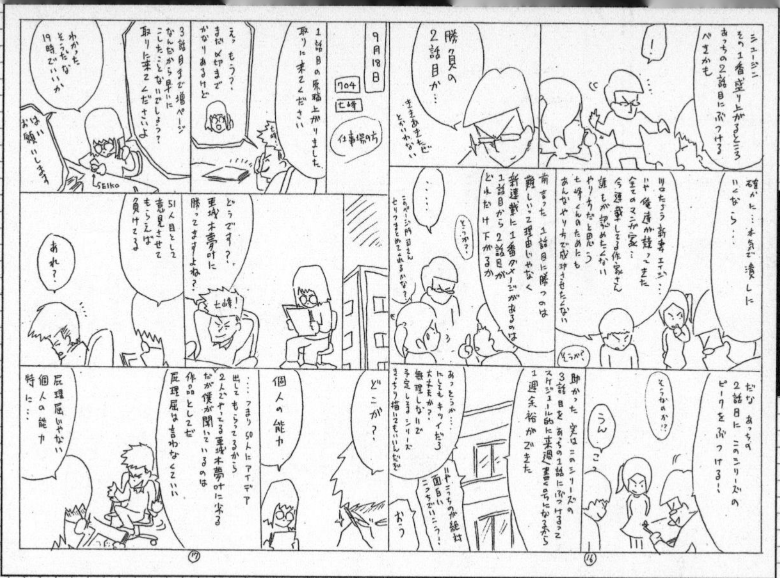
シュージン その1番盛り上がるところ あっちの2話目にぶつけるべきかも
！
…
勝負の2話目か…
確かに…本気で潰しにいくなら…
リロたろう 新妻エイジ… いや俺達が競ってきた全てのマンガ家… 今連載してる作家さん 誰もが認めたくない やりかただと思う 七峰くんのためにも あんなやり方で成功させたくない
そうか
前言った 1話目に勝つのは難しいって理由じゃなく 新連載に1番ダメージがあるのは 1話目から2話目が どれだけ下がるか
そうか？
……
だな あっちの2話目に このシリーズのピークをぶつける！
そうなのか!?
うん
助かった 実はこのシリーズの3話目を あっちの1話にぶつけるってスケジュール的に来週まできつくなるから 1週余裕ができた
あっそうか… にしてもキツイだろ 大丈夫か？ 無理しなくて 予定してるシリーズ きっちり描いてもいいんだぞ
いや こっちの方が絶対面白い ここでいこう！
おう
9月18日
704 七峰
仕事場の方
1話目の原稿上がりました 取りに来てください
えっもう？ まだ〆切まで かなりあるけど
3話目まで増ページ なんだから早めに こしたことないでしょう？ 取りに来てくださいよ
わかった そうだな 19時でいいか
はい お願いします
どうです？ 亜城木夢叶に 勝ってますよね？
七峰！
51人目として 意見させて もらえば 負けてる
あれ？
どこが？
個人の能力
…つまり 50人にアイデア 出してもらってるから 2人でやってる亜城木夢叶に劣る だが僕が聞いているのは 作品として だ 屁理屈は言わなくていい
屁理屈じゃない 個人の能力 特に…

OBATA'S STORYBOARD

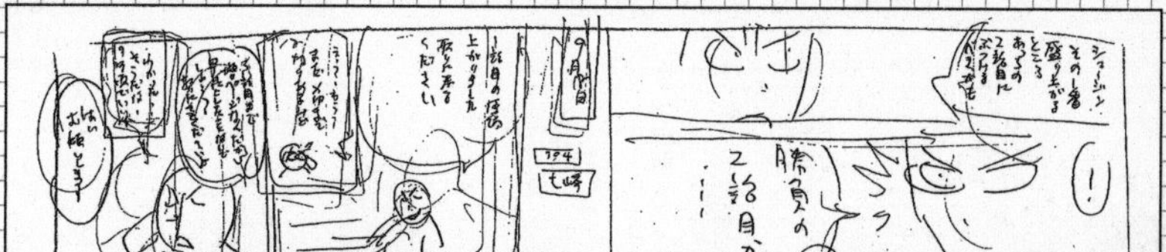

COMPLETE!

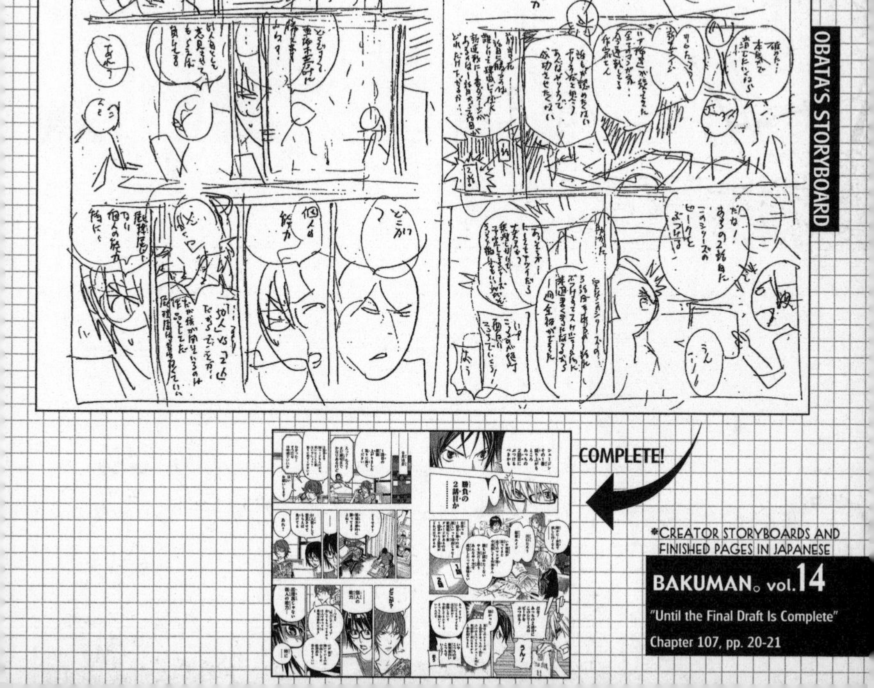

*CREATOR STORYBOARDS AND FINISHED PAGES IN JAPANESE

BAKUMAN。 vol.14

"Until the Final Draft Is Complete"

Chapter 107, pp. 20-21

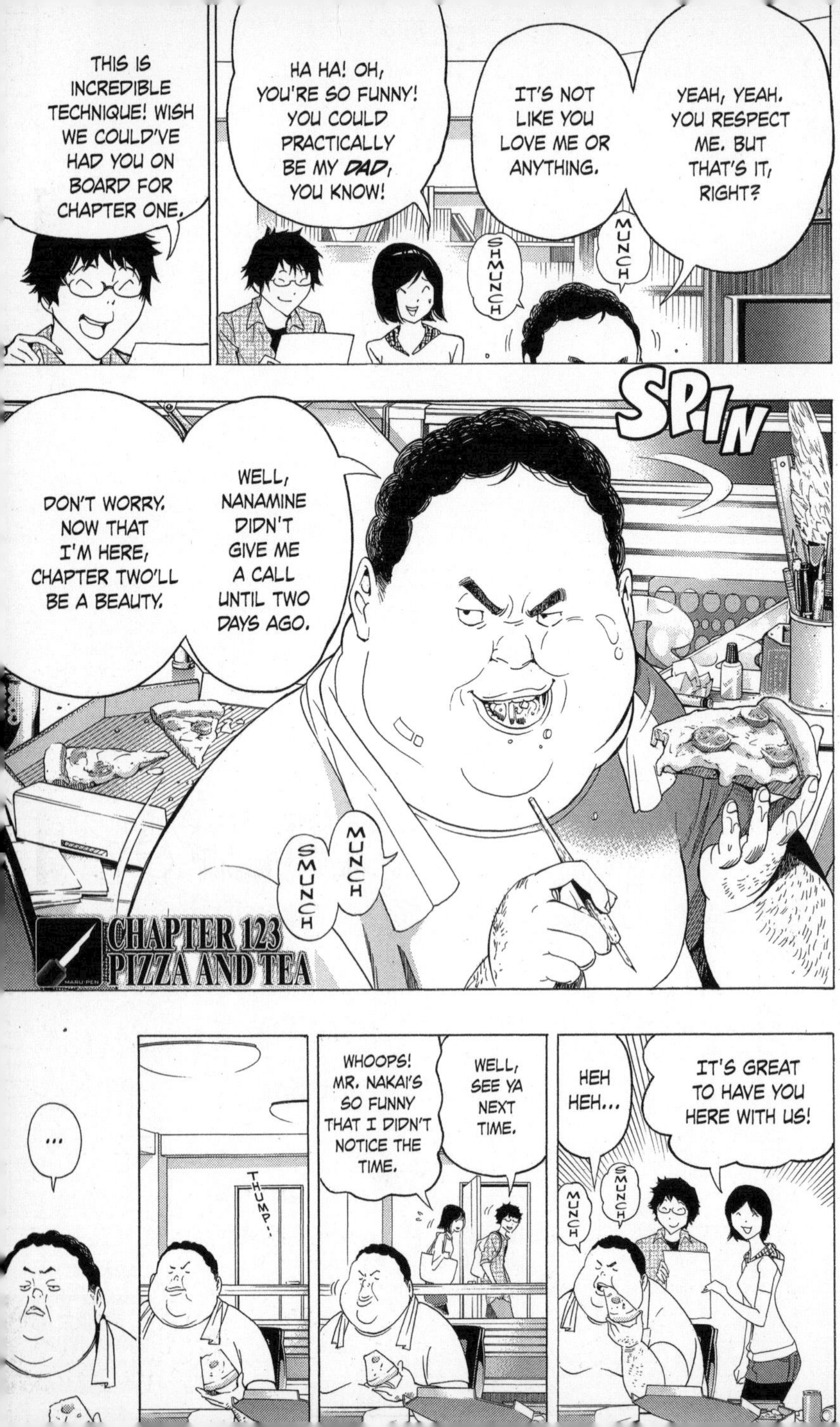
YEAH, YEAH. YOU RESPECT ME. BUT THAT'S IT, RIGHT?
IT'S NOT LIKE YOU LOVE ME OR ANYTHING.
MUNCH
SHMUNCH
HA HA! OH, YOU'RE SO FUNNY! YOU COULD PRACTICALLY BE MY *DAD*, YOU KNOW!
THIS IS INCREDIBLE TECHNIQUE! WISH WE COULD'VE HAD YOU ON BOARD FOR CHAPTER ONE.
SPIN
WELL, NANAMINE DIDN'T GIVE ME A CALL UNTIL TWO DAYS AGO.
DON'T WORRY. NOW THAT I'M HERE, CHAPTER TWO'LL BE A BEAUTY.
MUNCH
SMUNCH
CHAPTER 123
PIZZA AND TEA
IT'S GREAT TO HAVE YOU HERE WITH US!
HEH HEH...
SMUNCH
MUNCH
WELL, SEE YA NEXT TIME.
WHOOPS! MR. NAKAI'S SO FUNNY THAT I DIDN'T NOTICE THE TIME.
THUMP!!
...

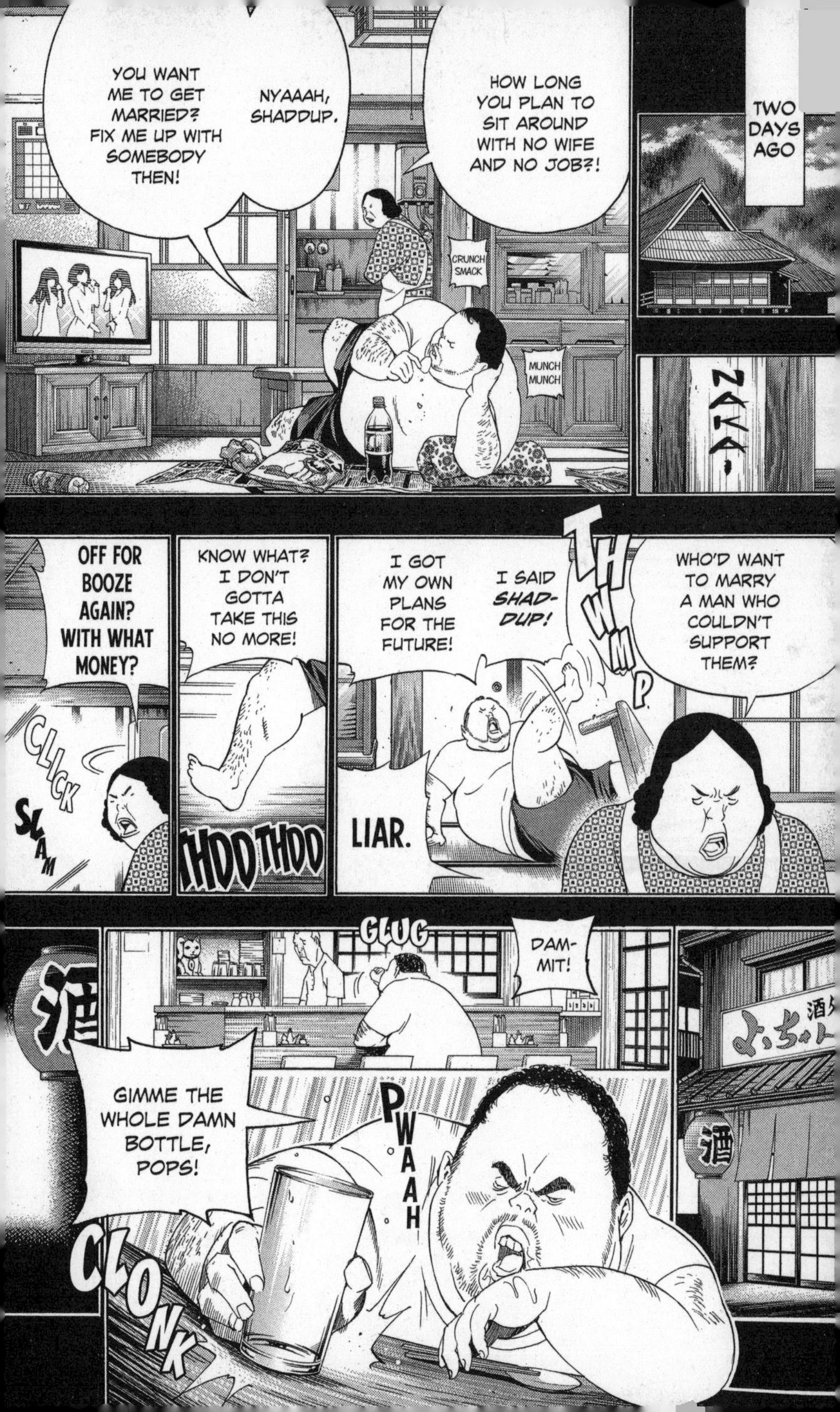
TWO DAYS AGO
NAKA
HOW LONG YOU PLAN TO SIT AROUND WITH NO WIFE AND NO JOB?!
NYAAAH, SHADDUP.
YOU WANT ME TO GET MARRIED? FIX ME UP WITH SOMEBODY THEN!
CRUNCH SMACK
MUNCH MUNCH
THWMP
WHO'D WANT TO MARRY A MAN WHO COULDN'T SUPPORT THEM?
I SAID SHAD-DUP!
I GOT MY OWN PLANS FOR THE FUTURE!
LIAR.
KNOW WHAT? I DON'T GOTTA TAKE THIS NO MORE!
THDO THDO
OFF FOR BOOZE AGAIN? WITH WHAT MONEY?
CLICK
SLAM
DAM-MIT!
GLUG
PWAAH
GIMME THE WHOLE DAMN BOTTLE, POPS!
CLONK

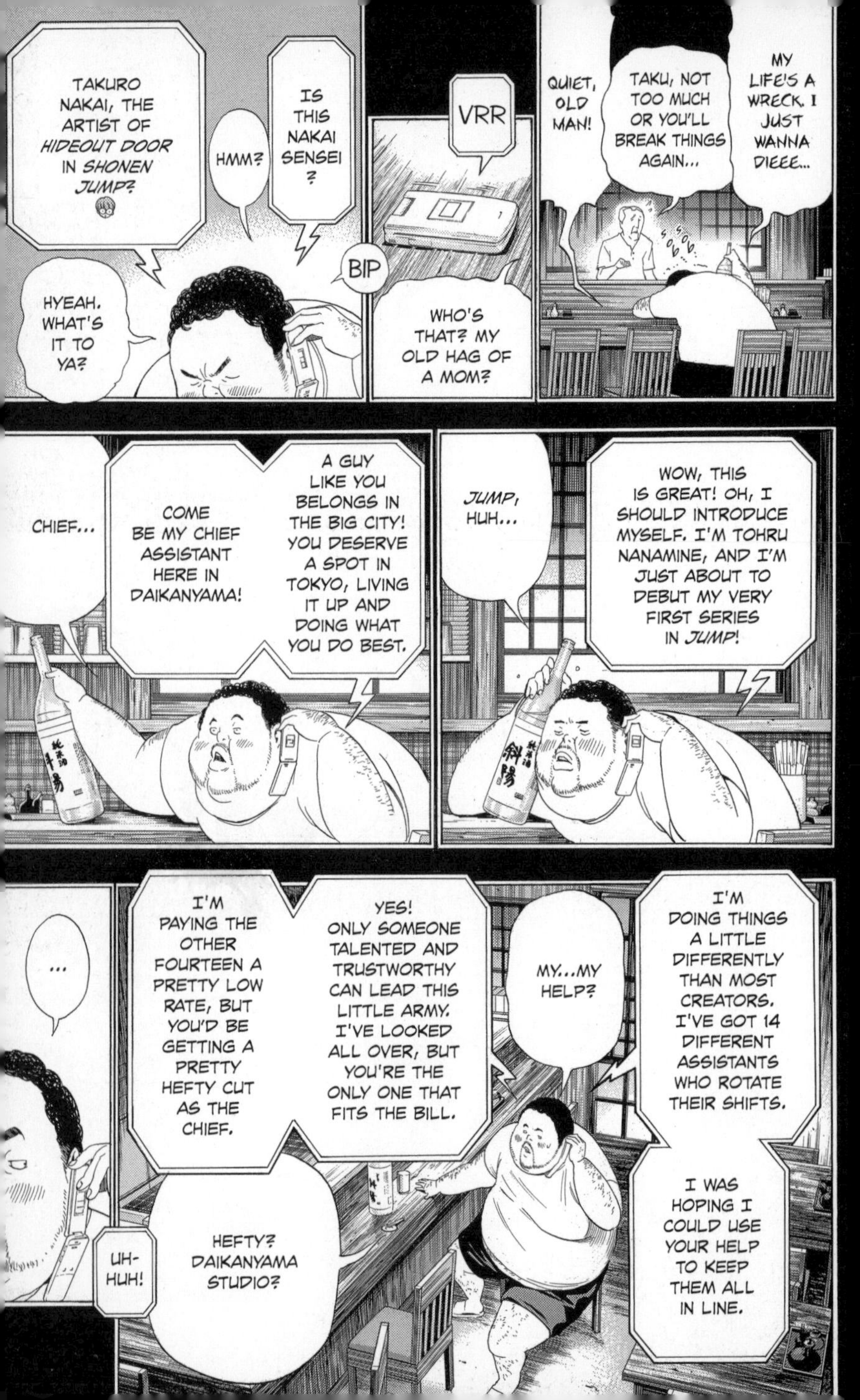
MY LIFE'S A WRECK. I JUST WANNA DIEEE...
TAKU, NOT TOO MUCH OR YOU'LL BREAK THINGS AGAIN...
QUIET, OLD MAN!
VRR
BIP
WHO'S THAT? MY OLD HAG OF A MOM?
IS THIS NAKAI SENSEI?
HMM?
TAKURO NAKAI, THE ARTIST OF *HIDEOUT DOOR* IN *SHONEN JUMP*?
HYEAH. WHAT'S IT TO YA?
WOW, THIS IS GREAT! OH, I SHOULD INTRODUCE MYSELF. I'M TOHRU NANAMINE, AND I'M JUST ABOUT TO DEBUT MY VERY FIRST SERIES IN *JUMP*!
JUMP, HUH...
A GUY LIKE YOU BELONGS IN THE BIG CITY! YOU DESERVE A SPOT IN TOKYO, LIVING IT UP AND DOING WHAT YOU DO BEST.
COME BE MY CHIEF ASSISTANT HERE IN DAIKANYAMA!
CHIEF...
I'M DOING THINGS A LITTLE DIFFERENTLY THAN MOST CREATORS. I'VE GOT 14 DIFFERENT ASSISTANTS WHO ROTATE THEIR SHIFTS.
MY...MY HELP?
I WAS HOPING I COULD USE YOUR HELP TO KEEP THEM ALL IN LINE.
YES! ONLY SOMEONE TALENTED AND TRUSTWORTHY CAN LEAD THIS LITTLE ARMY. I'VE LOOKED ALL OVER, BUT YOU'RE THE ONLY ONE THAT FITS THE BILL.
I'M PAYING THE OTHER FOURTEEN A PRETTY LOW RATE, BUT YOU'D BE GETTING A PRETTY HEFTY CUT AS THE CHIEF.
HEFTY? DAIKANYAMA STUDIO?
...
UH-HUH!

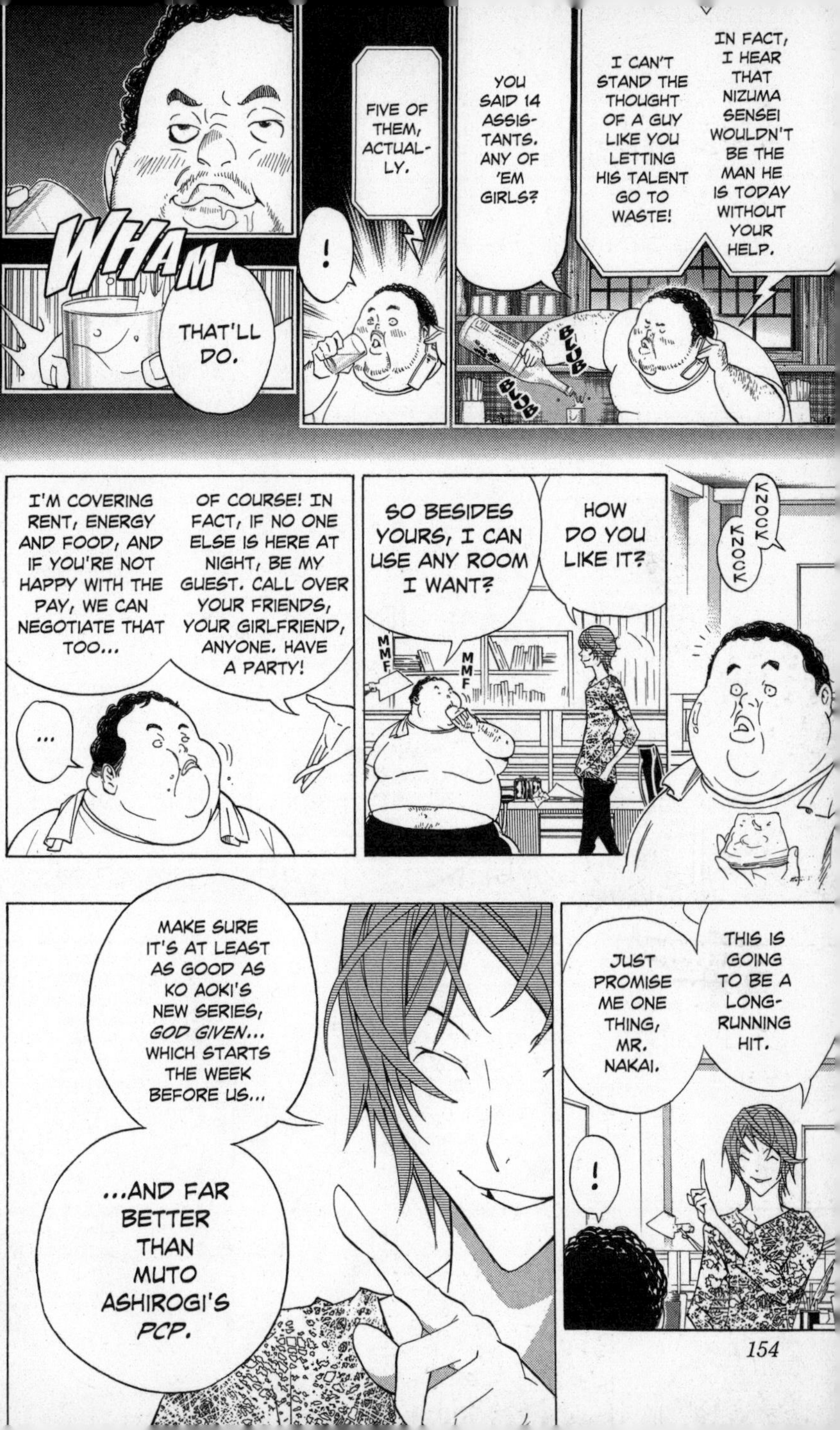
IN FACT, I HEAR THAT NIZUMA SENSEI WOULDN'T BE THE MAN HE IS TODAY WITHOUT YOUR HELP.
I CAN'T STAND THE THOUGHT OF A GUY LIKE YOU LETTING HIS TALENT GO TO WASTE!
YOU SAID 14 ASSISTANTS. ANY OF 'EM GIRLS?
BLUB
BLUB
FIVE OF THEM, ACTUALLY.
!
WHAM
THAT'LL DO.
KNOCK KNOCK
HOW DO YOU LIKE IT?
SO BESIDES YOURS, I CAN USE ANY ROOM I WANT?
MMF
MMF
OF COURSE! IN FACT, IF NO ONE ELSE IS HERE AT NIGHT, BE MY GUEST. CALL OVER YOUR FRIENDS, YOUR GIRLFRIEND, ANYONE. HAVE A PARTY!
I'M COVERING RENT, ENERGY AND FOOD, AND IF YOU'RE NOT HAPPY WITH THE PAY, WE CAN NEGOTIATE THAT TOO...
...
THIS IS GOING TO BE A LONG-RUNNING HIT.
JUST PROMISE ME ONE THING, MR. NAKAI.
!
MAKE SURE IT'S AT LEAST AS GOOD AS KO AOKI'S NEW SERIES, *GOD GIVEN*... WHICH STARTS THE WEEK BEFORE US...
...AND FAR BETTER THAN MUTO ASHIROGI'S *PCP*.

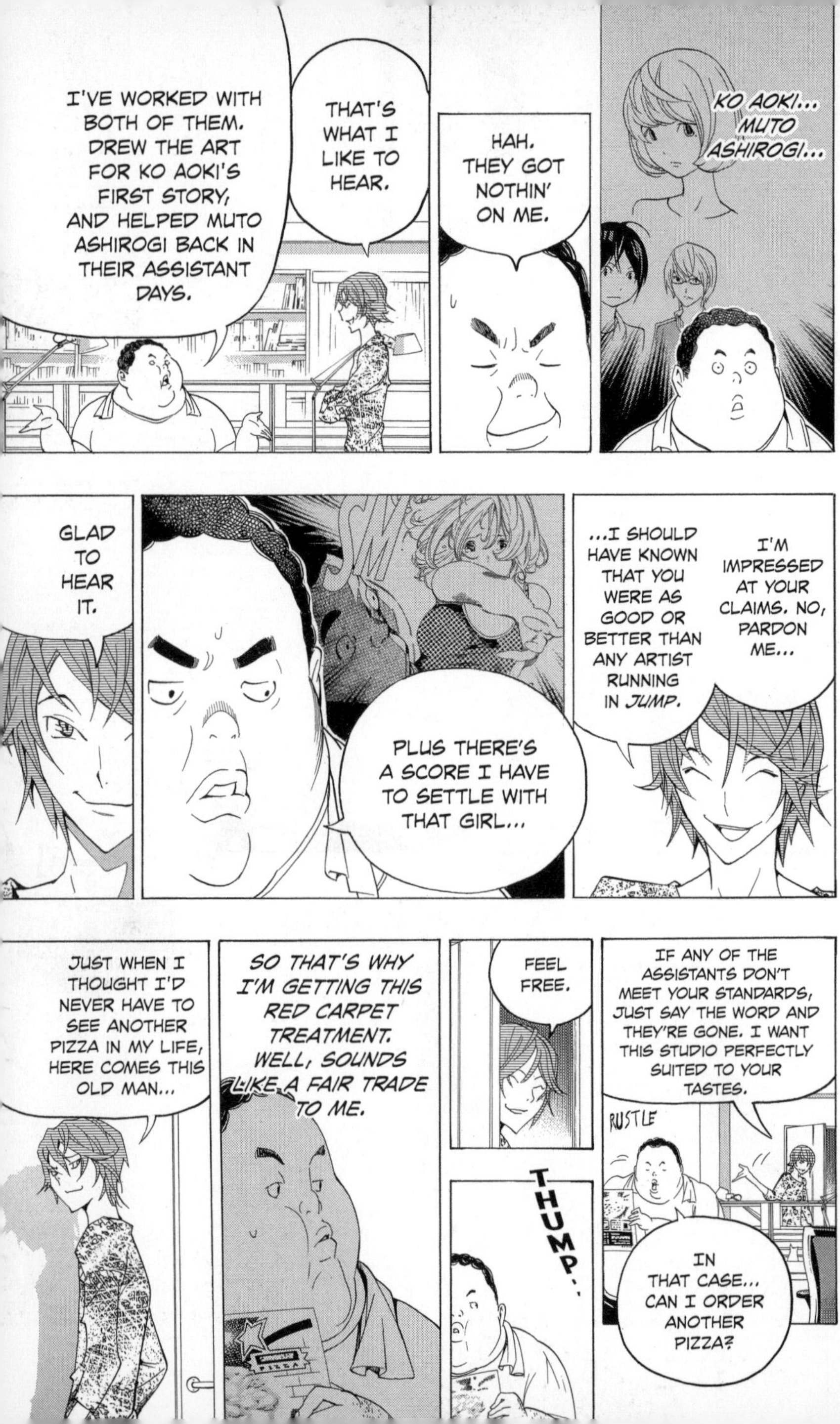
KO AOKI... MUTO ASHIROGI...
HAH. THEY GOT NOTHIN' ON ME.
I'VE WORKED WITH BOTH OF THEM. DREW THE ART FOR KO AOKI'S FIRST STORY, AND HELPED MUTO ASHIROGI BACK IN THEIR ASSISTANT DAYS.
THAT'S WHAT I LIKE TO HEAR.
I'M IMPRESSED AT YOUR CLAIMS. NO, PARDON ME...
...I SHOULD HAVE KNOWN THAT YOU WERE AS GOOD OR BETTER THAN ANY ARTIST RUNNING IN *JUMP*.
PLUS THERE'S A SCORE I HAVE TO SETTLE WITH THAT GIRL...
GLAD TO HEAR IT.
IF ANY OF THE ASSISTANTS DON'T MEET YOUR STANDARDS, JUST SAY THE WORD AND THEY'RE GONE. I WANT THIS STUDIO PERFECTLY SUITED TO YOUR TASTES.
RUSTLE
IN THAT CASE... CAN I ORDER ANOTHER PIZZA?
FEEL FREE.
THUMP..
SO THAT'S WHY I'M GETTING THIS RED CARPET TREATMENT. WELL, SOUNDS LIKE A FAIR TRADE TO ME.
JUST WHEN I THOUGHT I'D NEVER HAVE TO SEE ANOTHER PIZZA IN MY LIFE, HERE COMES THIS OLD MAN...

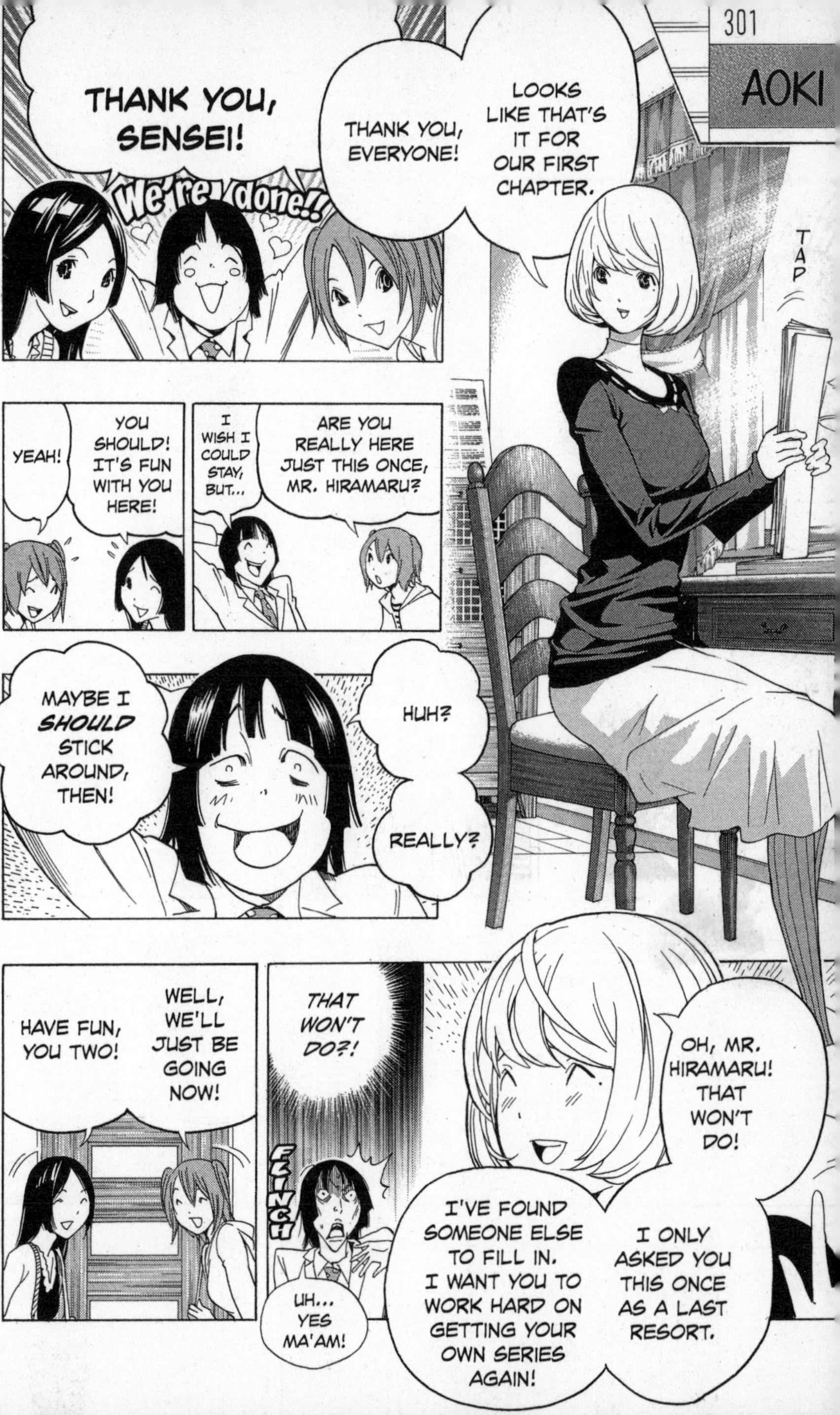
301
AOKI
LOOKS LIKE THAT'S IT FOR OUR FIRST CHAPTER.
THANK YOU, EVERYONE!
TAP
THANK YOU, SENSEI!
We're done!!
ARE YOU REALLY HERE JUST THIS ONCE, MR. HIRAMARU?
I WISH I COULD STAY, BUT...
YOU SHOULD! IT'S FUN WITH YOU HERE!
YEAH!
HUH?
REALLY?
MAYBE I *SHOULD* STICK AROUND, THEN!
OH, MR. HIRAMARU! THAT WON'T DO!
I ONLY ASKED YOU THIS ONCE AS A LAST RESORT.
I'VE FOUND SOMEONE ELSE TO FILL IN. I WANT YOU TO WORK HARD ON GETTING YOUR OWN SERIES AGAIN!
THAT WON'T DO?!
FLINCH
UH... YES MA'AM!
WELL, WE'LL JUST BE GOING NOW!
HAVE FUN, YOU TWO!

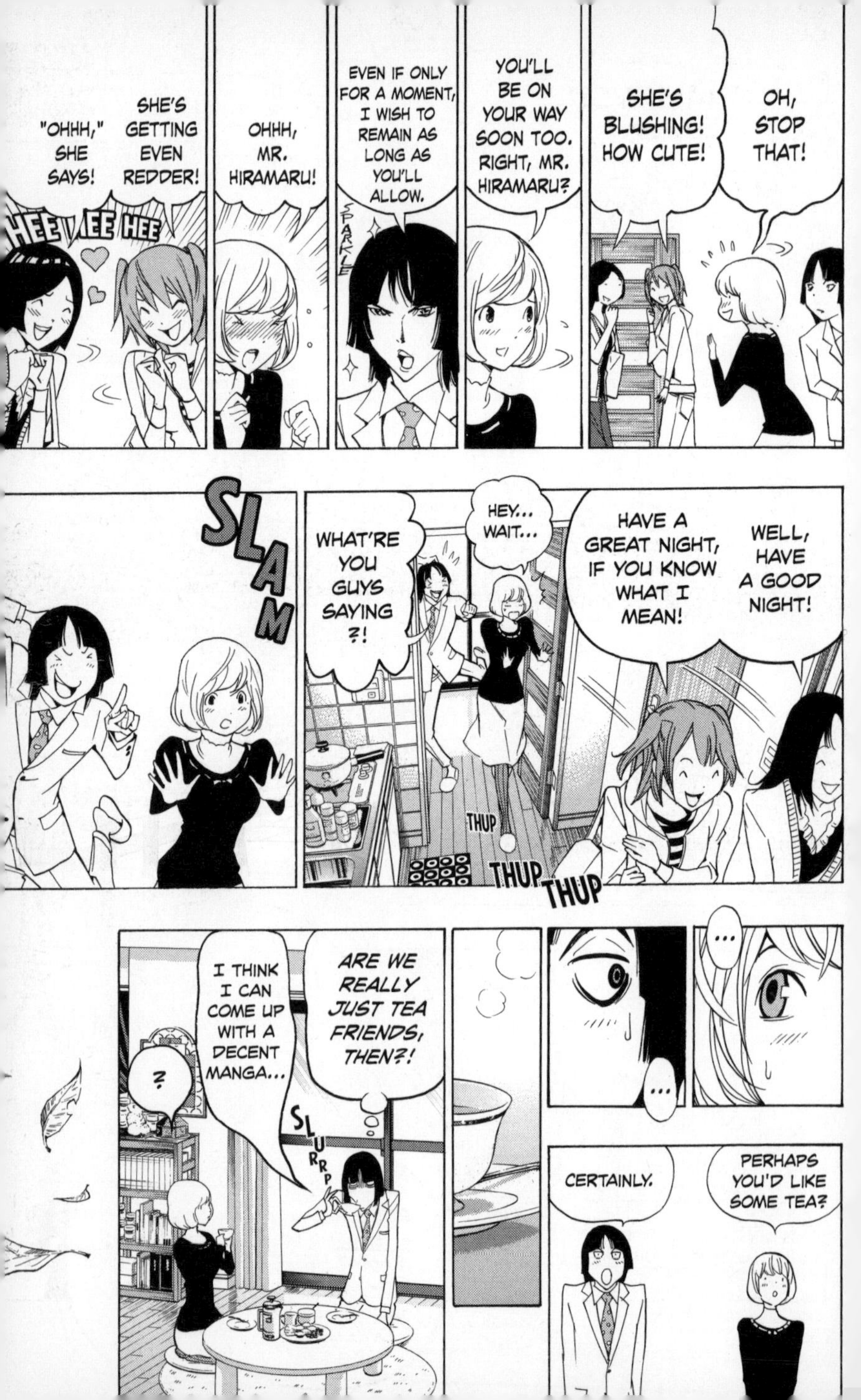
OH, STOP THAT!
SHE'S BLUSHING! HOW CUTE!
YOU'LL BE ON YOUR WAY SOON TOO. RIGHT, MR. HIRAMARU?
EVEN IF ONLY FOR A MOMENT, I WISH TO REMAIN AS LONG AS YOU'LL ALLOW.
SPARKLE
OHHH, MR. HIRAMARU!
SHE'S GETTING EVEN REDDER!
"OHHH," SHE SAYS!
HEE HEE HEE
WELL, HAVE A GOOD NIGHT!
HAVE A GREAT NIGHT, IF YOU KNOW WHAT I MEAN!
HEY... WAIT...
WHAT'RE YOU GUYS SAYING?!
THUP
THUP THUP
SLAM
...
...
PERHAPS YOU'D LIKE SOME TEA?
CERTAINLY.
ARE WE REALLY JUST TEA FRIENDS, THEN?!
I THINK I CAN COME UP WITH A DECENT MANGA...
SLURRP
?

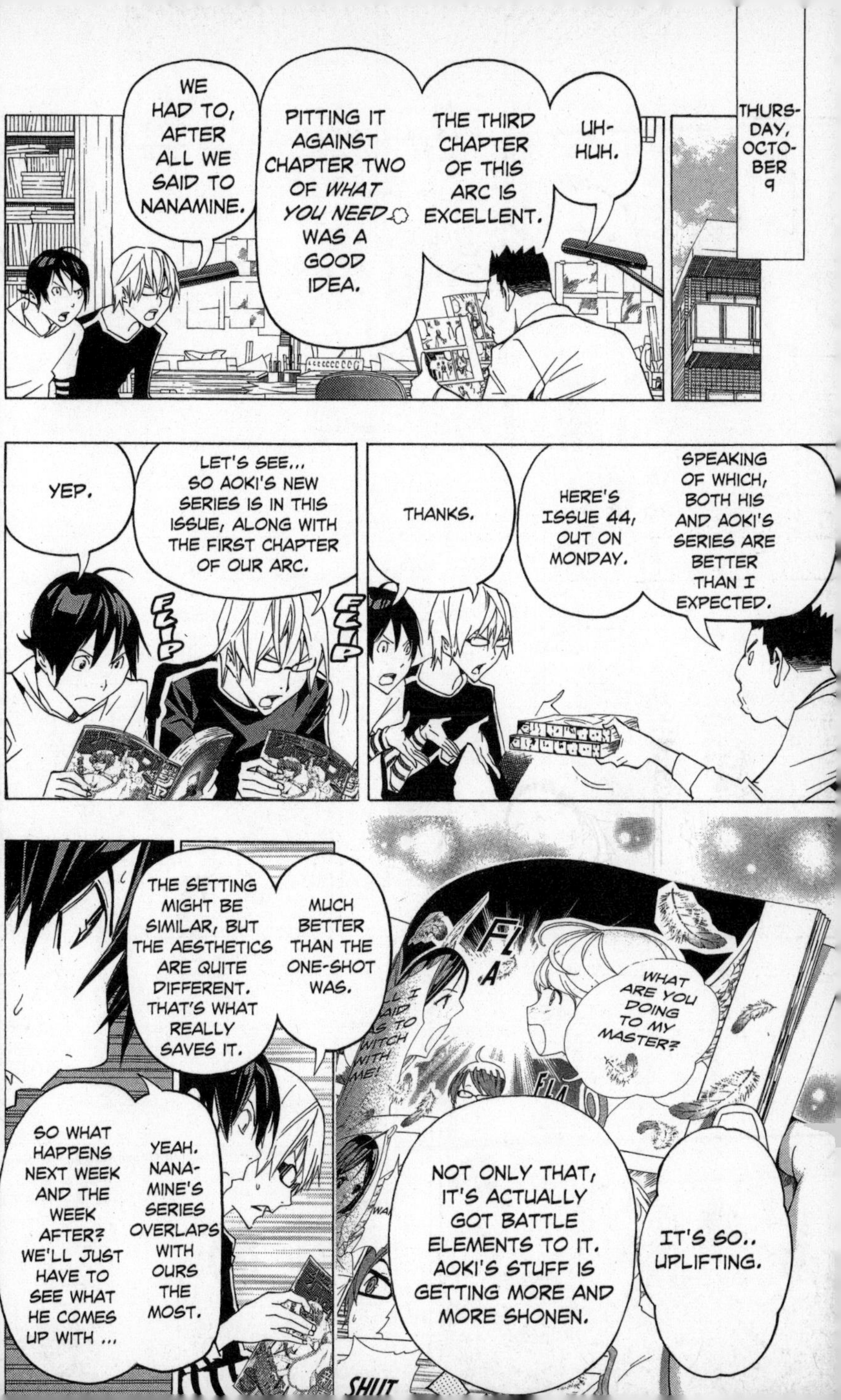
THURSDAY, OCTOBER 9
UH-HUH.
THE THIRD CHAPTER OF THIS ARC IS EXCELLENT.
PITTING IT AGAINST CHAPTER TWO OF *WHAT YOU NEED* WAS A GOOD IDEA.
WE HAD TO, AFTER ALL WE SAID TO NANAMINE.
SPEAKING OF WHICH, BOTH HIS AND AOKI'S SERIES ARE BETTER THAN I EXPECTED.
HERE'S ISSUE 44, OUT ON MONDAY.
THANKS.
FLIP
LET'S SEE... SO AOKI'S NEW SERIES IS IN THIS ISSUE, ALONG WITH THE FIRST CHAPTER OF OUR ARC.
FLIP
YEP.
FLA
WHAT ARE YOU DOING TO MY MASTER?
FLA
IT'S SO.. UPLIFTING.
NOT ONLY THAT, IT'S ACTUALLY GOT BATTLE ELEMENTS TO IT. AOKI'S STUFF IS GETTING MORE AND MORE SHONEN.
MUCH BETTER THAN THE ONE-SHOT WAS.
THE SETTING MIGHT BE SIMILAR, BUT THE AESTHETICS ARE QUITE DIFFERENT. THAT'S WHAT REALLY SAVES IT.
YEAH. NANAMINE'S SERIES OVERLAPS WITH OURS THE MOST.
SO WHAT HAPPENS NEXT WEEK AND THE WEEK AFTER? WE'LL JUST HAVE TO SEE WHAT HE COMES UP WITH ...
SHUT

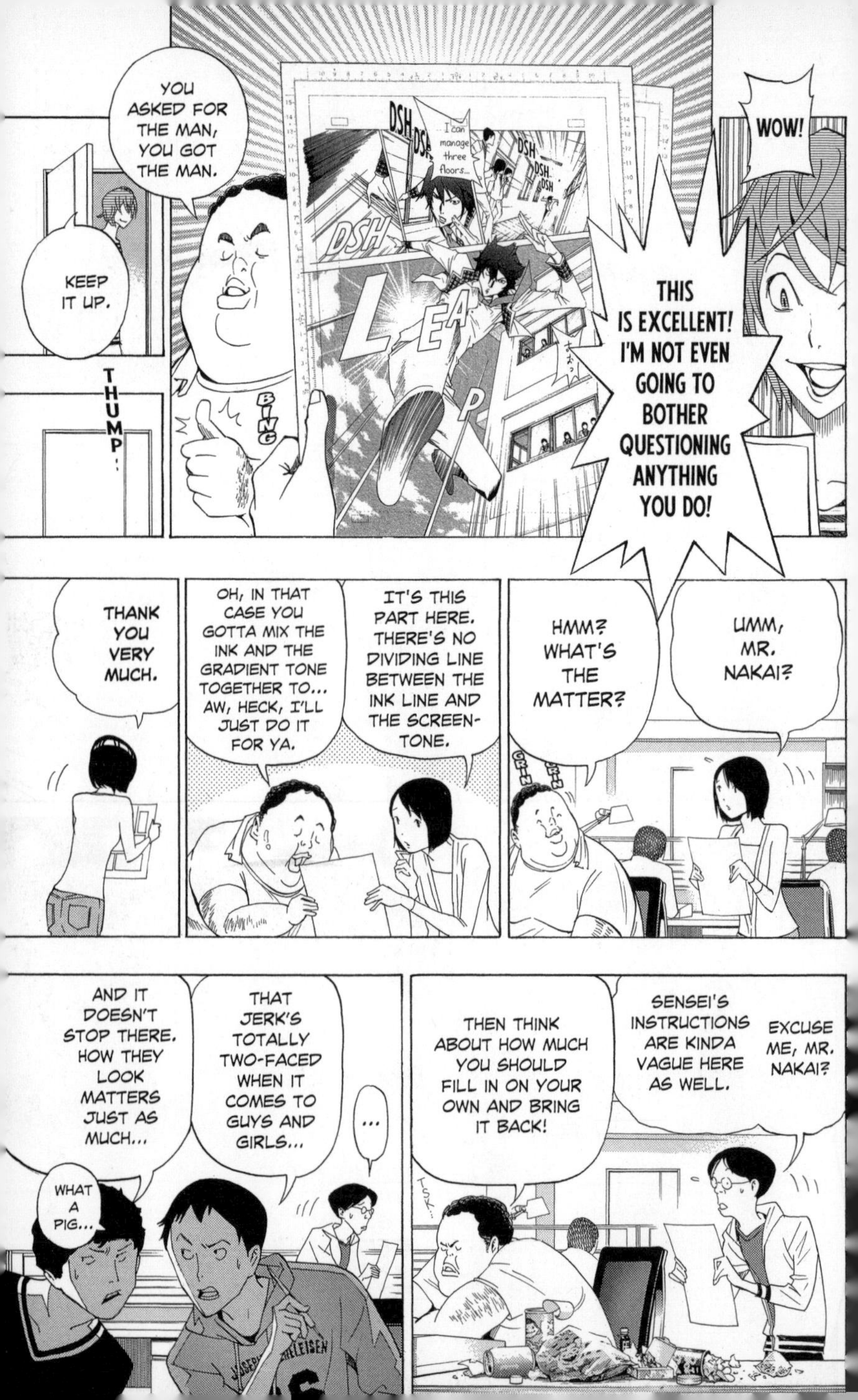
WOW!
THIS IS EXCELLENT! I'M NOT EVEN GOING TO BOTHER QUESTIONING ANYTHING YOU DO!
YOU ASKED FOR THE MAN, YOU GOT THE MAN.
DSH
DSH
I can manage three floors...
DSH
DSH
DSH
DSH
LEAP
BING
KEEP IT UP.
THUMP
UMM, MR. NAKAI?
HMM? WHAT'S THE MATTER?
GRIN
GRIN
IT'S THIS PART HERE. THERE'S NO DIVIDING LINE BETWEEN THE INK LINE AND THE SCREEN-TONE.
OH, IN THAT CASE YOU GOTTA MIX THE INK AND THE GRADIENT TONE TOGETHER TO... AW, HECK, I'LL JUST DO IT FOR YA.
THANK YOU VERY MUCH.
EXCUSE ME, MR. NAKAI?
SENSEI'S INSTRUCTIONS ARE KINDA VAGUE HERE AS WELL.
THEN THINK ABOUT HOW MUCH YOU SHOULD FILL IN ON YOUR OWN AND BRING IT BACK!
TSK...
...
THAT JERK'S TOTALLY TWO-FACED WHEN IT COMES TO GUYS AND GIRLS...
AND IT DOESN'T STOP THERE. HOW THEY LOOK MATTERS JUST AS MUCH...
WHAT A PIG...

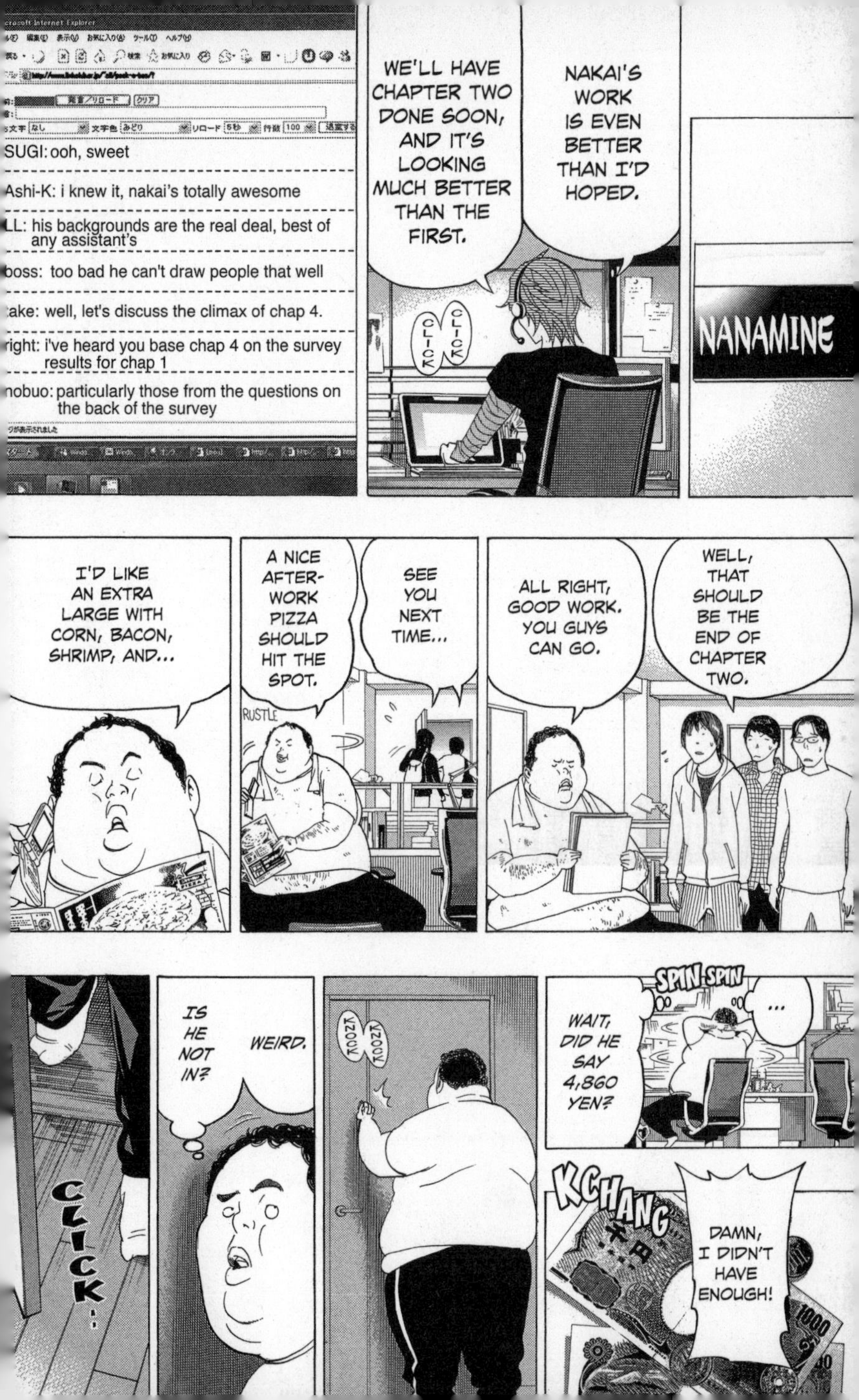
NANAMINE
NAKAI'S WORK IS EVEN BETTER THAN I'D HOPED.
WE'LL HAVE CHAPTER TWO DONE SOON, AND IT'S LOOKING MUCH BETTER THAN THE FIRST.
CLICK
CLICK
crosoft Internet Explorer
SUGI: ooh, sweet
Ashi-K: i knew it, nakai's totally awesome
LL: his backgrounds are the real deal, best of any assistant's
boss: too bad he can't draw people that well
ake: well, let's discuss the climax of chap 4.
right: i've heard you base chap 4 on the survey results for chap 1
nobuo: particularly those from the questions on the back of the survey
WELL, THAT SHOULD BE THE END OF CHAPTER TWO.
ALL RIGHT, GOOD WORK. YOU GUYS CAN GO.
SEE YOU NEXT TIME...
A NICE AFTER-WORK PIZZA SHOULD HIT THE SPOT.
RUSTLE
I'D LIKE AN EXTRA LARGE WITH CORN, BACON, SHRIMP, AND...
SPIN SPIN
...
WAIT, DID HE SAY 4,860 YEN?
KCHANG
DAMN, I DIDN'T HAVE ENOUGH!
KNOCK
KNOCK
IS HE NOT IN?
WEIRD.
CLICK

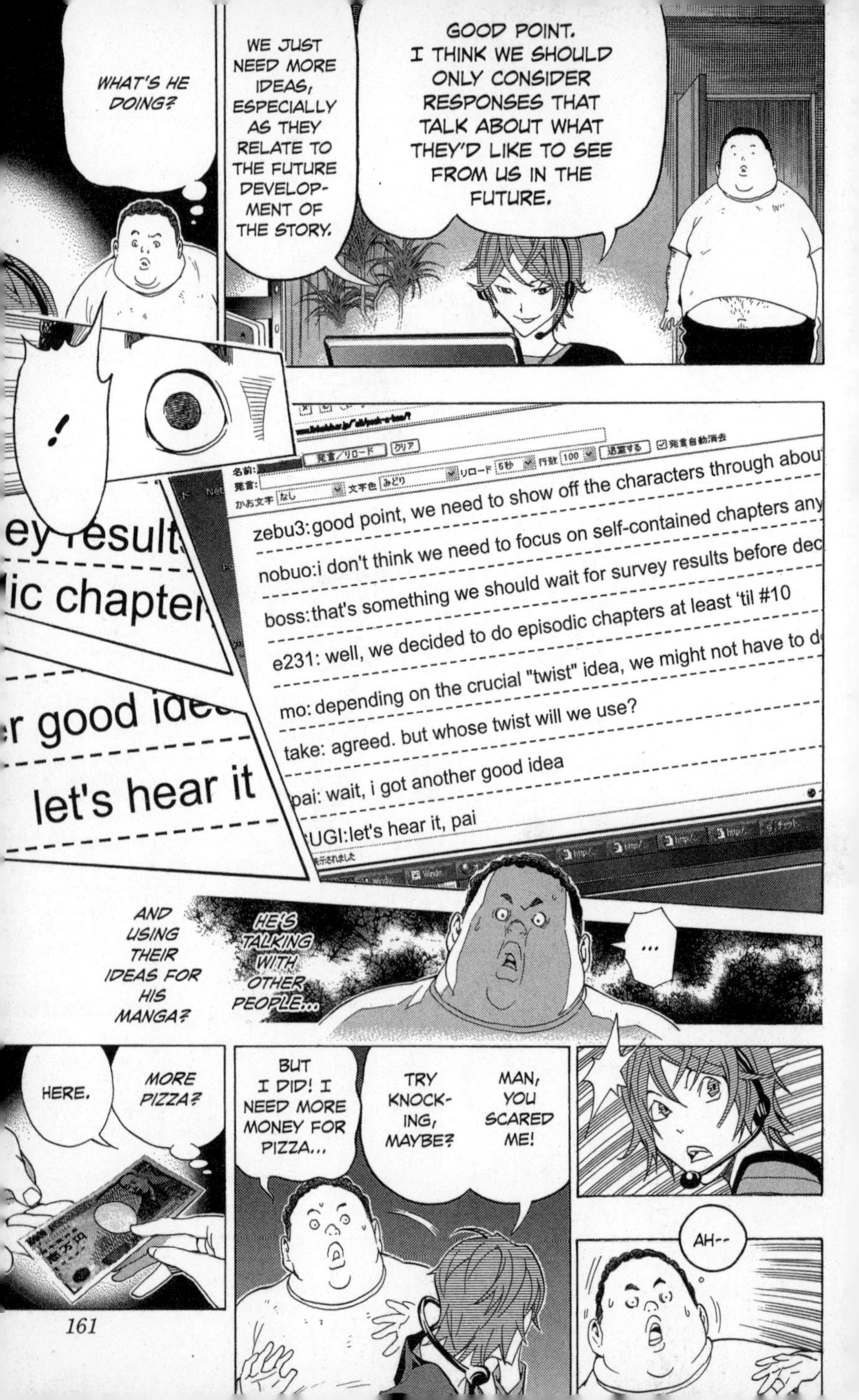
GOOD POINT. I THINK WE SHOULD ONLY CONSIDER RESPONSES THAT TALK ABOUT WHAT THEY'D LIKE TO SEE FROM US IN THE FUTURE.
WE JUST NEED MORE IDEAS, ESPECIALLY AS THEY RELATE TO THE FUTURE DEVELOP- MENT OF THE STORY.
WHAT'S HE DOING?
発言/リロード
クリア
退室する
発言自動消去
名前:
発言:
かお文字 なし
文字色 みどり
リロード 6秒
行数 100
zebu3:good point, we need to show off the characters through abou
nobuo:i don't think we need to focus on self-contained chapters any
boss:that's something we should wait for survey results before dec
e231: well, we decided to do episodic chapters at least 'til #10
mo: depending on the crucial "twist" idea, we might not have to d
take: agreed. but whose twist will we use?
pai: wait, i got another good idea
UGI:let's hear it, pai
!
ey results
ic chapter
r good ide
let's hear it
...
HE'S TALKING WITH OTHER PEOPLE...
AND USING THEIR IDEAS FOR HIS MANGA?
AH--
MAN, YOU SCARED ME!
TRY KNOCK- ING, MAYBE?
BUT I DID! I NEED MORE MONEY FOR PIZZA...
MORE PIZZA?
HERE.

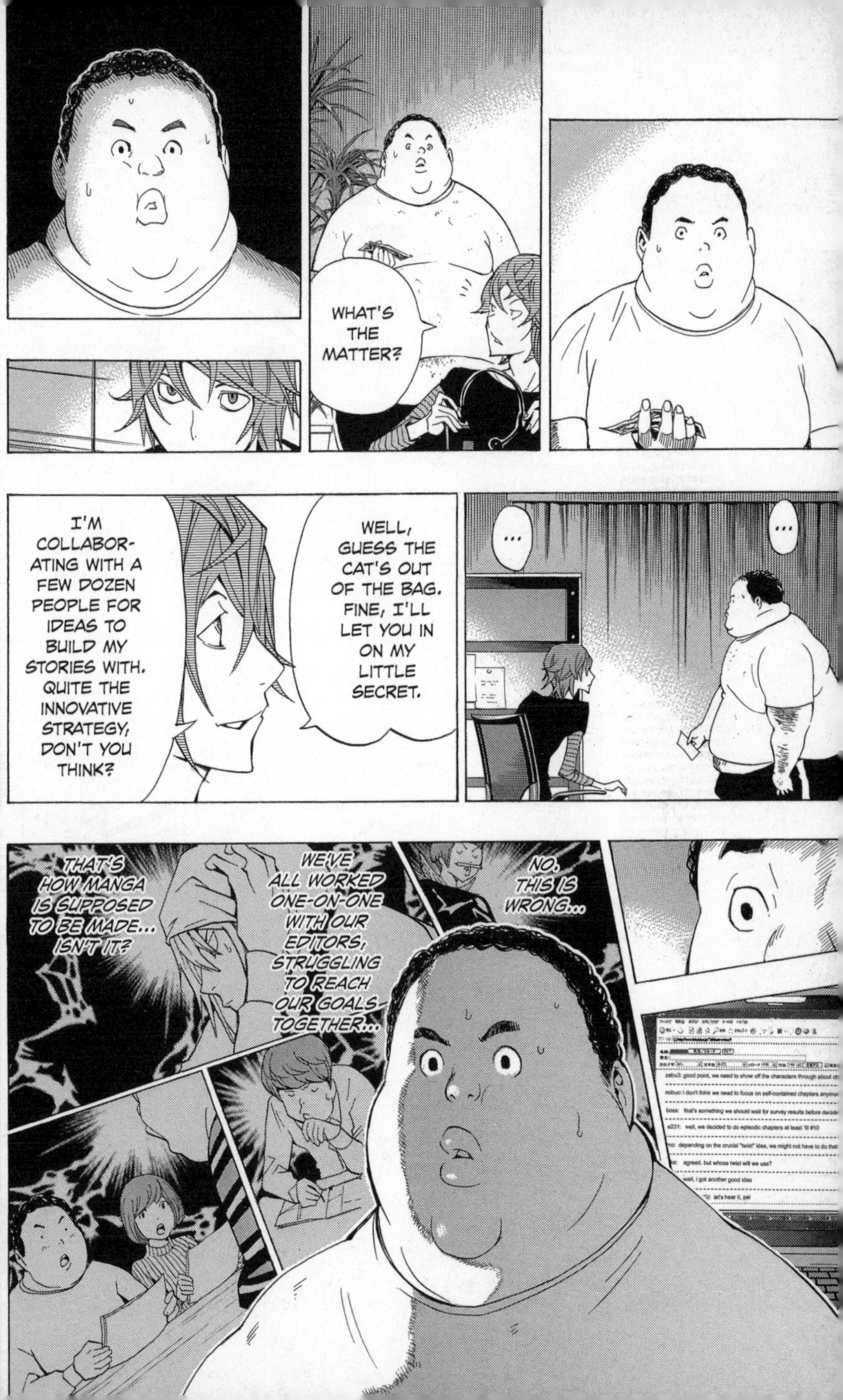
WHAT'S THE MATTER?
...
...
WELL, GUESS THE CAT'S OUT OF THE BAG. FINE, I'LL LET YOU IN ON MY LITTLE SECRET.
I'M COLLABOR-ATING WITH A FEW DOZEN PEOPLE FOR IDEAS TO BUILD MY STORIES WITH. QUITE THE INNOVATIVE STRATEGY, DON'T YOU THINK?
NO. THIS IS WRONG...
WE'VE ALL WORKED ONE-ON-ONE WITH OUR EDITORS, STRUGGLING TO REACH OUR GOALS TOGETHER...
THAT'S HOW MANGA IS SUPPOSED TO BE MADE... ISN'T IT?

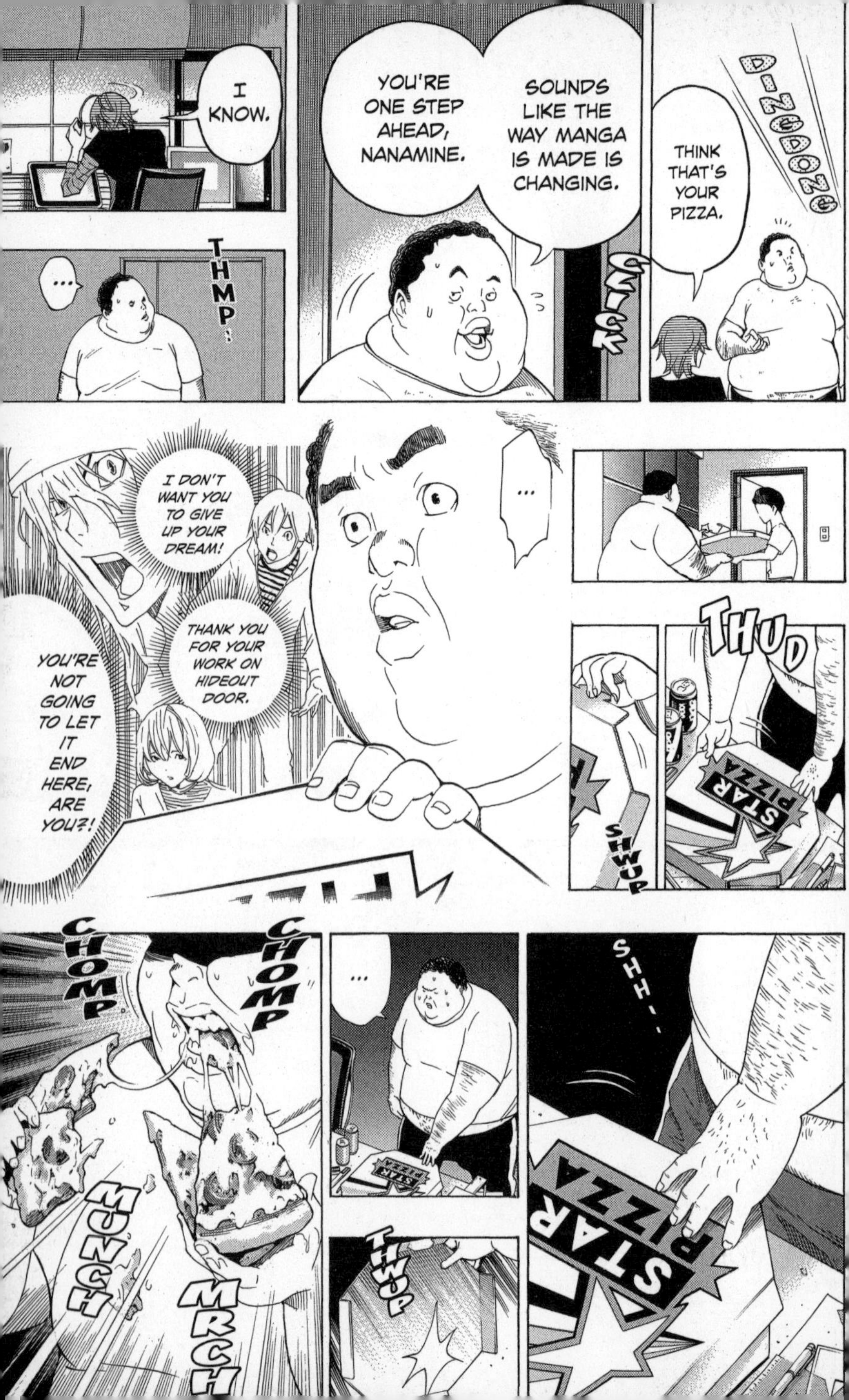
DINGDONG
THINK THAT'S YOUR PIZZA.
SOUNDS LIKE THE WAY MANGA IS MADE IS CHANGING.
YOU'RE ONE STEP AHEAD, NANAMINE.
CLICK
I KNOW.
THMP
...
THUD
SHWUP
STAR PIZZA
...
I DON'T WANT YOU TO GIVE UP YOUR DREAM!
THANK YOU FOR YOUR WORK ON HIDEOUT DOOR.
YOU'RE NOT GOING TO LET IT END HERE, ARE YOU?!
SHH..
STAR PIZZA
...
THWUP
CHOMP
CHOMP
MUNCH
MRCH

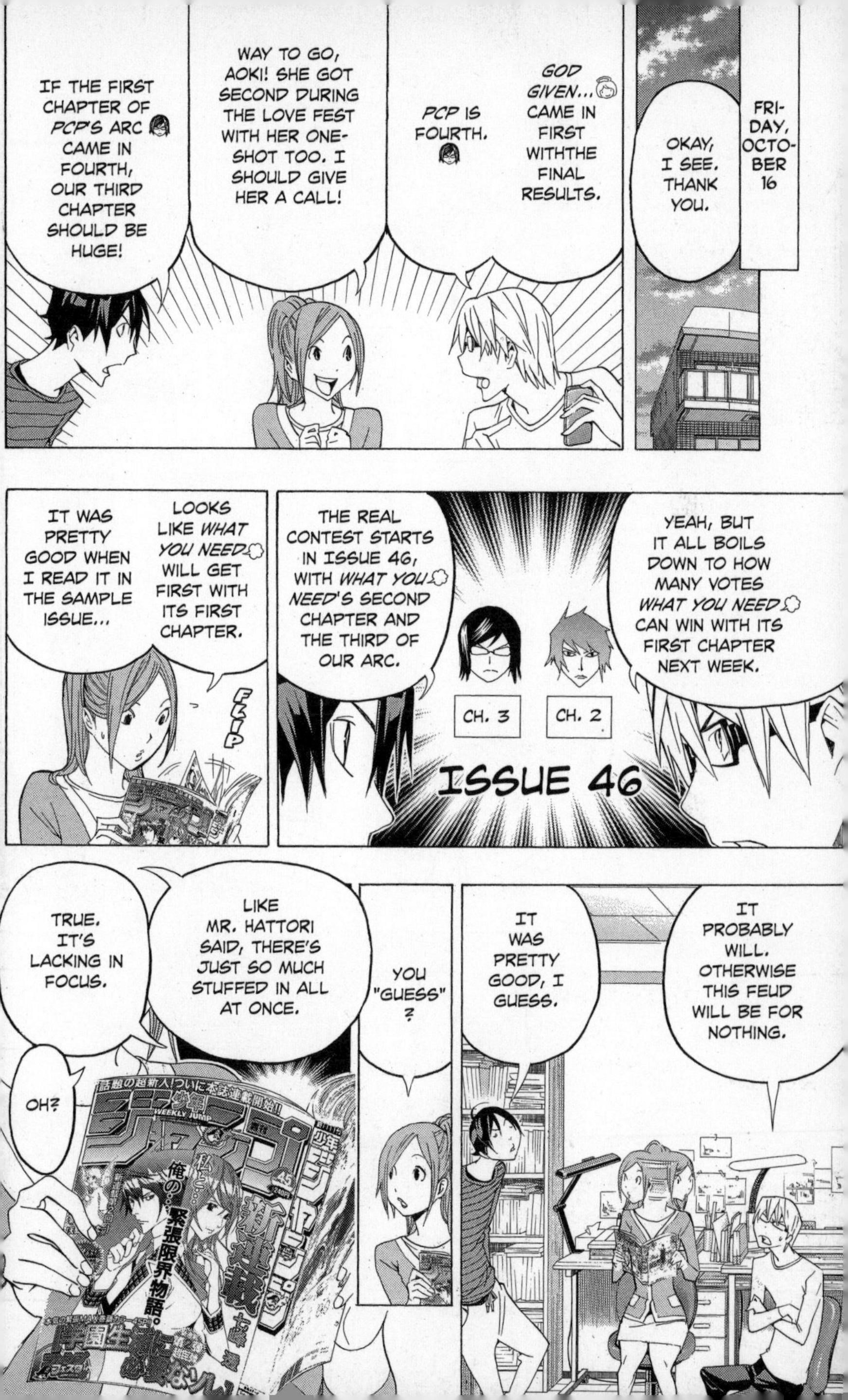
FRIDAY, OCTOBER 16
OKAY, I SEE. THANK YOU.
GOD GIVEN... CAME IN FIRST WITHTHE FINAL RESULTS.
PCP IS FOURTH.
WAY TO GO, AOKI! SHE GOT SECOND DURING THE LOVE FEST WITH HER ONE-SHOT TOO. I SHOULD GIVE HER A CALL!
IF THE FIRST CHAPTER OF *PCP*'S ARC CAME IN FOURTH, OUR THIRD CHAPTER SHOULD BE HUGE!
YEAH, BUT IT ALL BOILS DOWN TO HOW MANY VOTES *WHAT YOU NEED* CAN WIN WITH ITS FIRST CHAPTER NEXT WEEK.
THE REAL CONTEST STARTS IN ISSUE 46, WITH *WHAT YOU NEED*'S SECOND CHAPTER AND THE THIRD OF OUR ARC.
CH. 2
CH. 3
ISSUE 46
LOOKS LIKE *WHAT YOU NEED* WILL GET FIRST WITH ITS FIRST CHAPTER.
IT WAS PRETTY GOOD WHEN I READ IT IN THE SAMPLE ISSUE...
FLIP
IT PROBABLY WILL. OTHERWISE THIS FEUD WILL BE FOR NOTHING.
IT WAS PRETTY GOOD, I GUESS.
YOU "GUESS"?
LIKE MR. HATTORI SAID, THERE'S JUST SO MUCH STUFFED IN ALL AT ONCE.
TRUE. IT'S LACKING IN FOCUS.
OH?
WEEKLY JUMP

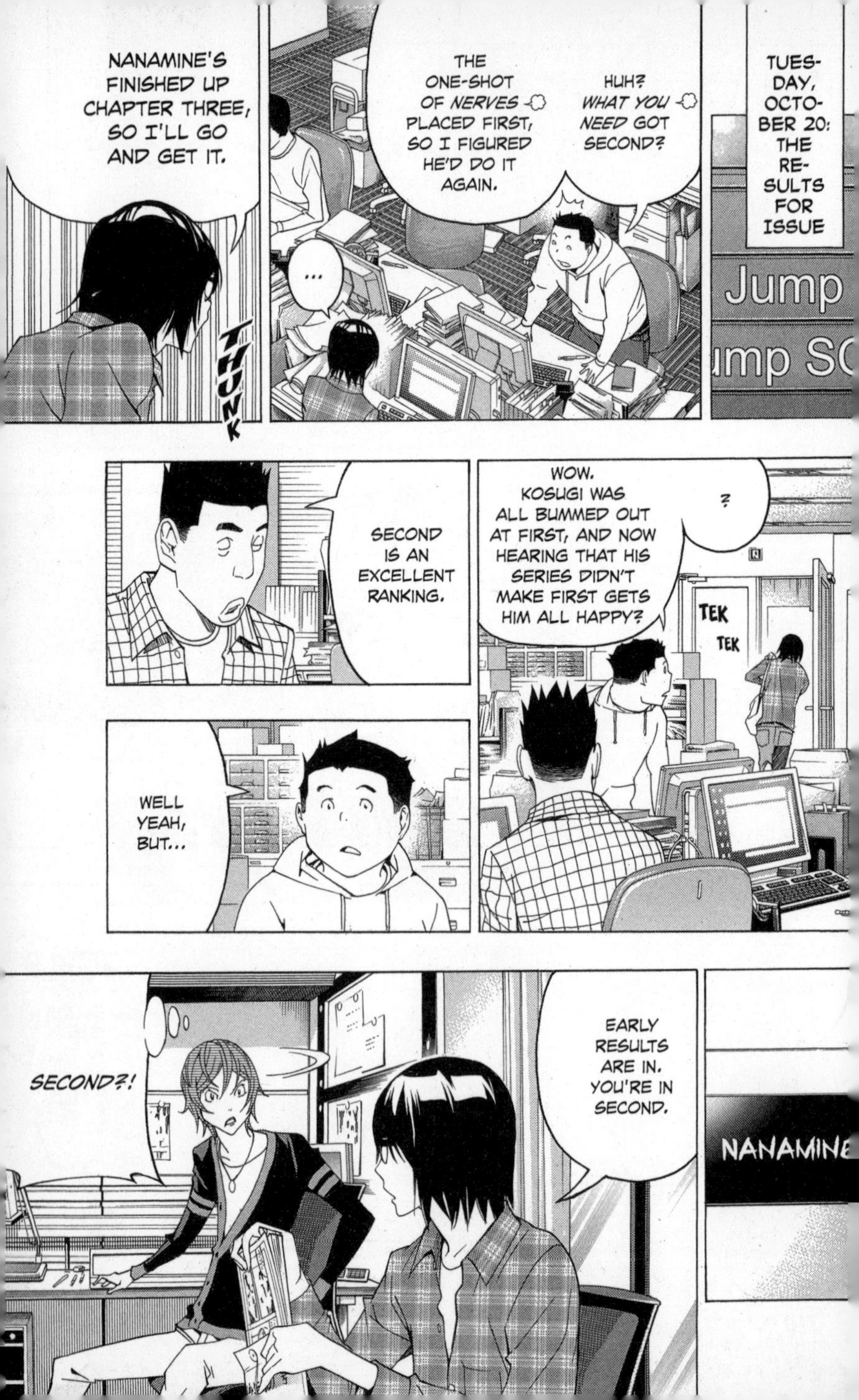
TUESDAY, OCTOBER 20: THE RESULTS FOR ISSUE
Jump
ump SC
HUH? WHAT YOU NEED GOT SECOND?
THE ONE-SHOT OF NERVES PLACED FIRST, SO I FIGURED HE'D DO IT AGAIN.
...
NANAMINE'S FINISHED UP CHAPTER THREE, SO I'LL GO AND GET IT.
THUNK
?
WOW. KOSUGI WAS ALL BUMMED OUT AT FIRST, AND NOW HEARING THAT HIS SERIES DIDN'T MAKE FIRST GETS HIM ALL HAPPY?
TEK
TEK
SECOND IS AN EXCELLENT RANKING.
WELL YEAH, BUT...
NANAMINE
EARLY RESULTS ARE IN. YOU'RE IN SECOND.
SECOND?!

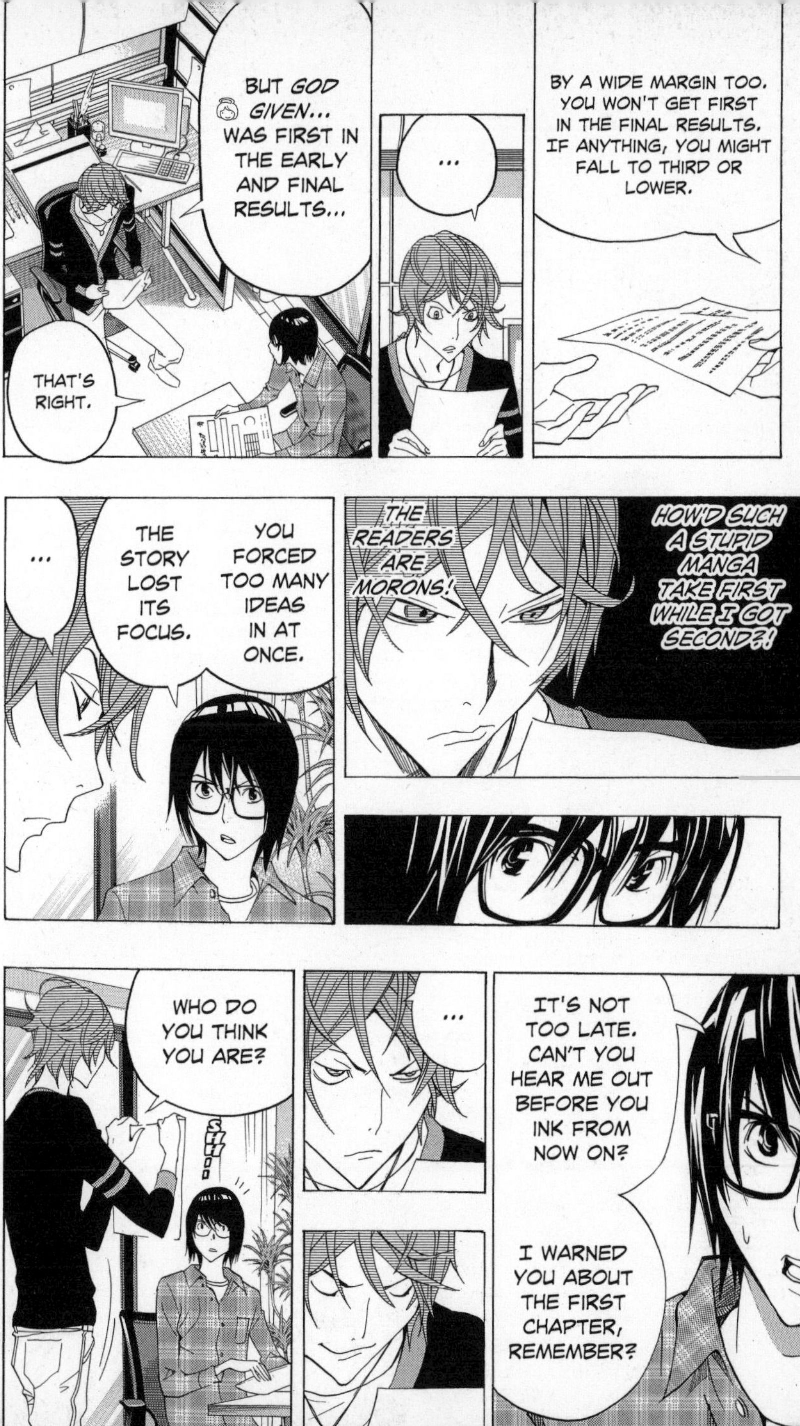
BY A WIDE MARGIN TOO. YOU WON'T GET FIRST IN THE FINAL RESULTS. IF ANYTHING, YOU MIGHT FALL TO THIRD OR LOWER.
...
BUT *GOD GIVEN*... WAS FIRST IN THE EARLY AND FINAL RESULTS...
THAT'S RIGHT.
HOW'D SUCH A STUPID MANGA TAKE FIRST WHILE I GOT SECOND?!
THE READERS ARE MORONS!
YOU FORCED TOO MANY IDEAS IN AT ONCE.
THE STORY LOST ITS FOCUS.
...
IT'S NOT TOO LATE. CAN'T YOU HEAR ME OUT BEFORE YOU INK FROM NOW ON?
I WARNED YOU ABOUT THE FIRST CHAPTER, REMEMBER?
...
WHO DO YOU THINK YOU ARE?
SHH...

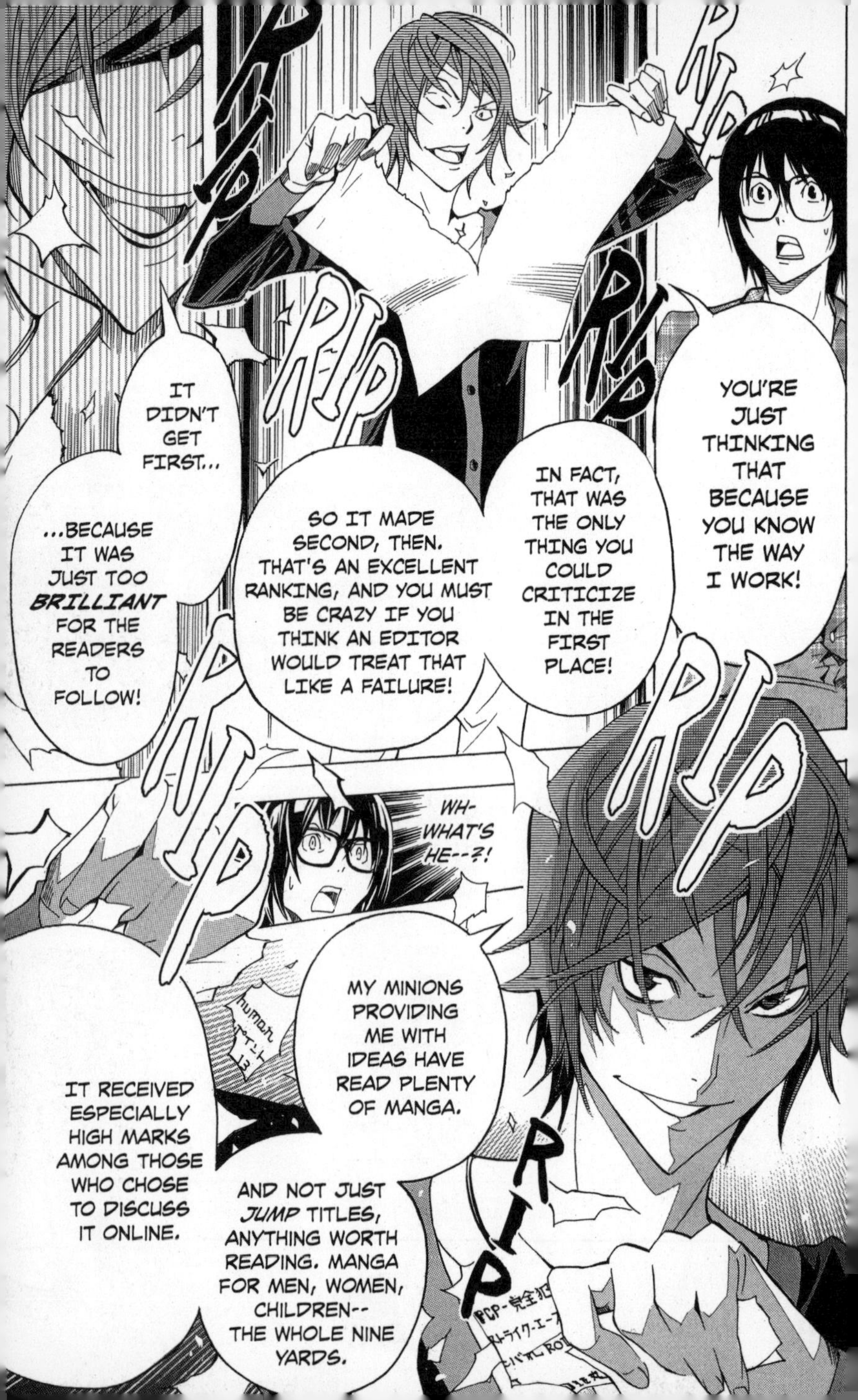
RIP
RIP
RIP
YOU'RE JUST THINKING THAT BECAUSE YOU KNOW THE WAY I WORK!
IN FACT, THAT WAS THE ONLY THING YOU COULD CRITICIZE IN THE FIRST PLACE!
SO IT MADE SECOND, THEN. THAT'S AN EXCELLENT RANKING, AND YOU MUST BE CRAZY IF YOU THINK AN EDITOR WOULD TREAT THAT LIKE A FAILURE!
IT DIDN'T GET FIRST...
...BECAUSE IT WAS JUST TOO *BRILLIANT* FOR THE READERS TO FOLLOW!
RIP
RIP
WH- WHAT'S HE--?!
RIP
MY MINIONS PROVIDING ME WITH IDEAS HAVE READ PLENTY OF MANGA.
AND NOT JUST *JUMP* TITLES, ANYTHING WORTH READING. MANGA FOR MEN, WOMEN, CHILDREN-- THE WHOLE NINE YARDS.
IT RECEIVED ESPECIALLY HIGH MARKS AMONG THOSE WHO CHOSE TO DISCUSS IT ONLINE.

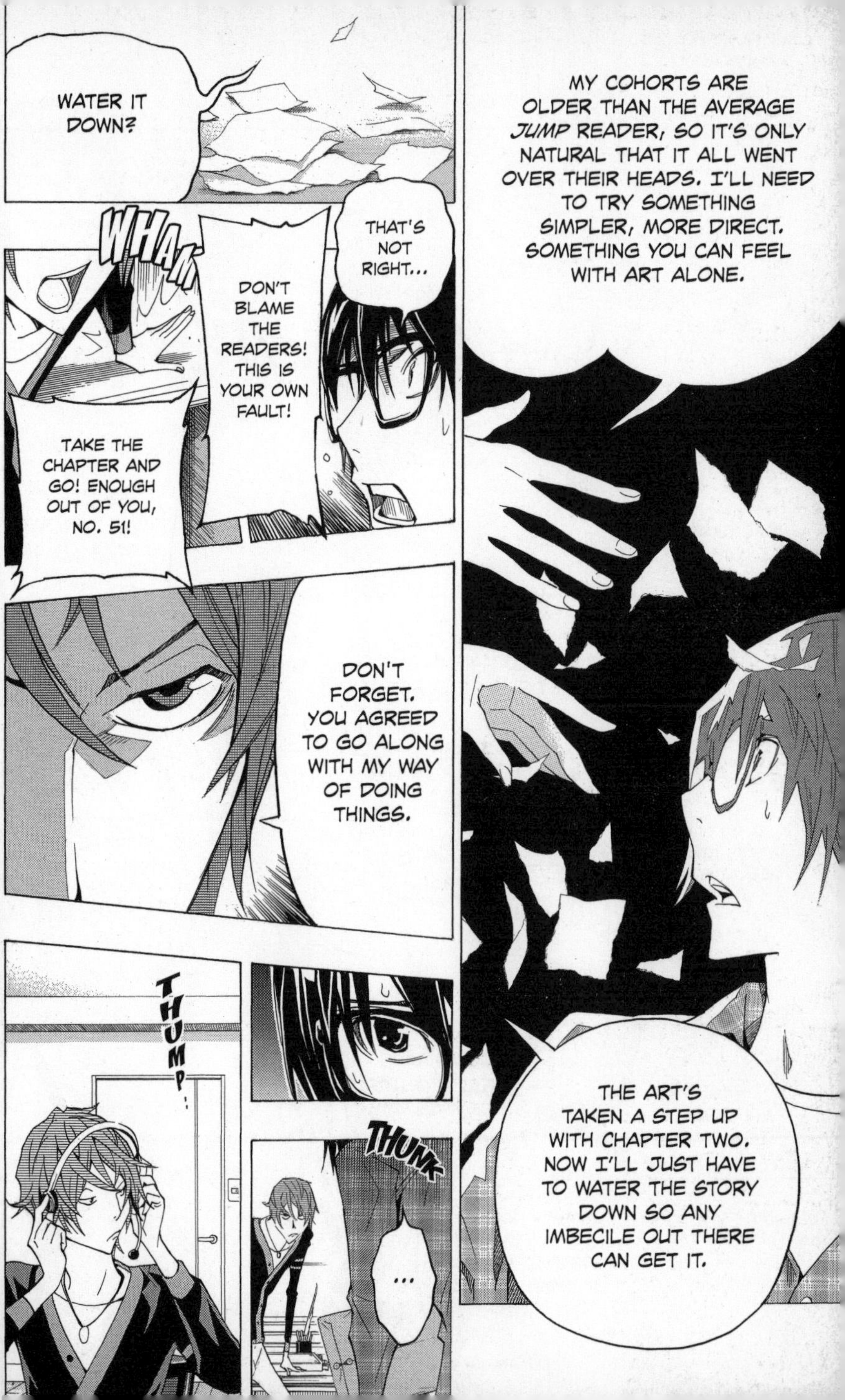
MY COHORTS ARE OLDER THAN THE AVERAGE *JUMP* READER, SO IT'S ONLY NATURAL THAT IT ALL WENT OVER THEIR HEADS. I'LL NEED TO TRY SOMETHING SIMPLER, MORE DIRECT. SOMETHING YOU CAN FEEL WITH ART ALONE.
THE ART'S TAKEN A STEP UP WITH CHAPTER TWO. NOW I'LL JUST HAVE TO WATER THE STORY DOWN SO ANY IMBECILE OUT THERE CAN GET IT.
WATER IT DOWN?
THAT'S NOT RIGHT...
DON'T BLAME THE READERS! THIS IS YOUR OWN FAULT!
WHAM
TAKE THE CHAPTER AND GO! ENOUGH OUT OF YOU, NO. 51!
DON'T FORGET. YOU AGREED TO GO ALONG WITH MY WAY OF DOING THINGS.
THUNK
...
THUMP

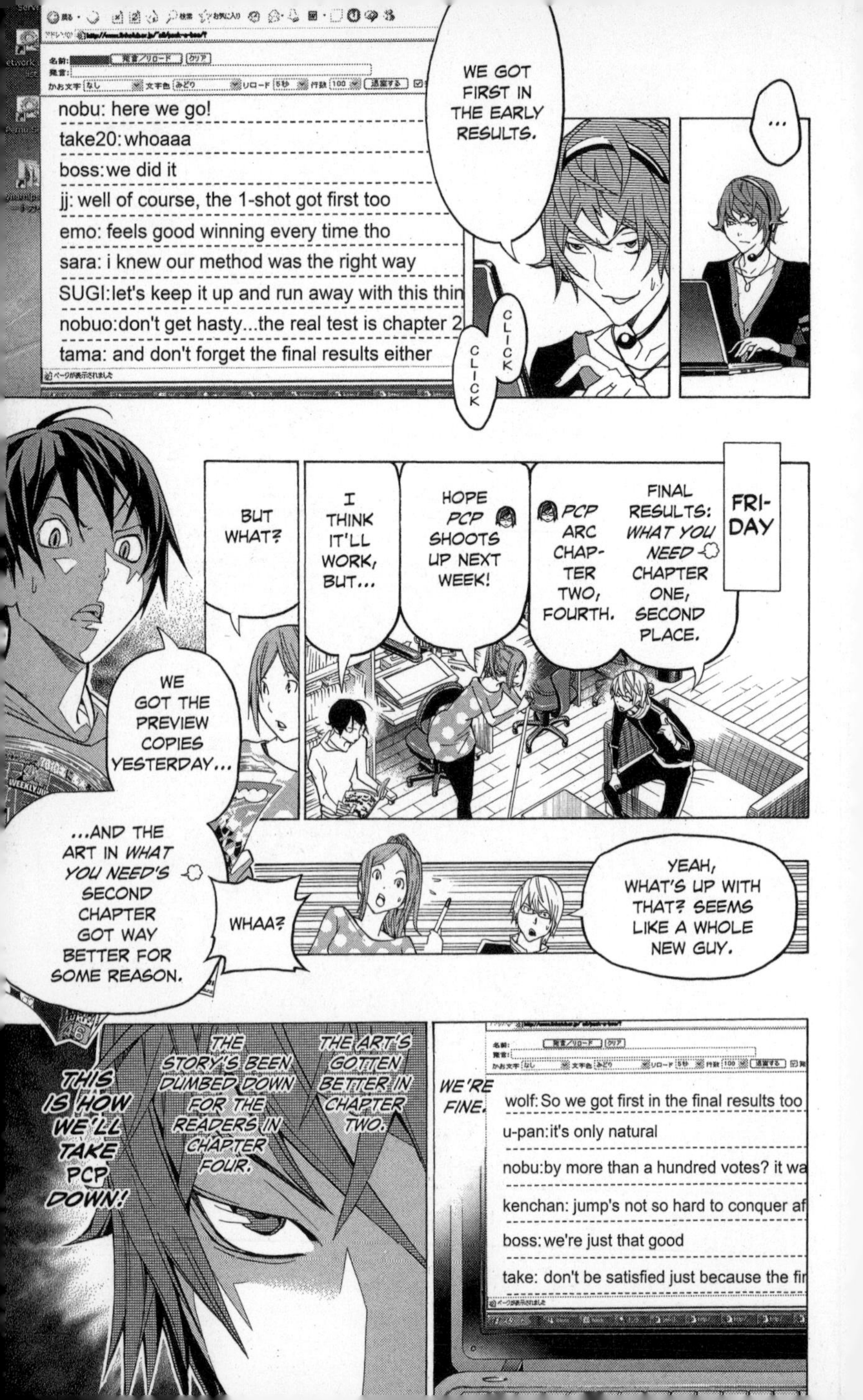
...
WE GOT FIRST IN THE EARLY RESULTS.
CLICK
CLICK
nobu: here we go!
take20: whoaaa
boss:we did it
jj: well of course, the 1-shot got first too
emo: feels good winning every time tho
sara: i knew our method was the right way
SUGI:let's keep it up and run away with this thin
nobuo:don't get hasty...the real test is chapter 2
tama: and don't forget the final results either
FRI-DAY
FINAL RESULTS: WHAT YOU NEED CHAPTER ONE, SECOND PLACE.
PCP ARC CHAP-TER TWO, FOURTH.
HOPE PCP SHOOTS UP NEXT WEEK!
I THINK IT'LL WORK, BUT...
BUT WHAT?
YEAH, WHAT'S UP WITH THAT? SEEMS LIKE A WHOLE NEW GUY.
WHAA?
WE GOT THE PREVIEW COPIES YESTERDAY...
...AND THE ART IN WHAT YOU NEED'S SECOND CHAPTER GOT WAY BETTER FOR SOME REASON.
wolf: So we got first in the final results too
u-pan:it's only natural
nobu:by more than a hundred votes? it wa
kenchan: jump's not so hard to conquer af
boss: we're just that good
take: don't be satisfied just because the fir
WE'RE FINE.
THE ART'S GOTTEN BETTER IN CHAPTER TWO.
THE STORY'S BEEN DUMBED DOWN FOR THE READERS IN CHAPTER FOUR.
THIS IS HOW WE'LL TAKE PCP DOWN!

OHBA'S STORYBOARD

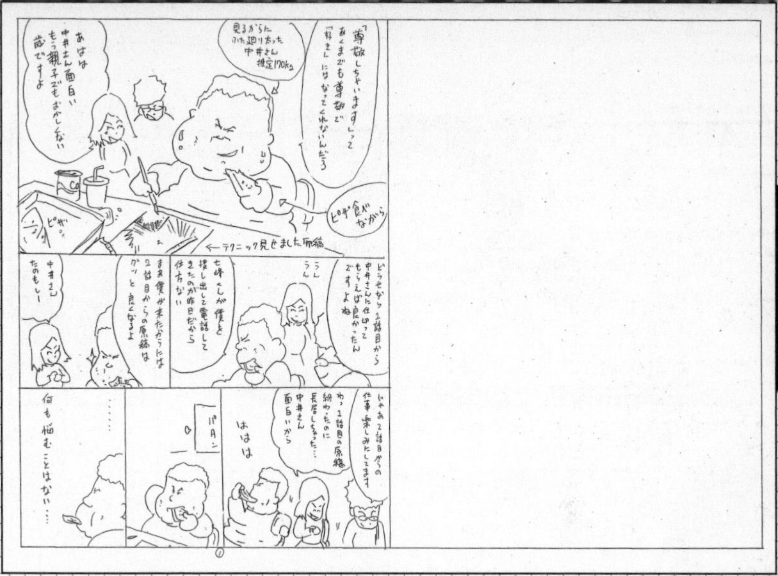
「尊敬しちゃいます」って あくまでも尊敬で「好き」にはなってくれないんだろ
見るからに ふた廻り太った 中井さん 推定170kg
ピザ食べながら
あはは 中井さん面白い もう親子でもおかしくない歳ですよ
ピザ
← テクニック見せました原稿
どうせなら1話目から 中井さんに仕切ってもらえば良かったんですよね
うん うん
七峰くんが僕を捜し出して電話してきたのが昨日だから仕方ない
まあ僕が来たからには2話目からの原稿はグッと良くなるよ
中井さん たのもしー
じゃあ2話目からの仕事楽しみにしてます
わっ1話目の原稿終わったのに長居しちゃった… 中井さん面白いから
ははは
パクン
……
何も悩むことはない…

OBATA'S STORYBOARD

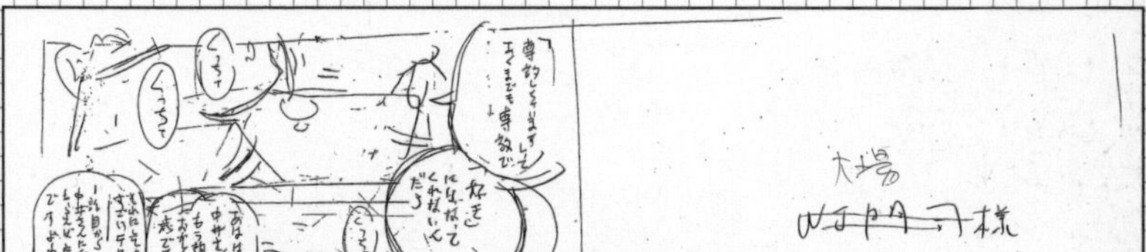
くっちゃ
くっちゃ
尊敬しちゃいますって あくまでも尊敬で 「好き」にはなってくれないんだろ
大場
WJ門司様
WJ門司
←ちょっと見にくいので 戻すかも

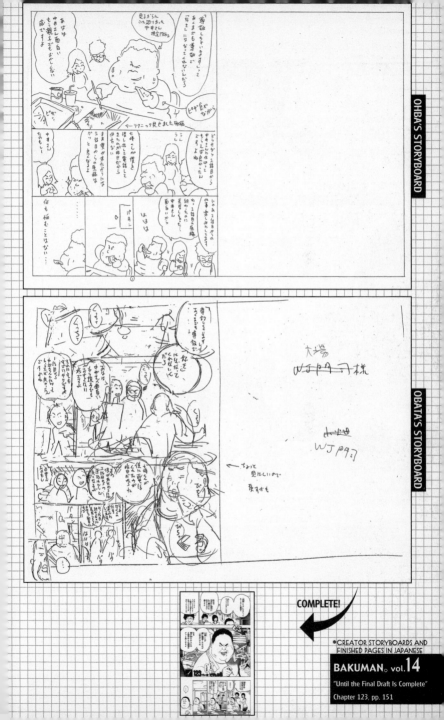

COMPLETE!

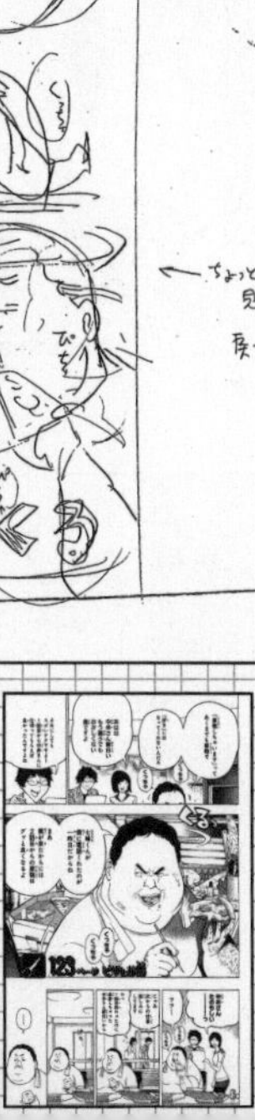

*CREATOR STORYBOARDS AND FINISHED PAGES IN JAPANESE

BAKUMAN。 vol.14

"Until the Final Draft Is Complete"

Chapter 123, pp. 151

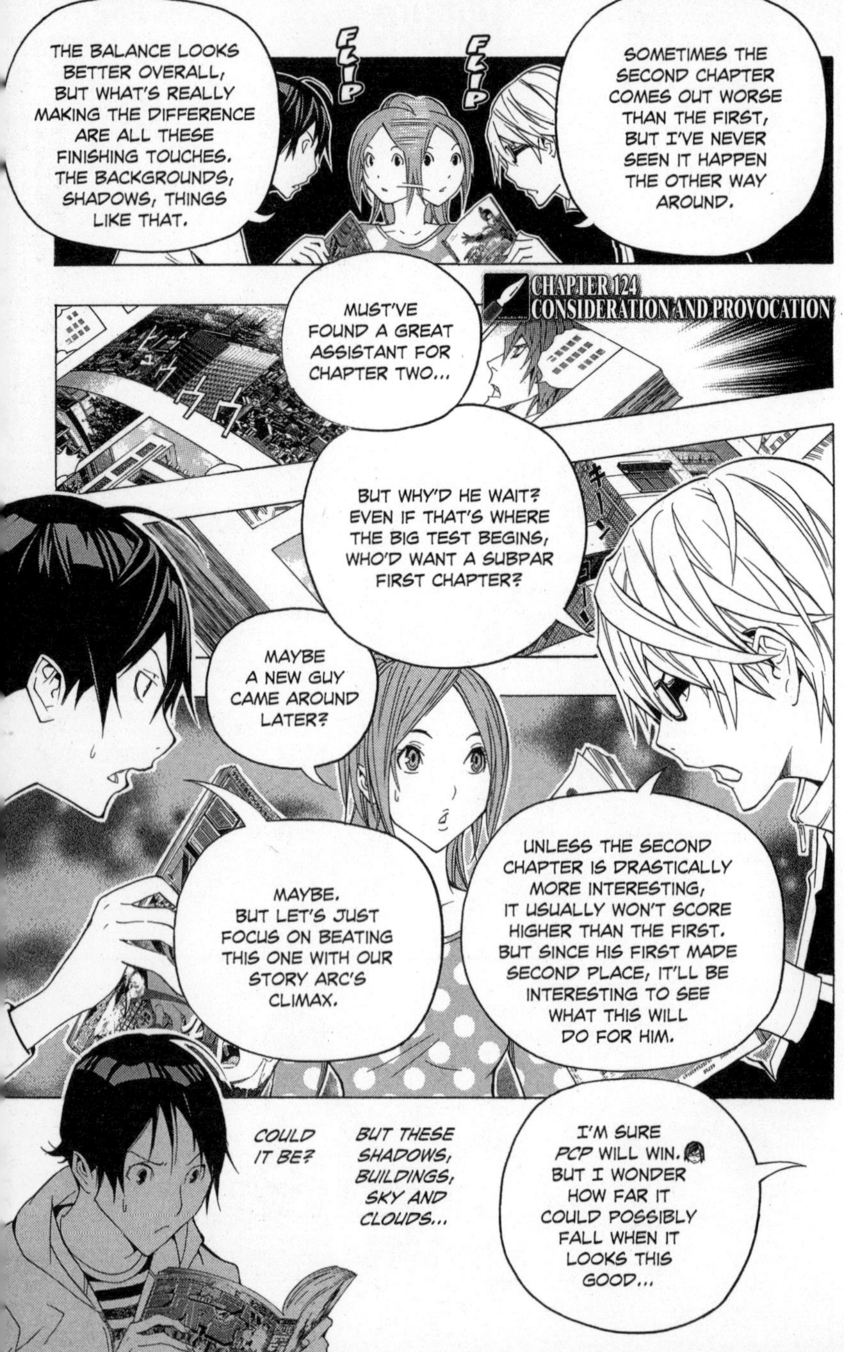
SOMETIMES THE SECOND CHAPTER COMES OUT WORSE THAN THE FIRST, BUT I'VE NEVER SEEN IT HAPPEN THE OTHER WAY AROUND.
FLIP
FLIP
THE BALANCE LOOKS BETTER OVERALL, BUT WHAT'S REALLY MAKING THE DIFFERENCE ARE ALL THESE FINISHING TOUCHES. THE BACKGROUNDS, SHADOWS, THINGS LIKE THAT.
CHAPTER 124 CONSIDERATION AND PROVOCATION
MUST'VE FOUND A GREAT ASSISTANT FOR CHAPTER TWO...
BUT WHY'D HE WAIT? EVEN IF THAT'S WHERE THE BIG TEST BEGINS, WHO'D WANT A SUBPAR FIRST CHAPTER?
MAYBE A NEW GUY CAME AROUND LATER?
UNLESS THE SECOND CHAPTER IS DRASTICALLY MORE INTERESTING, IT USUALLY WON'T SCORE HIGHER THAN THE FIRST. BUT SINCE HIS FIRST MADE SECOND PLACE, IT'LL BE INTERESTING TO SEE WHAT THIS WILL DO FOR HIM.
MAYBE. BUT LET'S JUST FOCUS ON BEATING THIS ONE WITH OUR STORY ARC'S CLIMAX.
I'M SURE *PCP* WILL WIN. BUT I WONDER HOW FAR IT COULD POSSIBLY FALL WHEN IT LOOKS THIS GOOD...
BUT THESE SHADOWS, BUILDINGS, SKY AND CLOUDS...
COULD IT BE?

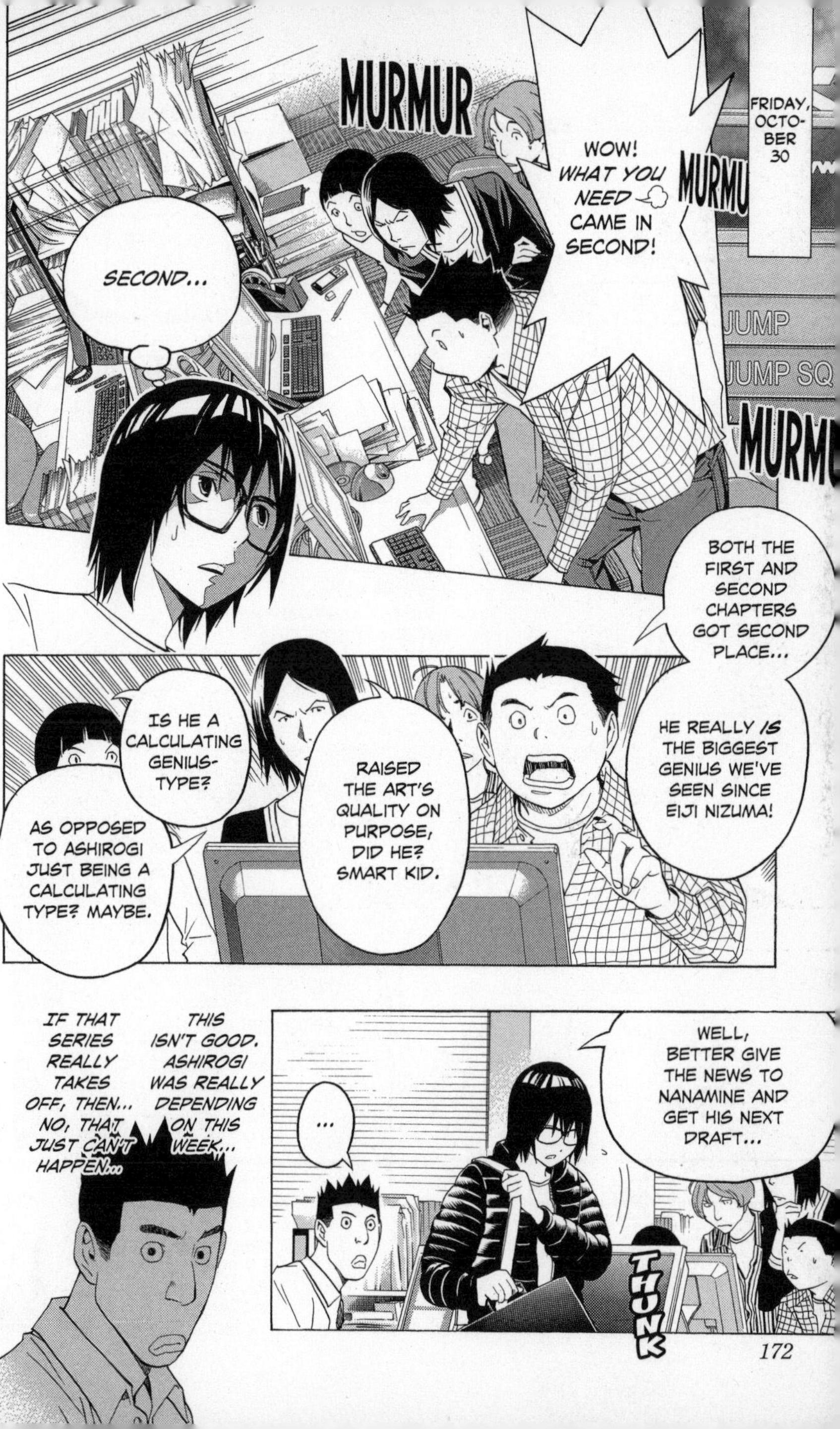
FRIDAY, OCTOBER 30
MURMUR
WOW! WHAT YOU NEED CAME IN SECOND!
MURMU
MURMU
SECOND...
BOTH THE FIRST AND SECOND CHAPTERS GOT SECOND PLACE...
HE REALLY IS THE BIGGEST GENIUS WE'VE SEEN SINCE EIJI NIZUMA!
RAISED THE ART'S QUALITY ON PURPOSE, DID HE? SMART KID.
IS HE A CALCULATING GENIUS-TYPE?
AS OPPOSED TO ASHIROGI JUST BEING A CALCULATING TYPE? MAYBE.
WELL, BETTER GIVE THE NEWS TO NANAMINE AND GET HIS NEXT DRAFT...
...
THUNK
THIS ISN'T GOOD. ASHIROGI WAS REALLY DEPENDING ON THIS WEEK...
IF THAT SERIES REALLY TAKES OFF, THEN... NO, THAT JUST CAN'T HAPPEN...

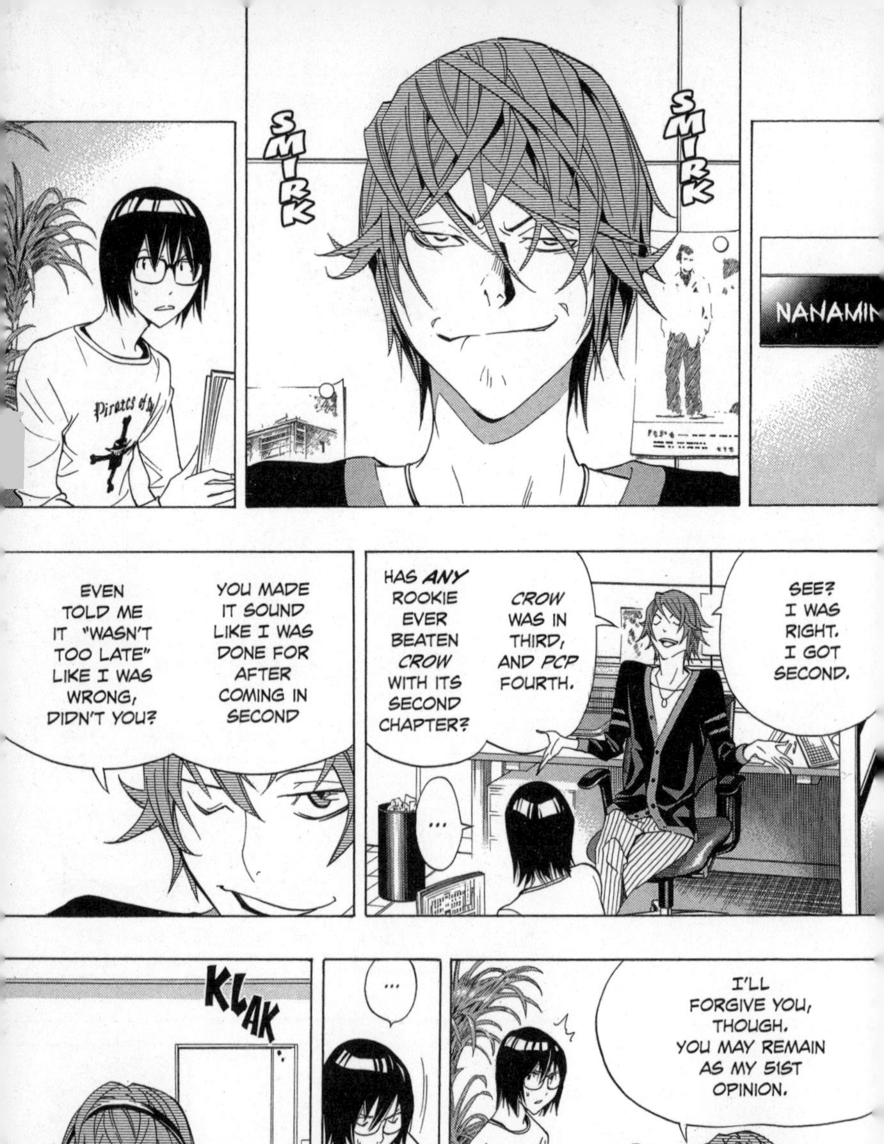
NANAMIN
SMIRK
SMIRK
SEE? I WAS RIGHT. I GOT SECOND.
CROW WAS IN THIRD, AND PCP FOURTH.
HAS ANY ROOKIE EVER BEATEN CROW WITH ITS SECOND CHAPTER?
...
YOU MADE IT SOUND LIKE I WAS DONE FOR AFTER COMING IN SECOND
EVEN TOLD ME IT "WASN'T TOO LATE" LIKE I WAS WRONG, DIDN'T YOU?
I'LL FORGIVE YOU, THOUGH. YOU MAY REMAIN AS MY 51ST OPINION.
NOW OFF WITH YOU.
...
RUSTLE
KLAK

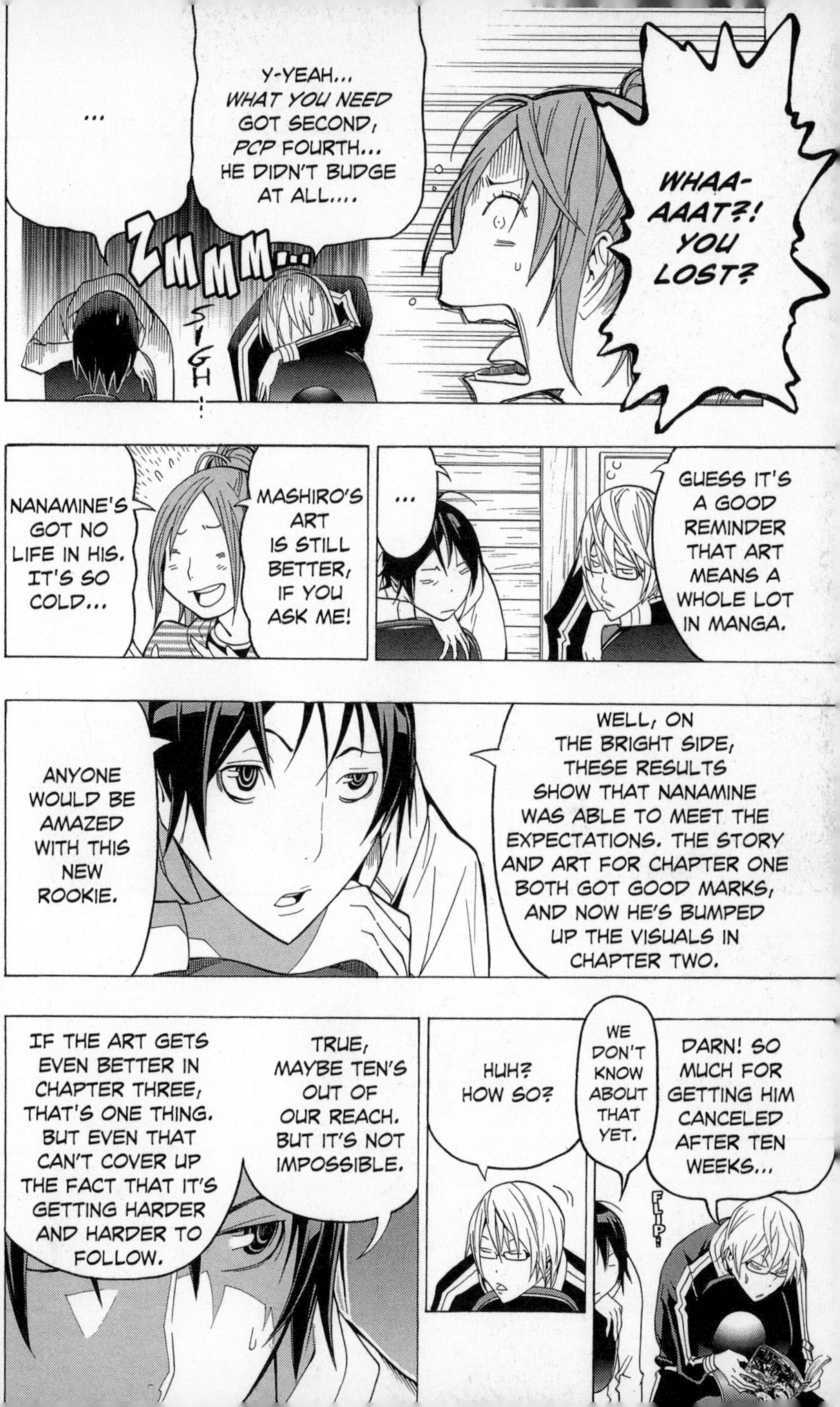
WHAA-AAAT?! YOU LOST?
Y-YEAH... WHAT YOU NEED GOT SECOND, PCP FOURTH... HE DIDN'T BUDGE AT ALL....
...
ZMMMM...
SIGH!
GUESS IT'S A GOOD REMINDER THAT ART MEANS A WHOLE LOT IN MANGA.
...
MASHIRO'S ART IS STILL BETTER, IF YOU ASK ME!
NANAMINE'S GOT NO LIFE IN HIS. IT'S SO COLD...
WELL, ON THE BRIGHT SIDE, THESE RESULTS SHOW THAT NANAMINE WAS ABLE TO MEET THE EXPECTATIONS. THE STORY AND ART FOR CHAPTER ONE BOTH GOT GOOD MARKS, AND NOW HE'S BUMPED UP THE VISUALS IN CHAPTER TWO.
ANYONE WOULD BE AMAZED WITH THIS NEW ROOKIE.
DARN! SO MUCH FOR GETTING HIM CANCELED AFTER TEN WEEKS...
FLIP!
WE DON'T KNOW ABOUT THAT YET.
HUH? HOW SO?
TRUE, MAYBE TEN'S OUT OF OUR REACH. BUT IT'S NOT IMPOSSIBLE.
IF THE ART GETS EVEN BETTER IN CHAPTER THREE, THAT'S ONE THING. BUT EVEN THAT CAN'T COVER UP THE FACT THAT IT'S GETTING HARDER AND HARDER TO FOLLOW.

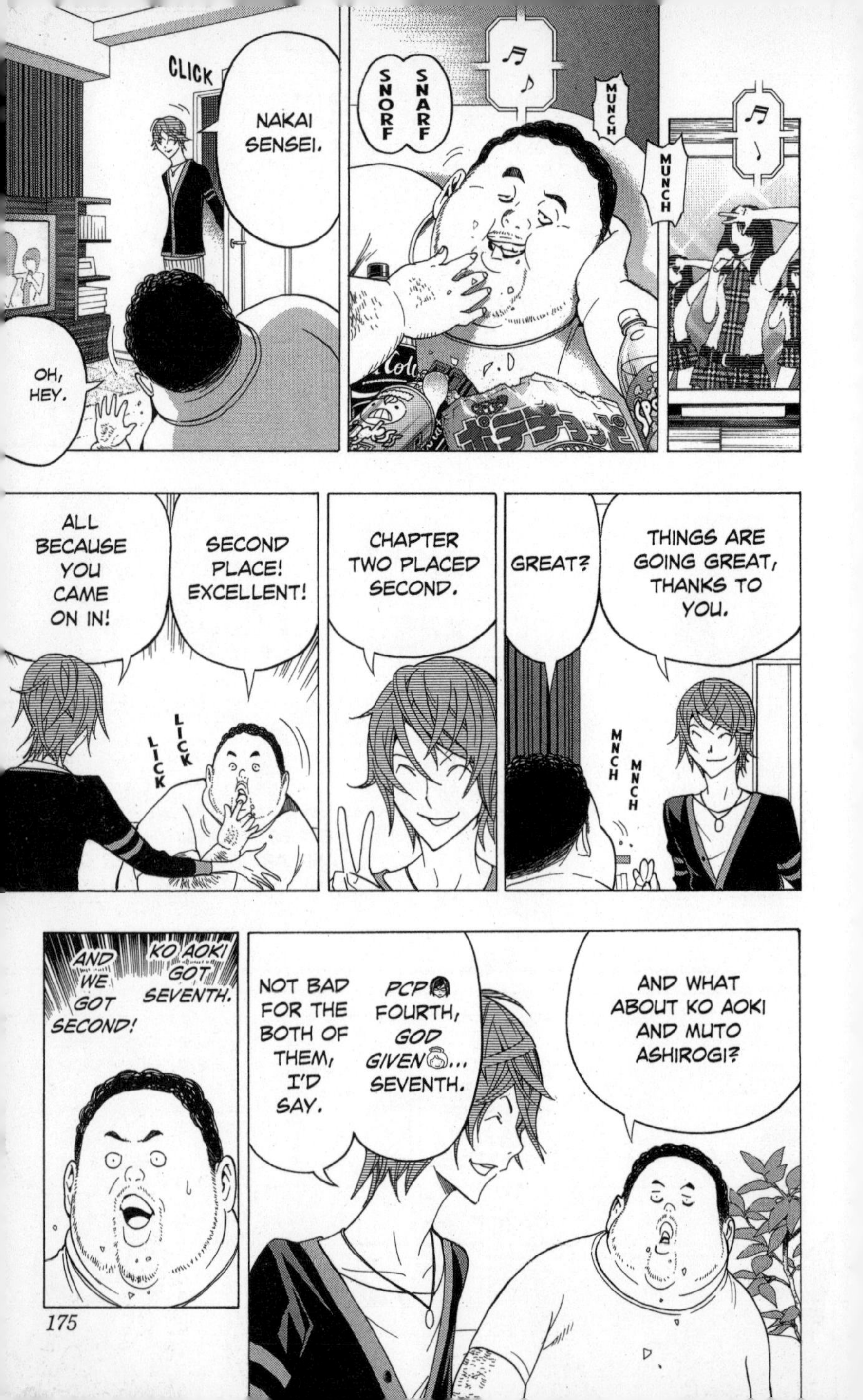
MUNCH
MUNCH
SNARF
SNORF
NAKAI SENSEI.
CLICK
OH, HEY.
THINGS ARE GOING GREAT, THANKS TO YOU.
MNCH
MNCH
GREAT?
CHAPTER TWO PLACED SECOND.
SECOND PLACE! EXCELLENT!
ALL BECAUSE YOU CAME ON IN!
LICK
LICK
AND WHAT ABOUT KO AOKI AND MUTO ASHIROGI?
PCP FOURTH, GOD GIVEN... SEVENTH.
NOT BAD FOR THE BOTH OF THEM, I'D SAY.
KO AOKI GOT SEVENTH.
AND WE GOT SECOND!

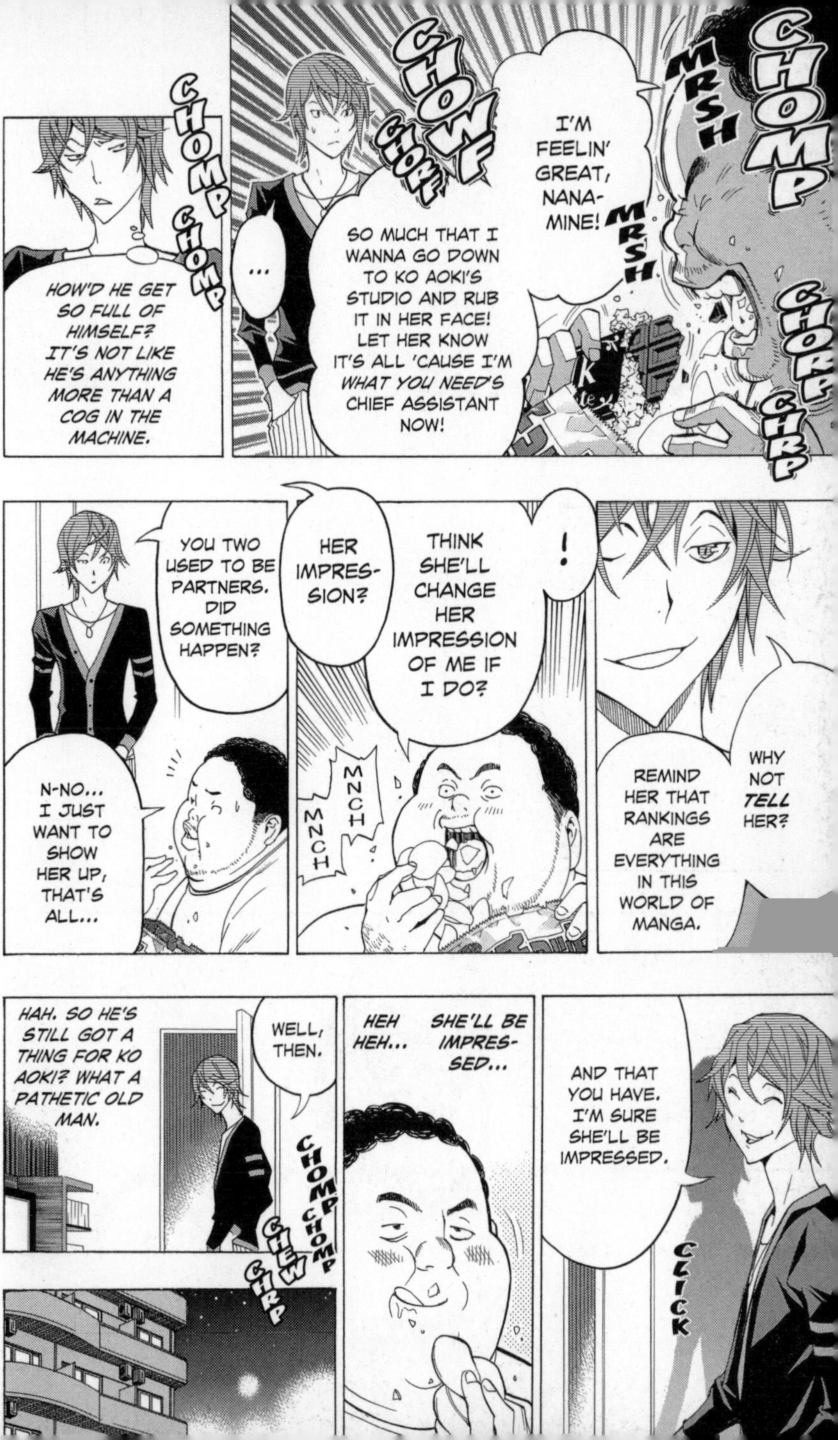
CHOMP
MRSH
I'M FEELIN' GREAT, NANAMINE!
MRSH
CHORP
CHRP
CHOWF
CHORF
SO MUCH THAT I WANNA GO DOWN TO KO AOKI'S STUDIO AND RUB IT IN HER FACE! LET HER KNOW IT'S ALL 'CAUSE I'M *WHAT YOU NEED'S* CHIEF ASSISTANT NOW!
...
CHOMP
CHOMP
HOW'D HE GET SO FULL OF HIMSELF? IT'S NOT LIKE HE'S ANYTHING MORE THAN A COG IN THE MACHINE.
WHY NOT *TELL* HER?
REMIND HER THAT RANKINGS ARE EVERYTHING IN THIS WORLD OF MANGA.
!
THINK SHE'LL CHANGE HER IMPRESSION OF ME IF I DO?
MNCH
MNCH
HER IMPRESSION?
YOU TWO USED TO BE PARTNERS. DID SOMETHING HAPPEN?
N-NO... I JUST WANT TO SHOW HER UP, THAT'S ALL...
AND THAT YOU HAVE. I'M SURE SHE'LL BE IMPRESSED.
CLICK
SHE'LL BE IMPRES-SED...
HEH HEH...
WELL, THEN.
HAH. SO HE'S STILL GOT A THING FOR KO AOKI? WHAT A PATHETIC OLD MAN.
CHOMP
CHOMP
CHEW
CHRP

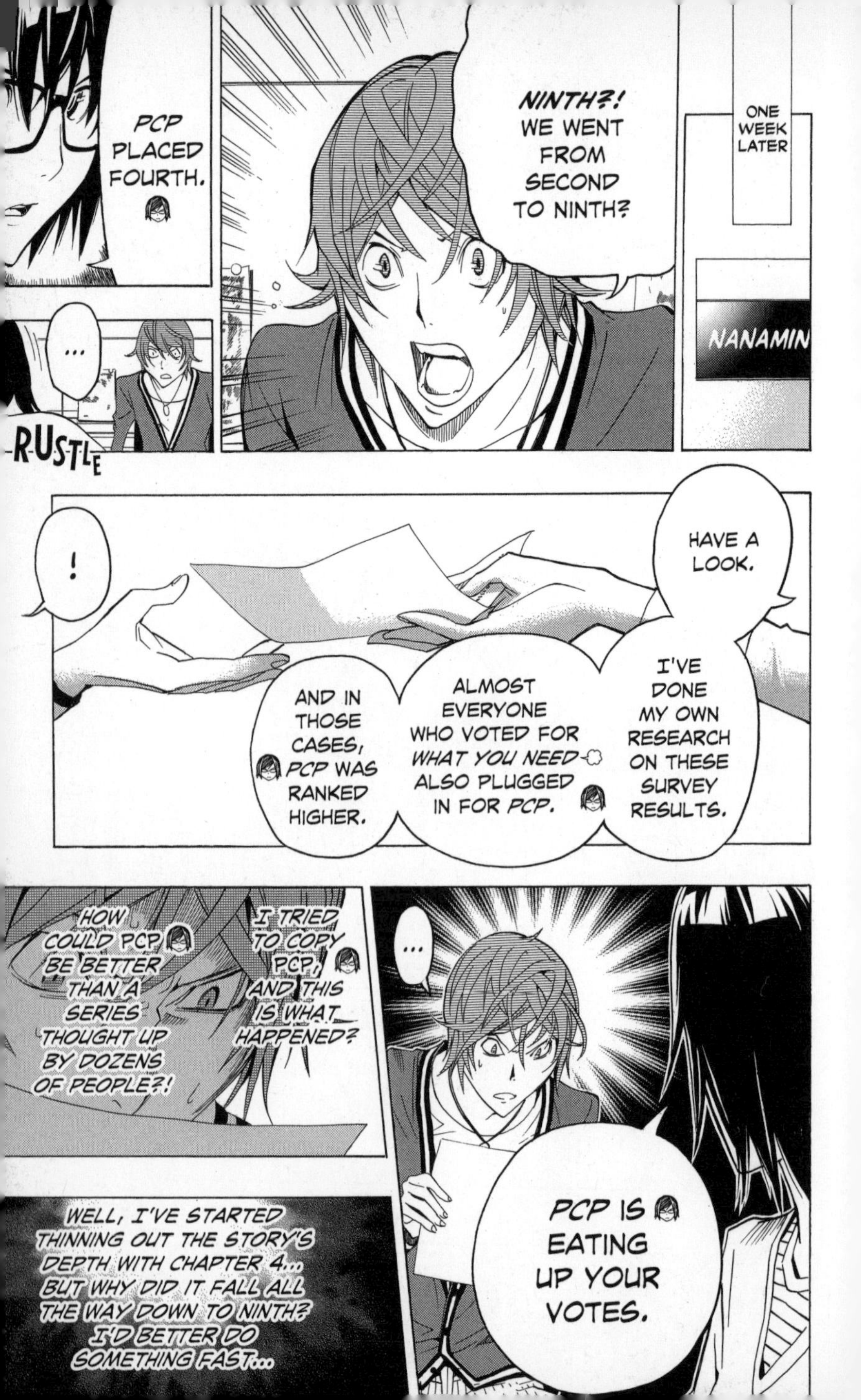
ONE WEEK LATER
NANAMIN
NINTH?! WE WENT FROM SECOND TO NINTH?
PCP PLACED FOURTH.
...
RUSTLE
HAVE A LOOK.
!
I'VE DONE MY OWN RESEARCH ON THESE SURVEY RESULTS.
ALMOST EVERYONE WHO VOTED FOR WHAT YOU NEED ALSO PLUGGED IN FOR PCP.
AND IN THOSE CASES, PCP WAS RANKED HIGHER.
...
PCP IS EATING UP YOUR VOTES.
I TRIED TO COPY PCP, AND THIS IS WHAT HAPPENED?
HOW COULD PCP BE BETTER THAN A SERIES THOUGHT UP BY DOZENS OF PEOPLE?!
WELL, I'VE STARTED THINNING OUT THE STORY'S DEPTH WITH CHAPTER 4... BUT WHY DID IT FALL ALL THE WAY DOWN TO NINTH? I'D BETTER DO SOMETHING FAST...

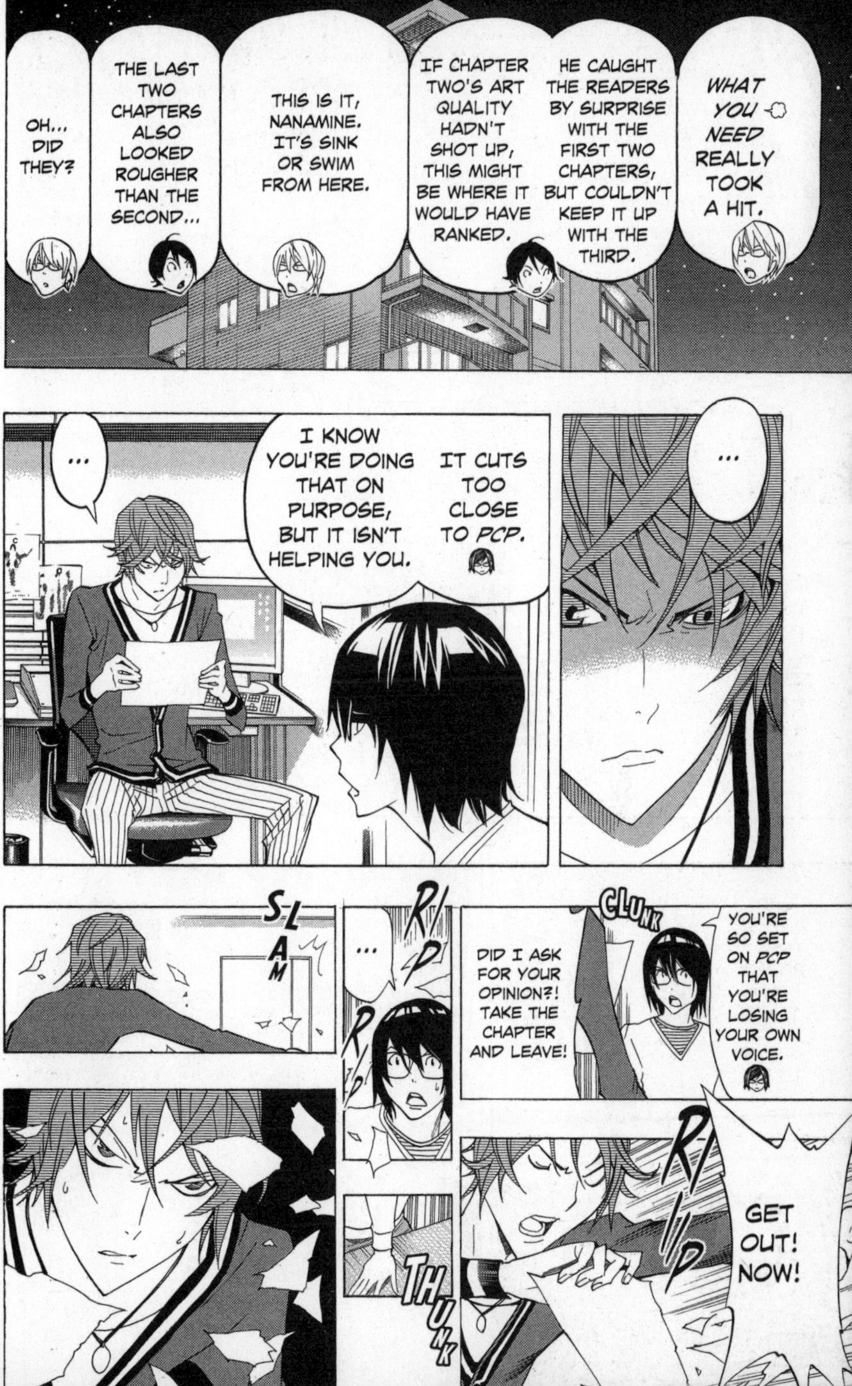

WHAT YOU NEED REALLY TOOK A HIT.
HE CAUGHT THE READERS BY SURPRISE WITH THE FIRST TWO CHAPTERS, BUT COULDN'T KEEP IT UP WITH THE THIRD.
IF CHAPTER TWO'S ART QUALITY HADN'T SHOT UP, THIS MIGHT BE WHERE IT WOULD HAVE RANKED.
THIS IS IT, NANAMINE. IT'S SINK OR SWIM FROM HERE.
THE LAST TWO CHAPTERS ALSO LOOKED ROUGHER THAN THE SECOND...
OH... DID THEY?
...
IT CUTS TOO CLOSE TO PCP.
I KNOW YOU'RE DOING THAT ON PURPOSE, BUT IT ISN'T HELPING YOU.
...
CLUNK
YOU'RE SO SET ON PCP THAT YOU'RE LOSING YOUR OWN VOICE.
DID I ASK FOR YOUR OPINION?! TAKE THE CHAPTER AND LEAVE!
RIP
...
RIP
SLAM
RIIIP
GET OUT! NOW!
THUNK

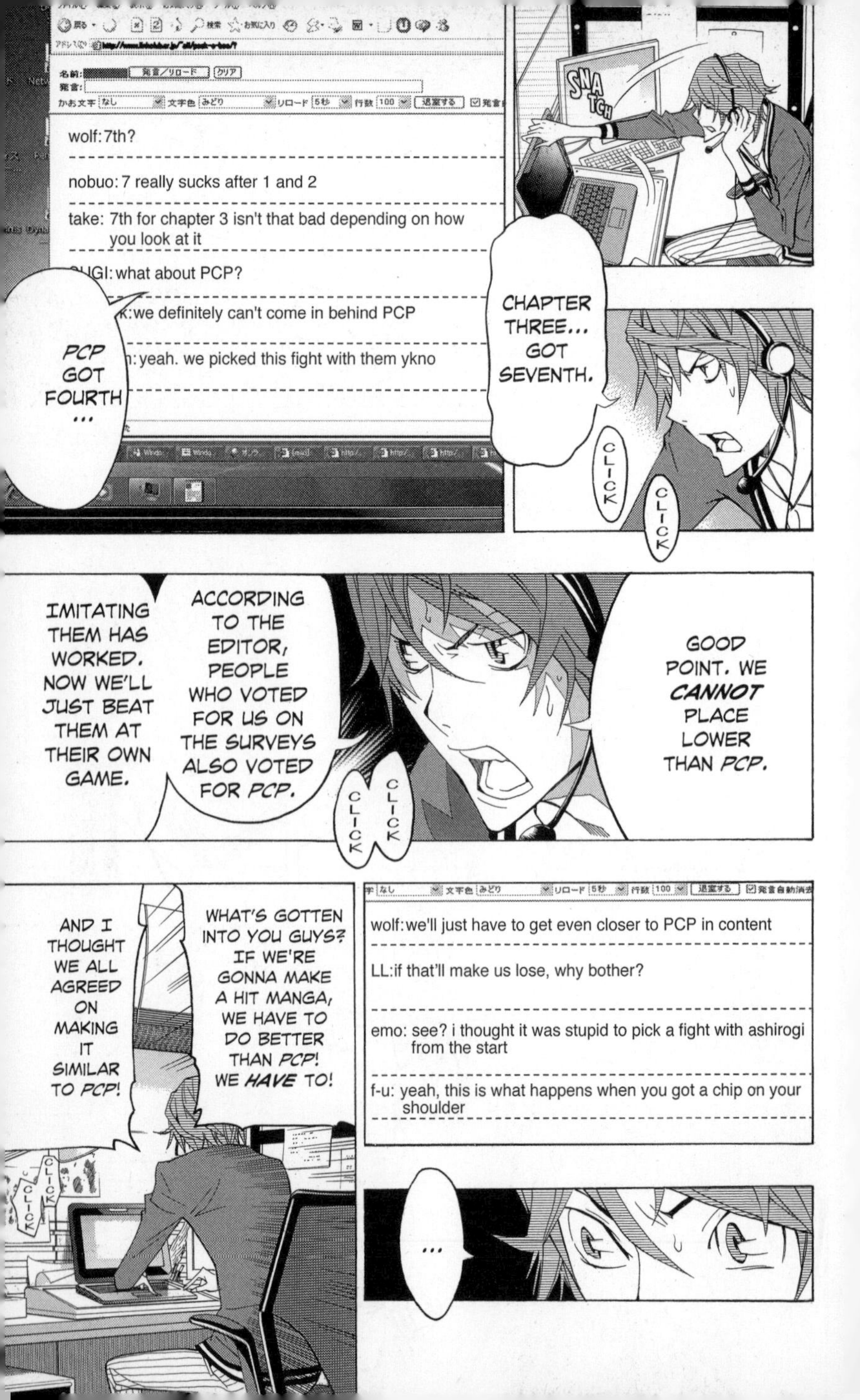
SNATCH
CHAPTER THREE... GOT SEVENTH.
CLICK
CLICK
wolf: 7th?
nobuo: 7 really sucks after 1 and 2
take: 7th for chapter 3 isn't that bad depending on how you look at it
UGI: what about PCP?
k: we definitely can't come in behind PCP
n: yeah. we picked this fight with them ykno
PCP GOT FOURTH...
GOOD POINT. WE CANNOT PLACE LOWER THAN PCP.
ACCORDING TO THE EDITOR, PEOPLE WHO VOTED FOR US ON THE SURVEYS ALSO VOTED FOR PCP.
IMITATING THEM HAS WORKED. NOW WE'LL JUST BEAT THEM AT THEIR OWN GAME.
CLICK
CLICK
wolf: we'll just have to get even closer to PCP in content
LL: if that'll make us lose, why bother?
emo: see? i thought it was stupid to pick a fight with ashirogi from the start
f-u: yeah, this is what happens when you got a chip on your shoulder
...
WHAT'S GOTTEN INTO YOU GUYS? IF WE'RE GONNA MAKE A HIT MANGA, WE HAVE TO DO BETTER THAN PCP! WE HAVE TO!
AND I THOUGHT WE ALL AGREED ON MAKING IT SIMILAR TO PCP!
CLICK
CLICK

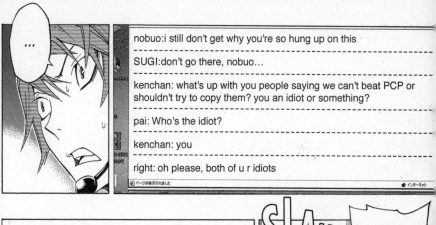

nobuo:i still don't get why you're so hung up on this
SUGI:don't go there, nobuo…
kenchan: what's up with you people saying we can't beat PCP or shouldn't try to copy them? you an idiot or something?
pai: Who's the idiot?
kenchan: you
right: oh please, both of u r idiots
...
SLAM
ANYONE WHO THINKS WE SHOULDN'T OVERLAP WITH PCP, GET OUT!
pai:see ya.
LL:well, it was a good waste of time, i guess
e231:guess i'm out...
osaru:whatever, you'll never win anyway
THIS IS WHAT HAPPENS WHEN WE START TO LOSE A TINY BIT OF GROUND IN THE RANKINGS?
NO, DON'T PANIC. I CAN'T AFFORD TO LOSE MY COOL AT TIMES LIKE THESE!
...
IN ORDER TO BE A HIT MANGA, WE MUST SUCCEED IN RANKING HIGHER THAN PCP. THAT MUCH IS CLEAR.
FOR THOSE OF US WHO UNDERSTAND THAT, LET'S CONSIDER WAYS TO ACHIEVE THIS IN A RATIONAL MANNER.
TAK
TAK

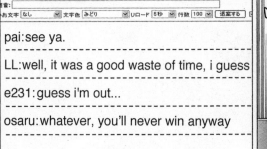

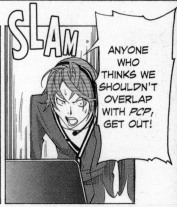

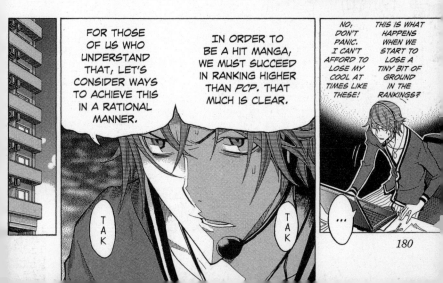

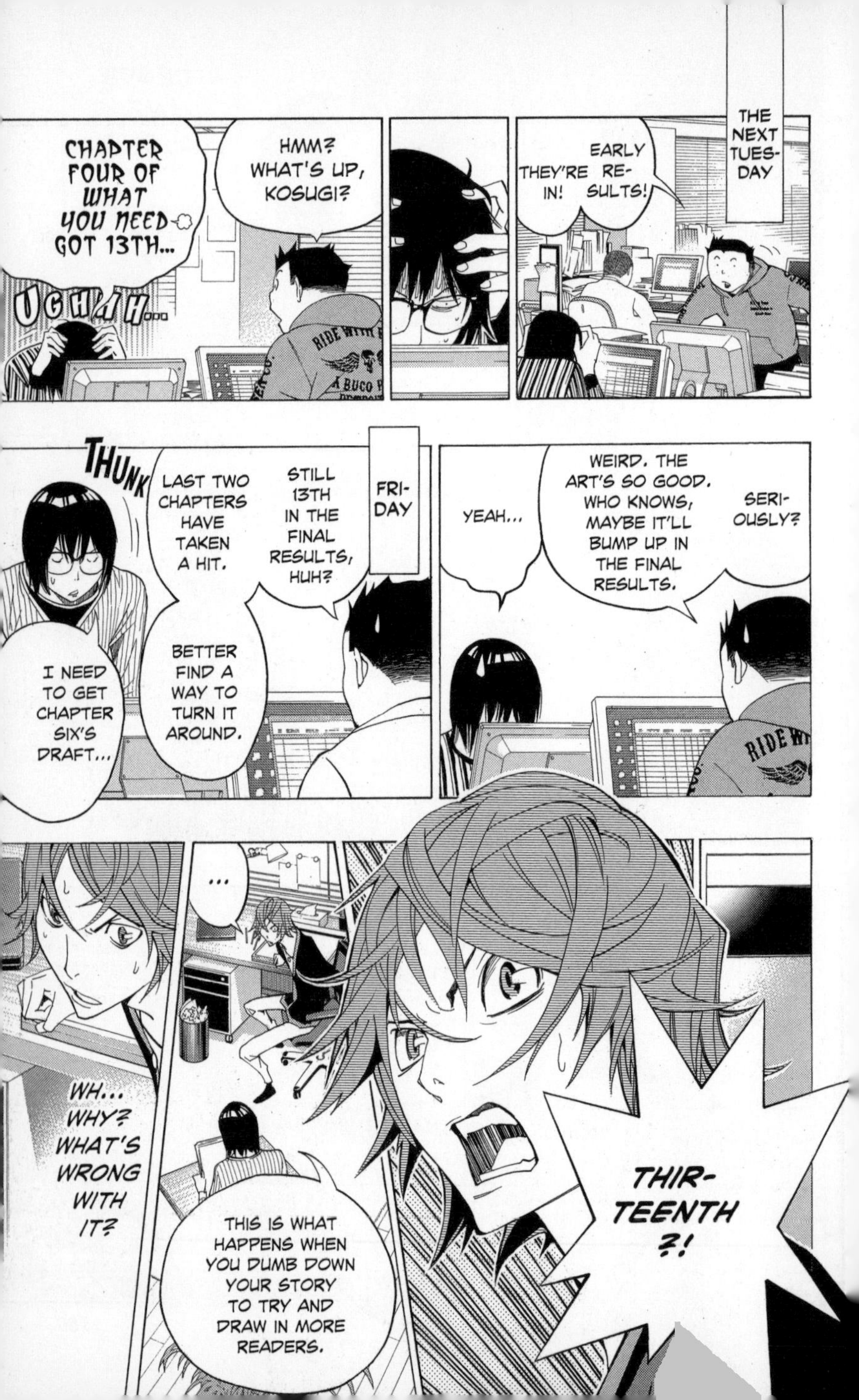
THE NEXT TUESDAY
EARLY RE- SULTS! THEY'RE IN!
HMM? WHAT'S UP, KOSUGI?
CHAPTER FOUR OF WHAT YOU NEED GOT 13TH...
UGHHH...
SERI- OUSLY?
WEIRD. THE ART'S SO GOOD. WHO KNOWS, MAYBE IT'LL BUMP UP IN THE FINAL RESULTS.
YEAH...
FRI- DAY
STILL 13TH IN THE FINAL RESULTS, HUH?
LAST TWO CHAPTERS HAVE TAKEN A HIT.
THUNK
BETTER FIND A WAY TO TURN IT AROUND.
I NEED TO GET CHAPTER SIX'S DRAFT...
THIR- TEENTH ?!
THIS IS WHAT HAPPENS WHEN YOU DUMB DOWN YOUR STORY TO TRY AND DRAW IN MORE READERS.
...
WH... WHY? WHAT'S WRONG WITH IT?

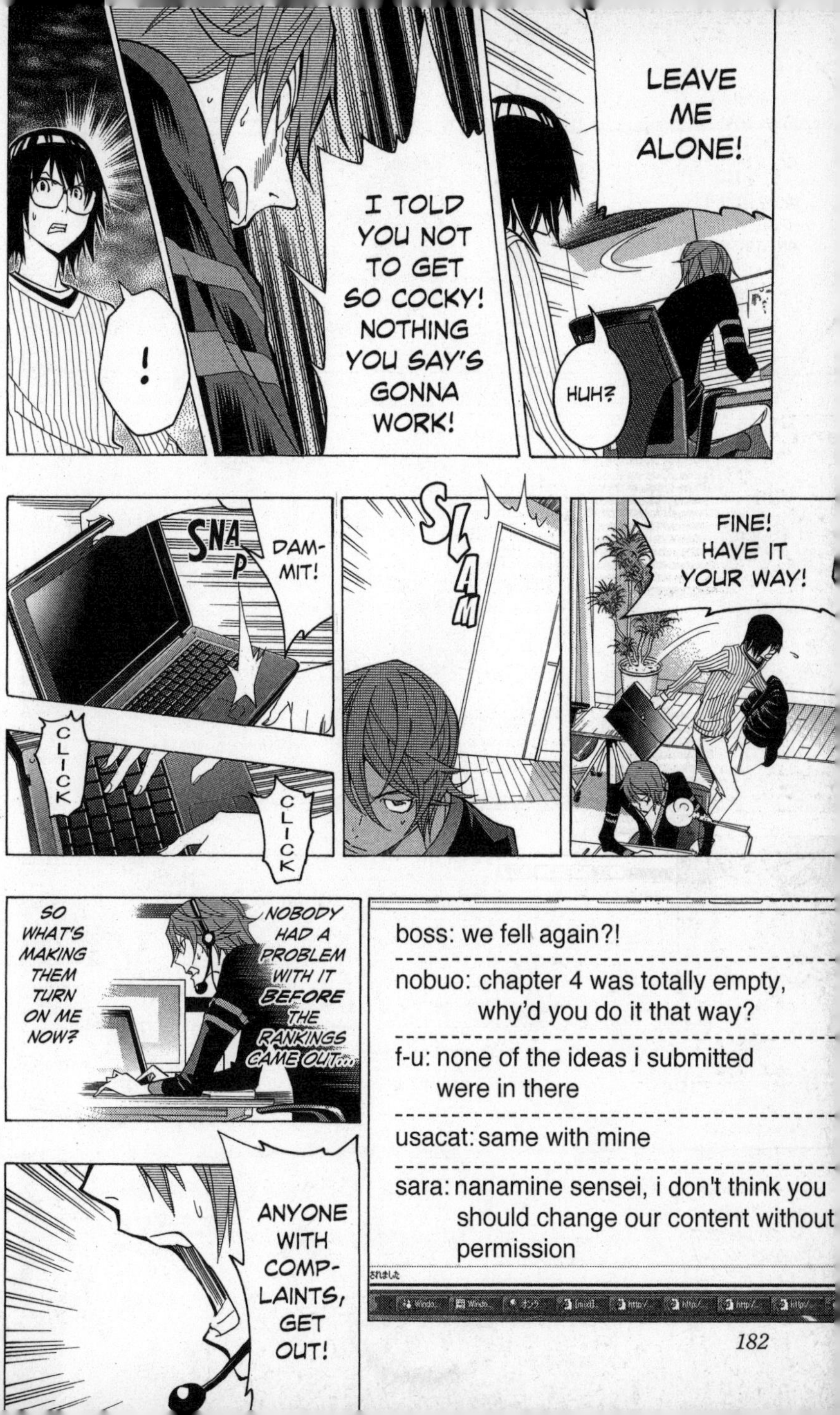
LEAVE ME ALONE!
HUH?
I TOLD YOU NOT TO GET SO COCKY! NOTHING YOU SAY'S GONNA WORK!
!
FINE! HAVE IT YOUR WAY!
SLAM
SNAP
DAM-MIT!
CLICK
CLICK
boss: we fell again?!
nobuo: chapter 4 was totally empty, why'd you do it that way?
f-u: none of the ideas i submitted were in there
usacat: same with mine
sara: nanamine sensei, i don't think you should change our content without permission
NOBODY HAD A PROBLEM WITH IT BEFORE THE RANKINGS CAME OUT...
SO WHAT'S MAKING THEM TURN ON ME NOW?
ANYONE WITH COMP-LAINTS, GET OUT!

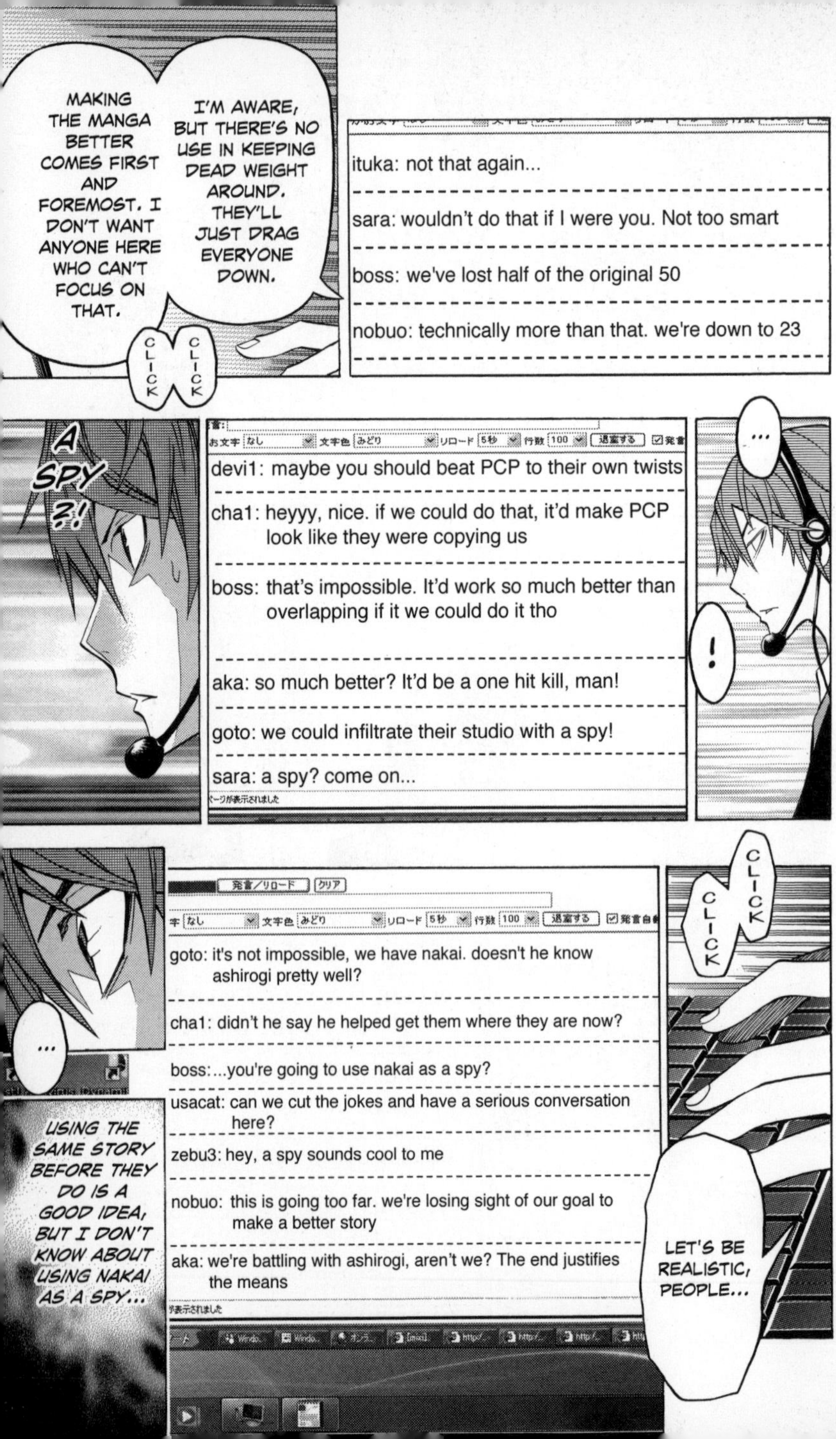
ituka: not that again...
sara: wouldn't do that if I were you. Not too smart
boss: we've lost half of the original 50
nobuo: technically more than that. we're down to 23
I'M AWARE, BUT THERE'S NO USE IN KEEPING DEAD WEIGHT AROUND. THEY'LL JUST DRAG EVERYONE DOWN.
MAKING THE MANGA BETTER COMES FIRST AND FOREMOST. I DON'T WANT ANYONE HERE WHO CAN'T FOCUS ON THAT.
CLICK
CLICK
...
!
devi1: maybe you should beat PCP to their own twists
cha1: heyyy, nice. if we could do that, it'd make PCP look like they were copying us
boss: that's impossible. It'd work so much better than overlapping if it we could do it tho
aka: so much better? It'd be a one hit kill, man!
goto: we could infiltrate their studio with a spy!
sara: a spy? come on...
A SPY?!
CLICK
CLICK
LET'S BE REALISTIC, PEOPLE...
goto: it's not impossible, we have nakai. doesn't he know ashirogi pretty well?
cha1: didn't he say he helped get them where they are now?
boss: ...you're going to use nakai as a spy?
usacat: can we cut the jokes and have a serious conversation here?
zebu3: hey, a spy sounds cool to me
nobuo: this is going too far. we're losing sight of our goal to make a better story
aka: we're battling with ashirogi, aren't we? The end justifies the means
...
USING THE SAME STORY BEFORE THEY DO IS A GOOD IDEA, BUT I DON'T KNOW ABOUT USING NAKAI AS A SPY...

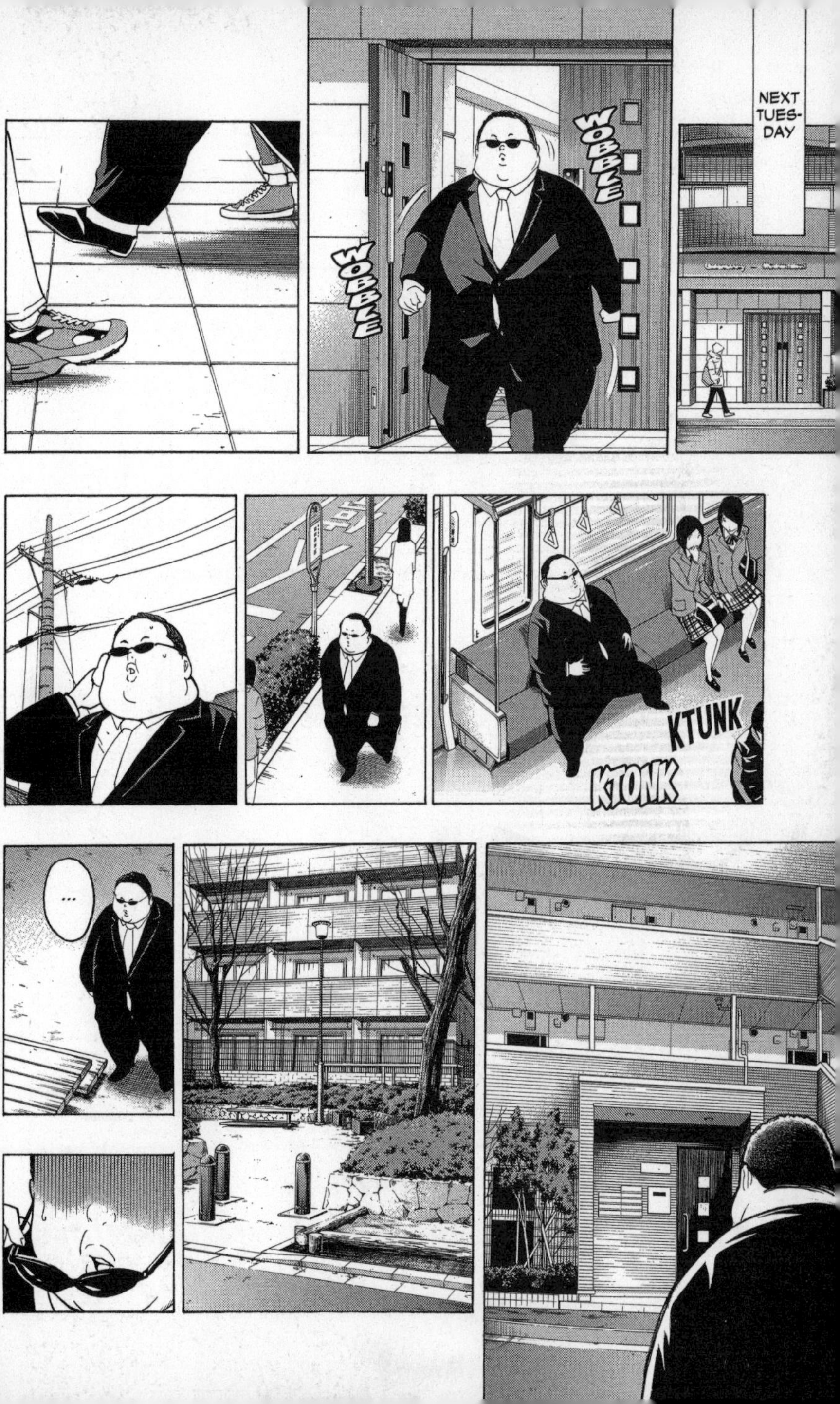
NEXT TUES-DAY
WOBBLE
WOBBLE
KTUNK
KTONK
...

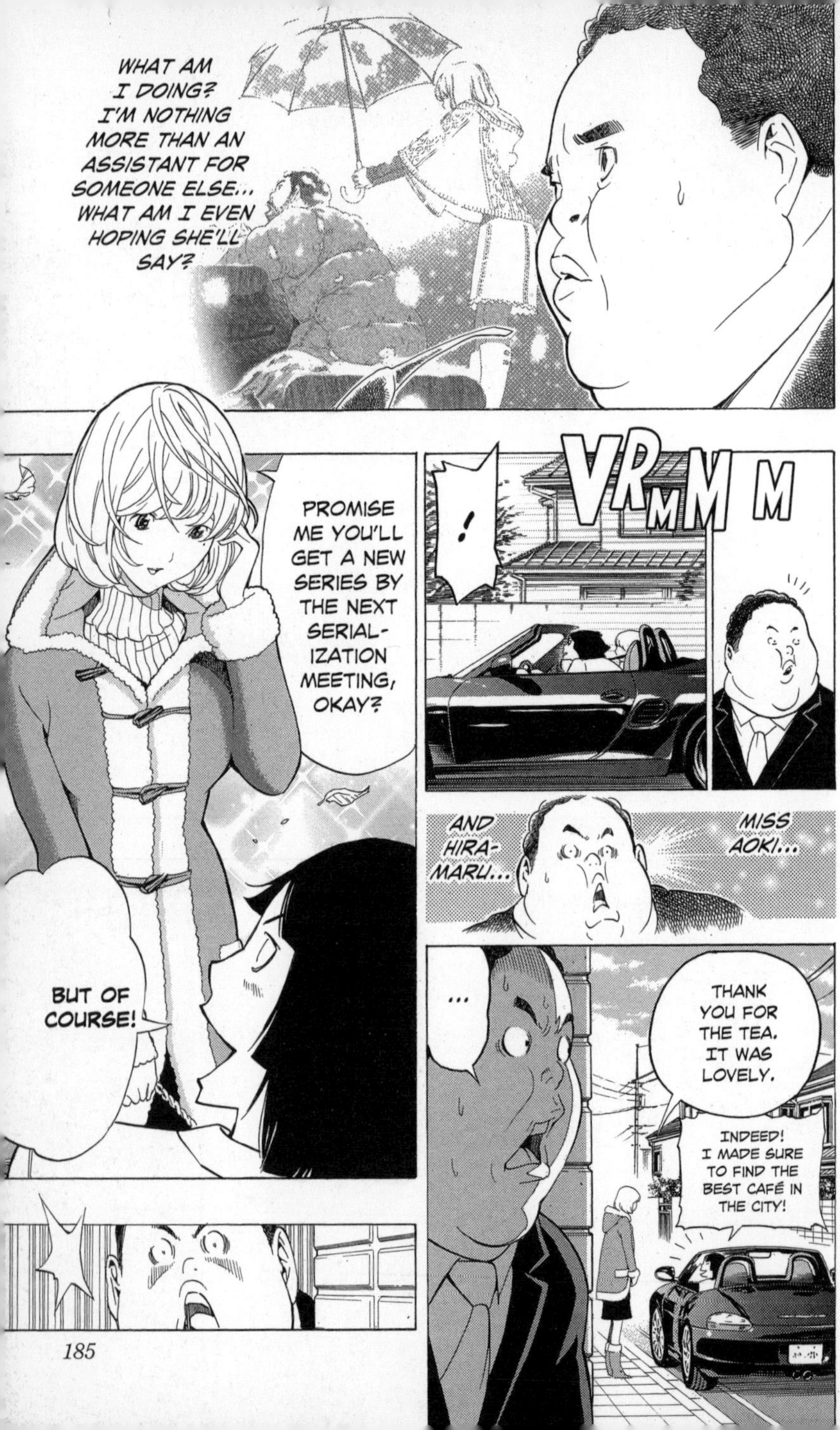
WHAT AM I DOING? I'M NOTHING MORE THAN AN ASSISTANT FOR SOMEONE ELSE... WHAT AM I EVEN HOPING SHE'LL SAY?
VRMMM M
!
MISS AOKI...
AND HIRAMARU...
THANK YOU FOR THE TEA. IT WAS LOVELY.
INDEED! I MADE SURE TO FIND THE BEST CAFÉ IN THE CITY!
...
PROMISE ME YOU'LL GET A NEW SERIES BY THE NEXT SERIALIZATION MEETING, OKAY?
BUT OF COURSE!

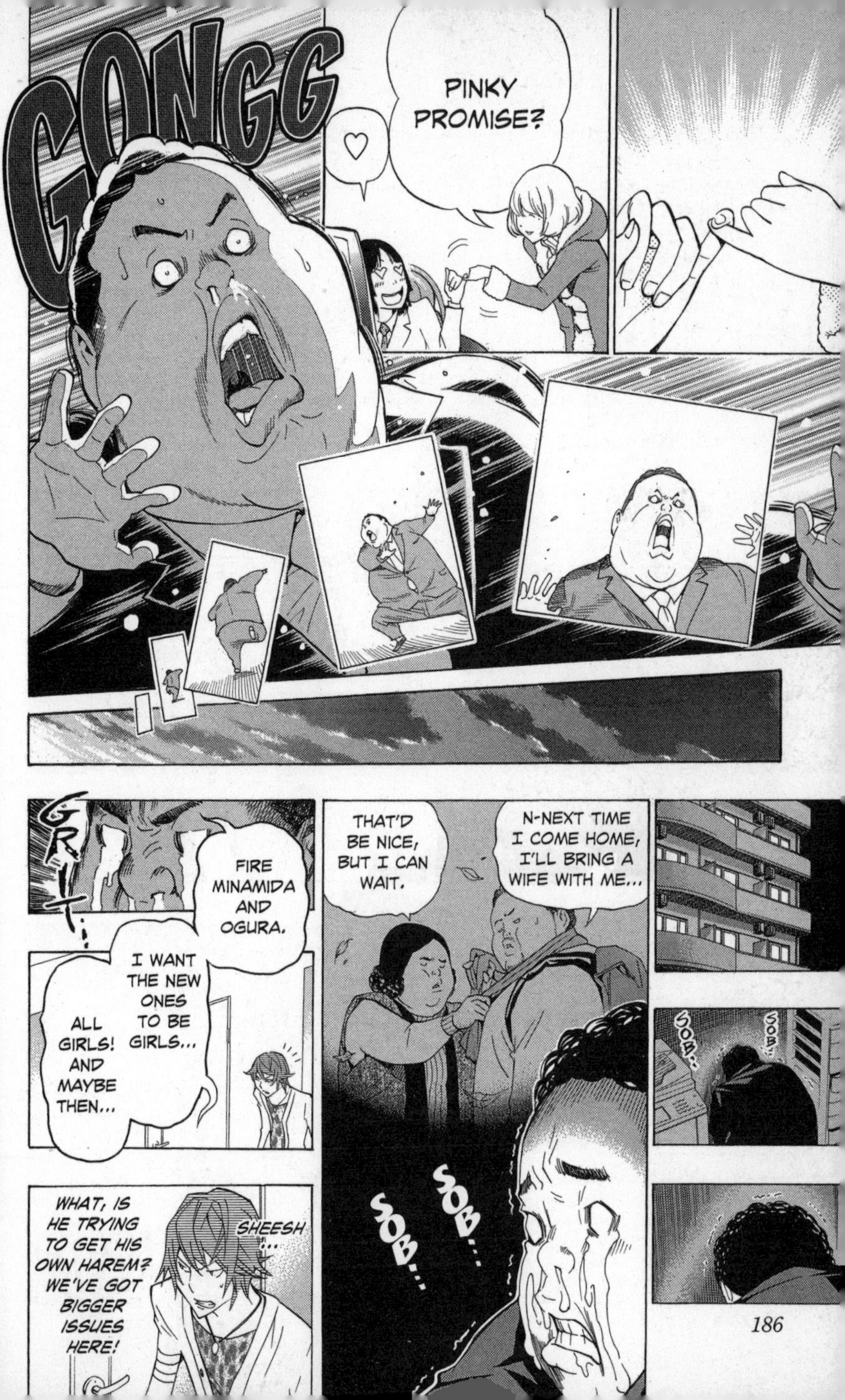
PINKY PROMISE?
♡
GONGG
SOB...
SOB...
N-NEXT TIME I COME HOME, I'LL BRING A WIFE WITH ME...
THAT'D BE NICE, BUT I CAN WAIT.
SOB...
SOB...
GRIT...
FIRE MINAMIDA AND OGURA.
I WANT THE NEW ONES TO BE GIRLS...
ALL GIRLS! AND MAYBE THEN...
SHEESH...
WHAT, IS HE TRYING TO GET HIS OWN HAREM? WE'VE GOT BIGGER ISSUES HERE!

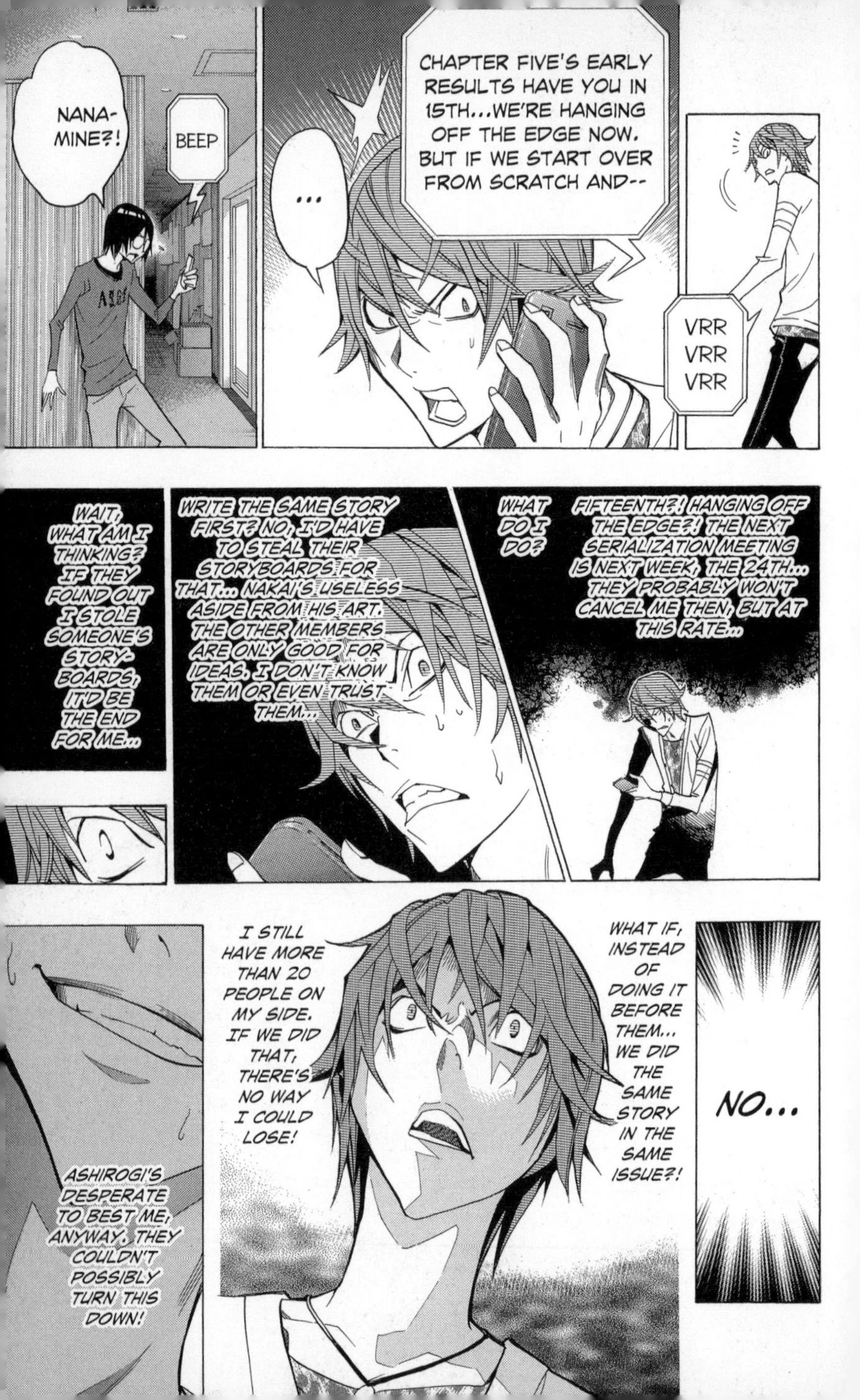
VRR VRR VRR
CHAPTER FIVE'S EARLY RESULTS HAVE YOU IN 15TH...WE'RE HANGING OFF THE EDGE NOW. BUT IF WE START OVER FROM SCRATCH AND--
...
BEEP
NANA-MINE?!
FIFTEENTH?! HANGING OFF THE EDGE?! THE NEXT SERIALIZATION MEETING IS NEXT WEEK, THE 24TH... THEY PROBABLY WON'T CANCEL ME THEN, BUT AT THIS RATE...
WHAT DO I DO?
WRITE THE SAME STORY FIRST? NO, I'D HAVE TO STEAL THEIR STORYBOARDS FOR THAT... NAKAI'S USELESS ASIDE FROM HIS ART. THE OTHER MEMBERS ARE ONLY GOOD FOR IDEAS. I DON'T KNOW THEM OR EVEN TRUST THEM...
WAIT, WHAT AM I THINKING? IF THEY FOUND OUT I STOLE SOMEONE'S STORY-BOARDS, IT'D BE THE END FOR ME...
NO...
WHAT IF, INSTEAD OF DOING IT BEFORE THEM... WE DID THE SAME STORY IN THE SAME ISSUE?!
I STILL HAVE MORE THAN 20 PEOPLE ON MY SIDE. IF WE DID THAT, THERE'S NO WAY I COULD LOSE!
ASHIROGI'S DESPERATE TO BEST ME, ANYWAY. THEY COULDN'T POSSIBLY TURN THIS DOWN!

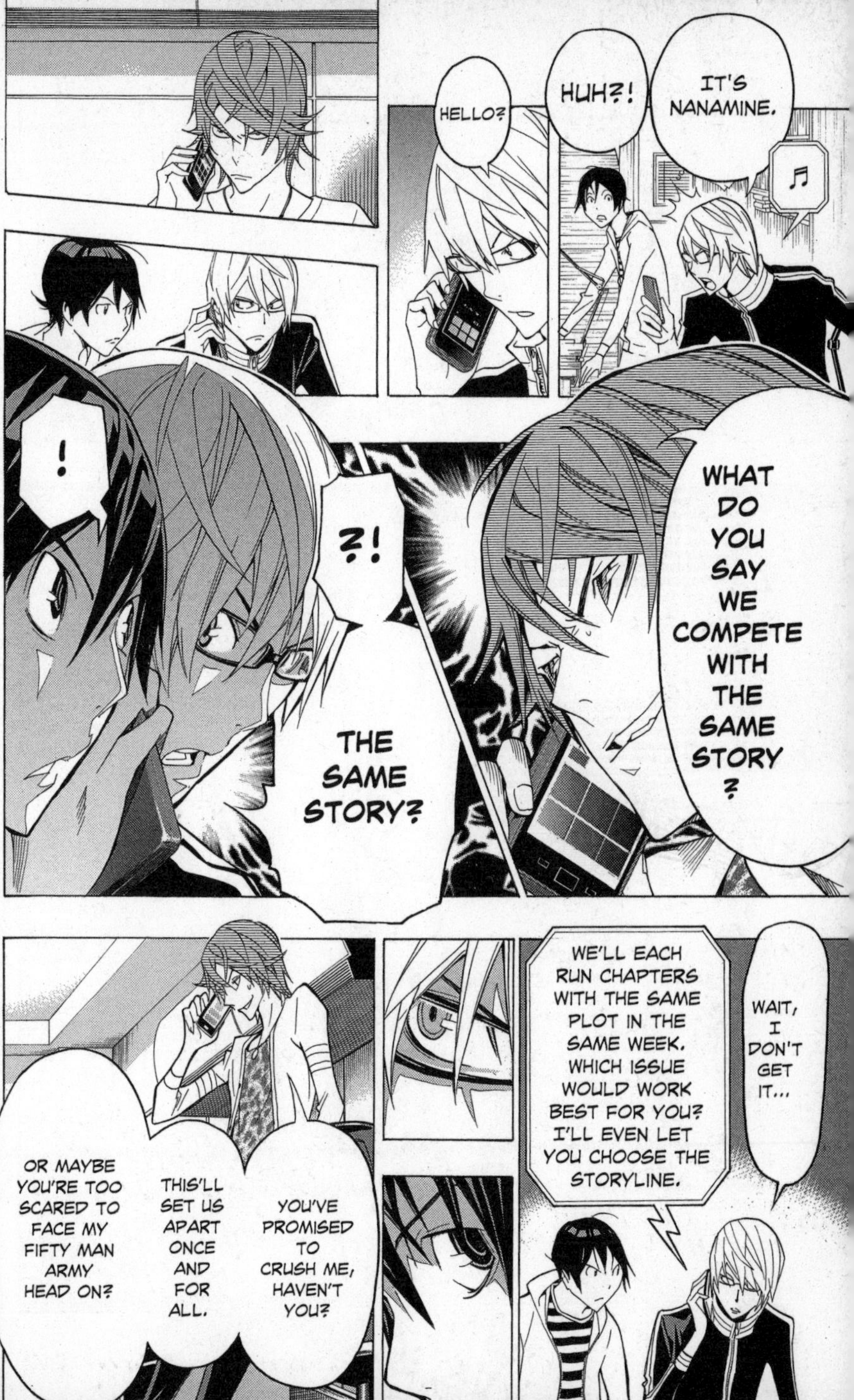
♪
IT'S NANAMINE.
HUH?!
HELLO?
WHAT DO YOU SAY WE COMPETE WITH THE SAME STORY?
?!
THE SAME STORY?
!
WAIT, I DON'T GET IT...
WE'LL EACH RUN CHAPTERS WITH THE SAME PLOT IN THE SAME WEEK. WHICH ISSUE WOULD WORK BEST FOR YOU? I'LL EVEN LET YOU CHOOSE THE STORYLINE.
YOU'VE PROMISED TO CRUSH ME, HAVEN'T YOU?
THIS'LL SET US APART ONCE AND FOR ALL.
OR MAYBE YOU'RE TOO SCARED TO FACE MY FIFTY MAN ARMY HEAD ON?

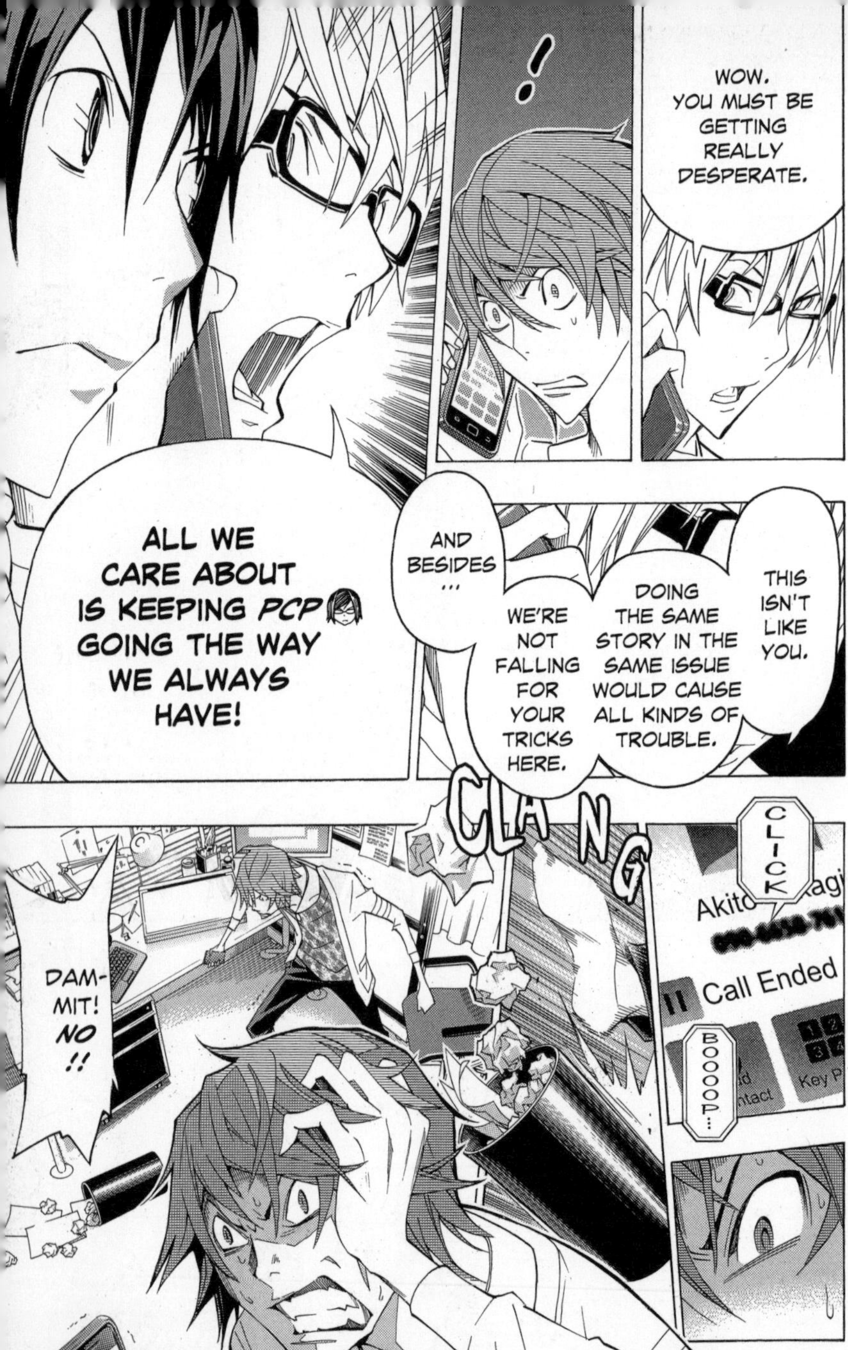
WOW. YOU MUST BE GETTING REALLY DESPERATE.
!
THIS ISN'T LIKE YOU.
DOING THE SAME STORY IN THE SAME ISSUE WOULD CAUSE ALL KINDS OF TROUBLE.
WE'RE NOT FALLING FOR YOUR TRICKS HERE.
AND BESIDES...
ALL WE CARE ABOUT IS KEEPING *PCP* GOING THE WAY WE ALWAYS HAVE!
CLICK
Call Ended
BOOOOOP...
CLANG
DAM-MIT! *NO!!*

14 Mind Games and Catchphrases (End)

OHBA'S STORYBOARD

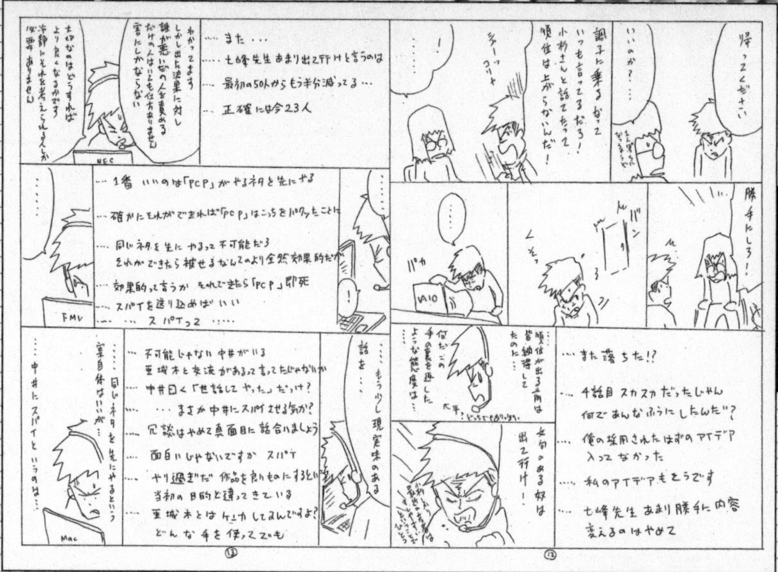
帰ってください
いいのか？……
調子に乗るなっていつも言ってるだろ！小杉さんと話てたって順位は上がらないんだ！
シーッ コリャ
！
……
勝手にしろ！
バン
くそっ
パカ
……
…また落ちた!?
…4話目 スカスカだったじゃん 何であんなふうにしたんだ？
…俺の採用されたはずのアイデア入ってなかった
…私のアイデアもそうです
…七峰先生 あまり勝手に内容変えるのはやめて
文句のある奴は出て行け！
順位が出る前は皆納得してたのに…
何だこの手の裏を返したような態度は…
12
……また…
…七峰先生あまり出て行けと言うのは
…最初の50人からもう半分減ってる…
…正確には今23人
大切なのはどうすればより良くなるかです 冷静にそれを考えられる人しか必要ありません
……
…1番いいのは「PCP」がやるネタを先にやる
…確かにそれができれば「PCP」はこっちをパクッたことに
…同じネタを先にやるって不可能だろ それができたら被せるなんてのより全然効果的だが
…効果的って言うか それできたら「PCP」即死
…スパイを送り込めばいい
…スパイって……
……
！
…もう少し現実味のある話を…
…不可能じゃない 中井がいる 亜城木と交流があるって言ってたじゃないか
…中井曰く「世話してやった」だっけ？
…まさか中井にスパイさせる気か？
…冗談はやめて真面目に話合いましょう
…面白いじゃないですか スパイ
…やり過ぎだ 作品を良いものにするという当初の目的と違ってきている
…亜城木とはケンカしてるんですよ？ どんな手を使ってでも
……同じネタを先にやるという案自体はいいが…
…中井にスパイというのは…
13

OBATA'S STORYBOARD

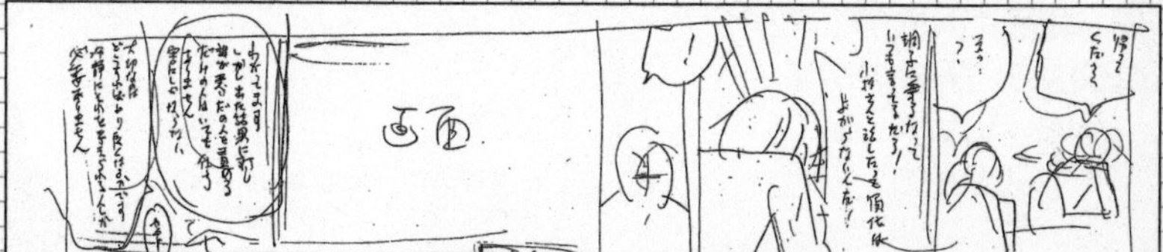

COMPLETE!

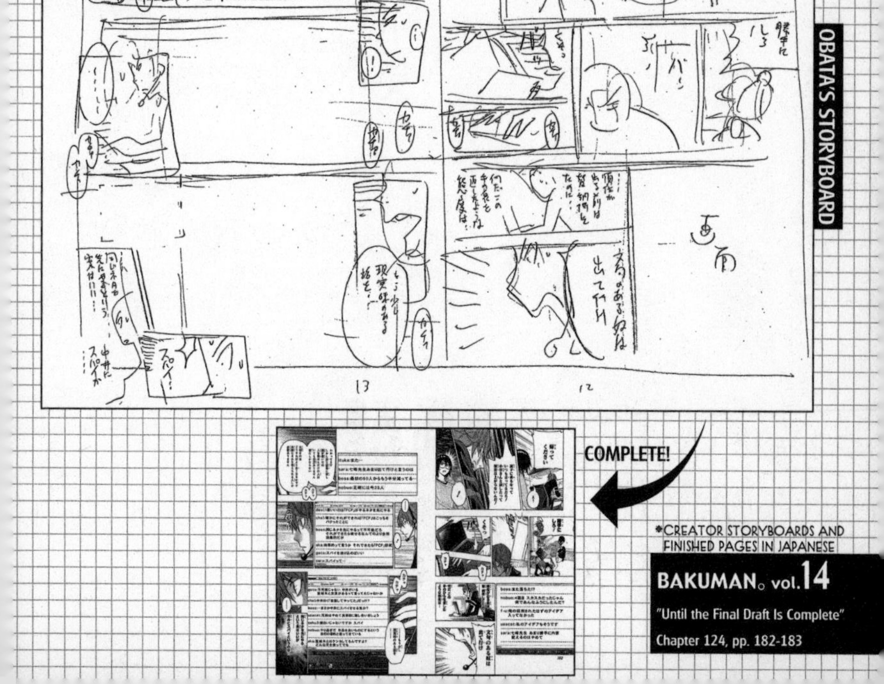

*CREATOR STORYBOARDS AND FINISHED PAGES IN JAPANESE

BAKUMAN。 vol.14

"Until the Final Draft Is Complete"

Chapter 124, pp. 182-183

BAKUMAN。

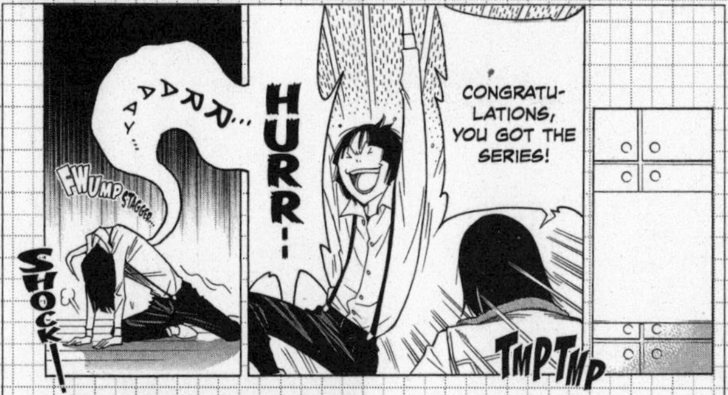
CONGRATULATIONS, YOU GOT THE SERIES!
HURR!!
TMPTMP
ARRR...
AAY...
FWUMP
STAGGER...
SHOCK!

In the NEXT VOLUME

As Tohru Nanamine starts falling behind in the *Weekly Shonen Jump* rankings, he gets desperate. Will his last ditch effort lead him to victory over Moritaka and Akito? And things go from bad to worse for Nakai when he gets into a fight with Hiramaru!

Available October 2012